SPHERES OF INJUSTICE

SPHERES OF INJUSTICE

THE ETHICAL PROMISE OF MINORITY PRESENCE

BRUNO PERREAU

THE MIT PRESS   CAMBRIDGE, MASSACHUSETTS   LONDON, ENGLAND

The MIT Press
Massachusetts Institute of Technology
77 Massachusetts Avenue, Cambridge, MA 02139
mitpress.mit.edu

© 2025 Massachusetts Institute of Technology

All rights reserved. No part of this book may be used to train artificial intelligence systems or reproduced in any form by any electronic or mechanical means (including photocopying, recording, or information storage and retrieval) without permission in writing from the publisher.

The MIT Press would like to thank the anonymous peer reviewers who provided comments on drafts of this book. The generous work of academic experts is essential for establishing the authority and quality of our publications. We acknowledge with gratitude the contributions of these otherwise uncredited readers.

This book was set in Stone Serif and Avenir LT Std by Westchester Publishing Services. Printed and bound in the United States of America.

Library of Congress Cataloging-in-Publication Data
Names: Perreau, Bruno, author.
Title: Spheres of injustice : the ethical promise of minority presence / Bruno Perreau.
Other titles: Sphères d'injustice. English | Ethical promise of minority presence
Description: Cambridge, Massachusetts : The MIT Press, [2025] | "Spheres of Injustice was published in French in 2023 by Éditions La Découverte." | Includes bibliographical references and index.
Identifiers: LCCN 2024023736 (print) | LCCN 2024023737 (ebook) | ISBN 9780262552264 (paperback) | ISBN 9780262382991 (epub) | ISBN 9780262383004 (pdf)
Subjects: LCSH: Minorities—Civil rights. | Minorities—Social conditions. | Equality—Philosophy. | Discrimination. | Cultural pluralism.
Classification: LCC JC312 .P4713 2025 (print) | LCC JC312 (ebook) | DDC 323.1—dc23/eng/20241129
LC record available at https://lccn.loc.gov/2024023736
LC ebook record available at https://lccn.loc.gov/2024023737

10   9   8   7   6   5   4   3   2   1

EU product safety and compliance information contact is: mitp-eu-gpsr@mit.edu

CONTENTS

ACKNOWLEDGMENTS vii

INTRODUCTION: WHAT IS A MINORITY? 1
1 SPHERES OF EXPERIENCE 19
2 MANAGING DIVERSITY 41
3 THE WEIGHT OF NUMBERS 65
4 ANTIMINORITY POLITICS 85
5 AFFIRMATIVE ACTION 107
6 CO-APPEARING 131
7 LEGAL ANALOGY 157
8 TOWARD MINORITY UNIVERSALISM 179
CONCLUSION: AN ETHIC OF INTERDEPENDENCE 203

NOTES 211
SELECTED BIBLIOGRAPHY 285
INDEX OF COURT RULINGS 315
INDEX OF INSTITUTIONS, ORGANIZATIONS, AND PLACES 319
NAME INDEX 327
SUBJECT INDEX 343

ACKNOWLEDGMENTS

The idea for this book began to take form in the early 2000s. At the time, I was a doctoral student in political science at the University of Paris I Panthéon-Sorbonne under the supervision of Évelyne Pisier. My research focused on filiation and the promotion of gender and sexual equality in France and Europe. I showed that so-called "recognition" policies were always paradoxical since they reinforced the primacy of the social reference group, the group to which individuals considered atypical were compared.[1] What system, then, should be put in place to ensure legal, social, and epistemic equality?

To address this question, I proposed that the journal *Pouvoirs* publish a special issue with the aim of reflecting on the ideas conveyed by "affirmative action." Daniel Sabbagh had just published a book devoted to the history and workings of this policy in the United States.[2] I wanted to gather contributions on the ways affirmative action transformed people's relationship to the law. The issue came out in 2004. In my article I argued that affirmative action was not a simple means of redistribution, but rather a minority conception of social relations in which decision-making was based on the situation of people who were socially dominated, economically exploited, and/or discriminated against in their lifestyles.[3] In my view, affirmative action was therefore the bearer of a new social theory based on interdependence and responsibility for others.

This observation was also rooted in my teaching practice. When I taught constitutional law at Sciences Po Paris, I mentored students who had benefited from *Conventions Éducation Prioritaire* (Sciences Po's affirmative action program), high school students from New Caledonia, and international exchange students. For nearly ten years I observed the impact of their presence with particular interest since I myself was a "class defector." My discovery of gay and lesbian cultures in Paris and my activist involvement with Act Up allowed me to cross other social lines before my move to the United States reshuffled the deck: my French identity became primary. These experiences permeate this book.

I put my thoughts on hold for several years to complete my work on adoption, bioethics, republicanism, and queer theory. My colleagues at the Massachusetts Institute of Technology (MIT) often encouraged me to resume my research on affirmative action. With this in mind, in 2019 I began writing *Spheres of Injustice* with the aim of advancing a minority theory of justice founded on the critical study of law, social mobilizations, and antidiscrimination policies in France and the United States.

Spheres of Injustice was published in French in 2023 by Éditions La Découverte. That same year two other works were published that also took up the notion of spheres. They explore how, in the global south, inequalities carry over from one sphere of life to another. Brazilian psychoanalyst Suely Rolnik's book, *Spheres of Insurrection: Notes on Decolonizing the Unconscious*, questions the way postcolonial neoliberalism directs the vital force of individuals toward the commercial sphere, to the detriment of creation and protest. Albeena Shakil and Gopal Guru edited a collective work—eponymous with this book—bringing together contributions on theories of justice in India today. Although these two books do not use Michael Walzer's theoretical framework, the coincidental timing of our publications illustrates the need to think more contextually about inequalities while reflecting on their connections. Engaging in this work from positions as distant as ours is one of the keys to destabilizing majority powers wherever they exist.

I could not have written this book without the support of Cynthia and John Reed at MIT; a Frederick Burkhardt Fellowship from the American Council of Learned Societies; and the Center for Advanced Study in the Behavioral Sciences (CASBS) at Stanford University, which welcomed me

ACKNOWLEDGMENTS

in 2019–2020. My exchanges with the CASBS teams and other fellows were critical, and I am grateful to all of them. The seminars organized by the Program in Critical Theory at the University of California at Berkeley enriched my work, and I am indebted to Judith Butler for inviting me to participate. I also would like to thank my colleagues and relatives who have contributed, directly and indirectly, to this work.

My appreciation also goes to Joshua Armstrong, who helped track down resources. Sciences Po's Presage program provided access to numerous books and articles. I am much obliged to its teams, especially Hélène Périvier and Violette Toye.

Finally, I would like to extend my appreciation to the team at the MIT Press for welcoming this book, especially my editor Gita Manaktala, whose benevolent guidance was essential. I thank Susannah Dale for revising the translation. Working on a book that borrows from law, continental philosophy, and political theory, all with a transnational perspective, is no easy task. Our discussions, often on the minutest textual details, provided opportunities to revisit my concepts and give them a more incisive spin. By focusing on minority experience, I twist and recast a very powerful French tradition of thought—that of universalism. I hope to shed new and different light on North American debates and, beyond that, provide critical tools to everyone around the world who stands for equality and freedom.

INTRODUCTION:
WHAT IS A MINORITY?

On July 13, 2013, George Zimmerman, a volunteer neighborhood watchman, was acquitted of shooting seventeen-year-old African American Trayvon Martin. In response, three activists and community organizers, Alicia Garza, Patrisse Cullors, and Opal Tometi, launched a large-scale mobilization against anti-Black racism. They coined the hashtag #BlackLivesMatter to create a solidarity network on social media. A year later, following the murders of two other Black men, Michael Brown and Eric Garner—both killed by on-duty police officers—Black Lives Matter urged large-scale street protests, first in Ferguson, Missouri, and then throughout the United States.

The Black Lives Matter network advocates fighting anti-Black racism—be it police brutality, mass incarceration, employment discrimination, and even obstruction of the right to vote—by tackling each of its specific forms. Black people experience racism differently depending on their gender, sexuality, disability, creed, family background, professional environment, and so on. Any powerful social movement must be able to provide responses that are appropriate to specific situations.[1] This observation may seem rather obvious, but it is no less corrosive in a highly segregated country.[2] If racism is recognized as having many different forms and requiring ad hoc policies, there is a chance that minority voices may proliferate and become uncontainable. For Black Lives Matter, the model of the nuclear family thus stands in the way of intercommunity and intergenerational solidarities, which are vital in any struggle for human dignity.[3]

The conservative reaction to the Black Lives Matter protests was not long in coming. Republican Senator Tim Scott, himself an African American, defended the #AllLivesMatter movement that was created to attack the work of Black Lives Matter while simultaneously echoing it. All Lives Matter sought to promote the idea that to fight against a particular form of domination is to deny the value of other human lives. Black Lives Matter, however, has never sought to compete with other social struggles; the movement simply holds that every struggle is worthy of its own attention.

Antiracism protests intensified after the murder of George Floyd, who was choked to death by four Minneapolis police officers on May 25, 2020. Although racist crimes on US soil have always occurred, the images of Floyd's final agonizing moments sparked a public outcry around the globe.[4] His life story also illustrated the social, economic, and legal difficulties of the Black population and the importance of systems of mutual aid. A former college basketball player, George Floyd had several convictions for armed robbery and drug possession before becoming involved in charitable work in his local parish. He worked as a bouncer in a bar but lost his job when the COVID-19 pandemic broke out; Floyd himself had contracted the virus shortly before his murder. He was arrested for allegedly using a counterfeit twenty-dollar bill in a nearby store and showed no signs of resisting the police. Throughout June 2020, protests spread across the country, and the police's handling of protesters was brutal in some cases. President Donald Trump called for violence against protesters,[5] and federal troops joined in the crackdown.[6] In just a few weeks, eight demonstrators were partially blinded.[7] The antiracism mobilizations brought together more young, white activists than Martin Luther King Jr. did in 1965 on his march from Selma to Montgomery.[8] On several occasions, these activists stood between law enforcement and Black and mixed-race protesters to defend them against police aggression.[9] Many citizens of Asian and Latinx descent—Asian Americans for Black Lives, for example—also participated alongside various LGBTQ and feminist groups.

The June 2020 protests in the United States were a catalyst for mobilizations against racism in France. On July 19, 2016, Adama Traoré, a

INTRODUCTION 3

twenty-four-year-old Black French citizen, was killed at the gendarmerie in Persan, a small city north of Paris, after attempting to flee an identity check. According to their own statements, the gendarmes used prone restraint during his arrest. They claimed to have placed the young man in a lateral safety position when he began to convulse, but firefighters who were called late to the scene refuted this version of events: they found his body lying face down on the ground with his hands handcuffed behind his back. The day after Adama Traoré's death, his older sister, Assa, led a committee to determine the truth about the circumstances of her brother's death. There were several obstacles to the investigation. The first autopsy ordered by the public prosecutor concluded that Adama died from asphyxiation owing to a severe infection; the second, from cardiopathy related to sickle cell disease. Since no specialists in these alleged diseases carried out the two autopsies, the family requested two second opinions, which invalidated the initial interpretations and concluded that he died from asphyxiation. After battling with the authorities for several years,[10] the Adama committee mobilized tens of thousands of people on June 2, 2020, outside the Paris courthouse, in defiance of the prefecture's ban on demonstrations. Another rally was organized on June 13, 2020, at the Place de la République in Paris. The placards and slogans directly echoed the US situation: "Black Lives Matter"; "Adama Traoré. George Floyd. I can't breathe. Stop police impunity"; and "Floyd in the USA. Traoré in France." A few days earlier, French photographer and street artist JR created a giant mural in Paris's tenth arrondissement, intermingling the faces of George Floyd and Adama Traoré.[11]

Numerous media commentators and elected officials objected to the comparison between France and the United States.[12] To them the French Republic, founded on an abstract vision of citizenship, should not be equated with "US communitarianism";[13] only isolated police abuses could be at issue.[14] Admittedly, France's differences from the United States are well established.[15] In the United States, police departments are local; weapons circulate in significant numbers; urban segregation is considerable; social protection (for example, health care, sick leave, retirement pensions, maternity leave, unemployment benefits) is contingent on one's occupation; and the voting system adversely affects poor populations, especially Black Americans (voting takes place during the workweek, driver's licenses are used as IDs, there are considerable lines at the polls, and redistricting and gerrymandering are often questionable). However, these specificities in no way alter the fact that, in both countries, racist violence is rooted in similar mechanisms that subordinate minority bodies.[16] These mechanisms are part of a long transatlantic colonial history whose legacy weighs heavily on contemporary practices,[17] including racial profiling.[18]

Beyond that, there is an even deeper reason for these transatlantic echoes. Confronted with images of George Floyd's murder, Black people could not but feel that their destiny was linked to his; that it might have been them, whether in Minneapolis or elsewhere.[19] On January 3, 2023, Keenan Anderson, Patrisse Cullers's cousin, was arrested following a car accident. Disoriented, he was tased to death by Los Angeles police officers. His last words: "They're trying to George Floyd me." Racism is not only the negation of unique lives and cultures; it is also characterized by the substitutability of people: a Black man jogging, a Black child holding a water pistol, a Black man dancing, a mixed-race woman in her car—all of these lives are seen as interchangeable and reduced to a worldview that associates Black or Brown skin color with danger.[20] The victims embody a type of presence that their tormentors are unable to imagine. To them, that presence is therefore literally omnipresent; it saturates their present. It becomes so destabilizing that it must be eliminated. Even if the modus operandi of transphobic, homophobic, sexist, Islamophobic, antisemitic, classist, or ableist violence are not the same—since they are based on material factors other than skin color and on histories other than those involving enslavement and segregation—the fact remains that all these forms of violence reduce individuals to a property. To be a minority is to face the possibility of the most radical erasure of uniqueness: minorities may not share the same experiences but rely on a system of thought in which one's very life can be swept away at any moment, just like other minority lives can in the most arbitrary way possible. Every act of violence, every interpellation of a minority person resonates through every other minority person's body. This phenomenon connects anti-Black racism in France with anti-Black racism in the United States.[21] It also connects the Black minority to other minorities, themselves connected to each other: while their interests may differ and even conflict at times,

INTRODUCTION   5

they all face the threat of the most radical desingularization, with no possible means of escape. As Claire Jean Kim puts it when discussing the COVID-19 pandemic, "We are not all in this together, or, more precisely, . . . we are all in this together very differently."[22] Not all minorities have access to the same resources: some are protected by their families, others are not; some are treated unjustly by the law, others are not; some are underrepresented, others are not; some are exposed to physical brutality, others less so; some are overexposed in the public space, others are invisibilized or cannot even access it. All, however, are overdetermined by the fate that has befallen them. For Frantz Fanon, to be Black is to experience an atomized presence in the world, made up of "the fragments . . . put together by another self."[23] To be a minority is to live in resonance with other minority lives, because all minorities, in their own way, experience atomization in majority worlds, of which they are the epistemic boundary.

RESONATING LIVES

Minority resonances are the subject of this book. What are their mechanisms and limits? Whom do they affect? Can they form the basis of a policy of collective emancipation? Movements that defend minorities always intervene "in the name" of the group they represent. They thus assume a certain internal cohesion and on this basis regularly call for a "convergence of struggles."[24] Yet there are dissenters within every minority group and differences of opinion between minority groups. Doesn't seeking to resolve such contradictions in "commonalities" fuel the power struggles that run through minorities? Isn't the desire to align minority struggles paradoxically tantamount to essentializing each group? This is the illusion that movements hostile to minority rights weaponize when they feed on polemics about cultural separatism, women-only meetings, competing forms of remembrance, or intergenerational conflicts. I maintain, to the contrary, that it is possible to stay true to each minority struggle without giving in to essentialist temptations. This implies moving from a logic of "commonalities" (*le commun*) to a logic of solidarity, of acting as one (*le comme-un*)[25] and, to do so, conceiving the notion of minority as *relational*.[26]

What exactly is a minority? US sociologist Louis Wirth, a member of the Chicago School, popularized the word. In a 1945 article, he explained that a minority is a "group of people who, because of their physical or cultural characteristics, are singled out, from among the others in the society in which they live, for differential and unequal treatment, and who, therefore, consider themselves to be objects of collective discrimination."[27] According to Wirth, the feeling of belonging to a minority group comes from two objective elements: one's specific characteristics and one's experience of being treated differently.[28] This definition still operates, even today, in antidiscrimination policies in the United States, France, and Europe. French law protects individuals on the basis of twenty-five criteria in various areas—employment, health, and access to housing—and for acts as diverse as insults, refusals of service, or even physical violence. The United States has a very similar system of "protected classes." There are nine such classes, which statutes or case law gradually incorporated into the law between 1964 and 2008.[29]

By defining differential treatment on the basis of predefined criteria, the French and US legal systems assume that the protected classes are constant and consistent. But these categories change over time,[30] and the way people identify with them varies considerably.[31] What, for example, constitutes a sexual minority? Feelings of love? Sexual acts? If so, which ones? The narrative identities of individuals? Cultural references? Types of socialization? Legal categorization reflects these complexities: over the years, sexual minorities have been designated using terms as diverse as "mores," "tastes," "preferences," or, more recently, "orientation."[32] The construction of sexual categories also depends on broader social transformations that do not affect all sexual minorities in the same ways; this is the case with women's work, contraception, the right to abortion, births outside marriage, the rise in celibacy, the fight against HIV, online dating, and so on.[33]

Moreover, a given individual can be a majority member in a given space and a minority member in another: reflecting on minority status means questioning the territorial or contextual anchoring of categories.[34] As sociologist Colette Guillaumin noted:

In certain social relationships, individuals belonging to minority groups have majority status; even if it is not fully exercised because it is limited by minority membership. With respect to Black Americans, all whites—be they women,

INTRODUCTION 7

workers, foreigners, Jews, etc.—are in a majority relationship. . . . For non-citizen foreigners, all nationals, whoever they may be, stand in a majority relationship to them. . . . We are therefore unable to define minorities or the majority in a symmetrical balance based on a set of stable and constant characteristics.[35]

The case of women is particularly revealing. All over the world they are, to varying degrees, minoritized in power relations (particularly economic and political); they are restricted in the free use of their bodies and obstructed in their movements by repressive customs and by the effects of violence and injury in both the public and the private spheres[36]—and yet they are in the numerical majority in many countries. Feminist movements have every reason to exploit this advantage to fight their battles. The same is true of Black people in South Africa, who face structural forms of oppression despite constituting 80 percent of the population. We must therefore overcome the "false dilemma" between number and power.[37]

This is no easy task. If being a minority is not about an essence or a status but instead about a relational association that is at once complex, changing, and polysemic, it therefore means recognizing that we all have within us a more or less significant minority part that connects us to others. In his reflections on voting, Nicolas de Condorcet demonstrated that no majority was mathematically possible in the event of a complex choice, since it is illogical to aggregate unalike preferences.[38] It follows from his work that every group is structured by minority dynamics that the group ignores, rejects, or accepts. However, grasping the complexities of these dynamics does not prevent certain individuals and groups of individuals from accumulating majority positions and thereby enjoying disproportionate advantages including economic power, rights, freedom of movement, and access to property, among others. Such privileges position them on the side of the universal, as if they embodied the group by default. Colette Guillaumin identified this perfectly: "Being in the majority (belonging to the majority) consists first and foremost in *not being* (Black, woman, Jew, gay, colonized, foreign, etc.)."[39]

A minority does not equate to a dominated *position*, as if it were merely the result of group discrimination on which to base a politics of difference;[40] difference always ends up becoming fossilized and in turn a source of discrimination under the influence of contrite majority discourses.[41] Nor should minority dynamics be a strategic *positioning* from which anyone can transform the social world—what Gilles Deleuze and Félix Guattari called "becoming minoritarian."[42] Minority dynamics is what emerges from the tension between position and positioning. It leads to thinking in terms of both identity and anti-identity. Identity is a necessary cornerstone that can, however, reduce the individual to a characteristic; critiquing identity makes it possible to escape objectification but deprives us of collective tools of resistance. This is the whole paradox of authenticity that Jean-Paul Sartre highlighted in *Being and Nothingness*.[43] The transformative energy that is characteristic of minorities therefore stems from the fact that, constrained by unfavorable power relations, they learn to live with contradictions they cannot resolve (whereas the majority may, wrongly, claim to have resolved these contradictions).[44] Because minorities are trapped within the language of the majority, they must both avow and disavow who they are.[45]

The question to ask, then, is not who is a minority and who is not, but whether the existence of a minority relationship to the social group does or does not generate a structural disadvantage. Shifting our perspective allows us to better understand how our lives are intertwined, and how each of us bears the presence of minority challenges. By the term "presence," I mean both the fact that there are to some degree people and groups of people—minorities—around each of us whose social identities are overdetermined by a relationship of domination; and, simultaneously, the fact that this presence resonates within each of us with a whole set of other minority experiences that (even though they do not necessarily shape our identities and are not considered bases for discrimination) influence our behavior and our sense of responsibility toward others. This conception of presence thus does not mean rejecting the mechanisms that protect minorities as they exist today, but it invites us to implement them in a more precise and flexible way, by examining minority relations in context. This approach should not only make it possible to fight discrimination more effectively but also to extricate ourselves from the rhetoric that antagonizes subjects based on the discriminations to which they are—or are not—subjected. Such rhetoric dominates the public debate today and breeds strong resentment against minorities.

INTRODUCTION

THE SOCIAL MEANING OF INJUSTICE

In *Spheres of Justice*, published in 1983, American philosopher Michael Walzer criticized political theories that were too blind to the sense of belonging.[46] In doing so, he was responding to the hypotheses of social-liberal philosopher John Rawls in his seminal work *Theory of Justice*, published in 1971.[47] Rawls put forward the notion of a "veil of ignorance" and used the metaphor of a sports team to describe the relationships of interdependence in a given society.[48] As we never fully know our social position, we might logically be inclined to accept the most protective modes of government if we were to need them. Moreover, as with team sports, individual satisfaction depends on collective achievement, as long as the rules of the game are respected and a certain balance is guaranteed among the team members.

These ideal types do not stand up to the test of facts. A social group is not a team; some members know their positions better than do others and have the wherewithal to take moral risks that may not be very protective. Moreover, although we are caught up in relationships of interdependence, not all our social interactions are comparable. Not all lives affect us the same way. Not all presences leave the same mark on us. Total commitment to the community is impossible both for moral reasons and for questions of energy and time availability.[49] We must therefore consider the principles of justice in more delineated spheres and study their circulation. Michael Walzer begins with the idea that social goods (whether moral principles, cultural practices, or material objects) have neither the same meaning nor the same value depending on the different "places" where they are conceived, produced, and shared—whether it is within the family, at work, in a public space, and so forth. Building a more egalitarian society requires taking these different meanings into account and examining how the possession of a social good in a given sphere can have an impact on the possession of other goods in other spheres governed by different principles of justice. This is what Walzer calls "complex equality": both the need to achieve equality in every sphere and the need to find a balance between them all.

Walzer is no relativist, however. He explains that "the idea that distributive justice is relative to the meanings of the goods being distributed is a universalist idea: it is meant to shape the distributive rules everywhere."[50] I support the idea that it is only possible to think about justice by taking into consideration the social meanings attached to it. However, I am proposing to base this reflection less on the possession of different social goods than on the deprivation of them. I therefore endorse a "hollowed" universalism. I argue that what binds individuals and shapes how they learn to be responsible toward others is less a matter of transcendental principles of justice than of the specter of injustice, whose haunting presence characterizes minority experiences.

The aim of this book is not to replace one philosophy of power with another or to support, where majority norms apply, a minority norm whose moral foundations would be equally fragile. Rather, it seeks to open new theoretical and practical horizons. What would happen if we were to admit that life was made up of minority relations in unique configuration and to varying degrees? Democratic systems today conceive of minorities as groups of people who deserve protection, in the hope of providing them access to the same living conditions as the rest of the population. There is a paradox here—the ideal of minority politics is to eradicate what constitutes minorities as such—and this runs through minority movements themselves. As philosopher René Scherer noted, "The use of the word minority . . . is odd because it is obvious that it carries with it a certain claim to 'majority.'"[51] This is why discourses that castigate irredentism often accompany recognition policies.

Minority presence disturbs the social order because it reveals that the majority is merely an unstable and contradictory aggregation of minority interests. The purpose of majority decision-making is to use discourses about what we have in common to mask the process by which any political community is constituted—itself a process in which the majority erases traces of its own origins to better embody the general will. Of course, some institutional arrangements allow for minority opinions,[52] but they remain part of a majority decision-making system. Yet not all individuals or groups stand equal before this system. Depending on the context, the minority mark will be more or less indelible. To get around this impasse, rather than propagating corrective measures, would it not be better to recognize that minority experiences shape all subjectivity and relations, and that "the" majority is always an artifact? This is the

INTRODUCTION

ethical work in which movements such as Black Lives Matter are engaged. Contemporary democracies still have to add an ethical dimension to the existing procedural dimension (election, deliberation, vote, execution, control) and normative dimension (custom, fundamental rights, and case law). By reviewing the legal and public policy mechanisms that regulate relationships of interdependence in a way that does not follow a majority logic, I hope to suggest lines of thought that will cast new light on our responsibility toward others and thus outline an ethics of presence and democratic learning that is so essential in the twenty-first century.[53]

THE VALUES OF DEMOCRACY

Spheres of Injustice takes a different look at current events. The battles minorities are waging around the world are not only battles for human dignity and respect of their fundamental rights. They are also about transforming the values on which democratic institutions are tacitly founded, such as deliberation, obedience, delegation, hierarchy, contradiction, and alternation. These transformations redefine the meaning of community, raising both hopes and concerns. Herein lies the value of a Franco-American study. The political systems of France and the United States draw inspiration from each other,[54] but the two countries also share a desire to be models for other democracies by creating, in Alexis de Tocqueville's words, a "public spirit."[55] By exploring minority policies that are interwoven across the Atlantic, I am offering an analysis that is more intercultural than strictly comparative and that suits already intertwined legal practices.[56] I thus wish to contribute to an "interpretative community" at the crossroads of two distinct but increasingly close legal traditions, those of common law (dominated by case law in the United States and in the United Kingdom's Commonwealth of Nations) and civil law (dominated by statute and the codification of law in continental European countries).[57] This is also why it is crucial to understand the joint formation of theories of justice in the US[58] and French contexts.[59] *Spheres of Justice* was published in the United States in 1983, at a time when Ronald Reagan's presidency was dismantling the welfare state and the critical category of race was being called into question.[60] That same year, France was pivoting to austerity and launching its process of decentralization. In

1983 the National Front, the main far-right party in France, also achieved its first electoral successes; and the first debates on "communitarianism" and the dangers of multicultural society in the United States began to flourish in the opinion press. Since that time, the French Left has had an increasingly pronounced conservative slant, both in ideological and network terms.[61] In the early twenty-first century, this slant materialized more concretely as several social-democratic figures took seats in conservative governments. The decline of a socialist doctrine on a national scale cannot be explained solely by the recent decline of party structures, since that affects all political currents to varying degrees.[62] It stems from the split between principles of freedom and equality within a state that is increasingly reduced to its criminal and police functions.[63] Contemporary polemics around questions of migration, diversity, memory, and even censorship are symptoms of this separation. *Spheres of Injustice* aims to revive the gesture of theoretical resistance that presided over the writing of *Spheres of Justice* in the United States. By exploring the way in which the idea of injustice affects all social relations, it seeks to open an alternative path: that of a minority ethics at the service of a social, legal, and political philosophy that is about both equality and freedom.

Spheres of Injustice comprises two parts. The first part—chapters 2 to 5—highlights the challenges facing the notion of minority today, both in France and in the United States (managerial drift, algorithmic computation, reactionary discourse, and competition between minorities). The second—which spans the final three chapters—addresses these challenges by presenting several conceptual tracks: co-appearance, *intra*sectionality, and minority universalism. These two parts follow a first chapter that introduces and builds on Michael Walzer's work. Issues related to gender, race, sexuality, and class compose the bulk of this book, insofar as the ethical reflection I am offering proceeds from a critical analysis of current social, political, and legal developments. However, *Spheres of Injustice* is not limited to these issues: the book also invokes several cases of discrimination related to age, health, disability, language, creed, or place of residence.

The first chapter, "Spheres of Experience," offers a critical rereading of *Spheres of Justice*. It begins by introducing Walzer's concepts of complex equality, pluralism, and social good. Returning to his work is even more

INTRODUCTION

necessary given the paradoxical reception of *Spheres of Justice* in France. During the 1990s, several neoliberal and neoconservative authors used the notion of "complex equality" to justify inequalities and denounce the so-called tyranny of minorities. But, like de Tocqueville before him, Walzer explains that tyranny is the exercise of an abusive majority power. Besides, *Spheres of Justice* was also unduly characterized as a multiculturalist theory, which considerably undermined Walzer's vision of democratic pluralism. Although his book recognizes that the meaning of justice varies from one sphere to another, it is not meant to advocate for self-sufficient communities but to better resist the normative hegemony that one sphere may exercise over another. Chapter 1 seeks to dispel these misconceptions while complementing Walzerian theory. It shows that the experience of injustice, much more than the ideals of justice, over-determines relationships to institutions. The distribution of social goods revolves, in fact, around three ways of experiencing injustice: direct, spectral, and witnessed.

The second chapter deals with the issue of managing diversity. It shows that the fuzziness surrounding the concept of minority is both its strength and its weakness. The term can be adapted to many situations, but it has become real business, especially since it is also a very powerful discursive tool in public debate, as evidenced by recent arguments over "cancel culture."[64] Chapter 2 shows that different minority configurations generate different forms of power. As numerous works in social psychology (and, in particular, those of Serge Moscovici) reveal, minorities have a real capacity to wield influence, but they still have to play by the rules of the majority and adhere to an imperative of consistency. Chapter 2 thus shows that the notion of minority is both versatile and fragile and that the influence it exerts is always mediated.

The third chapter deals with the weight of numbers. Relationships of dominance vary according to the size of the group concerned. Since women account for almost 50 percent of humanity, they do not experience the same kind of subjugation as linguistic, religious, and cultural minorities with far fewer people. Measures for determining what constitutes a numerical majority changed considerably over the twenty-first century. Strong political polarization in many Western countries resulted in new decision-making methods that favor consensus, at the risk of weakening the divisions that minority cultures need to exist. A proliferation of qualified majority systems made it possible for minorities whose interests are at stake to garner enough votes to block a majority victory. Finally, the deployment of algorithms also redefined the very idea of a majority: the principle of the greatest number ceded to the law of averages. In this context, deviations from the mean are codified as anomalies. A majority veil of a new type, seriality, covers up significant minority differences. To address these changes, chapter 3 presents a theory of community as jointed incompleteness.

Relative as it may be, the influence of minorities is coveted. The fourth chapter, "Antiminority Politics," analyzes how contemporary reactionary discourses in France and the United States have instrumentalized the concept of minority.[65] Movements hostile to the rights of minorities have presented themselves as the only true voice of the people, sidelining minorities among foreigners, stateless persons, and even international elites. According to these movements, minorities are a threat because their alleged power and deviance would make them more loyal to their own groups than to the nation.[66] This rhetoric has taken an unexpected strategic turn. In the name of their freedom of expression, reactionary groups are demanding to be protected as minorities. In France and in Europe, these groups have integrated the symbols and vocabulary of minority struggles into their antirevolutionary lexicon and rhetorical register. In the United States, similar groups have fought by taking their cases to the courts and invoking their First-Amendment freedoms. What political tools are left to minorities when their main detractors appropriate their cultural references?

The fifth chapter, "Affirmative Action," reflects on the obstacles minorities in France and the United States face in employment, university admissions, and access to housing. Affirmative action, or the oxymoronic term "positive discrimination" used in French, consists of a set of measures that provides targeted information to minorities, saves admissions slots for them, or creates new procedures to promote their recruitment and selection. The US Supreme Court recently put an end to some of these practices. On June 29, 2023, it ruled that race-conscious college admissions policies violate the Fourteenth Amendment's Equal Protection Clause.[67] Population flows, it is true, make the category of "minority"

INTRODUCTION

a complex one: for example, in most US universities, admission policies did not include African students; however, the internationalization of universities and the procedures used for selecting students, based partly on their life histories, have boosted the number of Black migrant and visiting students, while the population of American-born Black students has stagnated.[68] Obstacles therefore vary from one subgroup to another, although they are often rooted in the same criteria: primarily the place of residence, in addition to skin color.[69] Likewise, what defines a minority in one area or context is not necessarily applicable to another. In higher education, Asian Americans do not receive preferential treatment in admissions procedures because of their high academic performance.[70] They are nonetheless a minority and face stereotyping and discrimination both in society and throughout their education. Finally, the fact that grounds for discrimination are based on a list of protected classes promotes competition between minorities, since recognizing discrimination involves comparing one's own situation to that of other minorities.[71] Disability, skin color, sexuality, and gender, however, to use just a few examples, are subject to very different discriminatory mechanisms. Exclusion is not surveillance; surveillance is not rendering invisible; rendering invisible is not infantilization; and so forth. All the same affirmative action can be a powerful tool in the fight against discrimination when it combines a consideration of predefined criteria, reserved slots, procedures tailored for certain groups, and studying application files on a case-by-case basis. Using the example of the Priority Education Agreements (*Conventions Éducation Prioritaire* or *CEP*) at Sciences Po Paris, chapter 5 shows that affirmative action is necessary for institutions to be able to transform themselves and endure. Representation, based on a logic of delegation, always dilutes the contribution of minorities. Having mechanisms that ensure their full participation is essential to democracy, since those mechanisms bring together presence and reciprocity.

What is a policy of presence? Chapter 6, "Co-appearing," highlights several elements: direct speech, the value of experience, and the preservation of memory. The "convergence of struggles," however, to which certain minority movements adhere, masks antagonisms and dissent; it promotes a logic of aggregation that is the polar opposite of the idea of presence. Chapter 6 therefore invites us to step away from the mythology of "commonalities." To do so, it mobilizes the idea of "co-appearing" inspired by the work of Jean-Luc Nancy on "co-appearance" (or "compearance," in some translations).[72] "Co-appearance" refers to the fact that each person embodies something of others and *appears* on the social scene *with* them. Minority movements give life to other presences in their struggles, even when these presences contradict each other. They show that co-appearance is never fixed but activated by the tensions that run through it. Chapter 6 provides several examples: the media's treatment of the LGBTQ nightclub massacre in Orlando, Florida; police violence against Black people; the repression of social movements in France; and France's 2001 law recognizing enslavement as a crime against humanity. Chapter 6 shows that minority issues do not require a convergence of struggles, but rather social co-appearance that diversifies our connections to political time and space.

Chapter 7, "Legal Analogy," explores minority presence in the legal field. It starts with the way in which the notion of gender introduced flexibility into the understanding of legal categories. For a long time in French, US, and European antidiscrimination law, the principle of equality could only be applied once a difference in treatment had been identified and shown not to comply with the law.[73] This process required comparing minorities to the majority, thus placing the majority in a central position. By considering discrimination categories interdependently, invoking gender made it possible to break with this approach. The focus is now on measuring the dynamics of discrimination (its intensity, modus operandi, and duration) in context and in connection with other forms of discrimination. By analogy, gender can protect race, race can protect sexual orientation, sexual orientation can protect age, age can protect disability, and so on. All our fates are legally connected and marked by minority presence. This is what I call *intra*sectionality; it complements intersectionality as developed by legal scholar Kimberlé Crenshaw in "Mapping the Margins."[74] Proving discrimination at the intersection of several "protected classes" is not an easy task. The more criteria there are, the more difficult it is to establish the exact source of discrimination. Intrasectionality therefore contributes to overcoming the limits of traditional legal reasoning, which only considers discrimination in isolation and cumulatively. A broader view of interdependence thus emerges.

The eighth and final chapter, "Toward Minority Universalism," examines the relationship between freedom and interdependence. If the specter of injustice structures the moral spheres in which minorities evolve, its empire also extends to the majority. When minoritized individuals denounce an injustice, they see themselves reduced to their community of belonging. They are "minoritized" because they simultaneously experience recognition and dispossession. This process, however, also delineates the majority's scope of action, since individuals in a majority dread being, in turn, minoritized themselves. All moral spheres are therefore governed, however differently, by the specter of injustice.[75] This is what I call "minority universalism." This final chapter counters the morality of empathy by defending an ethics of learning that links the fates of the most privileged and the most vulnerable while continuing to take their specific characteristics into account. In doing so, it makes a new contribution to theories of ecology, while global interdependence makes individual and collective responsibility more difficult to pinpoint.

1

SPHERES OF EXPERIENCE

In 1983, US philosopher Michael Walzer, professor at the Institute for Advanced Study in Princeton, New Jersey, and author of the well-known book *Just and Unjust Wars*,[1] published a groundbreaking work: *Spheres of Justice: A Defense of Pluralism and Equality*.[2] The book stemmed from a course he and Robert Nozick had taught at Harvard in fall 1970. Entitled "Capitalism and Socialism," the course gave rise to two classics of contemporary political theory: Nozick's *Anarchy, State and Utopia*,[3] a libertarian perspective, and Walzer's *Spheres of Justice*, a pluralist one. In 1973, the magazine *Dissent* published Walzer's early thoughts on redistributive justice, "In Defense of Equality."[4] *Just and Unjust Wars* can also be read in conjunction with *Spheres of Justice*, since it analyzes how the meaning of war changes from one society to another, while *Spheres of Justice* reflects on different definitions of justice within a given society. *Just and Unjust Wars* asserted the need for a minimal universalism, without which there can be no shared understanding of the norms and customs that govern armed conflict. *Spheres of Justice* further explored shared understandings. The book introduced the idea of "complex equality" at a time when "simple equality" was under attack from Friedman-inspired neoliberal policies championed by Margaret Thatcher and Ronald Reagan. Complex equality points to equality not having the same meaning in different spheres of life. In families, public life, friendships or romantic relationships, in work or school, in the hospital, in retirement, in sports or leisure activities, we emphasize different values such as competitiveness, empathy, pride, solidarity, seduction, austerity, modesty, and transmission. Because simple equality can apply similarly across these spheres, it contradicts centuries-old moral principles that are deeply rooted in each community's belief systems. Neoliberal policies exploit these contradictions to persuasively show that the principle of equality is irrelevant. They can thus more easily justify lowering economic and social protection levels and in doing so extend their control of markets, laws, and bodies. For Walzer, the promise of simple equality is not enough to prevent neoliberal attacks on social justice. He therefore uses the concept of complex equality: he does not abandon a general principle of equality that applies to all spheres of life, but he adds a principle of balance between these different spheres. Advantages acquired in a given sphere should not result in privileges in other spheres.

In this chapter, I introduce Walzer's distributive theory, and I discuss the very unexpected reception of this theory in France. Intellectual circles close to the literary and philosophy magazine *Esprit* first introduced France to Walzer's work at a time when resistance to North American works was raging. During the 1990s, he was associated with the New Left, all the while suspected of endangering France's republican model. Since the early 2000s, Walzer has mainly been in demand for his writings on war and as a theoretician of multiculturalism. Yet his conception of shared understandings counters the moral self-sufficiency promoted by multiculturalist philosophies and the policies that flow from them, such as that of "reasonable accommodation."[5] In recent years, thanks in particular to the work of Astrid von Busekist, Justine Lacroix, and Simon Wuhl, lesser-known aspects of Walzer's work have gained prominence in France, especially his contributions to universalism and Judaism. Walzer has called for minimal morality, while reflecting on the irreducible diversity of social goods. Although this view still aligns with a majority logic, such a balanced position is invaluable for thinking about minority issues in our time. As a final step, therefore, this chapter seeks to recast the perspective of *Spheres of Justice* in the current context by showing that experiences of injustice contribute to shaping and connecting the moral spheres that Walzer discusses.

SOCIETY OF DISTRIBUTION

Spheres of Justice is based on the central idea that "human society" is a "distributive community." Walzer writes: "That's not all it is but it is importantly that: we come together to share, divide, and exchange. We also come together to make the things that are shared, divided, and exchanged; but that very making—work itself—is distributed among us as division of labor. My place in the economy, my standing in the political order, my reputation among my fellows, my material holdings: all of these come to me from other men and women."[6] Walzer draws this notion from Blaise Pascal's *Pensées*: he takes up the very powerful idea that "we live in the opinion of others."[7]

Using very concrete examples, he explores several spheres of justice that are both distinct and interdependent, including the family, the workplace, and public institutions. These spheres are constantly changing and are often specific to a given culture and political system. Walzer therefore does not make them his framework. Instead, he organizes his work around the study of social goods including membership, security and welfare, money and commodities, office, hard work, free time, and education. Walzer shows that these social goods change value from one sphere to another. He suggests, for example, that, within families, permanence takes precedence over the volatility that is typical of the market sphere.[8] The same applies to solicitude in romantic relationships: it must be exchanged throughout a relationship, whereas, in a commercial exchange, it only occurs in the initial act of sale.[9]

The same social good can mean different things in different spheres. This is why an everyday object functions differently as a gift to a friend and when it is used in a religious ceremony. As a result, the value of social goods depends on their context. Walzer believes that the value of social goods must not be affected by considerations outside the sphere in which they are exchanged: "Domination is ruled out only if social goods are distributed for distinct and 'internal' reasons."[10] As far as possible, the dominance of one social good over another should be eliminated. Physical strength, a name, or certain religious duties should not provide access to other resources such as consumer products, property, or political power. However, "no social good ever completely dominates the range of goods,"[11] because there is always the risk of encountering resistance: according to Walzer, "The struggle against the dominance of money, against corporate wealth and power, is perhaps the finest contemporary expression of self-respect."[12]

How should one judge whether social goods are distributed according to fair collective principles, when it is a question of both having and being?[13] Walzer believes that the best solution is to delve into the heart of the different spheres in which social goods are distributed. "Things slip away from the state's grasp," he says.[14] "There has never been a single criterion, or a single set of interconnected criteria, for all distributions."[15] He therefore rejects a single-tiered, monist approach to justice that would suggest there is "from Plato onward . . . one and only one distributive system that philosophy can rightly encompass."[16] In other words, pluralism is not only the fruit of human diversity and the variety of social goods exchanged; it also results from the fact that these exchanges' governing principles are themselves plural and the result of exchanges. "The struggle for control of the means of production is a distributive struggle."[17]

Walzer therefore criticizes overly speculative conceptions of equality. In order not to promote a rigid view of justice or exclude a number of situations and individuals, John Rawls favored the idea of an "original position" where everyone would be unaware of their exact place in the social space and would tend, for this reason, to retain the most protective definition of justice.[18] Apart from the fact that this "veil of ignorance" is more or less transparent and that some individuals have no interest in renouncing the sort of justice that serves them so well, Walzer points out that Rawls expected a world without community ties, as if the idea of justice were not marked by specific histories.

For all that, *Spheres of Justice* is not a complete questioning of the Rawlsian framework but rather its contextualization. From *A Theory of Justice* to *Political Liberalism*, John Rawls's theses have been driven by a concern for social justice, even if they have sometimes been read in a reductive way.[19] Rawls stands for justice to "maximize the expectations of those most disadvantaged."[20] Walzer acknowledges the importance of Rawlsian assumptions but questions their effectiveness in the real world.[21] He describes his own work, and that of theories that reflect on the meanings of justice in different communities of life, as a "corrective" to liberal theories of the political, such as Rawls's.[22]

To avoid the pitfall of a substantivist conception of justice, Walzer suggests that social goods be distributed according to the meaning they have for people. His statement is simple:

> All goods with which distributive justice is concerned are social goods. They are not and cannot be idiosyncratically valued. . . . Some domestic objects are cherished for private and sentimental reasons, but only in cultures where sentiment usually attaches to such objects. . . . There is no single set of primary or basic goods conceivable across all moral or material worlds. . . . Even the range of necessities, if we take into account moral as well as physical necessities, is very wide, and the rank orderings are very different.[23]

This variety stems from the historical character of the social goods that are exchanged. For Walzer, there are shared understandings among cultures, groups, or people, but the reasons for which a single thing is valued are different.[24] He thus proposes an antihegemonic theory of justice. This theory applies to the principles that govern exchanges. For example, merit, need, and money are not only intermediaries between different spheres of justice; they are social goods themselves, whose meanings vary. The idea of justice itself is negotiated and exchanged, and it fluctuates according to the contexts and the people concerned.[25]

If the distribution of goods is based on the meanings people assign them, is justice only possible at the individual level? For Walzer, meanings can and must be shared. This is the very condition for creating a sphere of justice. Some sort of agreement about lifestyles, values, and collective rules is necessary for a community to function. Such agreements are of course imperfect. Assessing merit is, for example, quite random; but if the *need* to agree is generally accepted, an exchange becomes possible.[26] Walzer's theory of justice therefore allows for different social circumstances as long as these differences do not create privileges in other spheres. He anticipates that the various manifestations of justice will break down to the point where they partially cancel each other out; he imagines "a complex egalitarian society" in which, "though there will be many small inequalities, inequality will not be multiplied through the conversion process."[27]

Several feminist authors, such as Susan Moller Okin, have criticized the weakness of this conceptualization in the face of the systemic and total nature of domination. Whereas Walzer, unlike many other theorists of justice, has taken the question of equality between women and men seriously, Moller Okin saw his conception of shared understandings as only possible in societies where minimal conditions of equality already exist.[28] For Walzer, however, such conditions are never so well attained as when the distribution of social goods in a given sphere makes it possible to imagine other modalities of distribution in other spheres, which broadens the field of equality: "Complex equality might look more secure if we could describe it in terms of the harmony, rather than the autonomy, of spheres. But social meanings and distributions are harmonious only in this respect: that when we see why one good has a certain form and is distributed in a certain way, we also see why another must be different."[29] Even with incentive measures, however, the conditions for equality are rarely met—which is highly detrimental to women.

Walzer addressed Moller Okin's reservations. He admitted that "arguments about justice can be developed across cultural boundaries and historical eras. . . . There is a minimal morality, a 'fine' conception of justice whose character is largely negative, which is probably rooted in human vulnerabilities and fears."[30] Walzer also reminded us that it is essential not to orient distribution methods even before an exchange, because this runs the risk of preventing "the appearance of shared understandings,"[31] particularly in the context of globalization. His concept of justice is not relativistic, but he is sensitive to the fragility of exchange and seeks to ensure that nothing can impede the emergence of new social meanings. It is therefore a liberal theory of justice since it is open to new practices provided they respect certain minimal, moral principles such as the rejection of cruelty.[32] Walzer calls himself a liberal Democrat and a liberal Socialist, but also a liberal nationalist and internationalist, a liberal communitarian, a liberal feminist, a liberal professor, a liberal intellectual, and a liberal Jew.[33] It is also in the name of liberal generosity[34] that he considers liberal capitalism to be an oxymoron.[35]

A COMMUNITARIAN IN PARIS

In France, *Spheres of Justice* was given a surprising reception, to say the least. As long-term editor of the magazine *Dissent*, as well as a civil rights and anti–Vietnam War activist, Walzer had always pleaded for greater equality among citizens through a democratic and egalitarian socialism committed to the realization of his ambitions.[36] His work was introduced in France and Belgium by those on the center Left who were engaged in the critique of totalitarianism and who supported pluralism and social planning.[37] Many belonged to Socialist French prime minister Michel Rocard's New Left or were Christian Democrats. From the early 1990s, even before *Spheres of Justice* was translated into French, it became a reference for the philosopher Paul Ricœur, a tutelary figure of *Esprit*,[38] and Michel Rocard himself.[39] During the 1990s, *Esprit* published many of Walzer's texts, as well as several interviews. Philosopher and editor Joël Roman gathered these contributions in a book entitled *Pluralisme et Démocratie*.[40] It was *Esprit*'s editor, Olivier Mongin, and a member of its editorial board, Stanford professor Jean-Pierre Dupuy, who welcomed the French-language translation of *Spheres of Justice* into their series at Éditions du Seuil in 1997.[41] Several of Michael Walzer's books were already available in French: *Exodus and Revolution* (1985) as *De l'exode à la liberté*;[42] *The Revolution of the Saints* (1965) as *La Révolution des Saints*;[43] *Regicide and Revolution* (1992) as *Régicide et Révolution*;[44] *Interpretation and Social Criticism* as *Critique et Sens commun*;[45] and *The Company of Critics* (1988) as *La Critique sociale au XXe siècle*.[46] Philosopher Christian Delacampagne also played an important role in promoting *Spheres of Justice*, devoting numerous talks and articles to it.[47] Several months after Éditions du Seuil published the book, Éditions Gallimard published *On Toleration* (1997) under the title *Traité sur la tolérance*,[48] in which Walzer examines different forms of toleration, from empires to multinational states. Walzer was directly involved in disseminating his work in France. He took part in several debates on democracy (for example, with Alain Touraine, at UNESCO in 1997) and gave numerous press interviews.

France's reception of Walzer's work on justice, however, came at a time when several people close to *Esprit* were defending "French-style multiculturalism."[49] Their willingness to make an exception signaled both an interest in and a distrust of burgeoning minority claims in the United States and Canada.[50] It was in this context that several contributors to *Esprit*, including Alain Finkielkraut, Luc Ferry, Pascal Bruckner, François Furet, and Danièle Sallenave, engaged in an all-out denunciation of "political correctness" and North American communitarianism.[51] Through a highly selective look at their country's history, they wrote essays extolling a French model created from scratch.[52] Following sociologist Irène Théry and philosopher Guy Coq, *Esprit* took aim at France's future Civil Solidarity Pact (*PaCS*).[53] In a series of articles that were very hostile to the reform, *Esprit* described legal equality between heterosexual or same-sex couples as a sign of the decadence of civilization and a threat to the "symbolic order."[54] This limited the distribution of *Spheres of Justice*, which relied on the very intellectual circles that violently refuted Walzer's conception of democratic pluralism.

This situation considerably limited the book's circulation in critical intellectual and activist spaces, particularly since Walzer's work on justice was also being introduced when several reports to the government were advocating scalable equality, particularly in schools. Walzer was thus held up as an example and associated with a certain rejection of the idea of equality.[55] And yet complex equality is not scalable equality. When Walzer encourages us to consider the meaning of justice in different spheres, it was not to relativize it, but rather to make justice more enduring. *Spheres of Justice* invites us to deconstruct the links between materiality and meaning and thus, like Axel Honneth's work,[56] is more in line with Ernst Cassirer's and Pierre Bourdieu's reflections on the production and exchange of symbolic goods.[57]

However, it would be inaccurate to describe the reception of *Spheres of Justice* in France as an aberration, since Walzer himself contributed to its intellectual positioning. As political scientist Mathieu Hauchecorne has suggested, *Dissent*'s legacy undoubtedly weighed heavily in the balance: critiquing self-management and traditional left-wing parties encouraged exchanges with *Esprit* through "positional homologies."[58] The Christian legacy of Emmanuel Mounier, *Esprit*'s founder, no doubt also contributed to the misunderstanding: a hasty reading of Walzer might suggest that the nonhegemony he defends presupposes a moral equivalence between spheres of justice, thus leaving the door open for a defense of religious agape and mysticism (as in the work of Luc Boltanski[59]). The reception of *Spheres of Justice* in France thus led to a distortion of the US debate. Although *Dissent* supported minority politics in the world, it was not, as Pierre Bourdieu and Loïc Waquant wrote, in the name of a "good humanist conscience" typical of the "old New York left" and characteristic of North American academic imperialism.[60] It is because the magazine, of

SPHERES OF EXPERIENCE

which Walzer was then co-editor-in-chief, supported a realistic conception of justice for which the struggle against domination did not require a convergence of social meanings.

At the same time, a more conservative wing rejected North American theories accused of promoting "the tyranny of minorities." The term had first been used to warn of the risk of European nations disintegrating under the pressure of autonomist movements.[61] Then, in 1992, in the wake of the sexual harassment allegations made against Clarence Thomas,[62] philosopher Philippe Raynaud popularized the term, claiming to overturn the Tocquevillian concept of "tyranny of the majority."[63] He argued that minorities had acquired so much influence across the Atlantic that they now had the upper hand over US institutions, particularly the judiciary. By trying too hard to avoid a concentration of power, special interests would end up capturing that power. According to Raynaud, "The segmentation of society into a heterogeneous set of 'minorities' [to be protected] ended up becoming the *sole* political project of US liberals. The result . . . is easy to understand: a democracy of 'rights' is above all a democracy of 'minorities.'"[64] Ignoring all relations of domination, Raynaud went so far as to describe the protection of minorities as a form of "confinement."[65]

However, the vulnerability of minorities is well documented. For Tocqueville, US democracy provided no real guarantee against an all-powerful majority.[66] Inspired by part 10 of James Madison's *Federalist Papers*,[67] Tocqueville showed that the danger of tyranny exists because the majority is at once a mode of representation, decision, and thought—which restricts the exercise of freedom:[68] "In America, the majority draws a formidable circle around thought. Within these limits, the writer is free; but woe to him if he dares to go beyond them. It isn't that he has to fear an *auto-da-fé*, but he is exposed to all types of distasteful things and to everyday persecutions."[69] For Tocqueville, the practice of criticism is as important as institutional checks and balances. Minorities are not to blame when they challenge sovereignty because it is tyranny that is at the root of their disaffiliation:[70] "If liberty is ever lost in America, it will be necessary to lay the blame on the omnipotence of the majority that will have brought minorities to despair and will have forced them to appeal to physical force. Then you will see anarchy, but it will arrive as a consequence of despotism."[71]

Walzer's definition of tyranny is fairly close; according to him, tyranny is "a particular boundary crossing, a particular violation of social meaning."[72] Distribution then becomes a monopolistic system.[73] He reminds us that "good fences make just societies,"[74] Complex equality stands in stark contrast to the state of tyranny that characterizes totalitarian regimes; complex equality is a "maximum differentiation as against maximum coordination."[75] To rule is not to dominate: to rule is to direct distribution.[76]

After 2000, Walzer's influence in France grew. In the context of the Second Persian Gulf War, he gave several interviews to the newspaper *Le Monde* on the issue of just and unjust conflicts.[77] Philosopher Justine Lacroix devoted a special issue of the *Revue internationale de philosophie* to Walzer that highlighted his universalism.[78] Simon Wuhl, for his part, questioned the Judaic heritage in Walzer's thought.[79] In 2020, a book of interviews with Astrid von Busekist repositioned Michael Walzer's work as critical of institutions and social norms, including those created by left-wing movements.[80] It also provided a better understanding of how his Talmudic readings contributed to his conception of exchanges and peace.[81] In February 2023, for *Spheres of Justice*'s fortieth anniversary, philosophers Félix Megret, Christian Berner, and Christian Lazzeri organized a symposium at the University of Paris Nanterre to discuss the critical relevance of the work. Over the past four decades, Walzer's theory of justice has indirectly inspired several French works devoted to moral relations. Bruno Latour's work on modes of existence is reminiscent of the Walzerian framework, even if the notion of "mode" introduced a more impressionistic conception of interactions.[82]

In this book, I apply Walzerian theorizing to the field of antidiscrimination law in France and the United States. The minimal morality to which Walzer refers in response to feminist critiques of his work remains, in fact, governed by a majority principle: "Our minimum morality," he wrote, "summarizes what seems to be the most important . . . to the greatest number of us."[83] This question arises several times in *Spheres of Justice* but is not resolved: "*What touches all should be decided by all.* But once one begins including all the people who are touched or affected by a given decision, and not just those whose daily activities are directed by it, it is hard to know where to stop."[84] If a minority Pandora's box causes trouble, it is because it forces us to think not only about whom a decision

SPHERES OF EXPERIENCE

affects but also in what form and with what intensity. *Spheres of Justice* criticizes the moral hegemony of one sphere over the other but does not characterize it. The notion of minority appears only three times and as a simple synonym for "small number."

In my view, however, the key task for a twenty-first-century theory of justice is to think from a minority perspective, a task that Walzer's work has enabled but not directly engaged. Benjamin Boudou summed up this approach perfectly with regard to the treatment of foreigners (subjected to rules established by nationals): "By considering the fundamental interests of all those who are affected by power rather than by membership, we give ourselves the means to think about the injustices that allow a group to exercise power over individuals who have no say."[85] To fight injustice, we have to change our perspective by thinking about a group based on what it excludes. Walzer is mistaken in thinking that microsites of resistance are incapable of undermining relations of domination. Michel Foucault did not leave subjects disarmed in the face of the capillarity of power, as Walzer claimed.[86] To pluralize is not only to multiply meanings; it is also to acknowledge the performative potency of minority practices on multiple scales.

THE TEST OF PLURALISM

Spheres of Justice is not a multiculturalist theory. Multiculturalism consists in recognizing the history and specificities of the linguistic, social, religious, and cultural groups who live in the same country by implementing various policies that support education, participation, creativity, and dialogue between the different communities. The overall goal of multiculturalism is to maintain cohesive social bonds by combining group recognition, intercommunity tolerance, and state neutrality.[87] The term first emerged in Canada under Pierre Trudeau's leadership. As early as 1963, the Royal Commission on Bilingualism and Biculturalism recommended promoting social and cultural diversity. On October 8, 1971, in a speech to the Canadian House of Commons, Prime Minister Trudeau heralded a new era of multicultural policies. From the outset multiculturalism had a hidden agenda: diluting Francophone demands for recognition—not to mention autonomy—among those of other minorities.

Multiculturalism promotes a vision of social groups as a sort of archipelago, reflecting a shift from a vertical to a horizontal conception of the social world.[88] In this context, the task of institutions is to recognize discriminated groups both symbolically and materially by establishing mechanisms to compensate for inequalities and by providing various forms of arbitration in the event of conflict. In that respect multiculturalist approaches are rooted in classical liberalism. On the one hand, they tend to conceive of institutions as neutral; on the other hand, they recognize social groups to maximize every individual's potential. This is not so with Walzer: for him, institutions are never neutral. Politics is both a sphere in its own right and a principle that cuts across other spheres: "The political community is probably the closest we can come to a world of common meanings. . . . Politics, moreover, establishes its own bonds of commonality."[89] Individuals and social groups are marked by both horizontality and verticality.

Canada's debate on multiculturalism culminated in its "reasonable accommodation" policies. The concept was developed in 1985 in a case in which a salesperson, who could not work on Saturdays for religious reasons, was demoted from a permanent employee to a casual employee.[90] "Reasonable accommodation" refers to the possibility of finding a balance between the fundamental rights of individuals and the general rules that could impose "undue hardship" on them.[91] Such accommodation is not unlimited since it must remain "reasonable." But owing to the strength of case law, what was a matter of case-by-case arbitration has taken the form of more general standards of accommodation relative to entire groups, in this case religious ones.[92] In this context Canadian public administrations and companies allow people of the Jewish or Muslim faith to take a day off during their religious holidays since the civil calendar only recognizes Catholic holidays.

This transition from individual to collective accommodation, however, reached its limits in Quebec. Several high-profile cases sparked a far-reaching debate on which standards it would be "reasonable" to accept in a culturally dominated province. The first instance came on the heels of a 2006 ruling by the Supreme Court of Canada in the *Multani* case on the issue of Sikhs carrying a *kirpan* (a religious ceremonial dagger) in schools. The court overturned a decision of the Quebec Court of Appeal and upheld the lower court's judgment in the name of reasonable accommodation, thus authorizing the student to carry his *kirpan* to school "in a wooden sheath and wrapped and sewn securely in a sturdy cloth envelope."[93] Another case raised the issue of gender equality. In 2007, the municipal council of the Quebec village of Hérouxville adopted resolutions on community life and the private sphere. Entitled "Code of Life," the text specified that "men and women have the same value. Consequently . . . we consider that killing women in public beatings, or burning them alive are not part of our code of life."[94] By referring to a "code of conduct," they were doing the opposite of what they claimed to defend, linking criminal acts to cultural practices. Other cases were also highly publicized, such as the request by some Hasidic Jews in the Montreal borough of Outremont to install frosted windows at a YMCA gym and the removal of pork from certain cafeteria menus to satisfy Islamic dietary restrictions.[95]

In February 2007, Prime Minister Jean Charest called for the formation of a *Consultation Commission on Accommodation Practices Related to Cultural Differences*, cochaired by historian Gérard Bouchard and philosopher Charles Taylor. The commission's mission was to take stock of the reasonable accommodations accumulated over the years, disentangle the existing lexicon, and make recommendations. A year later, the commission published its report, *Founding the Future: The Time for Conciliation*, which advocated developing diversity policies specific to Quebec.[96] The commission noted that Quebec society was *pluri*culturalist (i.e., that calls for the meeting of cultures around a common foundation, in which language plays a key role), not *multi*culturalist (i.e., founded on individual rights, recognizing the existence of isolated communities). In other words, reasonable accommodation was problematic in a society that itself was culturally dominated on a national level and that could not accept accommodations without fearing for its own existence. In France, these debates were mostly portrayed as the unsuitability of multiculturalism for French-speaking societies, thus shifting from a relational justification of exceptionalism (the circumstances of French-speaking cultures in Canada) to a cultural one (the values borne by French-speaking cultures).[97] Likewise, the shift from the legal sphere to public debate exacerbated differences of opinion, threatening accommodation in the long run.[98] In this respect, the Bouchard-Taylor commission's response was not entirely satisfactory, since it avoided the issue of a clear conflict between pluralism and "common values."[99]

Political scientist Sarah Song highlighted the risks of a multiculturalist siloing of cultures.[100] She cited two cases in which cultural traditions served to undermine women's rights in the United States. The first involved a Pueblo girl whose father was not a member of the tribe. According to custom she was not eligible for tribal citizenship, a condition sine qua non for accessing various social and medical systems provided by the federal government. The US Supreme Court declined to rule out of respect for tribal law.[101] In the second case, a man of Chinese origin was convicted of murdering his wife. His sentence was reduced to a minimum term because, after consulting an anthropologist, the court took into account the fact that Chinese tradition would allow the husband to retaliate in the event of adultery.[102]

Drawing on these two examples, Song criticized the congruence effect of gender norms between minorities and the majority, the boomerang effect (which causes locally tolerated, patriarchal norms to come back with greater force in society as a whole), and the diversionary effect (which reduces attention to gender inequalities).[103] Susan Moller Okin also criticized multiculturalism for adopting an overly idealized definition of cultural groups, to the point of reinforcing inequalities between women and men.[104] She argues that multiculturalism is unsatisfactory because it invariably ends up justifying illiberal values on the grounds that certain groups have not benefited from the conditions required to pursue equality. The impact of moral values on people thus moves into the background.[105] This is the case with Will Kymlicka. While his early work excluded illiberal groups from the scope of multicultural policies,[106] he then made an exception for national minorities.[107] In his view, the mission of liberalism is to give people the means to revise their traditional values, even if this involves recognizing these values in some way.[108]

The coincidental timing of the translation of *Spheres of Justice* in France and about the debates on multicultural policies in Canada led many political theory textbooks to classify Michael Walzer among the champions of multiculturalism, although his approach differed.[109] The Bouchard-Taylor commission sought to avoid conflict by confining each minority to its own moral sphere. It fragmented the principle of equality

SPHERES OF EXPERIENCE

by acknowledging that there were spaces where the general principles of law could be suspended. It sidestepped the cultural knot but did not sever it. In contrast, Walzer argues that the pursuit of shared understandings requires arbitration in cases of moral disagreements.[110] Because we are all "culture-producing creatures,"[111] however, he points out that there is no such thing as a "good" conception of justice.[112] This does not mean that justice lacks overall consistency. According to Walzer, "The relativity of justice follows from the classic non-relative definition, giving each person his due."[113] He insists that this fair share cannot be determined on the basis of general principles, even those that seemed to cut across areas such as free exchange, merit, or need.[114] Even though there are no single distribution criteria, Walzer nevertheless sketches out a few possible avenues:

There are an infinite number of possible lives. . . . A given society is just if its substantial life is lived in a certain way—that is, in a way faithful to the shared understandings of the members. (When people disagree about the meanings of social goods, when understandings are controversial, then justice requires that the society be faithful to disagreements, providing institutional channels for their expression, adjudicative mechanisms, and alternative distributions).[115]

In this sense, Walzer is first and foremost a pluralist. He recognizes both the diversity of cultures and the need to settle disputes over social goods and their distribution. Walzer gives the example of a village society that sets up a very unequal distribution of the grains it harvests collectively, and he concludes that any decision that might break this agreement would be tyrannical since the mode of distribution is based on a shared conception. However, he then immediately adds that this inequality may only be accepted on the surface.[116] He thus recognizes the importance of protective mechanisms *despite* the existence of these shared understandings.

Two mechanisms are necessary to avoid isolating cultures: paying attention to the threshold at which interests diverge, and examining the contribution to democracy that results from recognizing a particular rule as an exception to common law. As long as the question is framed solely from the perspective of what democracy can do for minority groups, the moral dilemma remains insurmountable. To make pluralism effective, the reasoning must be reversed.[117] Challenging the fundamental rights of sexual minorities does not qualify as freedom of expression, since this type of discourse is an attack on the freedom of others. Conversely, legally recognizing same-sex couples does not call into question freedom of expression or religious freedom. It does not infringe on people's right to express themselves as long as the opinion expressed is neither offensive nor defamatory, and it does not disturb the public order. Nor does it inhibit beliefs or their free exercise. It is therefore entirely possible to resolve moral conflicts between minorities without falling into relativistic biases.

But there remains the question of the threshold. At what point is a social practice recognized as a source for creating laws imposed in all moral spheres? There is no definitive answer to this question, but there are context-specific solutions. In democratic societies, the fact that some women wear a veil in no way prevents others from not wearing one. Therefore, no prohibition is normatively relevant.[118] However, despite this observation, we should not overlook the ways in which representations of women's bodies, and the clothes women wear or do not wear, are vectors of domination on a collective level. A depreciative representation may be partially offset by social status, place of residence, or financial resources, all of which may lead to less exposure.

Yet what does not harm a single individual can harm the group. A given practice may therefore be a minority *and* a majority practice. If the wearing of the veil has multiple meanings, it is because it does not have the same significance in different national political traditions,[119] at school or within the family,[120] or from one generation to another.[121] A minority group in a given country, such as Muslims in France, can perfectly well engage in majority practices in certain spaces and thus play a part in excluding other groups that nevertheless dominate them in another sphere.[122] Recognizing that certain social practices are both macro-minority *and* micro-majority practices allows us to better understand how one sphere of justice can come to dominate another. This is precisely where an approach based on injustice proves useful by making it possible to shift the discussion. Rather than focusing on a normative conflict between two groups of women, veiled or nonveiled, the notion of injustice raises questions as to why men do not have to wear veils, why all men wear the same clothes when performing certain functions (in business, finance, politics, etc.), and why they are less obliged to display their bodies in public places. Reversing our perspective thus enables us to put relations of domination back at the heart of theoretical work.[123]

THREE WAYS OF EXPERIENCING INJUSTICE

It is useful to conceive of moral spheres in terms of injustice because the experience of injustice contributes to shaping an idea of justice. When individuals reject discrimination, inequality, and hierarchy, they shape their normative background by aggregating scattered principles, challenging them, and reformulating them. "Without the new ideas of oppression and corruption," Michael Walzer tells us, "without the sense of injustice, without moral revulsion, neither Exodus nor revolution would be possible. In the text [Exodus] as we have it, the new ideas are shadowed by their older opposites: the sense of injustice by resignation, revulsion by longing."[124] It is precisely because we experience or witness actual or potential abuse that we rely on moral principles to help us get through such ordeals. Consequently, all theorization of justice is fieldwork; the principles of justice always emanate from the practices of injustice that they regulate and give meaning to. This observation gives political theory a sociological as well as a normative dimension.[125]

Yet injustice is not simply the other side of justice—its embryonic state in Plato[126] or its corrupted version in Machiavelli[127]—that is, a set of situations in which justice does not prevail or no longer does. Over the centuries, many philosophers of justice have staged an impossible dialogue between enthusiastic defenders of justice as a public good and despisers of human nature, which is inherently unjust.[128] Thus, injustice became a sort of rhetorical twin, which helped strengthen the idea of justice.[129] This pairing, however, made theories of justice subservient to the anthropologies that dominate each era and rendered them more "vulnerable to being criticized as ultra-rationalist, idealist, and angelist," explains Céline Spector.[130]

In fact, injustice has its own logic, its own history, and its own classification methods.[131] To theorize injustice is not to relativize the idea of justice; rather, it is to deepen it by paying greater attention to the historical and cognitive processes that connect the just and the unjust. For philosopher Judith Shklar, "Because we cannot possibly expect to agree on what we ourselves deserve and on what is owed to others . . . we constantly feel that injustice is being done, even by those who accept the legalistic ethos. Even the most impartial minds and fair-minded people, and especially those who are in a position to impose political or judicial decisions upon us, will seem unjust sooner or later."[132]

Injustice is the modus operandi of a whole set of social relations based on honor, debt, purity, idolatry, care, and so on. On a psychological level, injustice precedes justice (the formation of judgment in children begins with the experience of injustice). Phenomenologically, injustice is the driving force behind affiliation and disaffiliation in any given community. I therefore subscribe to philosopher Emmanuel Renault's observation that theories of justice require a paradigm shift. Until now, most theories have used the experience of injustice to justify their approach, but they have failed to make it a full-fledged philosopheme, as if injustice were too subjective to form a basis for solid conceptual work.[133] This is why the economist Amartya Sen mostly approaches injustice in a restrictive way. For him, one can speak of injustice only if there is a possibility of avoiding calamities.[134] Contributions centered on injustice remain rare, although there are a few notable exceptions, such as those of the philosopher Miranda Fricker: using the term "epistemic injustice," she highlights situations in which any prejudice removes all credibility from the individual (testimonial injustice) as well as situations in which there is a gap in interpretative resources upstream of any exchange (hermeneutic injustice).[135]

In contemporary Western democracies, legal thinking tends to equate injustice and discrimination—an injustice amounts to an unfounded and legally sanctionable difference in treatment. And yet institutions do not have a monopoly on determining what is just and what is unjust. The moral law governing the group (the family, the friendly community, the couple, etc.) establishes rules and provides its own, most often symbolic, modes of reparation. Individuals fight injustices because they need a group's approval; their own certainties are not enough (their conscience is lost and possibly found in the other).[136] It is therefore impossible to define injustice according to absolute criteria.[137] That is its virtue. It is in fact futile to try to circumscribe the idea of justice, except to claim to essentialize something absent, a mirage, or a "lost origin" for which institutional systems might strive to provide the least imperfect translation.[138] Justice is always prescriptive. It is neither truth nor goodness. It imposes principles that a society adopts at a given moment in its history. It is precisely because it is prescriptive, and by extension performative, that conceiving of justice through a reflection on injustice is so meaningful.

In this sense, my approach to justice resonates with that of Philip Pettit, who thinks against the grain when he discusses justice. He approaches social justice ("between the citizens of any one society"), political justice ("justice in relations between citizens and the government that rules their lives"), and international justice ("justice in the relations between different peoples of the earth") as the quest for nondomination.[139] The notion of injustice offers other advantages. Because injustice is linked, either directly or indirectly, to experience, it is much more flexible than the notion of justice, whose "Keynesian-Westphalian framework," a strong legal formalization, reduces its scope.[140] Theorizing injustice helps to avoid making the major principles of justice—such as equality, freedom, and solidarity—contingent, while simultaneously thinking about them in terms of their limits[141]—which avoids overessentializing them. In other words, to theorize injustice is to think about democracy from the wings.[142]

Centering injustice shifts the focus onto experience, and the experience of injustice combines three distinct but interdependent situations. First is the actual *direct experience* of injustice of persons who, because they belong to a given group, are subjected to discrimination, insults, violence, exclusion, and the like. Second is the *possibility* of injustice: even when a potential injustice does not materialize, its specter continues to hover over all minority people. Individuals may never have been violated in a public space yet still be fully aware that such violence exists and that they may fall victim to it at any time. Their freedom of movement, by anticipation, will be affected. Third is the *witnessing* of injustice. Injustice involving one's own group has a profound impact on one's mental health.[143] Injustice involving other groups acts both as a reassurance and a threat, thus compelling a certain disciplined behavior. Indeed witnessing the mistreatment of other groups reaffirms a privilege, as the witness is not actually in danger.[144] However, this show of injustice also places limits on the witness's freedom: witnessing an injustice perpetrated against a member of another group raises one's awareness of the boundaries that limit one's own action; to intervene is to risk being assimilated to the victim. As Sandy Alexandre has shown, there is an "ecology of lynching" in which the witness, whether direct or indirect, is also singled out.[145]

Any show of injustice is a general call to order: for the minorities concerned, for other minorities, and also for majority subjects whose experiences of injustice are, admittedly, fewer in number, less intense, and offset by their dominant position, but no less real. The resonance of these three experiences of injustice might be conscious or unconscious, accepted or denied, pleasurable or painful, but it is always the pivot of the subjective transactions between minority and majority individuals. We must therefore return to the Benjaminian sense of experience as a form of participation with the other.[146] An experience can be total (the sum total of structural, permanent, and powerful constraints) or more momentary and of lower intensity. In the latter case, it is not a vector of identity and does not justify any particular legal status, but it can be the basis of a renewed relationship with the other, thus linking minority and majority paths.

Such a change is only possible if experience itself is subject to critique. If conceived as self-truth, experience will fail to transform norms. It then merely substitutes one dogma for another since, as Joan W. Scott wrote, "The evidence of experience works as a foundation providing both a starting point and a conclusive kind of explanation, beyond which few questions can or need to be asked."[147] And yet should experience be excluded from the field of critical theory? What else can it teach us? Caroline Hau calls for experience to be conceived as a way of processing information:

While experience cannot be assumed to be self-evident and always reliable . . . it would be wrong to argue that experience is always "epistemologically suspect." One way of conceptualizing experience in cognitive terms is to look at it as involving a range of processes of organizing information, processes that, like all cognitive activities, involve constant reinterpretation, reevaluation, and adjudication. These processes do not have to be consciously or even fully elaborated.[148]

Conceived in these terms, experience introduces an essential factor in the apprehension of injustice: its relationship to time. Experience makes it possible to differentiate what is fortuitous from what is permanent, such as a structural lack of resources—affordable housing, for example.[149] When thinking in terms of injustice, structure itself becomes the subject of justice, that is, answerable to its norms.[150] Thicker conceptions of justice thus emerge.[151] Iris Marion Young talks about nonexploitation, nonmarginalization, nondisempowerment, noncultural imperialism, and nonviolence.[152] More recently, a US collective laid out a series of very similar

SPHERES OF EXPERIENCE

criteria: nondiscrimination, political equality, freedom, universal economic security, egalitarian pluralism, community, and sustainability.[153]

Injustice, then. But why think in terms of spheres? Wouldn't changing one of the terms of the Walzerian framework require abandoning its overall architecture? On the basis of numerous field investigations, sociologists Alain Bihr and Roland Pfefferkorn have established that the spheres of activity that correspond to Walzer's moral spheres overlap with each other. An injustice experienced in a professional sphere can thus cause other experiences of injustice in other spheres, be it in health, housing, or the public space.[154] To counter such permeability, Walzer responds with both moral and procedural pluralism: "Difference as a value exists alongside peace, equality, and autonomy; it doesn't supersede them. My argument is that all these are best pursued politically in circumstances where there are many avenues of pursuit, many agents in pursuit."[155] Walzer believes we must pluralize the idea of justice and also make it more complex. The greater the number of distinct social goods, the greater the possibility of justice.[156] This conclusion is undoubtedly optimistic. Walzer justifies it by referring to the moral obligation to choose. He writes: "For a pluralist, at bottom, is a man with more than one commitment, who may at any moment have to choose among his different obligations."[157]

This is where my perspective diverges from his. In the end, if pluralism results from a demand for choice, it is, in my view, too weak a response to domination. This version of pluralism presupposes, in fact, that community exists before moral choice, even though community manifests in the very act of choosing (or not choosing). Elsewhere Walzer also recognizes the limits of his assertion: "It is a mistake, and a characteristically liberal mistake, to think that the existing patterns of association are entirely or even largely voluntary and contractual, that is the product of will alone."[158] To avoid the dead ends of a purely associative conception of justice, Walzer proposes an antihegemonic model for the distribution of social goods, a model that can be improved by extending it. It follows that the further individuals are from the norm, the more the state must be present.[159]

This is a double-edged sword. When minority individuals criticize the government, they are readily suspected of being separatists, while the same criticism offered by someone in the majority would be seen as a useful contribution to the common good.[160] Social exclusion results as much from a demand to conform as from a condemnation of criticism.

Minorities make visible "the capacity of the state not to judge" majority subjects.[161] They raise the question of who among us has or does not have "the possibility of untying ourselves from what we have done."[162] This is why I am proposing an approach that centers on injustice. I am not taking a step in the direction of a political philosophy of the good; rather, I am relying on the fact that a minority position, both outside and at the heart of the majority worlds, can improve democracy. The distribution of social goods is not only a matter of ownership or possession; it is also a matter of dispossession. How can individuals "undo" the very justice system they depend on?

I have devoted this first chapter to Michael Walzer's theory of justice because I share his intellectual and human objectives:

> We need liberal democrats ready to fight against the new populism; liberal socialists who defend equality but oppose the frequent authoritarianism of left-wing regimes; liberal nationalists who resist contemporary xenophobic nationalisms, including those that are anti-Muslim and anti-Semitic; liberal internationalists who defend people in trouble across the border; liberal communitarians who oppose the exclusivist passions and fierce partisanship of some identity groups; liberal feminists who know when to use state power to promote gender equality and when not to; liberal professors who defend free speech on campuses; liberal intellectuals who not only "speak truth to power" but speak truth simply and always; and liberal Jews, Christians, Muslims, Hindus, Buddhists, and all the rest who stand against the unexpected return of religious zealotry.[163]

A program such as this one cannot be achieved without mechanisms for transforming subjectivities, strengthening participation, improving the distribution of goods, protecting the planet, and making political subjects more connected, in law and in practice. Many of these mechanisms revolve around the minority relationship to the other. Like Walzer, I am not promoting any transcendental principle. A shared understanding never precedes a relationship. However, I am proposing an ethics that tries to connect different experiences of injustice and, on that basis, to bring out more emancipatory forms of presence and learning. Minority experience is *comp*rehension in the sense that it is learning from injustice *with* others.

In the next four chapters, I will analyze the obstacles confronting the concept of minority today, primarily in France and the United States. In the final three chapters, I will then address these challenges by outlining a social, legal, and political theory of injustice and its various spheres.

2

MANAGING DIVERSITY

The United Nations Charter, adopted in San Francisco on June 26, 1945, made no mention of minorities. Three years later, the fifty-eight states that make up the UN General Assembly met at the Palais de Chaillot in Paris. On December 10, 1948, they adopted the Universal Declaration of Human Rights. The question of minorities was still absent. It was not until the International Covenant on Civil and Political Rights (ICCPR) of December 16, 1966, which entered into force ten years later, that certain minorities acquired specific protections. Article 27 of the ICCPR specifies that "in those States in which ethnic, religious or linguistic minorities exist, persons belonging to such minorities shall not be denied the right, in community with the other members of their group, to enjoy their own culture, to profess and practice their own religion, or to use their own language." France expressed a reservation about this article since it considers its territory indivisible, a principle set out in Article 1 of its 1958 constitution. Article 27's civil and political rights therefore do not apply to continental France, Corsica, or France's overseas territories.

The word "minority" encompasses very different realities in different parts of the world. It has also changed significantly over time. The word comes from the medieval Latin *minoritas*, itself derived from the Latin *minor*, which designated the smaller of two things or two people, sometimes the youngest or most vulnerable. In Middle French, the term was used to describe the status of a person who was not yet an adult and did not have full legal agency. In 1374, Charles V invoked this word when establishing the age required to succeed to the throne as fourteen.[1] The earliest evidence in Middle English is from 1483 (the Acts of Parliament of Scotland).[2] In the eighteenth century, the term "minority" began to designate the smallest part of a group, more particularly within the context of an assembly. This definition was first used in the context of Great Britain's parliamentary democracy before becoming established in France shortly before the Revolution. The terms "minority" and "majority" then became a subject of political, constitutional, and theoretical debates.[3] In the United States, the place granted to a minority in the electoral system, in the workings of Congress, and in the federal organization of the state (in its judicial system in particular) was central to the Philadelphia Convention of 1787, which led to the drafting of the Constitution.[4]

It was not until the beginning of the twentieth century that the notion of minority began to designate national, religious, linguistic, and cultural groups living in a country that did not share their characteristics. The development of international law helped spread this new meaning. Thus Article 93 of the Treaty of Versailles (June 28, 1919) required protecting "the interests of inhabitants of Poland who differ from the majority of the population in race, language or religion." Starting in the 1960s in the United States and the 1970s in Europe, the growth of antidiscrimination law refocused the notion of minority on discrimination resulting from stigmatized identities. This change proved all the more significant when numerous books and articles on multicultural society were published in the 1980s and 1990s in the wake of studies by Charles Taylor, Will Kymlicka, and Michael Sandel. "Minority" is the product of a long history. It therefore conveys different meanings, depending on the context: a lack of legal agency; numerical inferiority; a subnational cultural community; and victims of discrimination. The term can refer to both individuals and groups of individuals or both. This semantic blurring is both a strength and a weakness: a strength because the term "minority" can adapt to the new social, political, and legal configurations brought about by the intensification of social interactions in the era of globalization and new communication technologies; and a weakness because the very same term can be subjected to myriad corruptions, which tends to make it rather suspect, especially in highly centralized countries such as France.

To untangle these semantic issues and their political consequences, this chapter compares how France and the United States define their respective minorities and describes the ensuing constraints and forms of authority. Is there such a thing as minority power? I analyze the antidiscriminatory culture that has taken hold on some US campuses and which, seen from France and even at times within the United States, has become a highly contentious issue. More specifically this chapter addresses the impact of social media and the role of academic institutions. After revisiting the distinction between power and influence established by various works of social psychology (in particular those of Serge Moscovici), this chapter will then show that minorities have no direct power but rather a capacity for influence upon which new management techniques thrive.

DISTURBANCES IN THE LAW

It is not uncommon for social theories that claim the moral superiority of majority rule or, conversely, that place value on the role of minorities in a democracy to pay no attention to what constitutes a "majority" or a "minority."[5] This is entirely understandable. Majorities and minorities exist in specific, relational contexts, while also being part of a "transnational moment."[6] A linguistic minority that moves to a new country in which the majority officially recognizes and speaks its language would be left with little more than its minority history.

The use of the term "minority" is no simpler: in a given situation, some people will claim this label for themselves, whereas others will reject it. Some consider this piece of their identity to be fundamental; others regard it as secondary. It is therefore impossible to establish a definition of "minority" that is both exhaustive and stable. And yet it is precisely because its boundaries are so blurred that the notion of "minority" instigates social mobilization, inspires artists, and raises legal questions. The work of defining it is the very locus of its power.[7] This is what philosopher Ernesto Laclau called "the war of identities": a struggle to control the processes of defining oneself and others.[8] In this struggle for epistemic hegemony, our weaponry is unequal. Some people have the wherewithal to define themselves, whereas others are identified before they can even name themselves. It is this asymmetry that ultimately differentiates majority and minority. In other words, identity is at once the cause, the driving force, and the result of struggles between "social labels."

The law is one of the main spaces in which the fight over identities takes place. In France, as in the United States, the law establishes lists of criteria according to which different treatments are considered discriminatory. These lists or categories are more or less open-ended. For example, Article 14 of the European Convention on Human Rights (ECHR) uses "such as" to bring together a wide range of discriminatory grounds, from physical traits and beliefs to social practices. In France, the grounds for discrimination now number twenty-five: age; sex; social and/or national origin; membership or nonmembership, real or perceived, of an ethnic group; membership or nonmembership, real or perceived, of a nation or purported race; pregnancy; state of health; disability; genetic characteristics; sexual orientation; gender identity; political opinion; union activity; philosophical opinion; religious beliefs, or membership or nonmembership, real or perceived, in a religion; marital status; physical appearance; name; mores; place of residence; loss of autonomy; economic vulnerability; language; and bank account location. These criteria fall under different branches of the law (labor law, civil law, criminal law, etc.) and are not all codified. In 2016, Robin Medard Inghilterra tallied twenty grounds for discrimination in criminal law, twenty-one in labor law, eleven to thirteen noncodified grounds, and fifteen to sixteen focusing on the status of public servants.[9]

Antidiscrimination law in France has in fact developed gradually. It began on July 1, 1972 with the Pleven Law, which made "incitement to hatred because of origin or membership or non-membership of an ethnic group, nation, race or religion" grounds for criminal sanction.[10] A second milestone was the transposition into French law of the European directive of February 9, 1976, on the implementation of the principle of equal treatment between men and women as regards access to employment, vocational training and promotion, and working conditions.[11] Since then many provisions have been added in criminal, social, and civil law.[12] An independent administrative authority was created in 2004 (the HALDE,

High Authority for the Fight against Discrimination and for Equality) and absorbed into the office of the *Défenseur des droits* (Defender of Rights, an independent administrative authority enshrined by the French constitution) in 2011.[13] Finally, the law of May 27, 2008, brought some clarification to discriminatory categories but only for issues that were within the scope of European Union law.[14]

The United States experienced a similar shift: the protected classes were gradually extended to the public sphere, school, and the workplace. The first civil rights law was passed in 1875 but found to be unconstitutional in 1883. In 1954, the Supreme Court's *Brown v. Board of Education* decision declared racial segregation in schools unconstitutional. The Civil Rights Act of 1957 followed, reaffirming equal voting rights. Strictly speaking, the first antidiscrimination provision was included in the 1963 law on equal pay for women and men, although it was not very restrictive and allowed for numerous exceptions.

It was the Civil Rights Act of 1964 that formed the true basis of US antidiscrimination law: its Title VII protects race, religion, skin color, sex, and national origin against discrimination in the workplace. Sex as a criterion was not covered in the initial version of the bill. It was added by way of a House amendment introduced by Virginia Representative Howard Smith, whose purpose, it seems, was to derail the bill by overextending it.[15] Since then, the scope of the Civil Rights Act has expanded through the combination of new legislation and case law: the 1967 Age Discrimination in Employment Act protects people over the age of forty; the Pregnancy Discrimination Act of 1978 prohibits discrimination on the basis of pregnancy, childbirth, and related medical conditions (except within companies with fewer than fifteen employees); the Americans with Disabilities Act of 1990 prohibits discrimination against people with disabilities and requires reasonable accommodations at work; and the Genetic Information Nondiscrimination Act of 2009 prohibits employers with fifteen employees or more from using genetic data for hiring, promoting, or firing employees. Similarly, the Supreme Court's 2020 *Bostock v. Clayton County* decision included sexual orientation and gender identities in the sex category added in 1964.[16] There are fewer categories in US antidiscrimination law, but they remain very close to French criteria: sex, sexual orientation, gender identities, race, age, disability, belief, skin color, national origin, religion, and genetic data. Individual states also have their own systems to prohibit harassment, discrimination in the workplace, and violence on discriminatory grounds.

While there are real similarities between France and the United States, the way protected categories are defined is not the same. In the United States, case law considers that categories must relate to characteristics that cannot be changed, such as skin color, age, and the like. Body shape or size and certain physical attributes are therefore excluded, as clarified by *Rogers v. American Airlines*, in which the District Court for the Southern District of New York held that a company's policy regarding its employee dress code (in this case, prohibiting braids) did not constitute discrimination because employees could change their appearance at will.[17] This interpretation limited the scope of antidiscrimination law.[18] In Europe, the establishment of discrimination is more flexible and broader. Judges retain as criteria attributes that it would be unreasonable to expect anyone to renounce (for example, religion, sexual orientation, or a physical trait)[19] and specify that protected categories are not limited to "characteristics which are personal in the sense that they are innate or inherent to the person."[20]

Similarly, direct discrimination (or disparate treatment) and indirect discrimination (or disparate impact) are also assessed differently on both sides of the Atlantic. In the United States, case law defines the contours of disparate impact: it is any seemingly neutral provision that has adverse effects on a protected category. Thus, a measure that requires a US diploma to work in the United States would disadvantage citizens and residents from abroad whose qualifications are equivalent; they would then not be discriminated against directly (since they could still get a US diploma) but indirectly (since they would be significantly more exposed than others to the specific restrictions imposed by this measure). Since the Supreme Court's 1971 decision *Griggs v. Duke Power Company*, disparate impact in employment is prohibited.[21] In 1976, however, in its *Washington v. Davis* decision, the US Supreme Court refused to generalize the use of disparate impact on the basis of the Fourteenth Amendment; the decision only prohibits disparate impact when it is deliberate.[22] When, more than a decade later, the Supreme Court was required to evidence disparate impact using statistics comparing majority groups and minority group,[23] Congress overturned this decision by expanding the scope of civil rights statutes (Civil Rights Act of 1991).[24]

The picture is very different in Europe. In applying EU law, French law distinguishes more clearly between direct discrimination and indirect discrimination. The May 27, 2008, law specifies that "direct discrimination [is] the situation in which . . . a person is, has been, or will have been treated less favorably than another in a comparable situation," and "indirect discrimination [is] a provision, criterion, or practice that is apparently neutral, but likely to lead to . . . a particular disadvantage for persons compared to other persons, unless this provision, criterion, or practice is objectively justified by a legitimate aim and the means to achieve this aim are necessary and appropriate."[25] The European Court of Human Rights also extended the scope of indirect discrimination; it now takes into account socioeconomic context based on statistical data. The court thus recognizes the collective aspects of discrimination. This is the case when it uses data on the prevalence of domestic violence against women.[26] In the case of Roma children in the Czech Republic placed in schools for children with cognitive impairments, the European Court of Human Rights also deemed that a measure that has "disproportionately harmful effects on a group of people even if not specifically aimed at that group" can be considered discriminatory.[27] Finally, inaction was also characterized as indirect discrimination in the case of a refusal to investigate police violence with a presumed racist motive.[28]

Unlike US common law, which is essentially based on precedent, the French legal system is largely based on statutes, which brings its own set of problems since it compartmentalizes the fight against discrimination and leads to different definitions. Discrimination may consist of "less favorable treatment" under the Labor Code[29] (or a *distinction* under the Penal Code).[30] Some legal specialists have therefore wondered whether the fragmentation of antidiscrimination law might be detrimental to its effectiveness.[31] Others have called for existing antidiscrimination law to be gathered into a single code, without changing its content.[32]

Under these conditions, it is impossible to provide a legal definition that would cover all minority configurations. Several attempts have been made in Canada, where the issue of protecting First Nations people as well as linguistic and religious minorities comes up regularly. During the

1980s and 1990s, intense legal debates took place, resulting in greater flexibility in the presentation of evidence before judges.[33] Nevertheless, attempts to standardize the notion of minority have so far been unsuccessful. Jules Deschênes, a former chief justice of the Superior Court of Quebec, sought commonalities among minorities, not based on specific cultural, social, or ethnic characteristics.[34] He defined minorities as groups united by choice or by necessity and driven by a desire to survive in an environment that oppressed or persecuted them. This definition covered a wide variety of groups. However, it was limited to the Canadian context, where minorities, with the exception of women, are primarily groups that are both disadvantaged *and* smaller in number.[35] In other contexts, Deschênes's definition loses all relevance: despite being a numerical majority, the Black populations of South Africa during apartheid were minorities. Similarly, very large groups in absolute terms (Uyghurs, for example, numbering nearly 12 million in China) are also minorities in the same way as smaller communities (some 15,000 Roma people in France, for example). Furthermore, contrary to what Judge Deschênes suggested, a minimum number of people does not always constitute a minority. People suffering from orphan diseases are not a minority because society persecutes them, but rather because it ignores them, precisely because there are not enough of them. The need to survive as defined by Judge Deschênes is not a satisfactory criterion either. The forms of domination faced by minorities vary widely: persecution, exclusion, inferiorization, erasure, and so on. They seek not only to survive but to live, or, in the words of Spinoza, to "persevere in [their] being."[36] This is precisely why uniformizing legal definitions cannot resolve circumstantial differences between minorities.

PASSING

By extending its scope, French and US antidiscrimination law has come to define an implicit category encompassing people who do not receive any effective protection. It is not enough to have a legal arsenal to protect people: individual subjects must also have recourse to it. Extending antidiscrimination law may give rise to ambivalent reactions, and so the complexity and scope of the law often leads the most disadvantaged

MANAGING DIVERSITY

49

populations to opt out of measures that might benefit them.[37] For sociologist William Julius Wilson, this mechanism is a powerful factor in segregation, especially since executive and legislative bodies tend to refer the most contentious issues to the judicial sphere.[38] This transfer politicizes the procedure and undermines the law's image of neutrality, which exacerbates the phenomenon of self-disqualification as among the most precarious.[39] Besides, not all people recognize themselves in the existing legal categories, and there are others who would like to be recognized by the law but are not necessarily able to do so.

This issue is particularly salient for gay men and lesbians in matters of asylum: condemned to secrecy in their countries of origin, it is difficult for them to include proof of their sexual orientation in their asylum applications.[40] Once in their host countries, asylum seekers frequently live with family members or in communities from their own countries or other countries where homosexuality may also be heavily stigmatized, making it very difficult for them to gather new proof of their sexual orientation.[41] The authorities therefore rely on life stories to help them reach a decision, and the notion of minority takes shape as the procedure progresses, sometimes without material evidence. In France, the executive branch could use regulatory means to clarify the law of July 29, 2015, which recognizes sexual orientation as grounds for asylum, and thus allows visas to be issued on a declaratory basis, later supplemented by material evidence (testimonies, cohabitation, etc.). Yet no government has taken this step for fear of opening up a loophole in asylum policies. The risk of sexual orientation fraud is, however, largely a fantasy. As the education specialist Jane Elliott showed in 1968, members of a majority are much more aware of their advantages than they care to admit and are reluctant to relinquish them. In her "blue eyes, brown eyes" exercise, she encouraged her students to reflect on their unconscious privilege by establishing discriminatory rules (and therefore assigning privilege) based on the students' eye color. She found that, faced with the minority/majority alternative, the students always gravitated toward the majority option, which they perceived as less discriminated against.[42]

The fact that people may take advantage of antidiscrimination measures by posing as minorities is a form of reverse passing. In her novel *Passing*, Nella Larsen highlights the fact that a Black person may pass for white and thus avoid racial segregation.[43] Despite the immediate benefits of doing so, people who "pass" nevertheless live in constant fear of being discovered or punished by a system whose limits they expose. In this case, people's experience of race is similar to that of sexual orientation, in which minority individuals, raised in an environment that does not match their identity, learn to speak the majority's language and "pass," with varying degrees of success.[44] When it comes to cases of asylum, the opposite is feared: namely, that a nonminority person may pass as a minority person. One case of reverse passing made the headlines in the United States in 2015. Born in Montana to two white parents of Czech, German, and Swedish descent, Rachel Dolezal identified and passed as Black.[45] She fought against racism and became chapter president of the National Association for the Advancement of Colored People (NAACP). During an interview, Rachel Dolezal clumsily revealed the truth. She was forced to resign from the NAACP, not because of her skin color or her origins, but because she had lied, thereby trivializing the struggles of Black people. Dolezal, herself married to a Black man, continued to insist she was telling the truth. She called for a more subjective conception of racial categories, explaining that skin color, a relative characteristic if ever there was one, was elusive, so much so that passing was sometimes described as a "universal condition."[46]

Reverse passing also surfaced in public debate during the 2019 Democratic primary. The press revealed that Senator Elizabeth Warren, a candidate for the nomination, had indicated Native American ancestry when registering for the Texas bar in 1986.[47] In 2012, when she was the Democratic candidate for the Massachusetts Senate, her Republican opponent Scott Brown accused her of lying about her ancestry in order to be appointed as a lawyer, though her family heritage played no role in her hiring. In 2019, Elizabeth Warren recalled that, ever since childhood, she had heard the story of her Cherokee ancestry and that DNA tests proved it. She nonetheless apologized to the Cherokee Nation, because they alone had the right to determine whether or not she is a tribal citizen.[48]

Minorities are caught up in a complex relationship of identification and disidentification with legal categories.[49] If protected groups vary from one space to another, if some people are ineligible for them and others opt out on their own, how is one supposed to identify oneself

MANAGING DIVERSITY

as a minority before the law? Thomas Piketty found that few US citizens and residents check more than one box when several ethnoracial options are available.[50] Similarly, because these categories are not sufficiently precise, identification is not always possible. Piketty noted that, in British censuses, almost half of the people from Turkey, Egypt, and the Maghreb identify as "white."[51] In the United States, census racial data is principally used to enforce civil rights mandates against discrimination in employment, in the selling and renting of homes, and in the allocation of mortgages.[52] However, these censuses use rather vague and loaded terms, such as "Caucasian" to refer to white people.[53] Refining classification categories is not enough, either, to make self-identification easier because it is always polysemic. Checking the "white" box is not simply the result of inadequate categories; it is also a deliberate choice. In a highly hierarchical society, identifying with the majority can be a self-affirming gesture. Paula Moya has strongly criticized discourses that condemn "assimilation" as a form of betrayal of minority cultures.[54] It is certainly not uncommon for minorities to accuse their own group of failing to integrate, but this type of incrimination must be seen as more than just an allegiance to majority norms. It is also an attempt to better transform these norms by edging closer to the places where they are produced.[55]

THE POWER OF MINORITIES

If a minority group regains its rights and takes its rightful place in political, economic, and social life, to what extent does it remain a minority? Éric Fassin used the term "inversion" to describe the shift from the disqualification of homosexuality in the public debate before the *PaCS* (or *Pacte civil de solidarité*, civil unions legalized on November 15, 1999, and available to both different-sex and same-sex couples) to the disqualification of homophobia a few years after that act was adopted.[56] Even if individuals in a minority can acquire some sort of influence, they never entirely stop being minorities. Even when minorities acquire certain prerogatives, they can be withdrawn at any time. The possibility of being subjected to violence, insults, and invisibilization, among other things, remains a feature of all minority lives, whether "privileged" or not.

Green Book, Peter Farrelly's movie based on Don Shirley's story, illustrates a threat hanging over minorities. The main character, a gay Black man and renowned pianist who is integrated into white high society, goes on tour in the southern United States, where he experiences injustice and violence without the immediate protection of his social status (even if, in the end, his network ends up protecting him). This is where fiction meets reality: being a minority individual means living with the sword of Damocles hanging over you.

Harvard's Opportunity Insights project, aimed at promoting more egalitarian public policies,[57] has shown that the risk of downward social mobility is greater for racial minorities, especially Black boys from advantaged families: their economic and social capital is more likely to decrease compared to that of their white counterparts.[58] Similarly, recognition in a given space in no way guarantees the enjoyment of the most basic freedoms outside that space. For example, gender minorities encounter disparities in access to health care from one US state to another or from one country to another. These disparities have a negative impact on people, even when there is very little discrimination in their immediate living environment.[59] Moreover, minorities are the first to bear the brunt of economic and social crises, owing to a lack of direct access to the political agenda.[60] Finally, no rights are guaranteed for life. Political regimes change and legitimize themselves against the previous legal order: it is not uncommon for minorities to be ousted from the national narrative[61] and for surveillance practices to be put in place.[62] Despite the possible "inversion" of the minority question, constraints stubbornly endure.

So what kind of power can minorities claim? This question has been the subject of numerous experiments in social psychology. They have all demonstrated that minority power is fragile, since it always requires the consent of the majority. In his classic work, *Social Influence and Social Change*, later published in French as *Psychologie des minorités actives*,[63] social psychologist Serge Moscovici shifted the spotlight away from the study of conformity and authority. Whereas standard works highlighted the considerable influence wielded by the majority over the shaping of minority judgment and opinion, Serge Moscovici argued that minorities also have the power to influence the majority and that the two phenomena are not mutually exclusive.

Several others, such as Solomon Asch, had already shown that certain minority types could resist conforming.[64] Moscovici went further by distinguishing between conforming and joining. At the end of the 1960s, he began designing experiments that measured the attitude of participants whom he asked to identify the color green or blue. He demonstrated that a response repeated in a firm and regular way could modify others' perception of colors, including when the response came from a small group of people.[65] In *Social Influence and Social Change*, he clarified this observation: minorities are not only anomic (i.e., passive), they are also nomic (i.e., active, in the sense that they affirm a worldview, a *nomos*).[66] Faced with orthodox or heterodox majorities, minorities may come to amplify their positions. In this context, if there is any conflict—if minorities instill any doubt within the majority group—changes may ensue.[67] Moscovici noted, however, that majority influence and minority influence are not of the same nature. Because the majority has the means of controlling the destiny of minorities (through coercion or empowerment), to exert its influence it only needs to gain respect for the standards it imposes in the public sphere (public compliance). Minorities, on the other hand, have to convert the majority to their worldview to garner support: the majority must internalize the minority's perspective to the point of being convinced (private acceptance). As a result, the threshold of influence that minorities must attain to influence collective decision-making is considerably higher. According to Moscovici, minorities must meet four main criteria: they must be consistent (both over time and within the minority group), be certain of the soundness of their positions, appear impartial, and be able to resist social pressure. Moscovici considers the consistency of minority beliefs to be the most powerful factor, to such an extent that persons can, on their own, transform majority opinion. In an appendix to *Psychologie des minorités actives*, Moscovici makes Aleksandr Solzhenitsyn the archetypal case of the "dissidence of one." He writes: "Faced with power and its impressive arsenal, Solzhenitsyn resists and does not bend; he sets himself a rule of insubordination, and he stands firm, regardless of what happens."[68] It is nevertheless possible to wonder whether, even in this case, the minority individual becomes an instrument of that majority, which typically finds another means of imposing its standards. This phenomenon is highlighted in numerous works published after Moscovici's; they show that the majority remains at the center of the game as a mediator of change. Thus the majority must perceive a minority position as nondogmatic for it to be accepted.[69] The majority gives itself the opportunity to organize its own discussions on the topic.[70] A minority's position is more likely to be supported if the majority takes it up as its own and if the minority's position suggests increased closeness to the views of the majority.[71]

These reservations prompt us to discuss Moscovici's conclusions outside the framework of his experiment. In fact he asked his participants to choose answers to questions that were not socially divisive (such as color perception). Nor were the samples he worked with in any way representative. In his 1969 experiment, the group consisted solely of women. Admittedly, his aim was not to characterize the prejudices against any particular type of minority or the dynamics within minority groups. Nevertheless, the perception of each minority had a considerable effect on its answers. Individuals are more likely to adopt the position of victims of discrimination when they share with them one or more minority identities.[72] Thinking about the connections between different types of discrimination also increases the propensity to adopt a minority point of view, whether or not one is a member of a minority group oneself.[73] Similarly, several studies have shown that women hold men who discriminate more accountable than they do women. In other words, belonging to the same gender group informs judgments about each person's responsibility.[74]

Finally, the field studies of psychologists Melanie Trost, Anne Maass, and Douglas Kenrick taught a crucial lesson: the influence of minorities is only strong if the issue in question is not controversial and if minority individuals adopt positions at odds with what one might expect of them; conversely, as soon as the subject of the discussion affects them directly, they face very strong resistance from the majority.[75] Minority groups are only recognized if they renounce aspects of their way of life and cultural practices: that is, if they adopt some of the majority's preferences.

This conclusion builds on the work of political scientist Elisabeth Noelle-Neumann, who formulated the "spiral of silence" theory.[76] This theory describes a group's role in shaping opinion. It shows that individuals anticipate the opinions of others and, in the event of a likely disagreement, censor themselves. The majority therefore carries considerable weight, both because it appears to embody general interest and because it arouses in others the fear of being sidelined. There is thus a premium placed on silence: minorities are far less exposed if they give up defending their opinions and interests. To break the spiral of silence, they must bring together several factors.[77] First, they must be sufficiently organized and united in their communities so as not to fear being isolated; second, they need to have adequate social and economic resources to compensate for the consequences of taking a stand; third, they also need to experience or have already experienced strong social exclusion to the point of not having anything left to lose; and, finally, they need to have a high enough level of education to situate their own stance within a broader history of dissidence.

As with Moscovici's theories, Noelle-Neumann's ideal type is tempered by the many exogenous constraints that weigh on minority groups. To prevail, their mobilizations have to be sufficient in number and have a constant supply of human and financial resources.[78] Moreover, minorities are less present in institutions, which creates a risk that their expertise and skills will not be passed down from one generation to the next. For the same reason, minorities have few tools to measure differences in treatment, which makes it difficult for them to have discrimination recognized, especially since individual cases of success distort the perception of inequalities at the group level[79] and slow down the process of collectively overcoming discrimination.[80] This phenomenon is particularly detrimental to populations of Asian descent in the United States, whose children are generally more likely to succeed at school.[81] A minimum level of well-being must also be reached for a minority voice to emerge. A negative self-image inhibits people's ability to speak out and thereby gain recognition.[82] Having access to mass media is essential for amplifying a message and requires the public to closely identify with what is being said, which involves adapting one's opinions to majority communication styles.[83] From this point of view, online modes of interaction do not radically change the situation. While anonymity may enable people to speak out, which seems to counter the "spiral of silence," it also perpetuates the isolation that characterizes some minority paths. Conversely, when online expression ceases to be anonymous, the pressure to conform to the majority becomes very strong again.[84]

Minorities' power depends on the context and the groups involved. Minorities have a different perception of their power and the demographic changes in which they participate depending on whether or not they are socially isolated.[85] The term "power" is therefore largely misapplied. Minorities can gain influence, but they remain dependent on the majority order. If circumstances change, their influence can disappear very quickly, as evidenced by recent US Supreme Court cases regarding religious freedom, abortion, and affirmative action.[86] Finally, minority influence is sometimes little more than a smoke screen. Institutions may promote "diversity" to legitimize themselves within certain management logics. This is the context in which we must understand the tensions around "woke" culture on some US campuses—which is far removed from the fantasies that keep the conservative media busy in Europe.[87] In what follows, I will show that the notion of minority falls under very different moral arrangements depending on the spheres in which it is brandished: in the administrative space, it is a mode of legitimization; in the academic space, it is a mode of communication; in the media space, it is seen as a moral referent; in the political space, it is a material and symbolic constraint.

BUREAUCRATIC INFLATION

In 2003, in the context of an appeal against the University of Michigan's admissions system, the US Supreme Court held that achieving diversity was a paramount objective, whereas the Fourteenth Amendment only prohibits discrimination.[88] The court thus endorsed a change in culture.[89] Ten years after *Brown v. Board of Education*,[90] the Civil Rights Act of 1964 addressed discrimination against women and national, ethnic, religious, and racial minorities. This act was first designed to end segregation in public accommodations and ban workplace discrimination.[91] Gradually extended to other groups, it is now dominated by a logic of diversity.[92] The reason for this shift is twofold. On the one hand, the gradual extension of the provisions contained in the Civil Rights Act was punctuated by successes and failures, with some groups struggling to gain recognition more than others.[93] The protection gap that could exist between one group and another made it necessary to design a system that went beyond a case-by-case logic. On the other hand, the Supreme Court began to rein in affirmative action policies in the 1970s, making it necessary to devise another justification for public action, in this case the pursuit of diversity.

In *Regents of the University of California v. Bakke* of 1978, the Supreme Court ruled that the admissions requirements of the University of California Davis School of Medicine violated the Equal Protection Clause of the Fourteenth Amendment and the Civil Rights Act of 1964.[94] Plaintiff Allan Bakke's admission scores were well above the average scores of other applicants. Although the school had available places, Bakke's application was rejected because the racial quota system stipulated that white applicants could only compete for 84 of the 100 places. The medical school then argued that its quotas served a compelling interest in light of the underrepresentation of racial minorities in the medical profession and that its goal was to build a diverse student body. However, the court rejected this argument, stating that there were other means of ensuring the representation of traditionally underrepresented groups. The court thus authorized the inclusion of race in university admissions criteria but considered quotas to be a form of racial discrimination against overrepresented populations. In his majority opinion, Justice Lewis Powell responded to the University of California's arguments on diversity. Using Harvard University admissions as an example, he explained that diversity should not be based on the criterion of race alone.[95] A conceptual reversal thus took place. Used by the University of California to justify race as a criterion, diversity served to soften and even limit its use. Sociologist Laure Bereni pointed out this paradox:

Diversity has imposed itself as a consensual norm in most liberal democracies, requalifying policies historically associated with the principle of equality. The success of this rhetoric, particularly among elites, stems from its ability to mask the hierarchies and antagonisms among social groups. Invented as a means of justifying the continuation of contested antidiscrimination policies, the discourse of diversity partially serves as a screen for the realization of egalitarian principles.[96]

Nevertheless, the mechanisms for fighting discrimination and promoting diversity are not necessarily mutually exclusive. Certain forms of hostility toward minorities, such as verbal abuse, censorship, or underrepresentation, do not constitute discrimination in the strict sense. In the eyes of the law, discrimination arises from very specific acts, such as unfavorable treatment or unfair dismissal. Diversity policies therefore come into play where the fight against discrimination reaches its limits. Diversity can usefully complement equality policies as long as it does not replace them.[97] It is therefore surprising to see diversity treated as a new public enemy[98] when it actually covers a wide range of situations.[99] During the 1990s and early 2000s, diversity became a means of justifying the management of certain large companies and universities. This was the context in which the notion took root in France. It then acquired another dimension, that of "liberal civicism,"[100] whose aim was to avoid conflict related to the republicanist paradigm of integration.[101] Yet differences of opinion are powerful tools of resistance against majority norms. Without disagreements diversity becomes a strategy for euphemizing disparities[102] and risks undermining the achievement of more substantial equality.[103]

This slippage can already be seen in anti-harassment policies in the United States: Title IX of the Education Act of 1972 prohibits discrimination on the basis of sex in any school or educational program funded by the federal government.[104] In the 1980s and 1990s, federal courts considered sexual harassment a form of discrimination under Title IX, first in employment and then in education. Yet, in 1998 and 1999, the US Supreme Court issued two decisions in which it ruled that any school receiving federal funds could only be held liable for the sexual harassment of students by their teachers or peers if it had "actual knowledge" of the facts and had reacted with "deliberate indifference."[105] The facts had to be serious enough to prevent the victim from attending school. This restrictive interpretation led the Office for Civil Rights (OCR)—the government agency responsible for monitoring civil rights within the Department of Education—to publish a long letter specifying the measures schools should take.[106] This "Dear Colleague Letter" focused less on mechanisms of identification and sanction and more on actions needed to change behaviors. It identified "sexual comments, jokes or gestures," "spreading sexual rumors," and "creating sexual e-mails or websites" as forms of harassment. OCR also encouraged schools to use the "single investigator" system, which gives a person appointed by the school's Title IX coordinator the authority to investigate and determine whether the person accused is guilty or not.

MANAGING DIVERSITY

This system was heavily criticized for not respecting due process of law and limiting the freedom of expression of both students and professors. The Dear Colleague Letter allowed plaintiffs to sue without divulging their identity, thus leaving those accused with no means of defending themselves. Northwestern University professor of media studies Laura Kipnis warned against the hijacking of the fight against discrimination and violence in universities. In February 2015, she published an article in *The Chronicle of Higher Education* denouncing the atmosphere of sexual paranoia in the administration at her university.[107] The article recounted the story of one of her colleagues, Peter Ludlow, who was accused of sexual assault and harassment after engaging in sexual relations with two women students. Ludlow resigned in November 2015 after the university determined that he was guilty of harassment. He had always claimed that these were consensual relations and that the inquiry, carried out by a panel outside the university, had fueled the prosecution. Kipnis also questioned the ingratiating logic of the university's administration and spoke of the infantilization of women.[108] Two other students, with the support of Northwestern University, then sued Kipnis for harassment, contending that her article was a form of retaliation that did not reflect the safe environment the university should provide for its students.[109] The president of the university was himself sued for writing an article defending academic freedom in the Kipnis case.[110] The students dropped their charges a few months later.

Kipnis then wrote a second article to chronicle her indictment, detailing in particular how the administration had orchestrated secrecy around the charges against her.[111] Kipnis maintained that by overprotecting the most vulnerable, the fundamental principles of justice were, paradoxically, altered.[112] In a book about the case, she denounced the collusion between university administrations and law firms specializing in investigation and arbitration, with no oversight or, at the very least, evaluation of their investigative methods.[113]

The Trump administration modified the "Dear Colleague" framework. In February 2017, Education Secretary Betsy DeVos withdrew the provisions on gender identity and then, in September of the same year, on harassment. On May 7, 2020, her department released new rules for addressing sexual assault on campuses. Colleges and universities would no longer be generally responsible for changing the culture of harassment but for dealing with specific cases of misconduct. Higher education institutions were required to organize their disciplinary proceedings as hearings in which witnesses could be cross-examined. The investigation should treat defense and prosecution in a balanced manner. On June 16, 2021, President Biden signed an executive order to ensure that educational environments remained free from gender discrimination and reintroduced grounds related to sexual orientation and gender identity. On June 23, 2022, the president asked that pregnancy be added to the list of protected categories in anticipation of the new limits imposed by the Supreme Court on the right to abortion.[114]

Like the Kipnis case, recent regulatory changes indicate how attention to discrimination has resulted in the establishment of powerful administrative services within universities. The ratio of administrators to students has doubled since the 1970s and has even tripled in places, especially since the beginning of this century.[115] These services have accomplished a considerable amount in many areas, for example the composition of the student body, equal pay for women and men, and building accessibility.[116] Their members are appointed by administrative and governing bodies to which they report exclusively. They present measures to academic bodies, such as the faculty, to be ratified, most often without the opportunity for amendment.[117] Diversity is now a career path and a profession, which involves specific training and the creation of a canon.[118] Yet the procedures that are put in place, however well-intentioned and effective they may be, are rarely in the hands of minority organizations.

It is in light of this new managerial configuration that one must understand "wokeness." The term "woke" comes from Black artists who, in the 1930s, called on people to be awakened to better resist segregation. In the mid-2010s, it became a rallying cry for the Black Lives Matter movement, which mobilized against racism and police violence in the United States, and criticized "too-centrist political viewpoints."[119]

Woke philosophy is described as a groundswell in certain reactionary media that cannot resist talking about it.[120] What they call "wokeness" (*wokisme* in French)[121] is not a spontaneous mobilization made possible thanks to perfectly neutral online platforms or the expression of an "offended generation"[122] thought to share psychic traits.[123] Claiming to be woke is nothing more than a traditional mobilization technique that encounters a wider resonance in a globalized media. This is the case of "cancellation," which, in situations where an institutional response may well be insufficient, consists of dismissing or dissing a person for saying or doing something felt to be discriminatory. Facilitated by the use of social media, cancellation extends the idea of dissent already present in the 1960s in the form of boycotts, demonstrations, or public information sessions (a function exercised today by "whistle-blowers").[124] Paradoxically that institutions mobilize around issues of diversity and harassment further highlights their shortcomings: the length of investigations, collecting testimony, and bias and rewriting the facts in cases investigating police violence.[125] Laure Murat thus considers that "the problem of cancel culture is one of an adequate, political response to impunity and a refusal to recognize, with whatever means at hand, what prolongs the pain of dispossession and recalls the mechanisms of oppression, discrimination, and domination."[126] It would, however, be simplistic to think of woke strategies as the only expression of a counterpower. A "cancellation" strategy also relies on institutions.[127] Lacking direct power over individuals, that strategy strives to disqualify them either to do the work of a failing institution or to have the institution sanction them. In other words, canceling can contribute to transforming an institution immediately or in a domino effect. But it must therefore act as both player and referee in a few emblematic cases.[128]

In a much-commented article, Harvard law professors Jacob Gersen and Jeannie Suk Gersen review the values defended by certain university administrations.[129] They show, for example, that terms such as "violence," "harassment," "aggression," and "inappropriate behavior" are not defined in internal regulations and are sometimes used interchangeably. This is the case with the surveys on well-being at work and on campus life that they reviewed.[130] The theme of respect recurs in all official statements on diversity, sexual violence, and labor relations, thus promoting norms about which sexuality itself should or should not be on campus, which the two jurists ironically refer to as "the foreplay bureaucracy."[131] As an example, they cite Georgia Southern University's annual report on campus safety: in 2015, it argued that "consent is a voluntary, sober, imaginative, enthusiastic, creative, wanted, mutual, informed, honest, and verbal agreement."[132] By defining consent in these terms, the administration produced a definition of "good sexuality," associating it with qualities such as honesty and creativity, which it was in no position to judge or promote. The shift from an institution that protects against violence to an institution that promotes a certain form of sexuality inevitably has an impact on minorities. The kinds of encounters the institution promotes, in fact, bear the stamp of a strong heterocentrism and a remarkable homogeneity of age and class.[133] The idea of a "safe space," initially intended as a sign of the institution's support of minority students, can also convey a restrictive conception of public space to the detriment of those whom it was intended to protect.

This paradox came to a head in 2017 during protests against Bret Weinstein, a professor of biology at Evergreen State College in Olympia, Washington. He wrote an email regarding a day when the campus was only open to people of color, explaining that it was necessary to consider the will of each individual to be present or absent. He was accused of racism, and his administration did not back him.[134] What followed were several weeks of unrest, his resignation, and a university weakened by a drop in enrollment after 2017. Although this sort of turmoil is rare on US campuses, the conservative media in Europe[135] weaponized these events against minority struggles and the #MeToo movement, just as they had done with critical gender and decolonial theories a few years earlier.[136]

The protection of minorities has become a very powerful identity marker for people under thirty-five in most Western countries, especially among the most highly educated;[137] this phenomenon is heightened in the United States where the under-thirty-five population is itself more diverse in terms of origins, race, and ethnicity.[138] On both sides of the Atlantic, there has been a change in rhetoric between the millennial generation (those who reached adulthood around the year 2000) and the next generation, known as Gen(eration) Z. The younger ones tend to have a more fluid notion of identities, whereas the previous generation focused more on breaking down identities.[139] Yet engagement in minority struggles makes it possible to forge links around shared struggles.[140] We should therefore understand the "woke" phenomenon within a logic of socialization around values borrowed from revisited diversity policies.[141]

The phenomenon is not unique to US campuses. Sociologist Roderick Ferguson showed that globalization is characterized by a propensity to aggregate with local cultures, in particular those that allow the expression of minority trajectories. This is true of advertising, television, social media, and the entertainment industry in general. Ferguson speaks of a "proliferation of minority difference."[142] Minority issues have thus become a new mode of communication, from which new norms and new ways of thinking emerge,[143] where critique and the reproduction of power relations are in tension.[144]

In this chapter, I have shown that the vagueness surrounding the concept of minority is both its weakness and its strength. The law struggles to grasp the complexity of minority categories, which sometimes makes it difficult to identify and implement protective measures. By constantly shifting the boundaries of existing categories, however, the notion of "minority" has also contributed to important legal transformations by protecting new groups and ushering in new fundamental rights. Still, this is a fragile situation. Minorities have acquired only relative influence: their demands are mediated by the majority, stifled by management culture, and, sometimes, reduced to a series of symbolic protests. They also face another challenge: the transformation of the law of numbers under the combined effect of the strong political polarization in the West and the rise of algorithms.

3

THE WEIGHT OF NUMBERS

Numbers are not, in and of themselves, a determining factor for whether a group is a minority. Minorities can only be defined *relationally*, relative to the power relations between two or more groups or individuals in a given context. Contextual features include spatial limits (determined by language, population mobility, borders, etc.); different levels of interaction (from local to global, intimate to distant); a complex institutional framework (codified, jurisprudential, or customary); and multiple, subjective temporalities (individuals do not mobilize their identities with the same intensity at each moment of their existence and in all their social experiences). In this web of constraints and opportunities, some people develop more or less intense relationships of solidarity around shared cultural references. Minority groups indeed emerge from exogenous and endogenous processes. This is why a minority cannot be reduced to a number. It can be made up of a large number of people and even account for more than half of a given population. Conversely, a group that is a majority in its relations to other groups may be made up of a small number of people. Does this mean that numbers play no role in a group's makeup or in the relationship between majorities and minorities? Definitely not. Minority groups consisting of large numbers of people do not experience the same kind of oppression as minority groups consisting of only a tiny fraction of a given population. Minority groups can also use numbers to their advantage: #MeToo provides a good illustration of a mobilization that was strengthened by mass effect. The question of numbers has even become a legal issue in its own right: in cases of alleged sexual violence, can the number of (male or female) plaintiffs be considered an incriminating factor for lifting or prolonging a statute of limitations?[1]

In the United States, demographics favor certain minorities. By 2040, ethnic and racial minorities (as opposed to "non-Hispanic whites") will have become a numerical majority.[2] This trend is largely due to the increase in the population of Latin American and Asian origin. It is even more striking in the under-eighteen age group, with the non-Latinx white population expected to account for 36 percent of minors by 2060.[3] The demographic argument is, however, a double-edged sword since it makes use of majority logic. In France, those in favor of parity (equal representation of men and women in parliament) put forward the fact that women made up more than half of humanity[4] to circumvent the notion of so-called quotas that the Constitutional Council had deemed incompatible with the constitution.[5] Parity, however, has not directly benefited other minorities, who cannot claim to represent half of the world's population. Parity was initially conceived as an instrument to boost women's entry into politics (in a logic similar to affirmative action and in a context of debates on recognizing immigrant populations in France[6]), but the demographic argument closed the door on other groups.[7] In the United States, there has been a rise in hostile opinions among non-Hispanic ethnic minorities as the Hispanic population has grown.[8] As Ariane Chebel d'Appollonia notes, "Levels of both tolerance and intolerance vary significantly across societal spheres. Whites, for example, can support affirmative action programs while being reluctant to share their neighborhoods with non-whites. Hispanics and non-whites can live in segregated neighborhoods while being integrated in the labor market."[9]

While numbers are an important feature of minority movements, they do not guarantee success. Numbers are never absolute. In this spirit, Gilles Deleuze and Félix Guattari put forward the idea of "becoming a minority."[10] In a 1990 interview with Antonio Negri, Deleuze clarified its outlines:

THE WEIGHT OF NUMBERS 67

The difference between minorities and majorities isn't their size. A minority may be bigger than a majority. What defines the majority is a model you have to conform to: the average European adult male city-dweller, for example. . . . A minority on the other hand has no model, it's a becoming, a process. One might say the majority is nobody. Everybody's caught, one way or another, in a minority becoming that would lead them into unknown paths if they opted to follow it through. When a minority creates a model for itself, it's because it wants to become a majority, and probably has to, in order to survive or prosper (to have a state, to be recognized, to establish its rights, for example). But its power comes from what it's managed to create, which to some extent goes into the model, but doesn't depend on it. A people is always a creative minority, and remains one even when it acquires a majority: It can be both at once because the two things are not lived out on the same plane.[11]

According to Deleuze, a majority is a norm; no one can ever be completely in a majority. But does this mean that a population is always a "creative minority," as he asserts? When a population dons the populist garb, it imposes the weight of numbers and wreaks havoc among minorities, since it claims to embody the entire social world to the point of no longer recognizing its plurality.[12] In other words, the idea of "becoming" is itself changeable. When a group embarks on a task of deconstruction, it acquires new tools of domination in the process itself. I therefore distance myself from the idea of "becoming a minority" when Deleuze maintains, in his *Abécédaire*, that "the majority is nobody; the minority is everybody. That is what it means to be on the left: knowing that everyone is a minority. And that is where the phenomena of becoming take place."[13] By considering "majority" to be an empty category, Deleuze tends to deprive minorities of tools of resistance; how does one identify discriminations if the group against which a minority is evaluated is an empty category?[14] While nobody is dominant in every area, some groups nonetheless accrue disproportionate advantages. Similarly, embarking on the "unknown paths" that Deleuze speaks of has a cost. The Deleuzian minority-becoming is based on a fairly homogeneous conception of the subject and pays too little attention to the material conditions required to pursue "minority-becoming." What is more, one person's minority-becoming ends where another's begins. Rather than generalizing the idea of becoming, it seems to me more pragmatic and constructive to jointly consider the crosscutting nature of minority dynamics and the uniqueness of minority groups, thus showing a certain "fidelity to minors" as an "event in the making."[15]

This chapter examines the making of a "minority" in a context of upheaval in modes of power allocation and decision-making. Strong political polarization in the West, with the rise of extremist parties and the weakening of governing parties, has led to the development of a philosophy of consensus that relies on negotiation to resolve conflicts. I will show that this approach is deeply unfavorable to minorities: the majority (which settles moral disagreements in favor of one group but ensures everyone's interests by adhering to a minimal morality) can sometimes restore minorities' agency. Today the algorithm revolution is reshuffling the deck. Algorithms have taken over whole areas of social life where they value averages and in so doing tend to marginalize minority cultures regardless of technical adjustments. After reviewing these three different logics of aggregation in a democracy—consensus building, majority rule, and algorithmics—I will propose a different approach, based on the interdependence of individual positionings rather than on numerical size or regularity.

THE LIMITS OF CONSENSUS

The question of numbers is a political issue. In the United States, media commentators often use the expression "the tyranny of the minority," which refers to parties that access power with a minority of votes and act against the general interest.[16] In the United States, the Electoral College members are appointed in each state, and they elect the president every four years. There are as many electors as there are members of Congress. Since the states are represented equally in the Senate, the electoral system overrepresents less populous states. The winner-takes-all system takes care of the rest: all one needs to win a state's electors is to lead. Candidates who win a large number of states by narrow margins and lose heavily in other states can still be in a position to win the election. It is therefore not uncommon for presidents to be elected with fewer votes than their opponent—which raises questions about the democratic nature of elections.[17] It is in this very particular context of electoral federalism that the expression "tyranny of the minority" is used. It was

THE WEIGHT OF NUMBERS

frequently used between 2016 and 2020, since President Trump drew on White House resources for partisan purposes without guaranteeing the opposition's rights.[18] The tyranny of the minority is thus as much a consequence of the electoral system as of a faulty, transpartisan ethic.[19] Such strong, political polarization destabilizes the entire constitutional system, which is based on the pursuit of political balance and even compromise.[20] The United States is currently in the grip of deep democratic uncertainty: rules for allocating power no longer guarantee a fair rendering of the public interest.[21]

In this context, many political scientists are working to develop new paths for decision-making. They seek to reduce the distortion of the current political system, whose strong ideological divide between Democrats and Republicans prevents a healthy balance of power. The logic of consensus requires, first of all, a more faithful representation of opinions, and second, mechanisms that organize the convergence of points of view. Proportional voting may seem the right way to bring about the first stage, but it leads to scattered representation and more frequent changes of alliance. Political parties and their leaders thus end up with considerable weight, and the people they represent lose control over decision-making. Proportional representation is therefore often counterbalanced by measures that moderate its effects (a threshold to qualify for representation, mixed systems combining majoritarian and proportional representation, or even smaller voting districts). However, even if it were feasible to establish a representational system more closely aligned with the population's composition and opinions, such as drawing lots,[22] one major obstacle would remain: how would the effective participation of minorities be guaranteed? France has the blocked vote parliamentary procedure and Article 49.3 of the Constitution, which allows a law to be passed without a vote, unless a motion of no confidence against the government is tabled and voted on by a majority of representatives. These mechanisms require parliamentary minorities to enter into risky alliances to achieve their goals (only one motion of no confidence has ever been passed during the Fifth Republic). In the US House of Representatives, Republicans use the "majority of the majority" rule (known as the "Hastert rule"): the majority speaker will not bring a bill to the floor for a vote without the support of a majority of the majority, thereby depriving the minority of the means to act.[23] Changing modes of representation therefore accomplishes little without establishing decision-making procedures in a more collegial framework, one in which minority voices can carry some weight—as is the case in the judicial sphere, where judges may express their disagreement with the court's decision by issuing "dissenting opinions," making it possible to thwart unanimity. This is the practice followed by the US Supreme Court and the European Court of Human Rights. Dissenting judges' opinions are not merely erased: they are published and discussed, providing a solid basis for a change in jurisprudence.

Besides issues of representation, a consensualist approach promotes methods of deliberation focused on resolving disagreements by bringing opinions together in so-called overlapping consensus.[24] This is the thinking behind opinion-sampling experiments such as "America in One Room": in 2019, Stanford University professors James Fishkin and Larry Diamond organized an initiative aiming to overcome the partisan gridlock that has characterized American political life for decades.[25] "America in One Room" involves surveying the opinions of a number of citizens before bringing them together and moderating an organized discussion to monitor how their views evolve. Experience shows that views can converge very quickly and that the convergence tends toward "moderate" views—which means that a certain number of Democratic voters who supported "progressive" measures have been known to abandon their positions in favor of a compromise and a better opinion of voters opposing them and vice versa.[26] But is it always good for minorities to temper their views? Pursuing an ideal of ideological convergence implies remaining relatively indifferent to the content conveyed. This is also confirmed by experiments that seek to show to what extent the automation of online moderation can be transposed to decision-making in a democracy.[27] The pursuit of consensus undermines the representation of minority interests, since all boundaries are destined to dissolve within a large, deliberative space characterized by "non-opposition."[28] Minorities, however, because of the domination to which they are subjected, will survive the deliberative process only if they can rely on robust political boundaries[29] and a strong identification with the people who represent them.[30] The search for convergence fails to take this into account and tends to

THE WEIGHT OF NUMBERS

weaken democratic practices: embodied ideological disagreements give way to cosmetic oppositions borne by interchangeable representatives.[31]

The logic of consensus not only dims minority voices; it also rests on a set of beliefs that is detrimental to them. The idea that conversation is the ideal setting for undoing prejudice overlooks the fact that it can just as well reinforce it:[32] the conversation can be based on an erroneous understanding of others' beliefs. The resulting consensus is then only superficial.[33] Philosopher Monique Deveaux admits as much: "My approach to mediating conflicts of culture emphasizes open deliberation and proposes negotiation and compromise as tools for reaching resolutions. As such, the account of democratic legitimacy I am reaching for here cannot guarantee a liberal outcome: Participants to deliberation may ultimately choose to preserve customs that are nonliberal in some regard (such as the decision not to prohibit polygamy in South Africa)."[34] For Monique Deveaux, however, any other approach to cultural conflict tends to idealize deliberation by imposing conditions or limits on it. The procedure then ends up suffocating itself. The solution she proposes is to organize a deliberation without trying to reach "strong consensus."[35] As long as the process is robust, she believes it is preferable to allow uncertainty to hover over support for a decision. However, this uncertainty can only disadvantage minorities: there will always be some doubt as to whether people actually support the means of protection they need, which will inevitably make these means more ephemeral. For this reason, Hélène Landemore and Scott Page go one step further, arguing for the persistence of disagreement, which they call "positive dissensus."[36] This improves the acceptance of public policies, since each party knows what to expect at the end of the deliberation process. But this way of aggregating opinions has moral consequences that are just as problematic as the pursuit of consensus. It runs the risk of aggravating discrimination by assuming that all dissenting opinions are equal; some, however, actively sustain inequalities.[37]

Philosopher Chantal Mouffe has pointed out that antagonism is necessary for democracy to counter "the illusion of consensus."[38] Of course democracy implies forging "functional equivalents"[39] to organize a copresence of different views on the world. Such orchestration still requires accepting the asymmetry of values and their impact on relations of domination—failing which, relativism replaces pluralism, to the detriment of the most vulnerable: "to take account of the 'political' as the ever-present possibility of antagonism requires coming to terms with a lack of a final ground and acknowledging the dimension of undecidability which pervades every order."[40] The question, then, is how to ensure that antagonism, like consensus, is not detrimental to the most disadvantaged. How do we prevent the tools used to resist social exclusion from reinforcing epistemic hierarchies? I suggest we pay greater heed to the multiplicity of political temporalities.[41] Against the "one room" logic, we must admit that minority and majority agendas are not perfectly aligned.

MAJORITY RULE

Can majority decision-making serve minority interests? If decision-making is about selecting one of two options, can it help resolve minority competition? A kind of brute force characterizes majority rule. The person, party, or project that comes in first wins, regardless of the relevance of other alternatives. Majority rule is thus a vector of stability in appearance only.[42] Although it structures opinion, it purges it beforehand of all its contradictory elements.[43] There are three important criticisms typically leveled at majority rule. The first is technical. It addresses the actual method of calculation. Jean-Charles de Borda, Nicolas de Condorcet, and Kenneth Arrow have shown that majority rule is a pure artifact that only works if the options are simplified: for, against, and abstention. When the options are complex (i.e., may lead to several answers), no majority is possible since the order of preference between two options is no indication of the order of preference between one of these options and a third one. Borda developed a calculation method that ranks the choices by assigning a certain number of points to each.[44] Condorcet proposed grouping the options in pairs to determine who wins most often;[45] his method has the merit of thinking about representation and decision-making in a relational way. Economist Kenneth Arrow took Condorcet's proposition to a more radical level. Considering that no method can solve the majority paradox, the only coherent choice is that of a single individual.[46]

THE WEIGHT OF NUMBERS   73

Thus the aggregation of choices can turn out to be entirely meaningless because each person's participation is based on issues that are specific to them. Majority voting masks electoral relativism, but it does not solve it.

The second criticism is political. Majority rule distorts representation and prevents the fair expression of political ideas. Winning a majority of constituencies is enough to win an election, regardless of the total number of votes. On five different occasions, a US president has been elected with fewer votes than his main opponent. This was the case in 2000 when Democrat Al Gore obtained over 500,000 more votes than Republican George W. Bush. But the gap was wider than ever in 2016, when Donald Trump was elected with nearly 3 million fewer votes than Hillary Clinton. In the US electoral system, the lack of proportionality between the size of the electorate and the number of electors per state (sparsely populated states are overrepresented for the sake of equality among states) emphasizes the distortion of the majority. Even in the case of a uninominal ballot (a single position for a single constituency), such as in a French presidential election, majority rule remains politically questionable since it completely eliminates the losers and their ideas.

Finally, the third criticism is of a moral order. Why assume that a group, just because it has more people in it than another, is normatively better? A large number of people can be wrong while a few are right. Why should minorities follow the will of the majority? Minorities are not merely the outcome of an electoral count. Each embodies specific interests, a culture, a region, a language, a philosophy, and is shaped by an unfavorable power relationship. There is no reason to erase these elements simply because other groups are more numerous or organized in a way the voting system favors.

This last criticism has been at the heart of political theory since antiquity.[47] Among the ancients, majority rule was essentially justified by the idea of nature, as an extension of natural domination. In the medieval tradition, the majority embodied wisdom and was meant to ensure alignment with the good. In modern, liberal democracies, majority rule ought to steer deliberation toward the best possible choice. The rule is thus intended to be virtuous. In the eighteenth century, the development of market liberalism created specialized tasks and increasingly complex social structures. Group interests became increasingly pronounced: the balance of these interests gradually transformed into a balance of powers.[48] Majority rule was thus designed to ease the allocation of power.

Increased geographical mobility and ever more complex social identities during the twentieth century have called into question the usefulness of majority rule. New justifications have been offered: for John Rawls, majority rule is connected to a principle of reason, one that runs through both the majority and the minority;[49] for Jürgen Habermas, it elicits a search for truth;[50] for Joshua Cohen, it means a rise in generality—individuals would detach from their personal interest—and thereby allow more robust principles of justice.[51]

More recently, political scientist Hélène Landemore has put forward a new, normative proposition: majority rule is fair because it increases the predictability of a decision. Landemore argues that majority rule is the best option for finding fair solutions to the problems of our time, like a group collectively trying to emerge from a labyrinth. Since it relies on the "cognitive diversity" of the group, whose diversity increases with size, majority rule is the best.[52] In addition to the labyrinth metaphor's limitations, which she herself acknowledges,[53] her definition of cognitive diversity focuses on one aspect: the variety of opinions. If there is a multitude of worldviews, it is more likely that a collective intelligence will emerge and therefore majority rule will be fair.[54] And yet in its very etymology the notion of diversity is linked to that of divergence. Justice is guided by the possibility of a decision being challenged by those who will suffer the most from it. Variety is an important component of diversity but it is not the only one. The second limitation of Landemore's proposal is that it tends to reduce the notion of intelligence to knowledge, understood as knowledge of a given environment and the ability to make it more predictable.[55] Associating the two does not always play out in the real world. Philosopher Chantal Jaquet has shown that the social intelligence developed by class defectors—whom she calls "transclasses"—does not always emerge from a better understanding of the social world; it can result from some form of illusion and even "ignorance and self-blindness."[56] If defectors were able to imagine the number and size of the hurdles involved in social "ascent," they would likely give up. This is not a cognitive error;[57] collective intelligence consists partly of uncertainty and unreason, so that "improvisation," to borrow a concept from Yves Citton and Jacopo Rasmi, can also yield good solutions.[58]

THE WEIGHT OF NUMBERS

On the basis of all the procedural and normative limitations that I have just outlined, majority rule seems incompatible with minority interests, and this echoes Albert Camus's celebrated phrase, "democracy is not the law of the majority but the protection of the minority."[59] But the die is not cast, because any majority remains an artifact. True majority decisions are only possible if the choices are reduced to binary alternatives. Complex democracy is paradoxical because it gives rise to individually coherent combinations that are contradictory at a macropolitical scale. This does not mean that the majority is a minority that does not speak its name, but that its coherence is only superficial, since it is permeated by minority relations. Condorcet explained that submission to the will of the majority results from the need to have a common rule in accordance with reason and the interest of all. He wrote: "Each man can in fact genuinely bind himself in advance to the will of the majority which then becomes unanimous; but he can bind only himself; and he cannot engage even himself towards this majority when it fails to respect the rights of the individual, after having once recognized them."[60] Condorcet therefore went against the grain of the Rousseauist ideal type that posited a resolution of conflicts between majority and minority in the social contract, since for Rousseau the minority needs the majority, and vice versa.[61]

Although Condorcet highlighted the contradictions between modes of political association, he did not abandon majority decision-making (by substituting it with a mode of minority decision-making, thereby allowing the minority to always win). He simply drew attention to the minority dimension of any majority. For Condorcet, majority rule could be useful for minorities as long as the basis for representation is not individual autonomy but rather interdependence. It is possible to avoid the competing-minorities deadlock if we reject the logic by which minorities' struggles are grouped (which tends to homogenize and make one minority prevail over others) or stacked (which makes it difficult to envisage the global transformation of modes of domination). This impasse can be overcome through spontaneous engagement, as seen among certain libertarian and antiglobalization groups that are not governed by any particular rules of representation.[62] It can also be avoided by using a "super-majority" or "qualified-majority" system. Paradoxically, simple majority voting proves to be harsher for minorities than systems in which the majority threshold is higher. With a supermajority, minorities can block a majority victory. Qualified majorities (combining numerical majority with a substantial majority; for example, most Council of the European Union decisions require a threshold of 55 percent of states, representing at least 65 percent of the overall population) can also offer minorities a solution. They make it possible to maintain a very transparent decision-making process while enabling one or more minority groups to come together to influence a decision before it is made. Such minority-inflected majorities have two implications: first, that the logic of traditional political parties should be combined with the organization of decision-making bodies by interest group; and second, that when the vital interests of the concerned groups are at stake, the qualified majority is activated, although not generalized to all decisions (which could generate undecidability).[63]

THE ALGORITHM AND ITS "DIVIDUAL"

The question of numbers, which is already polyvocal, has become completely reconfigured in the digital age. Our algorithmic society is all about predicting behavior, both globally and locally. In this context, the uniqueness of social relationships remains, but it loses some of its importance: Dominique Cardon notes that, "given our ignorance of the causes that motivate the actions of individuals, computation gives up on the search for a model that would explain it *a priori*."[64] Using Deleuze's "dividual" to describe the disappearance of uniqueness in machine flows,[65] Cardon concludes that "algorithmic behavior is what remains of *habitus* once social structures have disappeared."[66]

Digital society is characterized by an unprecedented type of governance: while social control was once based on various mechanisms for distributing social goods and socially situating the people who produced, possessed, consumed, and exchanged them, the digital society includes personal characteristics (age, place of residence, gender, race, and creed, etc.) in probabilistic calculations that anticipate people's behaviors. It organizes the social world according to a logic of recurrence and regularity that overdetermines individuals by what constitutes them. Individuals lose control of the processes in which they are caught up: each of us leaves behind digital traces of our daily activities, for example when traveling, communicating, or shopping. Social control is achieved through a responsive but tight modulation of the mathematical tools that regulate these pieces of the self, regardless of what the individual concerned wants to do or not do with the information. Following from Louis Dumont's work on caste societies, anthropologist Marilyn Strathern used the term "dividuation" to describe the composite nature of the self in Melanesian society.[67] The term is now used to characterize the operating modes of algorithmic flows in which individuals are no more than units intended to improve mathematical tools.[68] This phenomenon is all the more powerful because we, as individuals, contribute to our own deindividualization when we consume, travel, or meet using applications, social networks, and search engines. We rely on measurement tools that are beyond us and guide our behavior without being fully aware of it. The boundaries of the self are thereby permanently modified.[69]

At first glance, it seems this great upheaval might benefit minorities: the automation of computation detaches individual choices from "neighborly" moral judgment; moreover, so much data is produced that gaps and data leaks can only increase. Since minority subjectivity varies greatly from one context to another, the digital society can open up new spaces and offer new tools for exchange and learning. The possibilities for reclaiming new technologies are endless: hackerspaces, fab labs, DiscoTechs, hackathons, #TechWontBuildIt, and IndyMedia, among others.[70]

Four phenomena restrict minorities in the era of algorithmic calculation. First, citizens have no control over algorithmic choices: certain rules are put in place after the fact,[71] but democratic modes of deliberation play no role in creating computational tools. Minorities continue to play very little part in designing the tools of measurement that concern them.[72] In addition, through their mathematical capacity, these tools customize the services on offer and create a culture in which it is more difficult for individuals to understand the general and impersonal nature of the law. Why follow a rule whose reciprocity is not perceivable?[73] Digital freedom loses sight of the collective horizon precisely because it is also dominated by a logic of consumerism.[74] Large digital companies regard individual profiles as career directions that people could change depending on the economic context.[75] This reasoning assumes that individuals occupy secure social positions and can easily switch from one identity to another. This is not always the case for minorities.

The second challenge stems from the fact that majority rule no longer has the same meaning in the algorithmic era. In democratic deliberation, majority rule hews to the law of large numbers: unanimity, qualified majority, absolute majority, or simple majority. In today's world of big data, majority is a matter of averages and deviations from averages. Algorithmic systems handle an infinite number of spaces characterized by specific behaviors, opinions, or tastes. Algorithms compare, prioritize, and align practices to better coordinate them.[76] The uniqueness of relationships thus disappears in favor of standardization. When two Black friends use the "N-word" online to signal community or when lesbians refer to themselves as "dykes," social networks such as Facebook seem to have just one response: censorship. Those algorithm-driven networks are unable to grasp the specificities of minority relationships and their multiple manifestations, such as the strategic reversal of insults.

A third challenge confronts minorities in our digital society. How can we safeguard minority cultures when memories are outsourced to servers and circulate, via algorithms, with those concerned having no control over the flow of information that affects them? The development of medical technologies such as nanorobots and implantable sensors is set to increase this outsourcing of data tenfold. Will a posthumanity emerge, fully connected to the sum of all the knowledge produced on a global scale, or will power relations be created anew, on a different scale and according to a new majority logic?[77] Stored on servers of varying capacities, not all data will be accessible and protected in the same way. Some dataspheres will be much more richly endowed than others and only accessible to the wealthiest and most powerful people.[78]

Finally, the law of large numbers enables us to predict future events with considerable accuracy, but it does evade a fundamental democratic principle: the exception proves the rule. When sociobiographical criteria make it probable that a person will commit a crime during their lifetime, be it a misdemeanor or a felony, the terms of justice are such that it must ignore this probability. Yet algorithms have already made their appearance in the legal system, particularly in tort and criminal law.[79]

THE WEIGHT OF NUMBERS

Similarly, criminological models that use residential location to establish the probability of criminal behavior create segregation.[80] Even in cases of proven allegations, defendants must still be given the benefit of the doubt; evidence can only be gathered after the fact, otherwise minorities would be locked into a collective fate, with no option for dissent.[81] Like the dystopian society depicted in Steven Spielberg's film *Minority Report*, the predictive logic of algorithms extends its reach to education, employment, insurance, and even credit. Under the pretext of rationalizing decision-making, predictive logic has amplified the main feature of contemporary Western societies for almost thirty years, requiring citizens to constantly assess the risks they are taking. In this way, institutions externalize control.[82]

It is therefore essential to take a "minority look" at algorithms. To do so, the only option is to study the ways in which digital dividuals express their experiences of injustice. This is precisely the aim of several initiatives that are seeking to improve the predictive capacity of algorithms by incorporating "sensitive characteristics" that need to be protected.[83] So far, the response to algorithmic inequalities has simply been to decorrelate predictive criteria from the results of predictions (what statisticians used to call "demographic parity"). Researchers at UCLA have also shown that improving algorithmic inferences for minority populations makes artificial intelligence perform better for majority populations.[84] An MIT team led by Professor Gregory Wornell has created algorithms that adjust for minorities in their statistical regressions with no loss of accuracy for the population as a whole.[85] These initiatives, however, only correct the majority logic of the algorithm without radically transforming it. Such a transformation would require the participation of minorities in designing the features, functions, and measurements that concern them—as well as the use of artificial intelligence to create minority communities more easily. This is the work that MIT's Data+Feminism Lab is undertaking to connect feminist groups across the globe who fight locally against feminicide.[86]

But here again majority logic is not far away. To connect feminist groups across borders, artificial intelligence makes no distinction between communities whose histories, concepts, and modes of operation are unique: this artificialization of cultural translation tends to sacrifice the vernacular in favor of a common-denominator logic.[87] Considerable work therefore remains to be done to ensure that algorithms can think from the margins and across the interstices and give those who use them some control over the rules of the game. Artificial intelligence is, in fact, nothing more than "the embedding of words and mathematical values": by aggregating behaviors in the form of data, today's algorithms tend to amplify biases (positively and negatively) by masking them behind the apparent neutrality of technology.[88] This is why the notion of minority is more essential than ever: it enables meaning to be restored to relationships that are overlooked by the empire of metrics and thus helps to ensure that the externalization of data and the rise of artificial intelligence do not amplify social domination beyond any democratic control. To this end, we need to consider the question of numbers in relation to the question of norms.

COMMUNITIES AND SERIALITY

Since the 1980s, the term "communitarianism" in France has been used to refer to a minority group's show of supposed disloyalty toward the Republic.[89] The term enables certain cultural practices to be disparaged without incurring the symbolic cost of such attacks.[90] Even endogamous majority groups are not suspected of communitarianism: the criticism of self-segregation can vary in scale.[91] The accusation of communitarianism thus reveals a specific fear of pluralism.[92] It claims to counter three different inclinations of minorities: an attachment to vernacular traditions that compete with the nation's cultural heritage; the growing influence of minorities within the state apparatus; and the promotion of strong, transnational identities that might compete with ethnonational subjectivities.[93] The majority group will tolerate certain minority cultural practices if it perceives them to be secondary for those concerned and if the minority shows its allegiance to the nation through a whole series of daily actions.

This is one of the reasons why most cultural practices of people of Asian descent are largely ignored or erased in France's public exchanges: they themselves are simultaneously confronted with very powerful stereotypes[94] and invisibilized in the public debate. Anticommunitarian

THE WEIGHT OF NUMBERS

rhetoric has become so loud that minorities can only make themselves heard by being collectively perceived as a threat to the republicanist framework.[95] Since racism is largely expressed within "close social relations," minorities of Asian descent, particularly those of Southeast Asian ancestry, are less inclined to file complaints and tend to be nonconflictual when reacting to derision, insults, and violence, especially since they do not always have the resources that would allow them greater recourse to the law.[96] The ban on conspicuous religious symbols in schools in France, which originated with the issue of the Islamic veil, conversely shows how the visibility of certain minorities is automatically perceived as dangerous. Anticommunitarian rhetoric targets minority groups and especially those who are gaining greater visibility (in terms of their numbers and the dissemination of their cultures) as well as those with obvious links to other cultures or minority groups abroad. Beyond populations of foreign heritage or descent, minority groups often have a transnational trajectory because they need to find resources wherever they can. This transnational dimension is, however, more biographical than ideological: Fabien Truong showed that conflicting loyalties, in the case of young suburban boys, do not result from transnational political projects but rather from encounters with several cultures.[97] The "liminal space" of minorities weakens the process of cultural "localizations," which nations operate by repeating, accumulating, and applying beliefs and cultural references over a continuous time period.[98] Transnational minority mobilizations do exist, of course, but they largely continue to rely on national imaginaries. The use of virtual tools such as the #BlackLivesMatter hashtag has created transnational networks of solidarity, but the motivations of participants continue to differ considerably from country to country.[99] And so the condemnation of communitarianism produces exactly what those who use the term fear: the separation of minority groups from the majority. This separation leads minority groups to organize themselves more autonomously and conceive of their relationship with the majority as a normative struggle.

To be visible, minorities must designate those individuals or groups of individuals that derive a direct or indirect benefit from the power relationship imposed on them.[100] Thus, they achieve an epistemic break that is vital for the invention of other ways of thinking, living, and acting collectively. However, because the figure of the enemy is systemic and permanent, it puts minority struggles at risk of becoming immobilized in a simulacrum: minorities then proceed to live behind a mask in an adverse power relationship, a facade that screens out the possibilities of a more effective and profound deconstruction of modes of domination. What is gained in activist cohesion in the short term is lost in the achievement of long-term goals, as the work of sociologist Mancur Olson has long demonstrated.[101] A powerful minority struggle requires the ability to reverse accusations of communitarianism without becoming a prisoner of that reversal. It is by asserting the strength of their "affective alliances beyond claims of similarity and community" that minorities can establish more favorable social dynamics.[102] Yves Citton rightly notes that new forms of commitment are "de-colonial . . . de-polemic . . . and de-competitive . . . , where the acceptance of our incompleteness must nourish relationships of complementarity and mutual aid, contributing far more genuinely to our survival and our well-being."[103]

Minority struggles must themselves submit to a process of deconstruction because any relationship of identification with a group is also a relationship of disidentification. To quote Didier Eribon, "It is because [minorities] must for so long *play at being what [they] are not* that they can later only *be what [they] are* by playing at it."[104] Because minorities are caught up in the majority's norm and language, they show how the other's presence is an experience of incompleteness: it is at once a hurdle and an opportunity to act. In existentialist terms, the experience of incompleteness can be summed up as follows: a minority being lives in a state of permanent tension between existing thanks to others and existing for others.

For Jean-Paul Sartre, the "serial ensemble" designates a sum of individuals whose lives are intertwined (they live in the same place, use the same language, rely on the same food production chain, etc.), but who believe their destiny to be independent of that of others.[105] They are prisoners of an atomistic way of thinking. The serial ensemble contrasts with the performance of "groups-in-fusion."[106] Such groups are made up of a set of people, each unique in its own way, that emerges from its isolation and invents ways of acting that resonate with each other. Even though minorities may not be permanently in fusion, this configuration is part of

THE WEIGHT OF NUMBERS

their arsenal. Using their experience of incompleteness, minorities demonstrate that an open community is possible; such a community does not sanctify what it *has* in common but it *acts* in common, *as one*, by making the bodily presence of its members a field of expression for other groups.[107] Thus minorities challenge algorithmic seriality by creating communities anchored in *acting and role-playing* rather than in characteristics that are common in every respect (the same living spaces, similar interests, etc.), characteristics that can be rendered mathematically.

This minority role-playing is precisely what Franco-Cameroonian author Léonora Miano explores. Among the Black French population, some claim to be binational (even when they are not), while others use ethnic and national criteria to define themselves, using a model akin to hyphenated ethnicities in the United States. Still others claim a mixed or simply a racial identity.[108] This wide range is constantly being reconfigured, which is why Miano coins the word "Afropean" to characterize any "person of sub-Saharan descent, born or raised in Europe."[109] This notion claims an ethnicity for people whose experiences are European and who, "unlike their ancestors, . . . only know life from a minority stance."[110]

Miano does not superimpose two spaces and two identities. She merges them into a hybrid entity that involves new ways of "being in the world" and "socializing."[111] This entity attests to the existence of open communities whose issues are sometimes—as is the case for Miano—far removed from the questions of cultural reappropriation that separate Europe and Africa: "I do not see a representation of sub-Saharan figures in the group of Black people in Dunkirk, the carnival attraction of the city,"[112] she explains, although this issue is essential for the many people who are constantly confronted with representations that deprive them of their agency[113] and leave the embodiment of the universal to white people.[114] "Wearing a sub-Saharan hairstyle or piece of clothing—in Africa that wouldn't bother anyone. People would see it as a celebration of their culture," she says.[115] Going against the grain of algorithmic probabilism, Léonora Miano thinks about power relations in terms of where they connect and distribute roles. Her perspective is reminiscent of that of the American historian Clarence Walker, who explained that the idealization of African heritage had a restorative function in the United States, but that it also led to the trivialization of the rest of the history of Africans on American soil as if it were secondary (thus reinforcing the feeling of illegitimacy of the populations concerned).[116]

Providing context is not the same as reifying culture. Within minority groups, a great deal of cultural transposition takes place. Majority references are interpreted and transformed. Cultural appropriation that erases the other must be questioned, for it creates domination through mimicry. But when cultural transposition seeks to introduce an ironic distance from oneself and one's community, it takes on an entirely different meaning. It promotes the emergence of hybrid cultures and creates untimely connections between and within minority and majority groups, connections of which that mathematical regularity struggles to make sense.

In this chapter, I have reviewed the challenges posed to minorities by the weight of numbers. Numbers can be both a constraint and a strategy for emancipation. While they make it possible to gain visibility and legitimacy, they are, for minorities, a Pyrrhic victory. By asserting its arithmetic strength, a minority risks excluding other smaller and less powerful groups. A group's expansion does not guarantee that it will pursue objectives that protect minority interests more generally. Numbers are a means of distributing social goods, governed by a hegemonic logic. For minorities, the idea of victory, even in the name of justice, is always a trap. Conversely, reflecting on the experience of injustice provides a better understanding of what constitutes a community, without falling into the numbers trap. Where consensus logic weakens minority cultures, majoritarian logic simplifies them, and algorithmic logic marginalizes them, taking into consideration what imperfectly links dissimilar groups makes it possible to foster an open, hybrid vision of community. This work is all the more necessary since minorities do not only face the challenge of large numbers. They also face the argument of the few. Across the world, reactionary groups maintain that they are minorities just like any others and that their freedom to discriminate is a fundamental right.

4

ANTIMINORITY POLITICS

The expression "tyranny of minorities" was coined in France during the 1990s; it is now commonly used among reactionary essayists and writers,[1] whether to denounce the wearing of the burkini,[2] the lack of civility in the suburbs,[3] protests against a philosopher hostile to the rights of sexual minorities,[4] or the destruction of statues of enslavers.[5] Jean-Yves Le Gallou, a theoretician of "national preference," has thus condemned the ethnic, parliamentary, sexual, and media minorities who "stand together and support each other."[6] French far-right journalist and columnist Éric Zemmour, who ran for president in 2022, also takes umbrage with the state "mothering" its minorities and divesting itself of its virile authority.[7] On the Left, the argument of the "tyranny of minorities" is more straightforwardly populist: the parties in power are said to favor racial, sexual, and religious minorities, from *Touche pas à mon pote* ("Get your hands off my bro," an antiracist movement founded in 1984) to marriage for all, turning the true Left-wing voters over to the extreme Right[8]—an argument that is contradicted by how little attention the Left has paid to minorities for several decades.[9] For instance, Benoît Hamon, the Socialist Party candidate for president in 2017, was accused by members of his own party of having betrayed the people in favor of vocal minorities.[10] In 2014, several Socialist leaders blamed their losses in municipal elections on the excessive presence of minority issues in the campaign.[11] The same type of argument exists in the United States: some liberal academics blame minorities for the political disenfranchisement of the middle class, appealing for "solid" liberalism to counter the "liquidity" of identity.[12] Others invoke "democratized despotism" and identity strategies of "occupation," and conclude based on a few high-profile cases that there is a new "dictatorship of identities."[13]

Although the fear of minority groups capturing political power is as old as reflections on majority rule and a sound constitution,[14] it is now being expressed in new forms. The majority is said to be subjected to the power of minorities to the point where it has itself become a minority and should therefore be protected by law. This claim is all the more paradoxical because it results from the struggle against the social recognition of discriminated groups—it literally forms an "antiminority" identity.

In this chapter, I will describe this strategic reversal and its impact on the relationship between ideology, law, and politics. I will also explore the consequences of these strategies for minority groups who, faced with activist competitors, lose some of their most effective tools for communication and mobilization. In the United States, antiminority rhetoric is rife in the legal arena: it is grafted onto the defense of white supremacism and religious freedom. Claimants argue that their freedom of religion entitles them to treat women and sexual and gender minorities differently, for example by refusing to provide a commercial service or social assistance. Their appeals have ingrained the idea that being in the minority simply requires a declaration and that majority and minority are somehow structurally similar. This rhetorical sleight of hand considerably weakens the moral foundation of minority movements. In France, only the Constitutional Council can judge the constitutionality of a text, and so antiminority rhetoric is more present in the streets and in academia: it is in the name of parity, antiracism, pacifism, humanism, and environmental protection that activists have called for action against marriage for all, Black organizations, and certain minority religious events. This is one strategic piece of a wider ethnonational puzzle that condemns the "great replacement" of Western civilizations and also affects parts of South America[15] and now North Africa. It seeks to promote a reworked version of counterrevolutionary thought in the wake of Christian movements that advocate a more sovereign Europe; its supporters call it "new humanism."

The purpose of this chapter is not to chart the movements that in Europe and around the world see the protection of minorities as a sign of civilizational decay. These various movements are driven by very different values depending on whether they are structured around charismatic leaders, a highly organized activist base, or more distant and less politicized networks of influence.[16] Antiminority political platforms are, moreover, changeable: they adapt in situ to the prevailing political culture. Thus certain alternative Right movements in the United States want to bring down the nation by replacing it with a transnational, white community; those movements simultaneously display a very strong attachment to national identity by transposing into their belief systems the civic patriotism that characterizes the United States.[17]

For sociologist Charles Tilly, it is precisely because social actors fight for their own interests that they create their own set of references that are supposed to legitimize them; as a result, an analysis of their discourse, when it does not seek to be all-encompassing, sheds light on their trajectories.[18] Ideology is not just a way of perceiving the social world; it is also a way of acting upon it.[19] Antiminority discourse allows political and religious groups to capture the expectations of a population seeking new points of reference to help it understand globalization and the major economic and social transformations occurring in the West.[20] This chapter analyzes several examples of antiminority interventions in French and US public debate, including essays, political speeches, legal actions, legislative proposals, militant posters, advertising campaigns, and conferences. The aim is to study how antiminority rhetoric instills new frames of thought, such as the denial of scientific truth, the distortion of history, the glorification of nature and the gendered body, the idealization of domesticity, and more generally the demonization of institutions. These discursive repertoires are not simply the expression of existing categories of thought: they actively shape them. As such, they are a cornerstone of power relations.[21]

FREEDOM OF EXPRESSION

The First Amendment to the US Constitution guarantees freedom of speech. At first, the Supreme Court refused to recognize this freedom in public places (*Davis v. Massachusetts*, 1897)[22] before admitting that one of the functions of the street was to allow public expression (*Hague v. IOC*, 1939).[23] First Amendment case law has become much more liberal, but it still imposes limits in cases of fraud, defamation, obscenity, child pornography, and incitement to violence.[24] Political speech is also highly protected. Before the First Amendment, US law considered antigovernment speech a criminal act. For several decades now, the Republican-dominated US Supreme Court has adopted a more restrictive definition of the public places in which freedom of expression can be exercised (it is limited in schools and airports, for example); it has nonetheless extended the protection of freedom of expression relating to deeply held opinions and beliefs. Reactionary religious movements therefore enjoy claiming their due from a legal system that they otherwise despise.

In 2012, the COO of the Chick-fil-A fast-food chain, Daniel Truett Cathy, spoke out strongly against same-sex marriage. The media soon revealed that his father's foundation funded anti-LGBTQ organizations, especially those that supported conversion therapy. Several LGBTQ groups called for boycotting the chain; in response, many conservative leaders, including Mike Huckabee, rallied behind the company. The Cathy Foundation changed its donation policy but continued to provide financial support to the Salvation Army, whose policies openly discriminated against LGBTQ people. In this context, the Texas Senate passed a bill on April 3, 2019, making it illegal to revoke the state-certified, professional licenses of lawyers, doctors, electricians, teachers, and so on for expressing "sincere religious beliefs."[25] The state senators rejected an amendment that included a nondiscrimination clause against LGBTQ people. The bill therefore paved the way for all kinds of discriminatory treatment in the name of freedom of religion. Supported by Lieutenant Governor Dan Patrick, the bill was sent to the Texas House of Representatives, which postponed it indefinitely. It was then taken up in another form by the Texas Senate, hijacking the language of discrimination for the benefit of Chick-fil-A. The governor of Texas, Greg Abbott, signed the bill into law on June 9, 2019, stating, "Discrimination is not tolerated in Texas. No company should be discriminated against simply because its owners donate to a church, or to the Salvation Army, or to any other religious organization,"[26] and calling the law a "victory for religious freedom in Texas." On March 26, 2021, the state of Arkansas followed in the footsteps of its neighbor. Governor Asa Hutchinson enacted a law authorizing medical providers to refuse to treat a patient on the basis of their religious beliefs or moral objections, except in emergency cases. While state antidiscriminatory health measures still apply on the basis of race, sex, gender, or nationality, the same is no longer true for abortion and hormonal treatments when they are not related to a disease.[27] These systemic changes therefore particularly affect women and transgender people.

On June 4, 2018, a Colorado baker who had refused to bake a wedding cake for a same-sex couple, citing religious reasons, received the US Supreme Court's support by a 7–2 majority (*Masterpiece Cakeshop v. Colorado Civil Rights Commission*).[28] Based on Colorado antidiscrimination law, the Colorado Civil Rights Commission found discrimination and ordered the baker to provide the service requested by his customers. In its review of the case, it also mentioned the ideologies of hatred that had led to slavery and the Holocaust. The US Supreme Court held that the Colorado Civil Rights Commission, by relying on such arguments, had failed in its duty to remain neutral. The court overturned the decision on this basis without really ruling on the merits, in particular on the difference, claimed by the baker, between the freedom of artistic expression and the obligation to provide a service. The association that represented the cake shop, Alliance Defending Freedom, commented: "Tolerance and respect for good-faith differences of opinion are essential in a society like ours."[29] Several federal courts found discrimination in several similar cases in which hostility to religious belief was not established.[30] Justice Sonia Sotomayor deftly attempted to overturn the decision of *Masterpiece Cakeshop v. Colorado Civil Rights Commission* in favor of minorities: in *Trump v. Hawaii* on June 26, 2018, she considered President Trump's decision to prevent the issuance of visas to citizens of Muslim countries to be a sign of religious hostility. The court did not follow suit.[31] Justice Sotomayor, however, demonstrated that the neutrality argument was biased, since the court did not apply it to all religions.

The same contradiction can be observed in a number of cases brought by private health centers known as crisis pregnancy centers (CPCs) which, while claiming to counsel pregnant women, discourage them from having an abortion. There are some 4,000 of these centers throughout the United

States. They are unlicensed and are often located near high schools, campuses, and duly authorized family planning centers, whose acronyms and keywords they borrow to their own ends. Although they have no medically qualified personnel, they often require their staff to wear medical uniforms to influence the women they see. Funded by Christian anti-abortion groups, CPCs aim to discourage contraception and abortion by citing the risks to the health and development of the fetus (which they call a "baby" or "child").[32] California's Reproductive FACT Act of 2015 requires all unlicensed reproductive and pregnancy counseling centers to post notices clearly indicating that they are not medical centers and that free sexual health and abortion help are available at licensed clinics and centers. The CPCs considered that the state of California had a discriminatory attitude toward them (called "viewpoint discrimination"). On these grounds, the CPCs challenged the constitutionality of the 2015 law all the way to the US Supreme Court. For political scientist Wendy Brown, "Petitioners use the First Amendment as a deregulatory power to perpetuate simultaneous concealment and expansion of their religiously motivated policy aims into public space."[33] By a 5–4 majority, the US Supreme Court held that the notice requirement violated freedom of expression because the FACT law forced members of CPCs to go against their "deeply held beliefs," whereas most of the licensed centers were excluded from the licensed notice requirement.[34] The court therefore found that the law specifically targeted unlicensed centers, that is, speakers not speech.[35] For Justice Anthony Kennedy, the FACT Act "is a paradigmatic example of the serious threat presented when the government seeks to impose its own message in the place of individual speech, thought, and expression."[36] This reasoning is somewhat surprising, since it overlooks the fact that members of CPCs have little respect for the law. The Court of Appeals for the Ninth Circuit also recalled that the requirement to communicate information about contraception was purely factual and professional and that the impersonal nature of the law could not be equated with an opinion. Behind its desire to protect individual convictions against the fundamental rights of minorities, the US Supreme Court expressed its distrust of social institutions as a whole, insofar as they resist both deregulation and the competitive model that considers public and private interests to be of the same order.[37]

On February 24, 2020, in *Fulton v. Philadelphia*, the Supreme Court also agreed to review the constitutionality of certain adoption agencies that were turning away same-sex couples. Philadelphia's Department of Human Services is responsible for fostering and finding homes for children who have been abandoned or are victims of abuse and neglect. To do so, it works with local grassroots organizations, a number of which are Catholic. After learning that one of them, Catholic Social Services (CSS), was systematically turning away same-sex couples, the city severed its contract with the organization, which then sued the city on grounds of freedom of speech and religion. On appeal the court found no infringement of CSS's First Amendment rights. The organization therefore decided to appeal to the US Supreme Court, arguing, "As a Catholic agency, CSS cannot provide written endorsements for same-sex couples which contradict its religious teachings on marriage. The mayor, city council, Department of Human Services, and other city officials have targeted CSS and attempted to coerce it into changing its religious practices"[38] In a unanimous decision, the Supreme Court found that the city of Philadelphia had imposed undue control on the Catholic agency.[39] According to the court, private child placement agencies, unlike public agencies, do not fall within the scope of its 1990 case law (*Employment Division, Department of Human Resources of Oregon v. Smith*), which provided that no neutral, generally applicable legal text could be challenged on the basis of religious freedom.[40] CSS was therefore justified in invoking its free exercise of religion against the city of Philadelphia. Justice Roberts noted that the city had the ability, through its human relations officer, to exempt its service providers from certain antidiscrimination provisions. It was therefore not justified in breaking its contract with CSS because that would amount to imposing specific constraints on it. Although the decision, which centered on contract law, had no bearing on *Employment Division, Department of Human Resources of Oregon v. Smith*, it signaled a pause in protections for sexual minorities by refusing to distinguish between beliefs and practices. It did not proclaim a right to discriminate, but it did not rule it out either.[41]

On November 20, 2020, the Court of Appeals for the Eleventh Circuit overturned Boca Raton and Palm Beach County's ordinances banning conversion therapy in 2017.[42] These therapies consider homosexuality a mental illness that can be eliminated through rehabilitation sessions, brutal physical activities, and the intervention of spiritual and religious guides. The ordinances banned all conversion therapies, including purely speech-based therapy. It is on this basis that two marriage and family therapists appealed, arguing that their patients were willing and that none of their advertising material claimed to be able to change sexual orientation, but simply induced new behaviors that enabled adolescents to resist their sexual desires and address their confusion about gender identity. The county and the city highlighted the health risks, particularly suicide risk, that these therapies pose to young patients; numerous professional associations such as the American Academy of Child and Adolescent Psychiatry also emphasized these risks. The court nevertheless ruled that the risks were not proven in the case in question and that there was no justification for restricting freedom of expression. Justices Britt C. Grant and Barbara Lagoa, who authored the majority opinion, had been appointed by President Donald Trump. The third Justice, Beverly C. Martin, in her dissenting opinion, pointed to the proven danger of conversion therapy and considered the court's decision "ethically inadmissible."[43] However, she stood alone: in 2017, the US Supreme Court had in fact already refused to review the state of California's ban on conversion therapy.[44] By refusing to intervene, the US Supreme Court upheld the ban but also refused to extend its principle.

Refusals to intervene, such as this one, are quite common. In 2017, the US Supreme Court declined to hear the appeal of a school in Gloucester County, Virginia, after the court of Appeals for the Fourth Circuit had found the school guilty of discrimination against a young transgender student, Gavin Grimm, who was denied access to the men's restroom. The case was sent back to the local courts. Gavin Grimm won in the District Court for the Eastern District of Virginia and then again in the Court of Appeals for the Fourth Circuit.[45] Both courts found that the school had violated Title IX of the Education Amendments of 1972 and the Equal Protection Clause of the Fourteenth Amendment. In February 2021, the school appealed again, this time to the US Supreme Court,[46] which once again refused to rule.[47] By not taking up the case, the court extended the ban on discrimination against transgender people in the eleven states that come under the jurisdiction of the Court of Appeals for the Fourth

Circuit. Under similar circumstances marriage was extended to same-sex couples in the United States. In 2014, the Supreme Court refused to consider the constitutionality of same-sex marriages at the request of five states (Utah, Oklahoma, Virginia, Wisconsin, and Indiana), as marriages had already taken place in nineteen others.[48] Its refusal led to other states joining the movement until the *Obergefell v. Hodges* decision of June 26, 2015, allowed same-sex marriage throughout the country.[49]

However, President Donald Trump's nomination of Amy Coney Barrett in September 2020 significantly shifted the political balance of the Supreme Court. The conservative justices now have a 6–3 majority, and the court's silences no longer carry the same meaning. Justice Amy Coney Barrett is affiliated with the Catholic Charismatic Renewal movement and opposes abortion; she was on the board of trustees of a private school whose internal policies were hostile to lesbians and gay men.

Inevitably, Barrett's nomination caused great concern among LGBTQ activists and their organizations.[50] The Supreme Court's political shift soon translated into action. A decision of June 24, 2022, authorized states to ban abortions.[51] Justice Clarence Thomas, in his majority opinion, called on the court to rule again on contraception, same-sex marriage, and the decriminalization of homosexuality.[52] In July 2021, the US Supreme Court had already declined to intervene and thereby put an end, once and for all, to the refusal of service against same-sex married couples (in this case, supplying flowers for the ceremony)[53] while the Washington State Supreme Court had, for its part, recognized that discrimination had occurred.[54] The US Supreme Court's hesitations are now a double-edged sword. They can be both a step toward extending protections for minorities at a local level and an obstacle to recognizing the discriminatory nature of refusals of service. In this context, Congress had to regain control. To prevent the new justices from overturning *Obergefell v. Hodges*, the Senate passed legislation (by 61 to 36) recognizing same-sex marriage and interracial marriage (Supreme Court jurisprudence was all that has protected the latter since 1967[55]) and preventing any reversal in jurisprudence.[56] In a prescient action, President Biden signed the bill into law immediately.[57] In a new case, a company that designs wedding websites refused, on the grounds of freedom of expression, to do business with same-sex couples, as required by the state of Colorado. On June

30, 2023, the US Supreme Court ruled that this refusal was constitutionally justified because it did not concern any specific person, that nothing required a company to adhere to the "message" Colorado wished to promote, and that freedom of (creative) expression could not be unduly restricted (since the company published custom-made stories).[58] The next day, President Biden asked Congress, as he had done regarding same-sex and interracial marriages, to pass the Equality Act to protect LGBTQ people at the federal level.[59]

The US Supreme Court's positions are all the more crucial since many lower courts anticipate its reasoning and use it to curtail the freedoms of sexual minorities and women. This was apparent in a decision by Judge Reed O'Connor, a former Republican congressional staffer, in his North Texas district on September 7, 2022.[60] The Affordable Care Act (or "Obamacare"), which brought in cost-sharing reduction subsidies, had established three drug regulatory authorities responsible for drawing up the list of preventive medical treatments covered by insurance at no additional cost to policyholders. O'Connor ruled that one of these was not legal, thus vindicating the plaintiff, an employer who deemed that the PreP HIV-preventive treatment encouraged homosexuality.[61] In the Fort Worth district, an employer can now select insurance plans that do not cover PreP, thus restricting its employees' health coverage and hindering the prophylactic strategy that could end an epidemic primarily affecting minorities.[62] Justice O'Connor's decision aligns with the US Supreme Court's ruling that an employer may, on religious grounds, opt out of the contraceptive mandate of the health plans it provides its employees.[63]

Taken together, these cases illustrate the ambiguity of free speech in the United States today. While Title VII of the Civil Rights Act of 1964 protects against discrimination based on race, sex, color, origin, and religion (extended, on June 15, 2020, to gender and sexual orientation by a US Supreme Court decision),[64] the argument for freedom of expression acts as a spearhead against minorities[65] because it tends to sanctify the basis on which the country's constitutional law was founded: religious freedom.[66] Thus, antiminority struggles in the United States are fought on the basis of personal convictions, since religious belief is morally valued for what it allows in terms of socialization,[67] compassion, and patriotism.[68]

APPROPRIATION STRATEGIES

French public law also recognizes freedom of belief, which was essentially shaped at the turn of the twentieth century when the state sought to free itself from the grip of religion. The strategies, developed by reactionary groups on both sides of the Atlantic, therefore differ slightly. In the United States, they rely on religious freedom, sometimes explicitly, sometimes more implicitly, and play the card of moral relativism. In France, they seek to avoid the argument of religious freedom in favor of a secular framework in which social harmony, and therefore the interests of the nation, are at stake. For French Catholic activists, this is also a means of avoiding the risk of recognizing other religions on an equal footing. From this perspective, antiminority struggles in France have a direct link with its nationhood. It is, in fact, in the name of the public good that the nation protects minorities against expressions of hatred: the Law on the Freedom of the Press of July 29, 1881, criminalizes defamation; the Pleven Law of July 1, 1972, punishes incitement to racist and antisemitic hatred, a framework extended to discrimination based on ethnicity, nation, race or religion under the Gayssot Law of July 13, 1990; and to sexism, homophobia, transphobia, and disability under the Law of December 30, 2004, with the same statute of limitations (one year instead of three months) following a further law enacted on January 27, 2014.[69] Finally, the Gayssot Law also criminalized the denial of crimes against humanity.

This different understanding of freedom of expression can also be seen at the European level. In a case combining several complaints, one of the applicants was an orthodox Christian sex therapist and relationship counselor who had been fired after refusing to work with a same-sex couple.[70] Contrary to US law, the European Court of Human Rights found that religious freedom could be restricted in an objective and reasonable way since the employer had a policy of nondiscrimination toward its customers. In the court's opinion, in sanctioning the applicant the state had not exceeded its margin of appreciation. If no system of values is a guarantee of freedom as such,[71] European law takes care to distinguish between belief and the expression of belief when the latter takes any freedom away.

The greater protection given to certain minority groups in France and Europe does not mean that they have become hegemonic. Minorities only gain recognition when they pledge allegiance to majority standards.[72] The new appropriation strategies developed by antiminority groups are not the result of a retreat from their values but rather the expression of a change of scale. They now give priority to targeted actions. Thus, the *Manif pour tous* (the main movement opposed to same-sex marriage in France) mobilized a whole visual arsenal inspired by the student revolution of May 1968 and the union struggles to secure paid leave and safeguard jobs in industrial areas devastated by offshoring. Some placards used red ink to depict abandoned factories, raised fists, tools, and so on. Some posters read: "Aulnay comes first [an industrial site closed due to offshoring], not gay marriage;" "We want work, not gay marriage;" and "Fraternity for growth." The marches also featured children dressed up as Gavroche, the orphan in Victor Hugo's *Les Misérables*, symbolizing unhappy, impoverished childhoods in nineteenth-century Paris. The *Manif pour tous* movement also borrowed the phrase "Get your hands off . . ." (our kids, marriage, etc.)—the slogan that had been coined by the "SOS Racisme," movement founded in 1984, proclaiming "Get your hands off my bro!" ("*Touche pas à mon pote!*")[73] In 2016, *Manif pour tous* called for a demonstration against a possible extension of medically assisted procreation to all women, using a poster depicting a heterosexual couple with two children (placed at the top and center of the image), an elderly man with a cane, a young boy with a skateboard, an overweight person, a same-sex couple, etc. Its slogan "Demonstrate as you are" (*Manifestez comme vous êtes*) sought to tap into the language of diversity policies. In November 2019, the organization put up posters in the streets of Paris depicting a young girl with multiple disabilities in a motorized wheelchair and calling on people to stand up for social progress by respecting fatherhood, motherhood, and difference.

Other movements drew on the minority register. The French Spring, a small anti-gay rights movement close to the Vatican chose a name that echoed the various revolutionary Arab Springs. It defined its struggle asfollows: "Against an unjust bill in the service of minority privileges that they seek to impose on us through violence, we express our personal refusal to be complicit in the Taubira project and all the programs that attack

ANTIMINORITY POLITICS

the weak, the poor, and the disenfranchised."[74] During the demonstrations against marriage for all in France, placards demanded "parity, first and foremost in marriage." Many demonstrators described their march as "Catho Pride."[75] The Catholic group *Les Veilleurs* organized street prayers against marriage for all at which participants declaimed work by Hannah Arendt, Aristotle, Albert Einstein, Mahatma Gandhi, Martin Luther King, Louis Aragon, Guillaume Apollinaire, and Albert Camus. Éric Lemaître, an activist with the *Veilleurs* in Reims, summarized things thus: "The new slaves are those individuals who follow their desires to the limit. Who are prisoners of themselves. . . . That's why we quoted Martin Luther King and that's why we sing the negro spiritual 'Let My People Go.'"[76]

Other symbols of resistance to injustice were mobilized. The Antigones, a group of young women dressed in white veils, claimed to be "feminine" rather than "feminist," and vowed to fight, like Polynices's sister, against the moral corruption of the law by the Taubira bill. The *Hommen*, a group of young, white men of slim build, dressed in colored trousers, took to the streets several times with their torsos exposed and covered with slogans against marriage for all. Their stated objective was to fight against the emasculation of public spaces as a result of the attacks of feminist groups such as the *Femen*, Ukrainian-born activists who regularly protest against the patriarchy by exposing their bodies, in particular their breasts, in public.

Rather than considering the "consubstantiality of social relations,"[77] reactionary ideology willingly uses the idea of intersection to denounce one category by using another—what sociologist Sirma Bilge calls "ornamental intersectionality."[78] During the debate in the second round of France's 2017 presidential election, Marine Le Pen embraced the cause of women, Jews, and gay people even though her party has been routinely singled out for antisemitic remarks for decades, and her presidential platform attacked women's freedom of choice (Le Pen spoke of "comfort abortions") and sexual minorities (to whom she denied access to marriage and parentage). Her aim was to highlight the risk that the "Islamization of France" would pose for women and sexual minorities; she thus linked them in the nation's collective imagination while denying them the most basic rights. She even played on a certain gender confusion, claiming political strength as a woman and emphasizing the presence of gay men in her entourage, starting with her campaign manager, Florian Philippot.

The distortion of the fight for equality produces harmful effects on minorities themselves since it creates a moral homology between a discourse of affirmation and a discourse of rejection. This homology was one of Emmanuel Macron's 2017 campaign themes. By asserting that groups and ideologues hostile to the rights of sexual minorities had "good reasons" for being so,[79] Macron appeared to ignore relationships of domination. In the United States, this rhetoric also surfaces in the writings of some liberal academics who call for conciliation between the different "tribes" of the progressive Left and the nationalist Right, and thus remain on the fence.[80] When President Trump signed an executive order on September 22, 2020, reminding all federal agencies and their contractors of their duty to treat their employees fairly regardless of gender or race, he also suggested that these categories were "divisive" and condemned any stereotyping by government contractors as sexist and racist.[81] Programs promoting equality and academic discussions on gender were both described in the negative, as practices that would not be prohibited, provided they "are consistent with the requirements of this order."[82] Directly challenged in their most basic rights by various reactionary groups, minorities are also threatened by antiminority reasoning.[83] By turning domination relations on their head, this doxa imposes a moral equivalence that deprives minorities of the very possibility of making the specificities of their situation heard, if not recognized. This antiminority reasoning, however, is paradoxical: it muzzles minorities by granting them considerable symbolic power. Without constraints minorities would be unstoppable. Antiminority reasoning thus inadvertently reveals the underlying problem of reactionary groups: an impossible quest for redemption.[84]

REDEMPTIVE POPULISM

Casting oneself as a victim of minority politics is not a new strategy. Whether in the civil rights movement in the United States or the struggle against colonization in France, victimization has always been about ensuring the "heroic redemption" of the majority culture.[85] However, claiming to be a member of the silent majority under the yoke of overpowering minorities is no longer simply a tactic. It is now a form of identity. Faced with major demographic changes in the United States and the diversification of the French population, majority identities are now taking shape.[86] This is particularly true of white identity which, for white supremacists, has become a genuine political project based on a feeling that they are the target of a new form of racism:[87] the superior race must reclaim its natural space before it becomes extinct.[88] White supremacist philosophy is a collective crusade. In the United States, it borrows from the myth of territorial conquest and expropriation of Indigenous peoples— one of the myths on which the country's official history has long been based. In this context, each wave of recognition of minorities has resulted in a more or less violent backlash: this is the case for reproductive rights and women's health today.[89] Every economic crisis has been accompanied by scapegoating: during the 2008 presidential campaign, the figure of "Joe the plumber"—a deserving white worker whose opportunities for professional growth were limited by redistributive legislation—was used to portray contrasting Black and Latinx populations as idlers who profited from the system.[90] While Latinx, Black, and Indigenous populations experience poverty rates nearly four times greater than non-Latinx white populations,[91] the "poor little white man's" discourse was skillfully orchestrated by the Tea Party (founded in 2009 in opposition to Barack Obama's fiscal policies) and more recently by political supporters of Donald Trump.[92] This discourse is centered on the victimization of white people and makes invisible the real mechanisms of poverty and exclusion, including those that severely affect white working-class and middle-class populations.[93] Its rhetoric is particularly effective because racism manifests itself as much through direct violence as through a set of insidious advantages that privileged populations tend to deny, minimize, or naturalize through "cultural racism."[94]

To claim white, popular redemption against minority "excesses," reactionary activists need to show that they have the support of the "people." During the Yellow Vests protests that began in October 2018 in France, the extreme Right tried to rally its movement to the cause. The protests began spontaneously as mobilizations against plans to increase the "carbon component" of the domestic consumption tax on energy products. The carbon component had been established in 2014 under the presidency of François Hollande, but Emmanuel Macron was planning to increase it. The Yellow Vests objected to fighting global warming on the backs of the poorest people, especially those in rural areas who could not do without a car. On November 4, President Macron quipped: "The same people who complain about the rise of fuel prices also demand that we fight air pollution because their children are suffering from illnesses."[95] The Yellow Vests, however, were not mobilizing against environmental protection policies, but against financial measures that did not primarily affect the most polluting individuals, through various taxes on high incomes and financial transactions. By drawing attention to the vulnerability of a whole sector of the population, the Yellow Vests movement initially crossed traditional political divides. But rioters infiltrated the movement, giving vent to their antisemitism, racism, and homophobia. The far-right National Rally Party also sought to side with the Yellow Vests, but without claiming to adhere to it directly since its authoritarian ways ran counter to the spontaneity of the movement and its professed lack of leadership. After several months of demonstrations, the Yellow Vests movement's demands changed: its support for the most disadvantaged was overlaid by a demand for direct political participation and a general hostility to the representative regime. This demand is characteristic of transitions from a popular movement to a populist one.[96] Direct participation is not, in itself, a guarantee of democracy; it must be exercised within a framework of fundamental principles and rights. In December 2018, the French government instructed its Economic, Social, and Environmental Council (*CESE*) to launch an online consultative platform to respond to the Yellow Vests' expectations and prepare for the major national debate organized throughout France starting on January 15, 2019. The *Manif pour tous* flooded the site with contributions calling for the abrogation of marriage for all, a demand that quickly topped the list of requests submitted.[97] The reactionary tendency of direct democracy is well documented: in California, Proposition 8, banning same-sex marriage, was passed by referendum on November 4, 2008.[98]

Populism combines the rejection of elites and a monolithic vision of the people within a dual "anti-system" logic.[99] In order to mobilize highly diverse individuals and groups of individuals, social movements tend to project their values, beliefs, and classification categories onto the rest of society.[100] Sometimes this projection replaces their programmatic framework.[101] Popular protest may then become vulnerable to various forms of hijacking. The National Front was long a party hostile to the Fifth Republic, elitist in its organization and with an urban electorate inherited from the Poujadist movements, which claimed to support "small businesses and the trades." This is why the National Front has already been ready to mobilize in the streets.[102] Jean-Marie Le Pen always emphasized his authoritarian streak: an attachment to security, social conformity, and obedience.[103] A shift occurred with the passing of the baton from his generation to that of his daughter, Marine Le Pen. The party's electorate is now more rural[104] and more female.[105] The party has also established a strong local presence, especially in northern France, an industrial region with high unemployment. Marine Le Pen wants to paint the portrait of a national people through which France can restore its identity. However, the notion of "people" is difficult to apply because, unlike the very abstract idea of "nation," it invokes specific social trajectories that do not always match the party's ideals. Indeed, the notion of "the people" is already the object of a nostalgic attachment within left-wing political movements that consider themselves to be its custodians.[106] This is why, in the reactionary space, a traditionalist wing has rallied around Marion Maréchal, Marine Le Pen's niece, now a supporter of Éric Zemmour, to work on rewriting the notion of a people, which it pits against a society of minorities.

COUNTERREVOLUTIONARY ETHNONATIONALISM

On February 4, 2020, several conservative and far right leaders from Europe, the United States, and Israel gathered at the Grand Hotel Plaza in Rome for a conference under the banner "God, Honor, Country. President Ronald Reagan, Pope John Paul II, and the Freedom of Nations." Among the participants were Newt Gingrich, former Republican speaker of the US House of Representatives; Giorgia Meloni, president of the *Fratelli d'Italia* group and now prime minister of Italy; Viktor Orbán, prime minister of Hungary; Marion Maréchal-Le Pen, a rising figure of the French far right and granddaughter of the founder of the National Rally;[107] and Yoram Hazony, an Israeli intellectual, author of *The Virtue of Nationalism*,[108] and chair of the Edmund Burke Foundation, itself a cosponsor of the event. The mission of this meeting in Rome was to rethink conservatism on the model of the alliance between Ronald Reagan and John Paul II—an alliance which, according to the organizing teams, had led to the fall of European communist regimes. The traditionalist European Catholics, the far-right Zionists, and the US Christian evangelicals claimed to have in common the rejection of economic liberalism, immigration, supranational legal norms, and progressive values in matters of family and sexuality.[109] Their rallying cry? The collapse of Western nations. But their message concealed major contradictions, namely the rejection of representative democracy for some and its acceptance for others;[110] the hierarchical authority of the charismatic leader for some and the federation of more autonomous local groups for others,[111] the support for liberal economic policies for some and antiglobalism for others,[112] the stigmatization of sexual minorities for some and relative indifference for others.[113] Since these tensions made it difficult to build a powerful and stable coalition, the challenge of the Rome conference was to shape a program of renewed conservatism that would not be built solely on the condemnation of social and political change in Western countries. Marion Maréchal's speech during the event left no doubt:

Our grand idea is that conservatism is not a norm; it is not a fixed doctrine. It is above all a cast of mind. This is why there are so many national expressions of conservatism. The genius of each people has in its own way translated the universal need for the conservation of society. . . . Behind our differences, we can all accept this word, "conservative," because we all support a common vision of humanity and its natural extensions: communities of different kinds, more specifically a national community. We are the new humanism of this century.[114]

The term "nationalism" came into use in Europe during the eighteenth century, just as the first nation-states were beginning to take shape. It referred to the exalted belief in the ideal of nationhood as a means of defining community boundaries and of enabling the proper exercise of political sovereignty. It was initially opposed to international economic liberalism before emerging as its ally from the end of the nineteenth century.[115] Nowadays the term "nationalism" has a broader meaning since it denotes both an ideology and the movements that claim it. It was for this reason that political scientist Walker Connor crafted the notion of ethnonationalism in 1973. He believed "nationalism" to be too broad. In his view, the idea of self-determination is at the root of nationalist aspirations. Nationalists believe in each nation's ability to determine its own borders and population and to entrust a state apparatus with the task of ensuring full control. Still, Connor insisted on the paradox of self-determination:[116] how can we grant ourselves this right only to deny it to others, particularly regional and transnational minorities?[117] Nationalists have only been able to overcome this paradox by basing the feeling of belonging on more or less homogeneous and exclusive ethnic criteria. Birthright citizenship promotes a powerful egalitarian ideal and was notably used to fight slavery when, before the Fourteenth Amendment, US citizenship was reserved for "free white persons." Yet in the long run it often ends up promoting national cultural traditions and subjugating will in favor of heritage. The invention of the figure of the foreigner forms an essential part of this ethnonational mechanism. The nonself defines the self.

To that extent, Maréchal's "new humanism" fits perfectly within the definition of ethnonationalism: the figure of the foreigner acts as a specter that threatens the nation and makes it possible to define, *a contrario*, what constitutes it. This enemy-from-outside poses a particular threat to the nation, which is weakened by minorities' troubling behavior. Foreignness is the breeding ground of the foreign. In her speech in Rome, Marion Maréchal provided an overview of what ethnonationalism means today: antiminority thought that denounces critical feminism, elitism, European construction, postcolonialism and Islamism, all under the same banner:

What remains of [the] French spirit in the era of ideological delusions such as postcolonial studies? What remains in a time of restricted freedom of expression and intellectual terrorism? . . . What remains when my country turns into the back room of Salafist ideology, at a time when 150 French districts are in the hands of the Islamists? . . . What remains, in the era of gender theory, inclusive writing and neo-feminism? . . . What remains, in these days of European technocrats and judges who ignore the will of the people? . . . What remains, at a time when minority lobbies take the law into their own hands?[118]

By repeating "What remains?" Marion Maréchal combines the condemnation of decline with victimization. Antiminority movements routinely decry censorship[119] although they regularly make the front cover of magazines[120] and have powerful political backers.[121] The "new humanism" also reflects a philosophy of predestination opposed to the ideal of individual emancipation that revolutions brandish as their banner:

> We reject the relativism by which each individual creates his own values. We believe in natural law, in universal ethics. We believe that individual will cannot be society's sole compass. . . . Edmund Burke already detected in the French Revolution the roots of the evil that gnaws at us: an abstract citizen of the French Revolution, detached from his land, his parish, his profession, is a matrix of the citizen of the world![122]

It was to counter this logic of emancipation that Marion Maréchal established a new school in the city of Lyon in 2018: the Institute of Social, Economic, and Political Sciences (ISSEP). This school is training the leading thinkers behind her "new humanism"; her speech in Rome was a direct product of their "expertise." The school also seeks to become a crossroads for ethnonational activists, companies, and students.

The counterrevolutionary ideology promoted by Marion Maréchal also has spiritualist overtones.

> Everyone here still has these terrible images in mind of Notre-Dame de Paris up in flames. Eight centuries of civilization almost vanished before our eyes. . . . Facing such a blaze, the French felt this intense need to preserve. . . . Miraculously, all that was essential was saved: relics, statues of saints, stained glass windows. Even the proud Gallic rooster, symbol of our nation, was found almost intact after the steeple collapsed. . . . I see in it . . . a call: to rebuild this roof that protects us and this steeple that connects us to the sky.[123]

"New humanism" sanctifies the nation's heritage. Its optimism contrasts with the disillusioned nostalgia of the "great replacement" theory, which maintains that people from the global South (Mexico, South America, the Arabian Peninsula, North Africa and Sub-Saharan Africa) and Asia are replacing white Western populations, with the consent of globalized elites. Renaud Camus formalized this thesis, inherited from Maurice Barrès's national right, in his 2011 book, *L'Abécédaire de l'in-nocence*. In 2019, the author pleaded for "remigration" and ran in the European elections under the Sovereignty, Independence, and Liberties Party (a member of the Marine Blue Rally far right coalition). This was after a previous attempt in 2014 to run on an "anti-replacement" platform in the constituency of southwest France and a 2012 presidential election candidacy that was aborted for lack of sponsorship (he rallied behind Marine Le Pen in 2017 and Éric Zemmour in 2022). Jean-Marie Le Pen and Marion Maréchal took up his defense of "remigration," while it was rejected by Marine Le Pen.[124] The idea now routinely features in public debate, particularly in the discourse of Éric Zemmour, who has been convicted several times for his "complicity in the incitement of racial hatred."[125]

The "great replacement" theory is also popular among US white supremacists. It was openly claimed by Steve Bannon, ex-adviser to Donald Trump in the White House, who was indicted for laundering public money in August 2020 through the We Build the Wall organization. Steve Bannon claimed to have been inspired by Jean Raspail's *Le Camp des Saints*.[126] Published in 1973, this novel foreshadowed the "great replacement": it condemned the media and the youth of May 1968, and feared that white women would succumb to men of color. It was also part of a long tradition of disillusioned, hate-filled novels denouncing decadence, but it had a more journalistic tone and thus a lampooning quality that would in turn serve as a basis for several later works[127] including Pascal Bruckner's *The Tears of a White Man: Compassion as Contempt*[128] and Michel Houellebecq's *Submission: A Novel*.[129] The great replacement theory has been widely disseminated on social media and used to justify the actions of several far right criminals.[130] In the United States, the El Paso shooter (August 3, 2019) wanted to prevent the great replacement of the US population. In New Zealand, the gunman who shot fifty-one people in two mosques in Christchurch, New Zealand, on March 15, 2019, also claimed to be fighting against the great replacement.

At the beginning of the French Revolution, Edmund Burke sanctified tradition against the ideas of the Enlightenment and praised the virile and noble values of the national spirit.[131] His words still resonate today in the idea of "new humanism" but with a new feature: it actively seeks to redefine the human being against minority subjectifications. Minorities are the screen onto which fantasies of foreignness are projected: at once near and far, familiar and inaccessible. As Walker Connor pointed out, "Awareness of the existence of other cultures can be acquired by way of the spoken or written word, or the telecommunication media, as well as by actual contact."[132] A minority figure is as much a fantasy of the unknown as a blindness to what seems known but is only accessible in the form of spectacle:[133] "new humanism" is a paradoxical reaction to the fact that, in complex societies, minorities remind the majority that its fantasies of uniformity are futile.

In this chapter, I have shown the protean nature of antiminority discourses. They combine victimization of the majority, instrumentalization of the freedom of expression, appropriation of minority tools and references, assertion of the moral homology between majority and minority, fear of demographic and cultural replacement, rejection of self-definition, ethnicization of belonging, valorization of traditions, and sanctification of the land. Each country manufactures its own antiminority discourses as it interfaces with others: anti-US sentiment and condemnation of 1968 thinking in France;[134] protectionism in the United States;[135] neofascism in Austria, Germany, and northern Italy;[136] anti-Europeanism in Central and Eastern Europe;[137] evangelical proselytizing in Brazil;[138] and so on. This is why the antiminority register makes it possible for heterogeneous movements to cooperate. It poses a significant threat to antidiscrimination policies because it corrupts its categories.[139] Faced with such an offensive, theories of justice will not last long. Antiminority groups merely have to claim an alternative principle of justice to sweep away minorities' rights and appropriate their cultural references and activist tools. Thinking in terms of injustice thus provides a strategic advantage: the law can only recognize groups if they provide proof of the harm they have suffered. It is therefore possible to distinguish between true and false minority claims. Such arbitration is all the more necessary as the notion of minority is also a victim of its own success in antidiscrimination law: more numerous, more mobile, and more complex, minorities must compete for public authorities' attention and thus obtain legal protection. Born of the Civil Rights movement, affirmative action policies are now facing this serious challenge.

5

AFFIRMATIVE ACTION

There are many ways to fight oppression: collective mobilization, civil disobedience, adopting laws that prohibit and sanction discrimination, and introducing public policies that ensure moral and financial reparation for the harm caused. Affirmative action is part of this list: it aims to improve access to education and employment for people from structurally discriminated groups. Affirmative action relies on a wide range of mechanisms: targeted information for discriminated groups; quotas; selection procedures that pay close attention to applicants' backgrounds according to race, gender, age, and the like; and mentoring and scholarship policies once candidates have been recruited. There are several types of affirmative action, depending on the combinations used. But they all have one thing in common: their affirmative dimension. Affirmative action is based on the premise that support for some will serve as an example and inspire others to follow in their footsteps. In the United States, affirmative action originated with the Civil Rights movement: its aim was to actively include members of historically excluded racial groups.[1] However, it suffered several major setbacks. The first was in 1978. In *Regents of the University of California v. Bakke*, the US Supreme Court prohibited racial quotas. This led to the development of race-conscious policies, but these too were ruled unconstitutional by the court on June 29, 2023, in the context of college admissions procedures.[2] Affirmative action is both a policy of recognition and a policy of redistribution. Today, it is being challenged for two diametrically opposed reasons: on the one hand it is blamed for giving undue advantage to minorities and, on the other hand, for not being inclusive enough, that is, for not taking more minority groups into account.

The entire history of affirmative action in the United States has been fraught with difficulties.[3] The US Supreme Court's 1857 decision in *Dred Scott v. Sandford* excluded Black people from citizenship.[4] In 1868, the Fourteenth Amendment put a symbolic end to the Civil War by establishing that all citizens are equal under the Constitution. Yet local laws that organized segregation remained commonplace, often in the Southern states.[5] In *Plessy v. Ferguson* (1896) the Supreme Court laid out its "separate-but-equal" doctrine,[6] whereby segregation was considered constitutional as long as the same schools, transportation, and health care facilities were offered to Black and white people. In practice, these arrangements were anything but equivalent, if only in terms of their financial endowment. It was not until *Brown v. Board of Education of Topeka* (1954) that school segregation ended.[7] Ten years later, Congress affirmed the principle of nondiscrimination by adopting the Civil Rights Act of 1964. A year later, President Lyndon Johnson proposed a new tool in the fight against racial discrimination: affirmative action policies in public employment.

The term "affirmative action" first appeared in the National Labor Relations Act (1935), which required employers to rehire anyone fired for unionism, but it was not until 1965 that affirmative action became an antidiscrimination tool in its own right. Since then, the fate of affirmative action has not been easy. In *Piscataway Township Board of Education v. Taxman* (1996), the Court of Appeals for the Third Circuit held that the decision to lay off a white teacher was unlawful after she was selected because of her race and despite being of equal seniority.[8] The proportional logic applied by the New Jersey high school was initially supported by the Clinton administration, which then chose to limit affirmative action policy to cases of hiring and promotion, not dismissal. The appeal procedure was therefore dropped in November 1997. Affirmative action in public procurement also came to a halt in 1995, when the US Supreme Court ruled that strict scrutiny should be applied to race-based classifications in order not to violate the Fifth and Fourteenth Amendments.[9] In universities, *Regents of the University of California v. Bakke* (1978) endorsed affirmative action but strongly limited its use by requiring individualized treatment of cases.[10] This was also true of *Grutter v. Bollinger* (2003), which determined that an admissions procedure that favors "underrepresented minority groups" does not violate the equal protection clause of the Fourteenth Amendment as long as it evaluates applicants as individuals and that race is considered among all other factors.[11] On the same day, in another case involving the University of Michigan, the court held that recruiting underrepresented minorities by automatically awarding them admissions points was unconstitutional because this practice was contrary to candidates' individualized evaluation.[12] These two rulings thus reiterated that taking race into account was only an added factor in decision-making.[13] This approach aligned with the court's case law in electoral matters. Over the past twenty years, the justices have moved toward a standard that is increasingly color-blind when redistricting aims to benefit underrepresented minorities.[14] *Shaw v. Reno* (1993)[15] and *Hunt v. Cromartie* (1999)[16] narrowed the scope of the race criterion in this area.[17] Even so, a US Supreme Court decision on June 8, 2003, specified that when districting already benefits a racial minority, the system must be sustained.[18]

The two decisions of June 29, 2023, followed several principles. The court first held that deliberately considering race as a factor for college admission "lack[s] sufficiently focused and measurable objectives" and perpetuates racial stereotypes. The justices also found that neither Harvard University nor the University of North Carolina had been able to demonstrate how affirmative action better served the purpose of diversity. Finally, the court explained that the admissions offices now have the option of taking race and ethnicity into consideration, but only when they review individual files. Applicants would then have to prove how these criteria are "concretely tied to a quality of character or unique ability."[19] Such reasoning is paradoxical, since race and ethnicity are bound to play a greater role in the makeup and examination of applications. Moreover, in southern states with numerous ethnic and racial minorities, it is difficult for applicants to stand out. Admissions rates for Black and Latinx minorities are therefore likely to fall more sharply there than elsewhere, creating new disparities. The justices ruled against affirmative action by a 6 to 3 majority in the case involving the University of North Carolina, and 6 to 2 in the Harvard case (Justice Ketanji Brown Jackson, who had formerly served on one of the university's committees, recused herself). Against Chief Justice John Roberts's majority opinion and the concurring opinions, Justices Kagan, Jackson, and Sotomayor authored strong dissenting opinions demonstrating that equality always requires differential treatment and that affirmative action is essential to even imperfectly overcome segregation.[20]

In the end, and contrary to its image in France, affirmative action has never really been a dominant practice in the United States. Before the June 2023 decisions, a significant number of employers implemented outreach policies before hiring, while elite universities and a few public authorities promoted race-conscious admission policies steered by diversity, equity, and inclusion offices. However, these practices have never been widespread.[21] US society has always been more integrationist than the idea of the "melting pot" would suggest from a European viewpoint.[22]

How can we make sense of the disparities between discriminated groups and offer provisions that are both specific and open? How can we criticize legal categories while using them as a basis for protecting people? In this chapter, I will analyze the challenges of competition between minority groups using the two cases contesting the affirmative action policies and practices at Harvard University and the University of North Carolina, which led to the recent Supreme Court decisions. Second, I will show that it is possible, at least partially, to overcome the instrumentalization of diverging minority interests by valuing the reciprocity of minority experiences. To do so, I will outline the development of affirmative action in France, whose basis is essentially territorial. I will show that pluralism requires critical work on the part of institutions.[23] Affirmative action is then no longer strictly a policy of recognition and distribution; it becomes a performative policy. To provide an example I will draw on my experience at Sciences Po in Paris, teaching and tutoring students admitted through the Priority Educational Agreements (*Conventions Éducation Prioritaire*—CEP—Sciences Po's affirmative action program) and students from New Caledonia.

COMPETITION BETWEEN MINORITIES

The cases that prompted a nationwide ban on affirmative action involved two elite universities: one private, Harvard University; and the other public, the University of North Carolina. Both appeals were brought by Students for Fair Admissions, an organization founded by conservative activist Edward Blum, a former Republican candidate for Congress and the author of several previous affirmative action appeals.[24] In the Harvard case, the plaintiffs alleged that the university discriminated against Asian American applicants. On the basis of admissions documents they had been able to obtain, they estimated that taking into account qualities such as having "a positive personality," "likeability," "courage," "kindness," "attractive person to be with," and "widely respected" had led to downgrading Asian American applicants because racial stereotypes do not associate Asian Americans with most of these qualities.[25] The university explained that the documents were incomplete and that the admission rate for Asian American students had increased from 17 percent to 21 percent while the group made up approximately 6 percent of the US population. The university also claimed to have taken into account a range of factors in a context in which the general admission rate is around 5 percent. Two Massachusetts courts, at trial and on appeal, sided with the university.[26]

However, this case took place against the backdrop of the US Supreme Court's political shift. The Trump administration had already attempted to challenge admissions policies that partially relied on affirmative action. On August 1, 2017, the *New York Times* reported that the Civil Rights Division of the Department of Justice was seeking attorneys to challenge race- and ethnicity-based affirmative action practices in universities. The term used by the Department of Justice, "intentional race-based discrimination,"[27] emphasized the discriminatory nature of affirmative action and was reminiscent of the French term "positive discrimination." Under the Trump presidency, the Department of Justice also launched an investigation into the admissions procedures of several other universities. It accused Yale University of discriminating against its white and Asian American students even though the investigation it had initiated was still underway.[28]

The fate of affirmative action was played out before a Supreme Court dominated by the most conservative wing of the Republican movement. In 2017, conservative Neil M. Gorsuch replaced another conservative, Justice Antonin Scalia, who had died in 2016, after the Senate succeeding in blocking Barack Obama's nominee until Donald Trump was elected. After Justice Anthony Kennedy retired in 2018, Donald Trump nominated both Justice Brett M. Kavanaugh and, after Ruth Bader Ginsburg's death in 2020, Justice Amy Coney Barrett. In June 2022, in just a handful of decisions, the Supreme Court called into question several rights and provisions essential to minorities. In *Dobbs v. Jackson Women's Health Organization*, it ruled that a Mississippi law banning most abortions after fifteen weeks was constitutional, thereby overturning *Roe v. Wade*, which had protected the right to abortion since 1973.[29] In *New York State Rifle & Pistol Association v. Bruen*, the court held that the New York State law limiting the carrying of firearms outside the home violated the Second Amendment.[30] In *West Virginia v. Environmental Protection Agency* the court restricted the powers of the Environmental Protection Agency, thereby curtailing possible regulations on carbon emissions from power plants.[31] In *Kennedy v. Bremerton School District*, the court ruled that a Washington public high school football coach had a constitutional right to pray on the field.[32] Similarly, in *Carson v. Makin*, the court ruled that the state of Maine violated the free exercise of religion because it excluded religious schools from certain public funding.[33] These cases demonstrate that the current US Supreme Court supports a two-tier conception of individual freedoms: they are absolute when it comes to majority claims (mass consumption, religious beliefs, carrying firearms) but relative when it comes to minority claims (abortion, sexual health). The collective consequences of the exercise of individual freedoms carry very little weight in this court's decisions. In such circumstances, it was inevitable that race-conscious policies would be banned.

In 2016, when the US Supreme Court had a Democratic majority, it nevertheless tried to protect affirmative action by giving it greater flexibility.[34] The court concluded, in the majority opinion of Justices Kennedy, Ginsburg, Sotomayor, and Breyer, that the courts should allow universities a sizable margin for maneuver without it being absolute. Barely a few years later, this interpretation no longer seemed sufficient.

Affirmative action was particularly fragile since the Supreme Court's Republican majority could also rely on polls that were hardly favorable to the practice. In 2022, according to a Pew Research Center survey, 74 percent of Americans thought universities should not consider race or ethnicity in admissions. While this opposition is more marked among white people, no group is overwhelmingly in favor of taking race or ethnicity into account, including Democrat voters or ethnic and racial minorities who benefited from this system.[35] California banned affirmative action in 1996 with Proposition 209. Twenty-four years later, via referendum, California voters again rejected a bill that would have made affirmative action legal in the state. It therefore remained prohibited for admissions and hiring, as it was in eight other states (Washington, Florida, Michigan, Nebraska, Arizona, New Hampshire, Oklahoma, and Idaho) even before the two Supreme Court decisions in *Students for Fair Admissions, Inc.*

Other proactive measures are conceivable, but they might not always be as effective. Some major universities in the United States, anticipating the June 2023 decisions, spent several months considering their options. For example, the president of Cornell University, Martha E. Pollack, created a committee of administration and faculty members to propose new mechanisms for recruiting students from minority groups, especially African Americans. Many universities, including Yale and MIT, joined forces to develop alternatives to affirmative action. Among the solutions elite universities considered were strengthening outreach programs in high schools located in underprivileged areas and guaranteed admissions for those whose results rank them among the top 10 percent of their schools. Since social and racial segregation overlap in most cases, this approach would make it possible to maintain a more satisfactory admission rate for students of racial and ethnic minorities—without which this overall rate could drop by half or more. Another solution is to abolish selection tests, such as the SAT, which tend to benefit students who are better educated and have greater access to "legitimate" culture. This is an ongoing effort that began during the COVID pandemic: around 80 percent of colleges and universities no longer require the SAT.[36] In France, the competitive entrance exam has long been the preferred means of admission to the *Grandes Écoles*. Sciences Po Paris, however, twenty years after signing CEP agreements with disadvantaged high schools and opening up a new recruitment path, decided to abandon the written section of its entrance exam in favor of a more individualized assessment of applications. Since the start of the 2021 school year, students enter Science Po Paris on the basis of each student's continuous assessment in high school, overall average in the baccalaureate exams, profile, motivation, and performance in an oral exam.[37] The CEPs now include about 200 high schools across France, including the overseas collectivities and regions, and since 2023, several vocational high schools.

Although affirmative action has always faced obstacles, it serves to illustrate a double epistemic conflict between minority groups as well as between minority and majority groups. Some organizations consider affirmative action policies, from outreach to diversity, to be unfair to minorities who do not directly benefit from them.[38] While Harvard University and the University of North Carolina denied downgrading the profiles of Asian American applicants, affirmative action policies were not open to those students. Even though, on average, Asian Americans do better than others in their exam results, they face strong stigmas in higher education and in society as a whole.[39] To benefit from affirmative action policies, however, Asian Americans have no choice but to prove that the discrimination they face is every bit as real as that suffered by other minorities. A paradoxical dynamic is thus created, in which minorities pit themselves against each other and even compete with each other[40] and thus lose sight of the main relationship of domination. Even today, many major US universities, including those that applied affirmative action policies, often use a thoroughly nepotistic system of "legacy" admissions, in which special attention is paid to applicants whose family members are university alumni. One study showed that this criterion increases the chances of admission by almost 20 percent.[41] Although very few official figures exist, the number of students whose families are tied to the university may be around a third of the total. Peter Arcidiacono, Josh Kinsler, and Tyler Ransom revealed that 43 percent of Harvard students are athletes, legacy students, children of university employees—especially professors—and students whose names appear on VIP lists kept by the administration (these students have personal connections to celebrities or patrons).[42] Nearly 70 percent of these students are white.[43] Nepotism and majority privilege are very closely connected.[44] And this pattern continues after the student is admitted. Legacy students benefit from the support of alumni via scholarships, associations, and tutoring schemes. Ironically, the ban on affirmative action ought to undermine legacy admissions as a hidden form of preferential treatment.[45]

The selection process in major US universities is a paradigmatic illustration of Walzer's theory of justice. Economic, social, and cultural dominance grants undue advantages in a sector that should be allocating places on the basis of its own criteria. Affirmative action strives to overcome this failing: at the individual level, it is a means of redistribution; on a collective scale, it is a means of representation. But affirmative action goes further than this: it brings together different groups struggling with injustice and can, on that basis, foster an ideal of reciprocity.

In the following paragraphs, I will explore this ideal by examining the conceptions of collective life that underpin affirmative action. I will show that, with the right selection and support systems, affirmative action can promote forms of collegial commitment in which the relations between the minority and the majority and between the minorities themselves generate reciprocal benefits, even when groups are at odds or in competition with each other.

LOCAL INEQUALITIES AND REDISTRIBUTION

Affirmative action is intrinsically linked to the history of racial segregation in the United States. However, it was originally conceived elsewhere.[46] In India in 1919 and 1935, the British introduced two electoral reforms establishing a categorical system of parliamentary representation for certain castes, as well as for women and Christian, Muslim, and Sikh minorities.[47] From the 1920s, the Soviets used preferential treatment in federal public employment to ensure a greater presence of non-Russian republics in their confederation.[48] In the French colonial empire, the notion of minority designated the Christian and Jewish populations who, although smaller in number, had more power than the rest of the population.[49] In the countries of the Middle East and the Maghreb, the term "minority" is currently no longer used in constitutional law, but mechanisms for the protection of religious minorities do exist there.[50] For example, Lebanon's Constitution provides for an equal number of parliamentary seats for Christians and Muslims.[51] In Jordan, there are quotas for Christians to access parliamentary office in proportion to their demographic numbers.[52] Historian Todd Shepard has unearthed administrative and military archives related to largely forgotten practices in French territory: French Muslims from Algeria benefited from affirmative action policies from 1956 to 1962.[53] The French government introduced a measure known as "exceptional promotion," a quota system in which 10 percent of all civil service jobs were reserved for Muslim Algerians. Two entire student year groups of the National School of Administration (ENA) were even reserved for them. Today, there seems to be some "general amnesia regarding the shaping of the French nation and the consequences of its colonial wars":[54] preferential treatment of minorities did indeed exist for many years on the basis of ethno-religious criteria and now survives in other forms. The French Republic thus established two coexisting, interdependent models. On the one hand there existed a model of citizenship based on a national narrative hostile to all forms of community, on extensive regulation of bodies, and on legal rules guaranteeing the indivisibility of territory and language. On the other hand, there existed a model of subcitizenship based on exceptional statuses (such as indigenousness in Algeria), unequal rights, and strict segregation. This tension is still simmering in today's public debate, in which rhetoric hostile to any difference in treatment clashes with accounts of various experiences of preferential treatment in political representation, education, and territorial organization.

The French Republic was not entirely built on the rejection of differential treatment.[55] Article 1 of the Declaration of the Rights of Man and of the Citizen of August 26, 1789, states that "men are born and remain free and equal in rights. Social distinctions may be founded only upon the general good."[56] This formulation both allows for and restricts such distinctions. This is how the notion of "justified discrimination" came to be developed: it consists of all the differences in treatment decided on for the general public good and recognized by case law (that of the Council of State alone before 1958, those of the Council of State and of the Constitutional Council after 1958, and a fortiori after 1971[57]). Affirmative action therefore appears as one justified form of discrimination among others whose motive is to reduce a given inequality.[58] Article 13 of the

1789 Declaration adds that "a common contribution is essential for the maintenance of the public forces and for the cost of administration. This should be equitably distributed among all the citizens in proportion to their means." Progressive taxation thus paves the way for redistributive social policies. These policies are made necessary by the existence of de facto economic, social, and cultural inequalities against which the republic must work to guarantee not only the well-being of its citizens but also its own survival. In the absence of effective measures, the republic would put its legal foundations at risk.

The welfare state must ensure both equal rights and equal opportunity by compensating for territorial inequalities. Thus, the Law of July 13, 1991, exempts businesses established in sensitive urban areas from business taxation. The French Constitutional Council has always recognized this type of policy. In its December 29, 1984, decision, it ruled that "the principle of equality does not prevent legislators from enacting measures, such as granting tax advantages, to foster the creation and development of an activity sector to contribute to the public good."[59] The only obligation for legislators is therefore to respect the principle of proportionality between the means and the objectives of the law. The Constitutional Council also ruled that facilitating the hiring of indigenous New Caledonians by the civil service was in the public interest and therefore the principle of equality could be justifiably applied.[60] This decision was justified only by the exceptional situation of New Caledonia because, although the council recognized the flexibility of the framework for applying the principle of equality, it continued to object to the recognition of personal and cultural identities that might give rise to specific treatment. Indeed, the council rejected quotas for women in municipal elections.[61] It also rejected the notion of "Corsican people, a component of the French people," the formulation used in Article 1 of the Joxe Law on the territorial status of Corsica.[62] It further rejected the inalienable right to use a regional language, a provision laid down in the European Charter for Regional or Minority Languages.[63] Finally, it censured a so-called "organic" law (a law passed by an absolute majority to clarify the constitution) authorizing preferential treatment for people "born in French Polynesia."[64] The council does allow for exceptions, however, under specific conditions based on territorial rather than identity-related criteria. Echoing the 1946

Constitution, the 1958 Constitution recognizes the specificity of France's overseas *collectivités* (*collectivités d'outre-mer*, COM) formerly called overseas *territoires* (*territoires d'outre-mer*, TOM).[65] The Constitutional Council thus recognized the partial legislative autonomy of these *collectivités* as long as that autonomy did not concern overseas *départements* (DOM) and *régions* (ROM)[66] or metropolitan France (including Corsica.)[67] Articles 37–1 and 74 of the Constitution, part of the revisions of March 28, 2003, authorize any territorial community to intervene on an experimental basis in the domain of competence usually reserved to parliament (Article 34). That experiment is considered complete when it has been transposed to other territorial communities or when it makes up a territorial community with a special status. A group of territorial communities may also select a lead community (Article 72, paragraph 5). Since the 2003 constitutional revisions, the overseas *départements* and *régions* may adapt the law in certain areas, an option that was previously reserved for overseas *collectivités*, but a national law must authorize them to do so (Article 73). The 2003 constitutional revision was in keeping with measures to support the most disadvantaged territories. The law of November 14, 1996, created "urban free zones" where common law exceptions could be applied to support economic activity, regional development, and cultural and educational policies. The entire scheme must be renewed every five years.[68] Thus, the French Republic allows adjustments to the principle of territorial indivisibility laid down in Article 1 of its constitution: permanent or semipermanent for the overseas *collectivités*, *régions*, and *départements*,[69] experimental for metropolitan France. France compensates for situational inequalities using preferential treatment when they are territorially based.

According to the economist Thomas Piketty, France's territorial approach is based on the principle that "people from immigrant backgrounds and from various discriminated groups are generally overrepresented within the working class, particularly among workers and employees."[70] Despite "free zone" provisions, however, schools with a large proportion of racial minorities are the least well-endowed financially with the lowest average salary for teachers (they are more likely to have a temporary contract, be younger, and work part-time). Thomas Piketty concludes that an ambitious social policy is a prerequisite for any

AFFIRMATIVE ACTION

antidiscrimination policy while "antidiscrimination rhetoric has some-times been used to mask a rejection of any ambitious egalitarian policy."[71] He thus suggests prioritizing needs: social inequalities first, then societal and cultural discrimination. Such prioritization is artificial. Marriage for all was a social policy that changed the conditions of access to common residence, retirement, survivor's pension, inheritance, taxation, health-care, and so on.[72] Accessibility in cities is also a social issue, since it affects anyone who cannot use individual means of transportation. Controlling police activity is an issue both of race and of spatial segregation. Hierar-chizing the social and the societal is tantamount to validating the reac-tionary rhetoric that presents minorities both as privileged populations and as second-class citizens whose concerns are not essential to the gen-eral public's expectations.[73] Finally, the distinction between social and societal serves to reinforce the neoliberal logic that impoverishes the wel-fare state and expects private spheres, such as the family, to replace it.[74] Several researchers have shown that policies to support minorities con-verge with policies to fight poverty. For example, this is the case in ter-ritorially based affirmative action in India.[75] For this reason legal scholar Libby Adler has called for a "redistributive turn" in minority politics.[76] This is one of the challenges of affirmative action policies today: rather than artificially separating minority groups,[77] they must implement mechanisms that include all social groups.

THE PERFORMATIVE TURN

The CEP agreements were established at Sciences Po in 2001, at the initia-tive of the school's director, Richard Descoings, and the project manager, Cyril Delhay.[78] Their premise is territorially based and their philosophy is centered on minorities. A special entrance exam was offered to stu-dents schooled in several suburban high schools with which Sciences Po had signed partnerships. While some applauded Sciences Po's initiative, many condemned it in the name of republican universalism.[79] The con-troversy very quickly became an electoral issue. In 2002, Jacques Chirac's reelection as president of the republic against the far-right leader, Jean-Marie Le Pen, did not bring about a partisan restructuring. Chirac formed government teams made up of loyal followers, beginning with his two successive prime ministers, Jean-Pierre Raffarin and Dominique de Ville-pin. Meanwhile, Nicolas Sarkozy, in disgrace ever since he had supported Edouard Balladur over Jacques Chirac in the 1995 presidential race, was beginning to regain power, buoyed by his appointment as minister of the interior. On November 22, 2003, he came out in favor of "positive dis-crimination" for the "Muslims of France,"[80] making it one of the symbols of his modernity in politics against Chirac's supporters and the govern-ment's Left wing. Noting the failures of republican integration, he raised the possibility of reserving positions in the senior civil service for Muslim citizens.[81] In the space of a few days, both the prime minister and the president of the republic had disavowed him. Nicolas Sarkozy also came under fire from some on the Left. The chief secretary of the Socialist Party, François Hollande, remarked: "I sense in Mr. Sarkozy a very liberal, Anglo-Saxon notion that seeks representation through religion. It is the idea of equality that we must defend.[82]

The Socialist Party and its allies of the "plural left" (with the exception of the Green Party) were very hostile to the introduction of exceptional measures in the context of public service exams. This hostility originated in another policy. In 1999, the constitutional revision that preceded the adoption of parity[83] was the subject of fierce controversy, since it was no longer a question of basing difference in treatment on territorial grounds. Originally, parity was conceived as a faster, more effective way to coun-ter the exclusion of women in politics.[84] But public discussions took on a different tone—that of the "feminization" of politics.[85] By choosing to defend parity in the name of the fundamental division of humanity between women and men, the Socialist Party adhered to the argument of certain differentialist feminists: parity should reflect the anthropological separation of the sexes, a difference considered distinct from all the others, and even more fundamental than other differences.[86] By refusing to make parity just one corrective mechanism among others, the Socialist Party thus displayed its mistrust of any policies favoring underrepresented groups. Equality could only be "conditional equality."[87] However, the constitutional revision of July 23, 2008, on the modernization of institu-tions enabled a more flexible and broader application of the principle of parity. Article 1 of the Constitution now specifies that "statutes shall promote equal access by women and men to elective offices and posts as well as to positions of professional and social responsibility."[88] In the wake of this amendment, the "Copé-Zimmermann" law of January 27, 2011, on the balanced representation of women and men on boards of directors and supervisory boards and on professional equality imposed a minimum quota of 40 percent of members of each sex. Anthropological parity has therefore given way to simple accounting logic. The 40 percent threshold may seem more arbitrary than the 50 percent threshold, but both establish a general objective without taking into account the situation of the professional sectors concerned. In 2020, for example, the Ministry of the Civil Service sanctioned the City of Paris under the 2011 law for having appointed 60 percent women as administrative directors or deputy directors, although the ministry acknowledged that adjustments were needed.[89]

Given this background, it is surprising that French law remains so restrained about the possibility of favoring the representation of other minority groups. The notion of race, for example, appears in Article 1 of the 1958 French Constitution: "France shall be an indivisible, secular, democratic and social Republic. It shall ensure the equality of all citizens before the law, without distinction of origin, race or religion."[90] This formulation is based on the preamble to the 1946 Constitution which, at the end of World War II, was intended to stress its disapproval of racist ideas. However, because the negative formulation "without distinction" does not positively endorse the equality of categories, "race" is not used in compulsory censuses, a decision confirmed by the Constitutional Council on November 15, 2007.[91] Demographic and sociological research—on which public policy is often based—routinely makes use of this notion. Failure to take into account the categories by which people are discriminated against, mistreated, and/or inferiorized is tantamount to blindly obstructing the principle of equality itself. On July 12, 2018, the National Assembly's deputies voted to rewrite Article 1 to remove the notion of "race" and introduce that of "sex":[92] "[France] shall ensure the equality of all citizens before the law, without distinction of origin, sex, or religion." How can the notion of sex not be sexist, if the notion of race is considered fundamentally racist? In the absence of agreement with the Senate and in a tense political climate after the Yellow Vests' demonstrations, the text was withdrawn and a new constitutional bill "for a renewal of democratic life" was introduced in the assembly on August 29, 2019. The proposed revision of Article 1 retained the initial wording and added the following sentence: "It guarantees the preservation of the environment, biological diversity, and the fight against climate change."

In 2020, however, Amélie de Montchalin, then minister for transformation and public service, announced that "access paths for applicants from modest backgrounds" would be created for competitive entrance exams for senior civil service positions, as well as for magistrates and commissioners.[93] Unlike the CEP agreements at Sciences Po and Nicolas Sarkozy's plans in the early 2000s, this announcement did not spark controversy—attesting to a shifting outlook on affirmative action in France. Changes are currently underway, although they remain very modest at this stage: besides geographical criteria and the criterion of sex, French law only allows *"very slightly* preferential"[94] treatment, for example in the case of subsidized jobs for people with disabilities, which are too limited in number to change general recruitment procedures.[95] Still, affirmative action is recognized at the European level.[96] As law professor Hélène Surrel has noted, the European Court of Human Rights now considers that Article 14 of the convention implies "a positive obligation for States to treat differently individuals who are in different situations, and therefore to establish the necessary distinctions to correct *de facto* inequalities, as [it] recalled in *J.D. and A. v. United Kingdom*, of 24 October 2019, concerning distinctions based on disability and status as a victim of gender-based violence in relation to housing benefits."[97]

The term "positive discrimination" is still widely used in France for "affirmative action." Although it emphasizes the opposite of discrimination, it is still pejorative; it performatively rejects the equality it seeks to promote. By considering affirmative action primarily a form of discrimination, it essentializes the legal categories concerned. This is why a policy defined as one of affirmative action and one defined as positive discrimination, while relying on the same measures, will not have the same effects since their respective impact depends on the symbolic force attached to them. Admittedly, the US distinction between outreach policies (increasing the pool of applicants from a discriminated group) and affirmative action policies in the strict sense (allocating a certain number of jobs to members of a discriminated group before 1978, promoting diversity and race-conscious admissions policies since then) rarely figures in discussions in France.[98] Since the history of France does not provide any particular distinction between the two, this shortcoming can be overcome and does not warrant the oxymoron "positive discrimination." In fact, affirmative action seeks to combat the chronic underrepresentation of a number of social groups, less by reserving places for them than by increasing their means of accessing institutions, as Science Po has done. Affirmative action works toward collective equality that does not sacrifice individual paths.[99] It strives to articulate abstract universalism and concrete pluralism. This is a fragile mooring and must be constantly reset: affirmative action cannot, on its own, claim to resolve "the dilemma of belonging."[100] It is nonetheless an essential tool for affirming the legitimacy of minority trajectories and cultures and questioning the hegemony of institutionalized majority cultures. It is therefore both material and performative.

A PEDAGOGY OF RECIPROCITY

Affirmative action is never more powerful than when it is rooted in a relational conception of social identities. I would therefore like to examine it in a personal context. I taught and mentored students from priority education zones at Sciences Po from 2001 to 2010. Although I came from the provincial middle class and was the first member of my immediate family to get an advanced university education, I became responsible for speaking for the institution to which I had not been admitted.[101] My years on the high school science track had left me entirely unprepared for the entrance exam to Sciences Po Paris and so of course I failed, without the slightest awareness of what was at stake. The general knowledge section of the exam focused on existentialism, of which I had only heard from my favorite television series, *Who's the Boss*, in which one of the characters, a cleaner for a wealthy advertising executive, was going back to school. Because I was unable to read "existence precedes essence," I heard the quote as "existence precedes the senses."[102] Though I could no doubt turn this into a theoretical discovery today,[103] back then I sat one of the most selective exams in higher education armed with nothing but this one televisual memory. My results on the entrance exam to Sciences Po Lyon were no better, but the school also took into account my grades on the baccalaureate exam as an admission criterion—and that is how I got in. A few years later, when enrolled in a doctoral program in political science at the University of Paris 1 Panthéon-Sorbonne, I discovered quite by chance that it was possible to become an adjunct professor before having defended a dissertation—information that other doctoral students seemed to take for granted.

And so I started my career in the early 2000s teaching constitutional law, first at the University of Paris 12 Val de Marne and then at Sciences Po, where I was responsible for tutoring the first students in the CEP program. Selected on the basis of a special set of competitive exams, these students were supported with a great deal of information and guidance both before and after they entered the institution. One-third of this first CEP class enrolled in my courses. A few years later, Sciences Po established an outreach program for high school students from New Caledonia, for whom I also provided guidance and educational support. Within a few years, the internationalization of Sciences Po had also transformed its student body.[104] From 2008 to 2010, I was entrusted with the academic supervision of exchange students on the Paris campus. Over the months, I set up a logistical support system for those who were experiencing severe social exclusion in Paris, whereas they had enjoyed high levels of social well-being in their countries of origin thanks to their high academic achievements.

Becoming a teacher and then project manager at Sciences Po led me to reexamine my own career in light of that of my students. Many had parents who were diplomats, journalists, doctors, lawyers, publishers, and so forth. They had grown up in the leafy districts of western Paris and still lived there, and it took me several class sessions to fully convince myself that I had a legitimate right to be there. Although I had the knowledge required to train these students in the rudiments of the law, I feared that I would be found out. Who was I, after all, to "speak the law" at Sciences Po? Several members of my family were sure I would succeed in life and, right or not, they finally convinced me. I embodied my family's dreams of a brighter future. But the confidence they had in me depended on their social position and was no longer sufficient in a world that was entirely foreign to them. If social verdicts, majority norms, and nepotism are enduring, it is because they operate upstream and downstream of all

AFFIRMATIVE ACTION

entrance exams.[105] The ease acquired in a dominated social space is precisely how class subordination works outside of it.

The students selected through the CEP helped me to get my bearings at Sciences Po. Their presence signaled that there were several legitimate ways for both students and teachers to get there. I made it a point of honor to ensure that all of my students questioned their relationship with Sciences Po and understood what they could gain from having various ways of accessing the institution. After a few weeks, those of my students who were selected through the written exam and on the strength of their applications acknowledged that they would probably not have passed the CEP exams, which favored oral communication and were equally demanding. This acknowledgment created a new dynamic in the classroom. The CEP students were initially ill at ease but soon began to show signs of confidence and pride. In a kind of domino effect, the children of teachers and students who had been raised in the provinces and experienced an "ambiguous consecration"[106] also began claiming the uniqueness of their educational careers. Students from privileged backgrounds, too, came to reflect on their trajectories, no longer considering themselves the natural heirs of the institution. This dynamic did not, however, compensate for all the disparities in resources and networks, whether in terms of access to books, extracurricular activities, housing conditions, daily commuting time, and so on. Moreover, my own presence conditioned some of what happened in the context of the classroom. Students from the most privileged backgrounds no doubt used my analyses purely as a strategy. I once overheard a small group outside of class disparaging their Sciences Po education. Since the institution was open to profiles other than their own, they felt the need to distance themselves by somehow claiming that they did not need to be there. Conversely, the students selected via the CEP exam had little choice but to adhere to the school's precepts and present an image of individual success.[107]

A number of key questions then arose. How can we ensure that affirmative action does not become an individual "rescue" operation within a social system that is constantly adapting to better preserve its hierarchical nature?[108] How can collective transformation be initiated and then sustained? What did it mean to open up elite recruitment if the notion of elite itself was not called into question? In a statistical study compiling 515 studies on the prejudice that arose during encounters between different social groups, Thomas Fraser Pettigrew and Linda Tropp showed that contact alone was not enough to shift normative lines. Without long-term institutional work and appropriate conceptual frameworks, prejudice is barely reduced.[109] Support is therefore key to meeting the challenge of minority competition. My practice shows me that proposing ad hoc solutions is only relevant if they are combined with a critique of the institution (which requires the creation of minority studies within the institution itself[110]) and a pedagogy that values reciprocity. Would it then be possible to resort more frequently to affirmative action? Such an approach would mean taking better account of minority experiences in all hiring procedures (paying attention to applicants' personal background, disparities in their educational resources, and the impact of their social network, etc.). This kind of attention would go hand in hand with a strengthening of affirmative action in areas facing issues of representativeness and multifactorial exclusion mechanism (in public employment, positions of responsibility in large companies, university admissions, etc.). Conversely, where discrepancies in ability are evident despite the elimination of these factors, affirmative action should not take precedence over the common good.[111]

Similarly, affirmative action cannot be applied in areas that require certain specific characteristics. For example, European law does not require that all jobs be available to everyone. The European Court of Justice ruled to this effect: requiring an eye test to become an airplane pilot,[112] for example, or disqualifying applicants from becoming firefighters for physical reasons.[113] Thus, extending affirmative action does not mean putting an end to all forms of selection but rather diversifying recruitment criteria and methods whenever possible. Monitoring the socioeconomic circumstances of people who have benefited from affirmative action must go hand in hand with monitoring the socioeconomic circumstances of the general population, that is, undertaking both a local and a global analysis of the conditions for the production and fair distribution of wealth.[114] This means rebuilding a legal system acculturated to minority culture,[115] without which any change to the rules is insufficient.

Affirmative action can be both implemented and disqualified symbolically. Only flexible systems can stop this. If the fight against discrimination is limited to predefined categories, the people concerned have no choice but to conform to them to be protected by the law. As the law shapes perceptions of discrimination,[116] legally protected categories must be constantly adapted so that affirmative action does not become counterproductive—what the anthropologist Jean-Loup Amselle has called "affirmative exclusion."[117]

There are certain methods for achieving this result. For example, French trade unionists at Peugeot who got fewer promotions than other, nonunionized employees invented the "panel method."[118] This method involves studying the career paths of groups of people with very similar profiles except for one given characteristic. This cross-referenced examination makes it possible to consider the structural effects while redressing individual discrimination. Similarly, the fight against discrimination requires an extensive information drive before any decision-making: antidiscrimination training in educational institutions, mediation in companies, and support in handling complaints, among others. Since February 2021, France's Defender of Rights has provided an online platform to enable alleged victims of violence and discrimination to receive support and guidance from specialists.[119]

My experience at Sciences Po also shows that antidiscrimination measures have a certain preventative effect. It is easier to develop a pedagogy that values reciprocity when the law draws clear boundaries between what is allowed and what is not.[120] Affirmative action is in itself an "argumentative constraint"[121] and an "act of persuasion."[122] This is the logic used by the European Court of Justice in ruling that any statement designed to exclude a given category of the population is considered discriminatory in itself even if it does not result in the exclusion or refusal of admission of a given individual (these cases involved the manager of a Romanian football club who made homophobic statements and the manager of a Belgian company who expressed his hostility to the recruitment of so-called "allochtones" or nonnatives).[123] Although the court sanctioned the chilling effect of discriminatory statements and reversed their dynamic, its focus on speech raised the question of the burden of proof.[124] Discrimination need not be preceded by discriminatory words; making remarks that are prejudicial to the dignity of persons may not translate materially. This is why the context needs to be assessed as carefully as possible. Freedom leads to irreducible plurality, making absolute equality impossible to achieve at any given moment; conversely, equality can be oblivious to the variety of experiences, masking inequalities, and reducing people's freedom by imposing undifferentiated treatment on them. Only contextual responses can overcome this aporia and produce "positive-sum judgments."[125] This is the case with affirmative action when it partakes of a logic of reciprocity. It promotes a minority system that yields greater freedom by implementing equality. This is what Etienne Balibar calls "equaliberty."[126] This combination rejects policies that isolate individuals through decontextualized recognition.[127]

According to French administrative and constitutional jurisprudence, equality is only possible in a comparable situation,[128] unless there is an exception provided for by law and/or the Constitution: "If the principle of equality before the law implies that similar solutions are applied to similar situations, it does not follow that different situations cannot be the subject of different solutions."[129] However, any comparison implies a reference norm, which, case by case, covers up minority cultures and removes them from the public space. By standing as a bulwark, affirmative action makes the majority hegemony visible, forces it to define itself, and thus attempts to reintroduce a certain normative equilibrium. Affirmative action in favor of Black Americans in the United States forced white people to identify themselves as such and to realize that they themselves benefit, by default, from systematic preferential treatment.[130] Affirmative action will not reverse a static balance of power but does strive to create a new dynamic in which majorities and minorities are considered relationally. It is a tool to resist the norm, from which a subjectivized identity can emerge. Affirmative action is not rooted in a predetermined identity but in the very movement away from subjection. Reduced to biological, social, historical, geographical, or linguistic criteria, it cannot avoid competition between minorities and the reduction of individuals to a series of predetermined categories.[131] Conceived in a critical relationship with the institution and accompanied by a pedagogy of reciprocity, affirmative action invites a minority hermeneutic of the republican tradition by aligning with Condorcet's political philosophy. In his draft constitution,

Condorcet designed a collective organization of deliberation based on reviewing institutions at regular intervals; establishing reforms within a long timetable; facilitating cooperation among citizens (Condorcet considered that representatives were no more democratically competent than those they represented); multiplying the number of decision-making bodies; and teaching individuals to be mindful of their sovereignty.[132] These are all mechanisms that resonate in affirmative action today.

In the last four chapters, I have offered a legal and political analysis at the crossroads of social psychology, the archaeology of discourse, cultural analysis, and pedagogy. I have explained that, in France and in the United States, the concept of minority faces many obstacles because it has not been conceived in a relational way: conceptual opacity, changing calculation methods, hijacking by reactionary groups, and competition between minority groups. In the last few paragraphs on the CEP, however, I have suggested that it is possible to restore the corrosive force of the notion of minority. I will expand on this idea in the next three chapters. First, I will present a theory of the subject built around the idea of minority presence. This philosophy of social co-appearance enables me to reformulate the rhetoric of the "convergence of struggles" and the "coalition." I will then demonstrate the usefulness of analogies between the different categories protected by the law. More broadly, I will propose the notion of intrasectionality to describe the legal expression of minority lives and temper the shortcomings of the notion of intersectionality. Finally, I will show the value of a minority universalism for reflecting on responsibility toward others in a context of globalization and ecological crisis.

6

CO-APPEARING

On June 12, 2016, Omar Mateen, a heavily armed gunman, walked into Pulse, an LGBTQ Latinx nightclub in Orlando, Florida. He shot dead forty-nine people and wounded fifty-eight others. In the hours following the attack, one TV journalist after another repeated the same refrain: tragedy had struck a nightclub in a quiet neighborhood, plunging many families and an entire city into mourning. Local law enforcement officials reported the story of the shooting and the number of victims. Neighbors and onlookers bore witness. TV discussions ensued about the possibility of a terrorist attack and an assault on the United States. A few hours later, an armed man carrying explosives was arrested near the Los Angeles Pride parade. Although his motives were not clearly established, the investigation quickly showed that this was no terrorist network. The media's tone began to change. Was the Orlando massacre an isolated act? Had the shooter planned his assault? Had he been plagued by internalized homophobic and transphobic feelings? The following day, none of the headlines in the French press, except in *Sud Ouest*, acknowledged the LGBTQ aspect of the ordeal.[1] In the United States, many of the reactions online and in the press were similar: "We could all have been killed"; "This is an attack on the country." Nor did the television networks, the press, or social media show any interest in the fact that Pulse was a Latinx club. The lives of the victims, who were of different cultures, languages, and social backgrounds, were shrouded in the logic of official mourning and its spectacle, a logic that put the nation, biological family, and marriage first and foremost.[2]

At his speech to the press, however, Barack Obama praised the courage of the LGBTQ community and spoke of Pulse as "a place of solidarity and emancipation."[3] Two years later, based on forensic cell phone evidence, the FBI concluded that the shooter had chosen the Pulse nightclub at the last moment and that his attack was not a hate crime targeting LGBTQ people.[4] During the incident, Omar Mateen had posted on Facebook, pledging his allegiance to the leader of the Islamic State of Iraq and Syria. He described his actions as a means of vengeance against the US. Still, it is no less striking that anti-LGBTQ hatred is one of the driving forces behind terrorism (ISIS, which had apparently been a source of inspiration for Omar Mateen, was known to release propaganda videos of supposedly gay men being thrown off buildings). The overexposure of LGBTQ people to violence is part of this puzzle, whether directly or indirectly. To dissociate the political, cultural, and psychological motives that lead to violence is to refuse to consider its systemic dimension.

A similar scenario unfolded on November 19, 2022: a shooter who identified as nonbinary shot five people dead and wounded dozens of others at Club Q, an LGBTQ bar in Colorado Springs. The social pressure described by the club's regulars, no doubt also experienced by the assailant himself, may help to explain how such tragedies can occur.[5] This time, the US media immediately recognized that homophobia and transphobia had motivated the attack and that it was part of a long history of discrimination: the *New York Times* chose to publish a full-page rainbow flag riddled with five bullet holes.[6] The French media followed suit, describing the shooting as a hate crime against the LGBTQ community.[7]

How do minority struggles become visible? Is the recognition of certain minorities detrimental to others? How can the majority express its solidarity with minority struggles without making them invisible? In a photographic sense, the very thing that makes a subject visible also erases some of its texture and relief. The gaze restores its substance and breathes life into it. Any politics of visibility then is a politics of perception. It is not a passive recording of reality: it is an active construction of the social world.[8] Visibility strategies therefore have a downside in that they give minorities greater access to the public sphere but at the cost of having images of themselves controlled—and this control is all the stronger when the images give the illusion of fully capturing their subjects. They immobilize minorities and thus expose them to potential violence, both individually and as a group. Furthermore, a reverse shot of the gaze reveals other forms of exclusion. What stays in the shadows so that a subject can be exposed? Minorities do not all have the same resources to play with and shape their images because they have different bodily markings. This is why, throughout this chapter, I will lay out the idea of minority *presence* rather than visibility. Of course, presence does not escape the gaze of the other, but it is more intransitive. Presence does not imply that self-image is converted into recognition. Because it imposes itself as an established fact, presence questions the authority of the gaze. Because it is characterized by its imprint in space, it reconfigures close relationships between people.

I will first address the main ways of understanding how minorities relate to each other: the first is the convergence of struggles; the second, coalition; the third, parallax. I will then explore what, beyond the strategies for coordinating minority struggles, feeds subjective resonances from one minority to another before discussing violence as a marker of minority bodies and minorities' spectral relationship to memory. I will conclude by examining the ways in which minority presence affects the majority experience—an essential basis for reducing inequality and discrimination, where framing the majority group as the enemy is only temporarily effective. I will use Jean-Luc Nancy's theory of *co-appearance* (or "appearing with") to demonstrate that the two dimensions of minority presence are interdependent: minorities' occupation of the social space and majority subjects' understanding of their own minority dimension(s) in contact with minorities.

CONVERGENCE, COALITION, PARALLAX

In the public realm, minorities experience insults, threats, and violence, sometimes inflicted by law enforcement itself. For example, the 1969 Stonewall uprising in New York is considered a turning point in the history of LGBTQ movements in the West, when trans, lesbian, and gay people, many of them Black and/or Latinx, set up barricades along

Christopher Street in an effort to stop police raids and abusive arrests. Still today, women face harassment on streets all over the world, they are war trophies in many armed conflicts, and contraception is not universally free or available. The elderly are neglected or abused. People with disabilities are excluded from public spaces owing to the inaccessibility or unsuitability of many spaces. In the United States, the incarceration rate of Black people is five times higher than that of white people.[9] Everywhere, minority bodies are surrounded by violence. Such control, whether direct or indirect, does not take the same forms and does not have the same consequences, but it does create a very particular "minority condition" in the sense that minority bodies are conditioned by the *possibility* of violence. From this perspective, minority lives always resonate with each other, even when their objective interests diverge[10] and are a source of conflict, even within the same group.[11] Although minority groups can be very heterogeneous in their beliefs and moral values, they always have, from experience, some awareness that minority issues concern them all.[12] This does not mean that their awareness is always engaged and put to the service of others. Indeed, one minority may target another, giving itself the illusion for once of being on the dominant side. Hans Mayer highlighted this strategy of avoiding one's own condition, which he called "hypertrophy of assimilation."[13]

There are two ways of settling this kind of conflict. The first is to agree on a set of minimum moral values. For writer James Baldwin, these values all tend toward one principle: human dignity.[14] But how should dignity be defined? According to the classic division highlighted by Isaiah Berlin,[15] it can be about positive values (such as the "right to respect for private and family life" enshrined in Article 8 of the European Convention on Human Rights) or negative values (nonviolence, nonexclusion, noninterference, etc.)—both of which are related in practice. As I will show in the next two chapters, this is a tenuous approach because disagreements can extend all the way into questions of values (after all, what exactly is family life?).[16] This requires a complex theory of justice. I share Norman Ajari's reservations when he notes that "Black dignity cannot be discerned from the principles of moral law, for violence disfigures even reason itself. It doesn't benefit from any positive law, for the state doesn't protect Blacks but puts them to death."[17] However, minority lives are not only confronted with powers that kill (necropower); they also caught up in institutional apparatuses that run their lives (biopower), as if they were living on borrowed time: social welfare, medical care, and education are dispensed in dribs and drabs and on condition of belonging. Biopower and necropower are inseparable.[18]

The second method is more process-oriented than normative. Several authors have defended the convergence of social struggles in the context of environmental dependence.[19] The idea of convergence is common in left-wing movements such as Les Engraineurs, a French antiglobalization citizens' collective, or the Convergence of Struggles group created by activists from the newspaper *Fakir* at the time of the Nuit Debout movement's occupation of public squares.[20] Convergence appeals as much to a "nostalgia for a party of the masses," as to the dream of a "revolution" or "the coming insurrection": in other words, the spontaneous federation of social struggles in a revolutionary movement.[21] But toward which struggle should minorities converge? Is the convergence of struggles not a way for the traditional trade unions and political Left to conceal a strategy to subsume proliferating minority struggles that had hitherto been relegated to the margins of their political agendas?[22] Who would become the movement's spokesperson?

For example antiracist and LGBTQ movements draw on very different subjective experiences. LGBTQ people are very rarely brought up in LGBTQ families. At some point they must find external resources, learn from their peers, and build their own community of like-minded friends who support their sexual choices, regardless of how much support they receive from their families. In Western Europe and the Americas family law has changed profoundly over the last three decades. A family is no longer legally defined as strictly heterosexual; nonetheless, it remains highly heteronormative. Family life is based on domesticity, the gendered division of roles, and social endogamy. Sexual and gender minorities are enjoined to conform to this "one-dimensional" life.[23] This constraint does not weigh on all minorities, however. In the vast majority of cases, the family remains a safe space, albeit a fragile one, for Black and mixed-race people. Its function is to act as a buffer against violence.

James Baldwin recalls that his father explained this idea to him after a white police officer shot a Black soldier accused of disturbing the peace at the Braddock Hotel in New York in August 1943, triggering riots in Harlem and the destruction of several white-owned shops.[24] The experience of racism remains biographically primary for Baldwin, which leads him to articulate his oppressions contextually: "The sexual question comes after the question of color; it's simply one more aspect of the danger in which all [B]lack people live."[25] What can converging struggles possibly mean to people who, as Baldwin says, are themselves the site of divergence? Intersectional movements live at the crossroads of several minority experiences, rearranging them in a multitude of ways. The search for convergence inevitably betrays a desire to reduce the complexity of the modes of resistance to oppression[26] and subjugate them to a majority agenda within minority groups. From this perspective, I subscribe to several of the arguments of Afropessimism, a current of thought which, in the wake of Frantz Fanon, maintains that not all forms of oppression are symmetrical. When Kehinde Andrews speaks of Blackness, he points out that it is a minority condition that is not accessible to everyone.[27] As Norman Ajari summarizes, "For Afropessimists, the Black condition must be understood, treated, theorized from within."[28] However, I believe that having a privileged relationship to one's own oppression does not preclude conceiving ways of resonating with other minority conditions. Like Norman Ajari,[29] I disagree with the second strand of Afropessimism, which argues that the Black condition should not be "harnessed as a breeding ground for examples, metaphors, or analogies by theories and political agendas in which [B]lackness is only one question among others, lost in the middle of a chain of equivalence."[30] Analogy is always ambivalent. It can erase a minority group just as it can make it more powerful by leading other groups to think and speak its language. It is entirely a question of context. Equivalence does not mean indifferentiation, but rather equal value. Thus, considering minority resonances between Black people and other groups is not at odds with grasping the specificities of racial capitalism, as Cedric Robinson does,[31] or the role of Black men in the production of white male dominance, as bell hooks does.[32] Of course, as Frank Wilderson claims, analogy can "mystif[y], rather than clarif[y], Black suffering."[33] But analogy also makes it possible—as long as it is not a simple comparison to a reference group—to highlight the gap between various experiences. In this way, analogy enriches our understanding of

CO-APPEARING 137

what is specific and what is transversal. The challenge of minority presence is as much one of autonomy as of interdependence.

The idea of coalition pursues this dual movement. It recognizes the unique features of each minority and offers an alliance guided by a common interest, namely to overthrow a multifaceted, oppressive system. In a 1967 speech, Martin Luther King Jr. spoke of a "coalition of conscience."[34] Coalitions do not seek convergences of movements but rather their tactical arrangements, so that a collective push can take place. While the struggles remain separate, the organization and expertise can be shared. Coalitions have been a prominent political instrument in the United States ever since the "rainbow coalition." On April 4, 1969, a group of individuals founded an antiracist, multicultural movement anchored in a logic of class struggle. The members were Fred Hampton, an activist member of the Black Panther Party; William Fesperman of the Young Patriots Organization (a left-wing organization based in Chicago created to support poor, young, white migrants from the southern United States); and José Cha Cha Jiménez of the Young Lords (another Chicago-based organization that started as a street gang and focused on helping and educating Latinx people, especially Puerto Ricans, and people from Central and South America).[35] Many other groups joined them, including the Lincoln Park Poor People's Coalition and, later, Students for a Democratic Society (a student association representing the New Left); the American Indian Movement (a grassroots movement founded in 1968 in Minneapolis to fight against the poverty of Native American communities in city centers and police violence); the Red Guard Party (a youth movement of Chinese Americans who fought poverty and repression in the United States and supported China's Cultural Revolution; and the Brown Berets (a movement in support of Chicano farmers, opposed to the Vietnam War, and in favor of making the southwest of the United States independent). The coalition helped to ease community relations in Chicago but eventually fell apart after a tactical unit backed by local police and the FBI assassinated Fred Hampton in December 1969. Mel King, a member of the Massachusetts House of Representatives, used the term "rainbow coalition" in his 1983 mayoral campaign in Boston; and the Reverend Jesse Jackson, a candidate for the Democratic presidential nomination in 1984 and 1988, also took up the term, founding the National Rainbow Coalition before launching his first primary campaign. At the time, Jackson said, "We must forgive each other, redeem each other, regroup, and move on. Our flag is red, white and blue, but our nation is a rainbow—red, yellow, brown, black and white. . . . The white, the Hispanic, the black, the Arab, the Jew, the woman, the native American, the small farmer, the businessperson, the environmentalist, the peace activist, the young, the old, the lesbian, the gay, and the disabled make up the American quilt."[36] In 1996, Jackson merged the National Rainbow Coalition with Operation PUSH (People United to Save Humanity), an organization he had founded in 1971 to provide economic and social support to Black communities. Mel King in turn founded the Rainbow Coalition Party of Massachusetts in 1997, which merged with the Green Party in 2003. Barack Obama's presidential success in 2008 and, to a lesser extent, in 2012 were often attributed to the mobilization of minorities in the wake of Fred Hampton's Rainbow Coalition.[37] And yet the Green-Rainbow Party ran as an alternative to the Democratic and Republican Parties.

In France, coalition strategies are not uncommon among minority rights movements. Such was the case with the Act Up Paris initiative in May 1997 and its manifesto "We are the left."[38] The movement emerged in the context of three events: the general strikes of December 1995 in defense of public services; the Pasqua law of August 24, 1993 (which made access to care conditional on legal residence); and the Debré law of April 25, 1997 (which considerably tightened conditions enabling undocumented migrants to obtain residence permits). Act Up brought together a large number of minority rights organizations to put pressure on the parties of the Left in the run-up to the legislative elections of May 25 and June 1, 1997. Its manifesto asserted: "The official left will not win the elections without us. Because we are the real left. We are the left that fights and has always fought on the ground, for its own living conditions and for everyone else's. For foreigners, the unemployed, gay people, women, the homeless; people with HIV, drug addicts, prisoners; for all those who suffer daily exploitation, repression, and discrimination."[39] Among the signatory organizations were: the *Sans-Papiers de Saint-Bernard* collective (supporting undocumented migrants); the *Syndicat de la magistrature* (a judges' union); the *Groupe d'Information et de Soutien des Immigrés* (an information and support group for migrants); the *Mouvement français pour le planning familial* (a nonprofit organization providing reproductive and sexual health care); the *Fédération des Tunisiens pour une Citoyenneté des deux Rives* (a Tunisian workers' union); feminist groups such as *Marie Pas Claire*, *Le Bus des Femmes*, and *Les Nanas Beurs*; Cabiria (an organization that supports sex workers in the city of Lyon); *Prévention Action Santé auprès des Transsexuels et Travestis* (an organization supporting transsexuals and transvestites); the newspaper *Vacarme*; *SOS-Homophobie* (an antihomophobia organization); *Autosupport Banlieue* (self-help projects); *les Sourds en colère* (a deaf association); and *Témoignage chrétien* (a Christian publication promoting religious tolerance); among others. Act Up Paris summed up its strategy as "minority solidarity."[40] More recently, in July 2011, Louis-Georges Tin created the equality and diversity initiative *Pacte pour l'égalité et la diversité*) as part of his think tank *République et Diversité*,[41] which was joined by other organizations and influential groups: *Mix-Cité* (a feminist organization); the *Mouvement français pour le planning familial* (a family planning association); the *Association des Parents et futurs parents Gays et Lesbiens* (an association supporting gay parents and prospective parents), the *Comité Idaho de lutte contre l'homophobie* (an antihomophobia organization), *Animafac* (a network of student organizations), the *Conseil Représentatif des Associations Noires* (a French antidiscrimination federation); *Graines de France* (an association that aims to strengthen individual and collective empowerment); *l'Association des paralysés de France* (an association supporting paralyzed people); *la Fédération des aveugles de France* (a federation providing support to visually impaired people); *la Charte de la diversité* (a collective for diversity created by the Institut Montaigne, a liberal think tank, in 2004); and *Terra Nova* (a center-left think tank close to the Socialist Party at the time). The *Pacte* put forward twelve general proposals to fight discrimination more effectively, such as creating a state department and an international observatory, establishing a "diversity label" for companies, and "integrating diversity issues more explicitly into school curricula." In such cases, coalitions demonstrate both their strengths and their weaknesses as they bring together people's demands but, in so doing, tend to dilute them.[42] They also face another challenge: the duration and intensity of discrimination vary significantly from one group to the next. Some minorities, therefore, have a greater interest in reforming institutions than in seeing new ones created.

Finally, the broader the coalition, the more a majority logic tends to prevail once again. Based on a questionnaire survey of 286 associations and a qualitative analysis of interviews with representatives from 40 of them, Dara Strolovitch demonstrated that a majority mind-set continued to prevail within groups defending minorities. She distinguished between mobilization issues that might concern the entire population, the majority of the group's members, an advantaged subgroup, and a disadvantaged subgroup. Her conclusions were clear: although the associations surveyed showed a deep and sincere interest in issues relating to disadvantaged subgroups, they invested far fewer resources in them unless they acted in coalition with other associations. In this case, however, most of the work involved in maintaining the coalition's momentum fell on the shoulders of the disadvantaged subgroups.[43] These groups therefore found themselves tossed from one dependency to another.

A third idea played a considerable role in the Black Lives Matter mobilizations, one defended by Assa Traoré and Geoffroy de Lagasnerie in their book, *Le Combat Adama*. It consists in intensifying one's own struggle—what BLM described as "being unapologetically Black"[44]—without dismissing other struggles or undermining their usefulness, because the force with which victories are won against an oppressive system can pave the way for the defense of other minorities:

You have to respect everyone's struggle. You have to respect everyone's values and how they see their own struggle. . . . On the other hand, I want to share some strength with you as you fight. We're here to give you all the strength we can in the struggle you are undertaking, the struggle you believe in, with your values and your principles. Even if I don't completely agree with everything [you say or do], I'll step forward and help you. . . . I'm not going to tell you you're talking nonsense. I respect your struggle, and we create alliances to give each other strength. On the other hand, you're also here to give us strength.[45]

It is still possible to be a witness, ally, or sounding board for a struggle that is not one's own without taking anyone's place. This position makes room for nonminority individuals. In this way, young, white protesters protected Black protesters by using their bodies as shields against the police during the June 2020 protests sparked by the murder of George Floyd. This new generation of activists, born out of antiracism protests, the Occupy Wall Street movement, the Green New Deal,[46] and the fight against homophobia and transphobia, rallied behind Vermont's Socialist senator, Bernie Sanders, during his campaigns in the Democratic primary in 2016 and 2020. It attracted new spokespersons such as Alexandria Ocasio-Cortez and Ilhan Omar. Impacted by a series of crises (September 11, water pollution in the poorest communities, the 2008 banking collapse, the COVID-19 health crisis, the war in Ukraine, inflation, etc.), these young radical activists wanted to tackle the root of the problems: a capitalist system protected by reactionary interests. Some, such as L. A. Kauffman, argue that "the more systems of oppression intersect with your life experience, the broader and more sweeping your vision of power becomes."[47] Kauffman believes in mutually reinforcing struggles. She suggested that new recruits bond with each other[48] through an exercise that concretely demonstrates how the oppression of some also constrains others.[49] This interdependence extends beyond national borders.[50] Jean Beaman summarized how Black identity is a vector of identification for young French people of North African origin: "Minority and marginalized populations may thus feel a sustained and genuine connection to blackness through, among other commonalities, similar experiences of inequality, without self-identifying as black."[51]

This new generation is not part of the long tradition of nonprofit activism[52] but rather of community organizing. Being an organizer is not about fighting for a cause or representing interests; it is about transforming an individual problem into a collective one by rallying people from one's own community first, then calling on other allies through meetings, rallies, or even cold calling. Organizers do not join already existing organizations but mobilize directly under the slogan "Don't agonize, organize!" In France, the Adama committee organized a series of mobilizations and actions (meetings, fairs, lectures, etc.) that brought together people from different neighborhoods. In the United States, community organizing emerged from a need for activist independence in a context where human rights associations were becoming highly professionalized as part of foundations or private social organizations.[53] In this spirit, a group of organizers launched the INCITE! collective in 2000, which challenges the profitability of the human rights defense sector.[54] Organizers mobilized by using direct exchanges via their networks of acquaintances, particularly online. Community organizing is also part of a broader logic of public education and training,[55] most often in poorer communities whose members are wholly absorbed by their everyday problems, whether related to school, unsanitary living spaces, or transportation. Community organizing is, then, mobilizing for change on a wider scale and an initiative to reorganize community life. ACORN (Association of Community Organizations for Reform Now), for example, is an interracial coalition that has been campaigning since 1970 on behalf of low-income families facing difficulties with housing, safety, health, and voting access in their neighborhoods.[56]

The intensification of separate struggles, however, runs the risk of incoherence. To what extent can some struggles be backed by others without the interests of one interfering with those of the others? Activists' vastly different situations necessarily create different expectations. This is particularly true when institutions begin to recognize and symbolically reward mobilization. When struggles take place in parallel, inconsistencies appear.[57] The only solution lies in conceiving the notion of minority in relational terms, as Michael R. Hames-García stated in his call for a realist conception of identities. He believes that poststructuralist theories, by revealing the constructed nature of identities, have suspended all judgment on the relevance of any particular conception of social ties or, at the very least, have only admitted it strategically. In his view, only certain epistemic configurations allow solidarity to be maximized among minority groups—in particular the relinquishment of control over other minorities' struggles.[58] This is how some feminist strategies have created coexisting movements with contradictory objectives and operating methods, for example between mixed and nonmixed groups.[59] It is therefore possible to allow for certain inconsistencies between minority struggles as long as we recognize that every struggle is in flux and adjusts to its goals, like a shifting point of view in a parallax displacement. Because the specter of violence haunts all minority struggles, they can open up to new connections but also, beyond that, to new ways of forming links with the majority.

BODIES OF VIOLENCE

The violence that law enforcement agencies inflict on Black and Brown bodies is disproportionate to the violence they inflict on the rest of the population. It is also a violence that is not met with any real counter-power. The many unresolved cases of police brutality caught on film raise questions about the impartiality of the justice system and respect for fundamental freedoms. In France, this question became highly sensitive in the wake of the Yellow Vests' demonstrations. Those protesting against the government's tax policy faced brutal police intervention techniques, leading to a very heavy human toll: one dead and nearly 2,500 injured protesters (including twenty-four who were partially blinded, and five who lost a hand).[60] More than 5,000 people were taken into preventive police custody with no legal grounds.[61] On June 8, 2020, the minister of the interior announced a ban on choke holds; however, a note from the director of the National Police specified that, although strangulation techniques would no longer be taught, they would continue to be "used with restraint and discernment."[62] In July 2020, Jacques Toubon, France's Defender of Rights, condemned the use of inappropriate techniques, in particular kettling, "preventive" arrests, and challenging the presence of journalists.[63] In the absence of prefectural authorization, arbitrary arrests took place during a number of demonstrations in support of Adama Traoré. One of the ways the state may claim a monopoly on legitimate physical violence is to exert it more forcefully on people whose low economic, social, and symbolic capital is less likely to expose the state to sanctions.[64]

According to the Defender of Rights, young men perceived as Black or Arab are twenty times more likely to be stopped and searched by French police than the rest of the population.[65] When Adama Traoré was stopped, he was with one of his brothers, Bagui, and it was Bagui whom the gendarmes had come to arrest as part of an investigation into extortion with violence.[66] Adama Traoré fled the scene knowing that he was not carrying his ID and had already been to prison twice. These facts need not be disregarded to prove structural racism. Black men make up around 35 percent of the US prison population (even though they represent around 6 percent of the country's total population), and they are both more often victims and more often perpetrators of misdemeanors and felonies.[67] The incarceration of Black people, especially men, stems in large part from a repressive policy on the use and sale of drugs. Legal scholar Michelle Alexander speaks of "new Jim Crow" policies.[68] Ariane Chebel d'Appollonia shows that the violence to which certain ethnoracial groups turn—violence they commit above all against themselves—is not simply a consequence of economic, educational, and residential disparities; it is also one of the only ways these individuals can gain visibility.[69] The use of violence is so much a part of the community's culture that there is a certain degree of habituation to it. Chebel d'Appollonia points out that resilience in the face of intracommunity violence is possible, but it is rarer in cases of intercommunity violence. She hypothesizes that violence is an anticipatory response to adversity.[70]

Justifying police controls and even violence in the name of legitimately repressing misdemeanors and felonies is disingenuous: the exemplary conduct of the police, as the holders of force, is the very condition of their legitimacy. On June 4, 2020, Arte Radio broadcast a documentary of recordings and messages from a WhatsApp group in which Rouen police officers poured out racist, sexist, homophobic, and Islamophobic insults and even calls for murder.[71] Even though an agent of the squad reported the police officers' actions in December 2019, and the matter was referred to the General Inspectorate of the National Police, the officers kept their jobs and were only referred to the disciplinary board once the media picked up on the case, proving that a structural problem existed within the police. A few days later, Jacques Toubon published his report on discrimination linked to one's racial and ethnic background. He explained that discrimination has a "systemic dimension" when it is reinforced from one sphere of life to another (employment, housing, family life, freedom of movement, etc.).[72] While some academics have called for caution in using the notion of "systemic racism" too broadly,[73] the real issue lies elsewhere: not naming a system euphemizes violence and reinforces impunity.[74] In July 2021, the newspaper *Mediapart* revealed that in 2019 the general director of the national gendarmerie had chosen to decorate the gendarmes who had arrested Adama Traoré for "remarkable commitment . . . and unfailing determination that bring honor to the national gendarmerie."[75] In November 2022, a new report confirmed that the "restraint" used on Adama Traoré had precipitated his death even though he was already in a "weakened state."[76]

The abuse of minority bodies is also a result of inaction on the part of public authorities. This is particularly true for disability policies in France. On December 13, 2006, the United Nations General Assembly adopted the Convention on the Rights of Persons with Disabilities (CRPD) which, in fifty articles, stipulates that member states shall undertake all appropriate measures to ensure the safety of persons with disabilities, their access to transportation, health, education, justice, work, voting, and so forth. The text emphasizes that people with disabilities must be able to "enjoy" and "exercise" their rights as a condition of autonomy, integrity, and self-worth. France ratified the Convention on February 18, 2010, and it came into force on March 20 of the same year. In 2011, the Defender of Rights, as an independent authority, assumed responsibility for monitoring the convention's implementation. Ten years after the convention came into force, Toubon published a report that was highly critical of disability policies in France, in line with the conclusions of the Special Rapporteur on the rights of persons with disabilities at the Office of the United Nations High Commissioner for Human Rights.[77] The Defender of Rights noted "significant shortcomings" in many areas such as the compartmentalization of child protection, violence against women with disabilities, the organization of emergency relief, the conditions for receiving migrants with disabilities, issues around medical consent, the weakness of systems for combating abuse, the precarious status of caregivers, significant delays in terms of accessibility, and so on.[78] Even before the 2006 Convention, the law of February 11, 2005, "for equal rights and opportunities, participation and citizenship of people with disabilities" had set a number of objectives relating to accessibility, personal care, and education. For example, it defined accessibility not on the basis of location but of "chains of movement" linking housing, transportation, work, leisure, health, etc. It also took into account motor, sensory, cognitive, and psychological disabilities. However, there has been no adherence at all to the timetable of incentives, training, and sanctions, particularly in the area of housing and transportation. The ELAN law of November 23, 2018, lowered the minimum rate of accessible housing in new constructions to 20 percent, whereas the 2005 law had set it at 100 percent. This law allowed the rest of housing to be "adjustable," that is susceptible to being redeveloped in subsequent renovation work. To a large extent, therefore, this system defers to the interests of the building sector, even though studies show that this approach does not yield satisfactory results.[79]

The rights of people with disabilities are therefore "vulnerable":[80] not only because they must count on political and social will, leading them to beg for rights, but also because inequalities and discrimination thrive under the effects of short-term profitability.[81] Institutions tend to confine disability to public policies of limited scope.[82] In 2023, the European Committee of Social Rights of the Council of Europe (ECSRC) also noted France's inaction in the area of disability. It considered the country to have failed to meet its obligations as a signatory of the European Social Charter.[83] This inaction is compounded by the mistreatment already observed in various closed specialized institutions and long denounced by disability organizations.[84]

In light of this situation, sociologists Pierre-Yves Baudot and Emmanuelle Fillion have called for a minority design thanks to which the needs of people with disabilities can benefit others: "Acting for the inclusion of people with disabilities makes it possible to renew and energize social participation for everyone. Live captioning makes discussion easier in a meeting, including for hearing people; low-floor buses make life easier for the elderly and parents pushing children in strollers."[85] Baudot and Fillion noted that the treatment of disability in France was initially based on assistance, under the law of June 30, 1975. The medical-social and nonprofit sectors were responsible for providing support for people: children's schooling, care and assistance for people with motor disabilities, and recruitment of people with cognitive impairments. Organizing nonprofits by type of disability curtailed the emergence of more radical solutions and restricted disability's overall impact.[86]

This depoliticization of disability-related issues in France is even more striking when compared to that of the United States. The US Disability Rights Movement emerged in the wake of the civil rights, feminist, and gay and lesbian movements in the 1970s, which enabled it, as a political minority, to challenge the ableist norm and establish the field of disability studies.[87] Minority activism is shaped by an ableist imaginary—starting with the very notion of "marching," which fails to include people with disabilities.[88] Europe's Freedom Drive, an event created in 2003 in Strasbourg, France, and now organized every year in Brussels by the European Network on Independent Living movement, fights against this trend. The event emphasizes autonomy and shows that activist collectives are mired in ableist assumptions. In the spirit of crip theory, it questions what accessibility is. Crip theory takes the pejorative term "crippled," reclaims it, and makes it self-assertive.[89] It challenges the notion of disability, which tends to focus on visible disabilities.[90] Crip theory shows how the body is minoritized in numerous ways. It endures both visible and invisible violence owing to ableist representations: infringements on freedom of movement, obstacles to enjoying their entitlements and rights, and the unavailability of care. These constraints are distinct and vary in intensity. They are, however, fundamentally linked because they all "condition" people with disabilities and only give them "conditional" access to majority spaces and temporalities.

DISRUPTIVE MEMORIES

During a parliamentary session in the National Assembly in February 2013, the then minister of justice, Christiane Taubira, spoke about marriage for all. Her remarks were particularly enlightening in addressing the issue of minority memories. The law of May 17, 2013, had been jointly written by the prime minister's office; the Ministry of Justice; the teams of then minister for family, Dominique Bertinotti; and several members of parliament, including Erwann Binet in the role of rapporteur. But it was Christiane Taubira who became the voice of reform. Echoing the words of Léon-Gontran Damas in his book-length poem *Black-Label* (1956), she formulated very directly the ironic point of view of minorities:[91] "We the beggars / we the few / we the nothings / we the dogs / we the skinny / we the Negroes. . . . What are we waiting for to play the fools / take a piss / over and over / against this dumb and stupid life / which is made for us."[92] The setting strengthened the reference: introducing poetic verse into a parliamentary forum accustomed to an entirely different mode of speech was already an affirmation. Christiane Taubira thus came to embody a unique minority presence. For a short time it seemed pointless to dress in the garb of the majority in order to be heard in public debate.

But can minority presence transcend majority representation? For Achille Mbembe, quoting Frantz Fanon, in a racist context to "represent" is always to "disfigure."[93] And yet, mirror representation is an integral part of the classical conception of representation: when decision-making power is delegated, resemblance is never far away. Representation is in fact part of a double paradox in which the respective autonomy of the representative and the represented cancel each other out and reinforce each other at the same time.[94] This is why, although resemblance is not an absolute determinant of voting, voters who are more removed from the political field tend to use the presence of minority candidates as a point of reference when deciding whom to choose. Conversely, the most politicized voters tend to minimize the impact of minority trajectories while acknowledging that a significant number of elected officials from minority groups can help transform public policies.[95] Isn't the delegation of minority voices always synonymous with erasure? We all carry within us voices that speak to us, enter into dialogue with us, and put us into words. Belonging to the majority stems from the ability to treat these voices as one's own. Confident that they possess a voice, majority subjects can consider delegating theirs since they know that they will find it in others. When minorities offer their voice to someone, they expect to experience a discrepancy. Unlike majority subjects, minority subjects do not know if they will recognize in those who "represent" them what they have entrusted them with. They cannot be fooled into thinking that representation is a simple delegation mechanism, transparent in itself, through which representatives "speak for" the represented. The mandate by which one person substitutes for another is always an appropriation. Gayatri Spivak has shown that representation is not just a relationship of substitution but also the very site of a rewriting.[96] A voice is not just "self-expression."[97] Self-expression always rests upon linguistic patterns that preexist the subject and give their words meaning. Voice is therefore also the expression of others whose presence is embedded.

Christiane Taubira's role ought therefore to be examined from the point of view of the type of delegation she enabled as a Guyanese woman and government minister. Through her commitments and the type of presence she embodied in an almost exclusively white National Assembly, Taubira was the vehicle through which largely invisible sexual minorities were able to make themselves heard. This has not, however, led to any significant increase in the visibility of LGBTQ people in politics. In France, a rhetoric of discretion—that is, an acceptable presence—characterizes how minorities are treated politically. Every minority group must achieve a certain degree of visibility to obtain rights but this should never become excessive or threaten the majority's hegemony.[98] Yet that is the risk the majority must face: not so much the forfeiture of its privileges (which are firmly anchored in family, cultural and educational structures, etc.) as the spectacle of minority cultures, which it no longer seems able to contain, to the point of feeling excluded. It was therefore no longer just a question of visibility and gaze but of presence and the performance of presence.

Christiane Taubira became the voice of minorities during the debate on marriage for all precisely because she had already instigated the law of May 21, 2001, recognizing the slave trade and slavery as crimes against humanity. The law requires that school curricula and research programs fully incorporate their study. It also provides for the establishment of ways to commemorate the abolition of slavery. The law caused a stir in France. Intellectuals and academics signed a petition warning against the politicization of history and the crimes of the past.[99] In 2008, two of the petition's signatories, Françoise Chandernagor and Pierre Nora, published a pamphlet following the Rendez-vous de l'Histoire de Blois festival.[100] They denounced the submission of history to the whims of legislators. To quell the controversy, a parliamentary information mission was created to better inform national representatives on issues of history and commemoration.[101] The Taubira law of 2001 called for a pluralistic vision of history.[102] It caused unrest by describing the fate of racial minorities currently living in France and the history of the slave trade and slavery as being inextricably linked. The law portrayed the work on memory, the possibility of preserving it, and the availability of archives as essential to the constitution of present identities. In so doing, it also revealed the power relations at work in the fabrication of memory.[103] History is not merely an inheritance to be deciphered. It is a complex set of facts and memories that flow into the present.[104]

By conceiving of justice as intergenerational, the Taubira law indirectly raised the question of reparations.[105] The issue of reparations has been the subject of numerous debates and appeals to the courts over the last fifteen years in France and elsewhere.[106] It is based on two complementary observations: it is impossible to "redress" crimes committed several centuries ago, given that the determination of responsibility would have no solid moral and legal basis today; and it is necessary to redress the structural consequences of the crimes committed—in this case the absence of sufficient attempts to ensure that the end of slavery would result in both the full exercise of citizenship from one generation to the next[107] and equal rights.[108] For philosopher Magali Bessone, "We must think about the continuity of the social arrangements in which the violation of rights occurred: thinking of our justice as reconstitutive justice points to our desire to take on board the structural nature of certain injustices."[109] Injustice is the enduring feature of any minority group over the long term. Even when structural inequalities or discriminations disappear, their consequences are so polymorphous that it takes a long time for injustice to fade and truly cease to exist. Even when redressed, such difference in treatment persists in the form of collective memory. The vertical resonance of a minority with its memory connects minorities to each other in a horizontal sense. Thus, a memory, such as that of the Holocaust, offers strength to other minority groups in their efforts to better understand their past and rally around it. Minority memories can therefore emerge in unexpected places and in unexpected forms.[110] All minority lives are inflected by such spectral memories, the ghostly presence of lives that, although gone or absent, are expressed in each of us.[111] As Judith Butler notes, "The body can and does become a site where the memories of others are transmitted. No memory is preserved without a mode of transmission, and the body itself can be precisely a mode in which your history becomes mine, or your history passes through mine."[112]

THE INCITEMENT OF PRESENCE

Another question then arises. How do the various echoes that bind minorities together reverberate on the shores of the majority? What differentiates majority presence from minority presence is that the latter, in James Baldwin's words, is always an "incitement."[113] It troubles taken-for-granted, psychic identity, since it causes the self to appear simultaneously as the object and subject of experience, thus redefining the standard distinction made in cognitive science.[114] It promotes a multimodal conception of identity[115] and, as anthropologist François Laplantine has also demonstrated, invalidates the conventional metaphysics of identity:[116] a body, a mind, a social role, and a legal personality.

The notion of identity grew out of the need, in the United States, to define oneself in relation to others in a large and disparate society that emphasized freedom and autonomy. Its use in the social sciences spread in the 1950s to discuss processes of subjectification and the way in which identity results from the appropriation of various institutional frameworks, be they family, religion, or residence.[117] In biology, the difference between self and nonself is for now established by immunological criteria, namely the boundary between what the body accepts as its own and what it attacks. Philosopher Thomas Pradeu finds this view unsatisfactory since it is not foreignness that triggers an immune response (there is such a thing as an endogenous tumor). And there are certain elements external to the body that it can accept perfectly well. Pradeu proposes a theory of continuous identity, in which the inclusion of the other in oneself[118] results in individuation. This theory has led him and fellow immunologist Edgardo Carosella to describe human beings as "mosaics of otherness."[119] Presence is therefore always a *co-presence*; otherwise, it would become a principle of order, and being would become an empty notion existing only in opposition to nonbeing.[120] The presence of the other does not create difference but a "gap."[121]

As the Pulse and Colorado Springs shootings with which I opened this chapter tragically demonstrated, the presence of minorities disrupts the social order in many ways. Such high levels of violence and invisibilization do not only arise when groups who suffer direct or indirect discrimination demand their rights; it is also their very presence that upsets a social order built around majority cultures. The majority is not satisfied with being more numerous and/or more powerful. It assures its hegemony by creating a "common world" in its image. By reasoning in terms of presence, I am attempting to break with this hegemony and think of minorities in their immanence. I am not attributing to them any virtue that the majority could not claim. The experience of exclusion confers no moral superiority. However, minorities' need to impose their presence has an effect on their feeling of belonging, their relationship to the law, the ways in which power is delegated, and their interactions with other social groups. What happens when minorities enter the public sphere, that is, when they appear without being invited or without playing the role expected of them? Starting with this sudden emergence,[122] Didier Eribon defends a minority existentialism in which what counts is not so much the position to which minorities are assigned as the way in which they use that position. When minorities take possession of the public space using their own codes, they pluralize political space and time, which then can no longer be dictated solely by the rules of the institutional and partisan game. Although it is clearly useful to fight for future social recognition and to uncover the traces of a concealed collective history, there are also effects specific to minority presence, which Jacques Derrida called "the present of presence."[123] Minorities deploy an intransitive energy, like Queer Nation's rallying cry: "We're here, we're queer, get used to it!" This minority present is not a "presentism,"[124] a homogeneous and frozen present,[125] closed in on itself and "autarkic."[126] The emergence of minorities in the public sphere reveals other narratives, other rhythms, other sound environments, other bodily expressions, etc. This presence expands the present toward multiple horizons, with no predetermined direction.

Not long after marriage for all and joint adoption for same-sex couples were legalized in France, the minister for family, Laurence Rossignol, stated that the extension of medically assisted procreation to lesbian couples—enacted by the promulgation of the bioethics law of August 2, 2021—"colonized" the rights of families.[127] There was nothing trivial about her choice of words. To speak of "colonization" implies that the presence of minorities necessarily took the form of an occupation, that of a majority territory that did not belong to them, either in fact or in law. Minorities would creep in like a "Trojan horse" and despoil legitimate majority cultures.[128] Their principle of action would be conquest and ownership would be their objective. Yet this is a projection of how majority cultures operate. Minority cultures develop by questioning the idea of an own and owned self, since they are spoken before they are able to speak. They demonstrate that ownership and nonownership are inseparable and that their territory—starting with language itself—is always already divided. The idea of presence therefore produces "effects of meaning" whose subjective consequences are considerable:[129] "To ask who you are is to avow that one does not know in advance who you are, that one is open to what comes from the other, and that one expects that no preestablished category will be able to articulate in advance the other's singularity."[130] Presence is always an event.

As Jean-Luc Nancy asserts, if the other exists by being present in each of us, the other is also the person *with* whom we *appear* to the social world.[131] *Co-appearance* conceives of the subject in a way that avoids the theoretical and political impasses to which calls for convergence and commonalities necessarily lead. Although they contain contradictions and antagonisms, these calls are driven by an imaginary of an appearance on the social scene *as a single being*: to be present is, in one and the same move, to make visible and to make invisible. "When I speak or understand," Merleau-Ponty notes, "I experience the presence of others in myself or of myself in others which is the stumbling block of the theory of intersubjectivity, I experience that presence of what is represented which is the stumbling block of the theory of time, and I finally understand what is meant by Husserl's enigmatic statement: 'Transcendental subjectivity is intersubjectivity.'"[132] Presence is then all the more powerful in that it is never fully decipherable: as François Jullien has written, the other is "recognized as unknown."[133] It is not about "appearing together," which would juxtapose two contradictory ideas, namely that several subjects share a social space or that several subjects form a whole.[134] With the idea of co-appearance, the question is no longer one of intersubjectivity, of one and the other, or even of both, but of "with." We co-appear before this "with"—the hyphen represents both a link and a gap that redefines sovereignty and responsibility.

Co-appearance calls for new forms of collective action that assert the specificities, even the exclusivity, of certain ties (family, friendship, sex, love, ethnicity, language, culture, region, nation, or religion) without being reproached for taking pleasure in them, since they are already bearers of other lives. It is thus possible to escape the "contradictory identity injunction"[135] that Sartre summed up as follows: "For a Jew, conscious and proud of being Jewish, . . . the anti-Semite reproaches [him] with *being* Jewish; the democrat reproaches him with willfully *considering himself* a Jew."[136] A relationship is truly a minority relationship when it avoids the trap of being authentically oneself in the face of the other. The other pluralizes the self, perforce renders the subject inauthentic, and in doing so enables it to exist outside of itself.[137] Minority experience also requires shifting away from the myths of belonging and ideal representation to consider presence in a more intransitive way. Jean-Luc Nancy argues that "want[ing] to say 'we' . . . is not at all sentimental, not at all familial, or 'communitarian.' It is existence reclaiming its due or its condition: coexistence."[138] Thinking about coexistence is not just a process of introspection. It is both a form of estrangement[139] and an opportunity for deployment: to co-appear is to project oneself into lives that are not one's own and to become "more than [one]self" in a kind of "exo-experience."[140]

What type of connection is established in one's relationship to the other's presence when the other is in the minority? The German sociologist Hartmut Rosa, one of the new generation of the Frankfurt School, has put forward the idea of a "vibrating wire" or an "experience or a condition, in which the subject is affected, i.e. touched, and moved by some segment of the world, outwardly directed emotional movement, with intrinsic self-interest (*libido*) and a corresponding expectation of efficacy."[141] He then broadens his reflection to address resonance as a relationship to the world in which subjects are affected by the world outside of them and express emotions outwardly toward it as well. Rosa specifies that *"resonance is not an emotional state but a mode of relationship."*[142] He thus opposes resonance and alienation, a relationship in which the subject and the world are indifferent to each other.[143] For Rosa, resonance can be horizontal (intersubjectivity), diagonal (relations to objects), and vertical (transcendence). The value of his theory of resonance lies in the fact that it takes into account the way in which intersubjectivity requires some degree of openness and some degree of closure to the world. Subjects can only welcome the world if they enjoy the necessary conditions to do so. Still, the idea of intercomprehension, within an "in-between" framework where subjectivity preexists interaction, continues to dominate in Rosa's theory.[144] This approach does not seem capable of fully capturing minority relationships in which subjects emerge jointly. There is no such thing as a majority subject without a minority subject and vice versa. The relationality in the idea of co-appearance is that of subjects who are inhabited by others and connect with the world based on how others resonate in them. This is a relationship of dispossession, which intensifies an individual's relationship with the world. For majority subjects, this means drawing on their minority experiences to connect with others; it means learning the limits of their sovereignty and allowing minority subjectivities *with* which they live to flourish.

Of course, this is never guaranteed. In her recent book, *Faut-il se ressembler pour s'assembler?* Nicole Lapierre aptly notes that "manufacturing 'another life' is not self-evident. It's a story strewn with pitfalls. Nothing is certain; that's what characterizes an event. Betting on it is always a gamble."[145] And yet what choice do we have but to create the conditions for minority resonances to occur? In another noted work, *Causes communes. Des Juifs et des Noirs*, Lapierre writes about "concrete humanism" forged by intersubjectivity, and she argues for the rediscovery of the philosophies of empathy that emerged in the wake of Robert Vischer in 1873 and are present in the works of several authors who reflected on the diaspora, such as W. E. B. Du Bois and Paul Gilroy.[146] While I share the same assumptions, my approach does not reify individual boundaries to the same extent. Co-appearance may mean acting for others, but it is also acting for oneself. There is no need to resort to an ideal of respect whose distribution is necessarily highly unequal and whose very definition is already an issue of power.[147] There is no need to conceive of collectives through the myth of the social contract when the reality of our presence is enough to create society. This is why I argue that subjectification should be considered in terms of how different experiences of injustice resonate and the ethical obligations that flow from them.[148] The Yellow Vests movement provided an opportunity for several such calls.[149] Student unions, the committee for the defense of Adama Traoré, railway workers, as well as several queer and feminist organizations rallied behind the Yellow Vests not only to support their movement but also to orient it toward greater solidarity.[150] Pierre Creton's film, *Le Bel Été*, released in 2019, reflects on hospitality toward other minority lives through the encounter between migrants and the rural world of the coast of Normandy. Even more recently, on January 17 and 18, 2020, the Comité de Libération et d'Autonomie Queer (a French queer activist group) organized a series of events to support the chambermaids at the Ibis-Batignolles Hotel in Paris who were entering the sixth month of their strike.

In this chapter, I have shown that, beyond a logic of convergence and commonality, another form of mobilization is possible. It contemplates the presence in oneself of the other in such a way that one always appears in the social world *with* the other. This co-appearance may be imposed or it may be assumed. When it is imposed, subjects can be destabilized, fearing they will lose themselves through the presence of others, to the point of feeling minoritized. They then seek to regain power over themselves through various means that drive out others in the hope of regaining what they believe to be their individual sovereignty. This majority logic is countered by a minority logic: letting the other live within oneself. Co-appearance then becomes an experience of "disorientation,"[151] since it refers us back to what Judith Butler calls the "unlived possibilities,"[152] that is, all the life potentials that comprise us. These unlived possibilities govern us. They guide our choices, our relationships, our likes and dislikes, and they give us our capacity to act collectively.[153] They also expose us to the gaze of others, since we then revisit the shame of wanting another life, of not loving our own enough: "[W]e are, however distinct, also bound to one another and to living processes that exceed human form. And this is not always a happy or felicitous experience."[154] The lives that pass through us remind us of our epistemic limits; we neglect certain possibilities of life that are too remote or too elusive. These unlived possibilities embed us in a performative chain: controlling others' practices, identities, and cultures ends up affecting who we are and how we are governed. The next chapter explores some of the forms this performative chain acquires in the legal field; it argues for analogical rather than comparative reasoning and lays out the idea of an *intra*sectional arrangement of legal categories.

7

LEGAL ANALOGY

Difference in treatment is not sufficient to prove discrimination. The difference must also be defined as illegal by statute or by case law. In France, the Council of State (the highest administrative court) puts the principle of equality of treatment in public service at the top of the hierarchy of administrative standards (*principes généraux de droit*) while specifying that differences in treatment may be allowed if the law provides for them, if there are appreciable circumstantial differences, or if reasons of public interest require it.[1] The Constitutional Council reasons in the same way, considering that "while the principle of equality does not prevent a law from establishing rules that are not identical with regard to persons in different situations, this is only the case when this non-identity is justified by the difference in situations and is not incompatible with the purpose of this law."[2] Similarly, the prohibition of discrimination laid down in Article 14 of the European Convention on Human Rights does not preclude specific situations from calling for differentiated treatment.[3] This distinction between unequal treatment and discrimination was made clear in the *F. v. France* case, heard by the European Court of Human Rights in February 2002, in which a gay single man had been denied approval to adopt.[4] The French government's representative argued before the court that there was indeed "an objective difference in circumstances between the family model that Mr. F. could offer a child and that of a heterosexual adoptive parent, whether single or married."[5] The court therefore found that the difference in treatment was based on the applicant's sexual orientation and concluded that it was discriminatory under a 1966 law allowing single persons over twenty-eight years of age to adopt, without any consideration of their sexual orientation. Nonetheless, in a complex interplay of abstentions,[6] the European Court of Human Rights also found that there had been no discrimination under European law because, in its view, Article 8 of the convention (on "respect for private and family life"), in conjunction with Article 14, was not applicable in the absence of a consensus regarding what constitutes a legitimate family in Europe.

Of course, political lines have since shifted. Social mobilizations in France and Europe led to the creation of civil union contracts and marriage for all as well as gay people's rights to jointly adopt in many countries. The European Court of Human Rights reversed its case law, condemning France for not granting approval to adopt to a woman in a relationship with another woman.[7] The court has often reiterated to member states that joining the Council of Europe requires making a commitment to equality. It has thus asserted that "only very strong considerations" can justify a difference in treatment on the basis of "sex."[8] The European Court of Human Rights now sanctions states that fail to take action against gender-based violence and allow a climate of hostility toward women to flourish.[9] In a recent judgment, the court condemned Russia for failing to protect a petitioner against violence by her former partner. In this case, the court immediately denounced the absence of appropriate legislation in the country.[10] Despite a very strong commitment, the court cannot completely free itself of the perceptions and prejudices that prevail within its member states since its authority depends in part on their accepting its judgments. It must therefore continue to adjudicate between good and bad differences.[11] The legal logic remains unchanged. Discrimination stems only from an illegitimate difference in treatment, which is assessed with respect to dominant social norms.

In this chapter, using French, European, US, and Canadian cases, I will show that the strength of the concept of gender lies in its capacity to reorganize this legal logic. Unlike the concept of sex, thinking in terms of gender makes it possible to think more flexibly about the relationship between biology, identity, and civil status and thus to broaden the definition of what is legally legitimate. Besides, the concept of gender is based as much on the idea of difference as on difference (of *differ*ing and *defer*ring, which I will come back to). This reasoning paves the way for a clearer understanding of multidiscrimination and intersectional discrimination. Indeed, the law can prove discrimination only by simplifying its process. If it goes beyond the examination of a few specific criteria (age, ethnicity, sexual orientation, nationality, gender, disability, etc.), it can no longer produce coherent comparisons, as each situation is irreducibly unique. The advantage of the notion of gender lies in its ability to establish discrimination by means of analogy rather than by comparison. Gender makes it possible to think about the connections between different categories—which I call *intra*sectionality.

GENDER: A USEFUL CATEGORY FOR POLICY MAKING

The concept of gender emerged in the field of clinical psychology and endocrinology in the 1950s and has since taken on numerous meanings. New Zealand psychologist John Money was one of the first to use the term to describe the social roles traditionally associated with the two sexes and the impact they had on his hermaphroditic patients.[12] The use of the term gradually extended to the fields of psychiatry[13] and sociology[14] and made it possible to designate everything that fell under social norms as opposed to biological data. It was intended above all to be descriptive. In 1986, the US historian Joan W. Scott gave it a more critical spin. She conceived of gender as a tool for questioning the construction of the very category of sex.[15] To her, gender must try to capture both the processes of categorization and the mechanisms by which people identify with categories. Two years later, philosopher Denise Riley developed this same approach in her seminal work, *Am I That Name?*[16] Their contributions mark a symbolic shift toward gender studies, characterized by transdisciplinarity, reflexivity, and concern for historicity. This shift is also marked by greater academicism, where feminist, feminine, and lesbian studies intermingled more closely with activist theories, albeit in very different registers.[17]

The concept of gender was quickly taken up in France as seen from the 1988 translation of Joan W. Scott's article by political scientist Eleni

Varikas.[18] The 1989 "Sex and Gender" conference was another turning point, bringing together some twenty contributors who explored the concept of gender in their respective disciplines.[19] The notion of gender did not become widespread, however; throughout the 1990s, it coexisted alongside other notions forged in the materialist tradition, such as "gender relations" (*rapports sociaux de sexe*)[20] and *sexage*—a term Colette Guillaumin coined that combines the notions of gender (*sexe*) and slavery (*esclavage*)[21]—the latter placing greater emphasis on the exploitation of women and the experience of male domination.[22] Unsurprisingly, the notion of gender eventually took off among researchers with the greatest international reach; French sociologist Éric Fassin, for example, who taught at Brandeis University and New York University in the late 1980s and early 1990s, wrote several important articles on gender[23] and edited the French version of Judith Butler's *Gender Trouble*.[24]

In this context of epistemological debate, European and international public policies brought about a wider dissemination of the notion of gender. The United Nations set out new strategies for promoting gender equality at conferences held in Nairobi in 1985, Cairo in 1994, and particularly Beijing in 1995.[25] The Beijing conference report urged member countries to implement gender mainstreaming, that is, to revisit all the policies that structured economic and social life with a view to achieving equality between women and men. As early as 1991, the third community action program (a set of public policies coordinated at the EU level) promoted gender mainstreaming.[26] The Amsterdam Treaty of 1997 confirmed this commitment by making the fight for equality between the sexes one of the principles of the European Union, without, however, using the term gender (Article 2 of the treaty). The concept of gender was not immediately integrated into the law in France, where there was a preference for an "integrated approach to equality" over gender mainstreaming. The law of August 6, 2012, on sexual harassment avoided any use of the word gender. After several deputies spoke out against the "anthropological revisionism" of gender and its theory during parliamentary debates, the term "gender identity" was dropped. Then, on December 7, 2012, these same deputies proposed that a parliamentary commission of inquiry should be established to examine the issue.[27]

It was not until the law of November 18, 2016, that the concept of gender identity was first considered grounds for discrimination in France.[28] It is true that in 2013, the National Consultative Commission on Human Rights had already called on lawmakers to comply with European and international law,[29] which had long since moved beyond gender mainstreaming strategies: the Yogyakarta principles were presented to the United Nations in 2007 and led to the enactment of the United Nations Declaration on Sexual Orientation and Gender Identity on December 22, 2008. In 2009, the report of the Council of Europe's commissioner for human rights, Thomas Hammarberg, recommended implementing the Yogyakarta principles.[30] The report served as the basis for the adoption of a resolution on April 22, 2015, calling on member states "to explicitly prohibit discrimination based on gender identity in legislation," to establish procedures for changing one's civil status by self-determination, to ban the sterilization and "compulsory medical treatment" of transgender people, and to consider a third gender option on official documents.[31] Several European Union directives also took gender identity into account, for example when assessing reasons for refugee persecution[32] or protecting victims of crime.[33]

Gender has therefore already extended the boundaries of legal protections for women and sexual minorities. Its semantic plasticity makes transposition easier from one legal level to another and serves to "legitimize" conceptual innovation.[34] However, the mechanisms for combating gender stereotypes[35] and protecting gender identities remain weak in France. The law of November 18, 2016, authorized a change in civil status without requiring medical interventions (any operation and/or hormonal treatment), but a high court (*Tribunal de grande instance*, now *Tribunal judiciaire*) must declare any such change valid on the basis of a sufficient gathering of facts.[36] Self-determination for transgender people by means of a simple declaration before a civil registrar was not retained. In addition, minors are not allowed to change their civil status, except in the case of emancipation. Only a person's first name at birth (minors included) can be changed by direct application to the civil registry office.

At the supranational level, the European Court of Human Rights has itself maintained an ambivalent position. While it condemns the sterilization of transgender people, it leaves states free to determine whether or not any civil status change procedure should be medicalized.[37] It holds that gender identity falls within the scope of Article 8 of its convention, which protects privacy, but that in the absence of any consensus on the matter at the European level it is up to states to decide which provisions apply to gender identity. The court therefore rejected a French intersex person's request to be recognized as being of neutral sex in their civil status.[38] Although the concept of gender as such is a vector of epistemological and legal transformations,[39] its potential has not yet been fully exploited.

DISCRIMINATION AND DIFFERANCE

The law is based on lists of classes protected against discrimination. Rather than extending the grounds of discrimination indefinitely at the risk of rigidifying each one, gender makes it possible to envision a more hospitable and flexible legal system under which the same class can protect different identities and difference is of little relevance. During the debates on marriage for all, a legislative change was proposed: namely, that the terms "father" and "mother" in the Civil Code be changed to *parent*.[40] This change would have transformed the system of presumptions for establishing filiation—itself based on childbirth (except in the case of anonymous childbirth, known as "delivery under X") and on the presumption of paternity in marriage (except for same-sex couples, for whom adoption is required)—on the basis of declaration of recognition at a town hall or the so-called possession of status, which is a notarized deed that establishes filiation when parent and child are manifestly considered as such. Transparenting also calls for a profound transformation of the legal system.[41] A woman can give birth with her own sperm, and a man can become pregnant with or without his own eggs. In many countries such as Belgium preserving the gametes of transgender people is encouraged before any surgical intervention. In France, some legal adjustments have been proposed but only when the filiation is already established. Thus, the May 10, 2017, circular provides for modifying the family record book so that any entries correspond to the gender identity of the parent.

But what happens when the filiation is not yet established? Why could a pregnant man not be legally recognized as the father? Why could a woman who conceives using her sperm not be recognized as the mother? The Montpellier District Court (*tribunal de grande instance*) heard a case in which the maternity of the mother, who had conceived using her sperm, was not recognized (as instructed by the public prosecutor and even though she had obtained prenatal recognition). The court offered two solutions, both of which were unacceptable: that the woman adopt the child (as any married same-sex couple would do) or that she change her civil status to reflect another change of gender.[42] In response, the Montpellier Court of Appeal (*cour d'appel*) suggested entering the term "biological parent" in the civil register. This met the parents' immediate needs (recognizing the kinship of the two mothers) but dealt with transgender filiation as a special case (since the law required the civil register to specify "father" and/or "mother").[43]

On February 12, 2019, the National Assembly, against the opinion of Minister of National Education Jean-Michel Blanquer, passed an amendment submitted by deputy Valérie Petit, which sought to include "parent 1" and "parent 2" on school forms (without, however, considering the possibility of multiparenting). The purpose of the amendment was to end discrimination against same-sex and transgender parents faced with joint "father-mother" categories in official documents.[44] Activists opposed to same-sex parenting objected vehemently.[45] On May 21, 2019, the Senate voted against this amendment at second reading. The reason it continues to raise objections has to do with the fact that gender makes will the foundation of law. As legal scholar Daniel Borrillo writes, gender is now "an element of legal personhood available to individuals as an essential component of their private life."[46]

Conversely, when, as another legal scholar Benjamin Moron-Puech has said, "Gender identity still lies in the shadow of the notion of 'sex,'" the situation for individuals is far from enviable.[47] A ministerial instruction of February 19, 1970, implemented via circular on October 28, 2011, stipulated that the most probable legal gender must be entered on the birth certificate and therefore in the civil register, thus giving the medical profession considerable responsibility. The District Court of Tours in central France had recognized a third category for "gender": "neutral gender" (*sexe neutre*).[48] But France's highest court of appeal ruled that "French law does not allow the inclusion, in civil status documents, of any indication of a gender other than male or female."[49] Its interpretation, conducted *in abstracto*, did not consider the claimant's interests.[50]

However, Article 16–3 of the French Civil Code provides that "the integrity of the human body may only be violated in the event of medical necessity for the person concerned or, exceptionally, in the therapeutic interest of others." Both in law and in practice, therefore, there is a tension between the "probability" of gender and the "medical" interest of the individual. The Council of Europe has estimated that nearly 1.7 percent of births present as intersex.[51] In 2017, a Senate report sounded the alarm about the situation of intersex individuals, pointing to abuses in genital reassignment procedures and a high level of discrimination against intersex people.[52] Similarly, even though Jacques Toubon, France's Defender of Rights, has not commented on the advisability of a third gender category for civil status, he has proposed that it be qualified as "intersex" or "neutral" if such a third category is adopted at a later date.[53]

The possibility of eliminating gender from among civil status options has often been brought up, but it would risk running counter to the needs of some transgender people for whom a change of civil status bears great symbolic importance—which is why legal scholar Benjamin Moron-Puech has suggested an optional declaration of gender in one's civil status.[54] This proposal, based on free choice, also has international resonance. For example, it features in a resolution of the Parliamentary Assembly of the Council of Europe[55] and in Danish and Argentinian laws that establish the principle of self-determination for the civil status of transgender people.[56] Germany allows birth certificates to be issued that do not mention gender; the Netherlands allows "gender undetermined" to be recorded on the birth register, leaving the individuals concerned to choose once they are old enough. India, South Africa, Malaysia, Thailand, New Zealand, Nepal, and Australia also allow a third choice on official documents.[57] These provisions show that it is entirely possible to think about the status of people without resorting to the idea of difference and that there is no true equality that is not global.[58]

The politics of difference has many harmful effects. It reinforces the internalization of stereotypes since it is on the basis of very limited categories that individuals can acquire certain kinds of recognition. Moreover, such recognition is double-edged because it is granted by a dominant culture to a dominated culture. The latter is therefore made subservient in the very act of being recognized. Finally, the politics of difference imposes a legal straitjacket that limits people's freedom; rather than inventing other statuses, minorities must work to conform to the difference assigned to them. Because the politics of difference claims to be advantageous in all circumstances,[59] it immobilizes minorities.

Minorities, however, do not all derive the same benefit from the same provisions. Some gain visibility, whereas others may find themselves further invisibilized. The politics of difference conceives of a subject's identity in binary terms—they are either affected by a norm or they are not. They are either discriminated against or they are not. They are either a man or they are not. They are either a woman or they are not. This approach to defining the principle of equality's scope of application is what has enabled constitutional democracies to ensure the formal cohesion of the law. As Eleni Varikas comments,

In the hierarchy of the Ancien Régime, where the absence of a common denominator for comparison was part of the political system that legitimized inequality at each level of the social hierarchy, the unity of the human race was not at risk. On the other hand, from the moment this unity becomes the fundamental source of human rights, inequality begins to appear arbitrary; unless there are such radical differences between beings that there can be no common denominator for comparison.[60]

With gender identities and the adjustments they require, difference ceases to be operative: gender identities prove that people can be simultaneously inside and outside a class or belong to several at once. The same is true on a theoretical level. The concept of gender invites us to radically transform the very idea of difference. Joan W. Scott, for example, proposed that we base our "political choices" on a "refusal" of the opposition between equality and difference.[61] Philosopher Françoise Collin called for disputation (*différend*) as a way out of the aporias of difference.[62] The point is not simply to recognize the plurality of differences, as the interpretation of legal standards would itself become contingent,[63] which would be detrimental to minorities above all. However useful plurality may be in the public space, it cannot resist being instrumentalized for long; this is the case with capitalistic uses of parity, what Réjane Sénac calls "profitable complementarity."[64]

Any rigorous conception of gender must accept that identities in a plural society are not different from each other, but that they do differ in that there is always a space between the subject and the class through which it is apprehended. Subjects are always out of sync with the way they are named; they never fully fulfill the role assigned to them by language and norms.

Jacques Derrida introduced the notion of "differance" to qualify this gap between subjects and institutions.[65] For him, identity is inflected by traces of the elements that serve to constitute it. Differance, then, does not force subjects into particularization; its "universalizing power" simply resides in the immeasurable rather than in generalization:[66] for Derrida, the universal is the way in which uniqueness bears the traces of everything it is not and never has been.[67] Gender can therefore be thought about as a hollow concept through all the minority memories expressed in it. It is this very specific characteristic that makes the grounds for discrimination more than just cumulative; they increase tenfold when they operate together since the traces of other scorned minority lives resonate through them. This is precisely what analogical reasoning is all about.

ANALOGICAL REASONING

Analogy denotes a meaningful relationship between two entities (a notion, thing or person), where what characterizes one makes it possible to understand the other better. Analogy is not a relationship of similarity, or even of resemblance, but rather a relationship of inference. Analogical reasoning does not compare cases but approaches them in parallel, drawing lessons from each unique situation. Analogical reasoning does not consider that ableist violence is *like* sexist violence but will put what concerns the one (its intensity, temporality, form, etc.) at the service of understanding the other. For one exists *with* the other. In this way, analogy makes it possible to assess complex situations without excluding from the scope of the law (and therefore from the application of the principle of equality) those individuals who do not have the "right difference" as far as public policy is concerned. The analogical approach is not new in the legal domain, particularly in countries where checks on legality and constitutionality are diffuse and/or several legal orders coexist (as is the case in federal states). Analogy can be used to make judgments without making the law inconsistent,[68] and to consider several grounds for discrimination without ordering them into a hierarchy.[69] Analogy may be closer or looser depending on whether it operates within the same branch of the law or shifts from one branch to another.[70]

As far as minorities are concerned, the use of analogy was initially prompted by the limited number of grounds for discrimination and their recent availability, which meant having to rely solely on existing legal grounds, even when they were removed from the case in question. Thus, the very first lawsuits alleging discrimination on the grounds of sexual orientation were filed on the basis of antiracist arguments.[71] They then became linked to sexist discrimination.[72] Gender discrimination itself was challenged on the basis of race.[73] In preparing *Reed v. Reed*, Ruth Bader Ginsburg, then director of the American Civil Liberties Union's Women's Rights Project, relied heavily on the analogy between gender and race.[74]

Of course, the proliferation of grounds for discrimination means that the analogy is not always needed today. However, minority identities bear the traces of this history, particularly since activism itself, because it is constantly interacting with the law, makes extensive use of analogical arguments.[75] Analogy therefore remains a structuring principle, even when legal interpretation techniques take other paths.[76] As law professor Janet Halley reminds us, in the US context, analogy is inevitable because it is intrinsic to the idea of justice. Given that the United States is the product of a segregationist system, race cannot fail to be omnipresent and therefore invoked by all types of social groups in their relationship with the law.[77] Nevertheless, Halley urges caution because, in using analogy, claimants tend to project some of their own traits onto other social groups. There is a fine line between the strengthening of ties between two discriminated groups and the subjugation of one by the other.[78] Any mediated form of recognition, however well-intentioned, can be a vector of discrimination.[79]

In Europe in the late 1990s, the Court of Justice of the European Communities considered that discrimination linked to what was not yet referred to as transition and gender identity was discrimination based on "sex."[80] However, it ruled out the protection of sexual orientation on the basis of "sex" in another case in which the partner of a British train company employee did not benefit from the reduced fares to which spouses of other employees were entitled (same-sex marriage was not yet available in the UK).[81] As the employee's partner, the claimant's reasoning was original. She argued that if she had been a man (therefore heterosexual), she would have benefited from the preferential fares. The court did not follow the same line of reasoning, but it is now tending to broaden its scope of review by categorizing an ever-increasing number of differences in treatment as direct discrimination.[82] For its part, the European Court of Human Rights readily uses a wider margin of appreciation to extend the grounds for discrimination.[83] It follows the same reasoning as the Court of Justice of the European Union in considering it necessary to treat people in different legal situations in the same way. For example, it ruled in favor of an Italian same-sex couple who applied for a residence permit on family grounds, even though these men did not have the right to marry.[84]

In Canada, analogy is at the heart of case law. To establish discrimination under Article 15 (1) of the Canadian Charter of Rights and Freedoms, the Supreme Court of Canada proceeds in a three-step framework. It states that discriminatory grounds are not exhaustive, that a discrimination provision always has a more general meaning, and that the grounds for discrimination are analogous.[85] This approach makes it possible to extend the protections granted to minorities by establishing connections between them. The court is thus able to include political convictions, method of conception, the fact of not having children, and of having been adopted.[86] Moreover each category of discrimination is itself pluralized. Thus disability covers a range of situations, such as stuttering, anxiety, depression, and even temporary disability, such as dependency due to accident or illness.[87] Finally, the court considers that recognizing these grounds for discrimination is permanent, and it imposes what constitutional law calls a "ratchet effect": a provision that cannot be reversed even at the level of provinces, which are expected to harmonize.[88]

As can be seen, analogical reasoning has encountered some resistance in Europe and North America, but its influence is strong. The concept of gender gives it an even broader reach. As law professor Gwénaële Calvès specifies, "The reference to gender, seen through the prism of gender stereotypes, therefore broadens the scope of the ban on discrimination on the grounds of sex."[89] She reports numerous specific cases: a woman deemed too aggressive by her employer,[90] a highly vulnerable sex worker of African origin,[91] a fifty-year-old woman undercompensated after a medical error, etc.[92] Gender can even create a link between sexual orientation and sex, as in the case of discrimination against a lesbian fired because her behavior did not conform to dominant heterosexual models.[93] Such attention to gender stereotypes allows the courts to "take the difference in treatment 'as it is'"[94] and, in doing so, to overcome the difficulties associated with combining several discrimination criteria. This approach, however, relies on the judge's ability to establish a link between stereotypes and difference in treatment. In the case of *Carvalho Pinto De Sousa Morais v. Portugal*, the European Court of Human Rights only resorted to the argument of stereotypes in the absence of truly comparable cases involving both age and "sex."[95] It thus considered that the claimant's undercompensation was related to prejudice about the loss of desire after menopause (she had undergone a gynecological operation leaving her with disabling neurological damage, particularly sexual).

Gender analogies serve to enrich antidiscrimination measures.[96] Nevertheless, analogical reasoning would be meaningless if it were just a more distant or vaguer comparison between two social groups (a trap that case law cannot always avoid).[97] Analogy implies considering each situation as unique and examining its own constraints. What is measured are not identities and cultures but the discriminatory consequences of a given social context for people. What is assessed are the negative effects; the groups themselves are not compared. What is examined, as a whole, is the relationship to the discriminatory context.

Sharon Rush considers analogical reasoning to be purely a matter of casuistry that fails to derive principles,[98] but I would argue that this is precisely one of its virtues. From an analogical perspective, the moral principles that structure a social group must be taken into account in assessing the impact of discrimination in each specific case, but they do not have to serve as general criteria. If this were the case, new forms of discrimination would inevitably appear in the very act of recognizing discrimination. US legal scholar Darren Rosenblum reminds us of this strong risk when he explains that discrimination arises when one culture erases another, even in legal reasoning: "Courts relying on traditional sexual and gender norms might deny sexual and gender subversive litigants and ignore their priorities," he writes.[99] He cites the example of the way in which monogamy and the exclusivity of romantic relationships were used to prove marital commitment and consequently to protect those relationships in the context of social housing—which, he reminds us, in no way reflects the lives of a large number of queer and intersectional people.[100]

INTRASECTIONALITY

How does the law deal with situations in which multiple identities intermingle to form a vernacular culture? In the United States, it has long been necessary to mobilize educators to combat the marginalization of young African American girls in the education system (low enrollment rates, rudimentary school equipment, more limited subsidies per student, etc.).[101] This mobilization has demonstrated the importance of building bridges between race and gender.

Yet neither the law nor the justice system has managed to address these intersections in a satisfactory manner.[102] Legal expert Robin Stryker has thus pointed out that employers who hire both Black men and white women will be able to prove that they are not discriminating against Black people or women, even if they refuse to hire Black women.[103] Joint research on the effectiveness of antidiscrimination measures in US labor law has also shown that legal actions brought on the grounds of several forms of discrimination are statistically less likely to succeed than legal actions brought on the grounds of only one.[104] Other legal experts have demonstrated that it is still currently more effective to fight against discrimination at the level of the social group than at the individual level.[105] The European Court of Justice has recognized that it is possible to deal with several grounds of discrimination simultaneously,[106] but it clarified in a recent case that combined discrimination could only be established if at least one individual ground for discrimination was present.[107] That conclusion renders any idea of intersectionality in European Union law virtually unworkable.[108] By the same token, even though French courts do not hesitate to extend certain grounds for discrimination, they fail to take into consideration the way in which several types of discrimination combine and reinforce each other. They continue to treat complex discrimination as a single discrimination or as a simple accumulation of discriminations.[109]

It was precisely to understand the dynamics of complex discrimination that legal scholar Kimberlé Crenshaw laid out the concept of intersectionality in two articles in 1989 and 1991.[110] She showed that gender-based violence has specific modes of operation depending on whether the women are Black, of mixed race, or white. Intersectionality does not just consider grounds of discrimination in combination; it also highlights the discriminatory catalytic dynamics that occur when several discriminatory factors are at play. In so doing, it offers a critique of the law, which it shows is too sectional in its grasp of differences in treatment.[111] It also challenges the way social movements tend to organize around a primary cause and, as a result, disregard minorities within the minority.

The concept of intersectionality thus contributes to the emergence of new voices in the public space. This movement is key to shifting frameworks of thought and transforming the law itself, based on a mechanism well known to political scientists: "The way in which the problem is posed, defined or identified determines, in a way, the manner in which it is dealt with; it indirectly disqualifies certain groups . . . and certain solutions which now seem unsuitable."[112]

Intersectionality, however, faces a major obstacle in law: the more complex it becomes, the less operational it is. How can the causes of discrimination be established with any certainty if too many factors are at stake? How can several specific cases be compared if the combination of grounds for discrimination ultimately makes each situation unique? Crenshaw immediately recognized this limitation, explaining that she was not trying to offer a "new globalizing theory of identity"[113] but to study convergence effects. In a recent article, she adds that intersectionality is just a series of "power music videos."[114] Highly contrasting dynamics intermingle at the intersection of several identities and cultures.

For some minorities, visibility is related to how their bodies are marked. Frantz Fanon writes of "epidermalization."[115] This is the case for race, certain forms of disability, and age. In other cases, particularly religion and sexual orientation, visibility is often a process of conquest affirmed through appearance, gestures, intonations, and references that make it possible to recognize oneself within the group and to be identified outside it using criteria over which the group has control. This strategy avoids the need to continuously state one's identity—that task falls to the majority, whose hegemony is thus challenged. It is not a question of a simple transition from darkness into light, as it is sometimes preferable not to be identified, for reasons of security or, more simply, of the time and energy available to do so.

Another factor at play is the fatigue of minority individuals; they are constantly enjoined to explain their circumstances or to be responsible for all of their own people.[116] Minority visibility is particularly variable because it depends on what the majority cares to see, giving minorities only a mediated consciousness[117]—which Maxime Cervulle literally and metaphorically calls a "white screen."[118]

Intersectionality is not only about considering the combination of several identities and forms of discrimination but also understanding which identities and which forms of discrimination do and do not fit together. This is what Didier Eribon analyzes in *Returning to Reims*. He describes how, for him, coming out of the closet as a gay man meant entering a social closet: "Basically, I had been convicted twice, socially speaking: one conviction was based on class, the other on sexuality. There is no escaping from sentences such as these. I bear the mark of both of them. Yet because they came into conflict with each other at a certain moment in my life, I was obliged to shape myself by playing one off against the other."[119] This subjective tension can also be observed within a given minority group and between minorities. The degree of visibility of some has a strong impact on the degree of visibility of others. It can expose them more or, on the contrary, partially eclipse them. Intersectionality is a knot of moral contradictions.

Transforming power relations is therefore only possible by contemplating how minority cultures are constituted and organized, and what values they convey.[120] Failure to do so means that intersectional politics tend to rely on agency as the primary remedy for domination with little regard for the moral dimension of belonging. Because each individual combines several group affiliations, intersectional politics expect, through a stacking logic, that minority coalitions will emerge. However, several writers

LEGAL ANALOGY   173

have pointed out the difficulties of a shift from the individual to the collective:[121] the notion of intersectionality provides a clearer understanding
of the internal differences within a given group, but it struggles to come
up with a satisfactory response to the divergent interests of minority
groups—and so tends to give priority to dominant interests.[122] Éléonore
Lépinard shows that agency can become a trap in which other people
are viewed in the light of their own capacity to act. Some women become
bad feminists in the eyes of others because of their clothing, profession,
or religion. At best, they are branded as alienated; at worst, as traitors to
the cause. Lépinard therefore argues for a feminist ethic of solidarity, proposing that people mobilize not in the name of the feminist "we," but on
the basis of a principle of responsibility for others, even when divergent
values are expressed.[123] This is also what political scientist Jodi Dean is
advocating when she speaks of "reflexive solidarity."[124]

I defend a similar point of view here: an ethic of responsibility that
understands the relationship to another less by comparison (my discrimination like/against yours; my freedom of expression like/against yours;
etc.) than by analogy—that is, by evaluating the relationships of equivalence that exist between complex and singular situations considered in
their own contexts.[125] The Constitutional Court of South Africa has been
pursuing this approach since 1998, when it heard a case of intersectional
discrimination based on gender, religion, and marital status.[126] Rather
than directly comparing this case with similar cases, the court brought
together a large number of decisions based on the criteria in question and
then sought to establish discriminatory bias associated with the combination of these criteria, examining which trends could be seen and in
what form. On this basis, the court made sense of the context of the case
and thereby rendered its decision.[127] An analogical perspective does not
consider individuals and groups of individuals in isolation but assumes
that we are governed by the government of others. The task of legal theory, then, is to consider the consequences of the presence of others on the
implementation of the principles of freedom and equality, rather than
seeking to establish them in seemingly transcendental values.[128]

The struggle for recognition therefore begins with the work of critical self-knowledge: scrutinizing the presence of others in oneself.[129]
This is why I speak of *intra*sectionality, as legal scholar Ido Katri does

in connection with transgender laws in the United States.[130] However, we use the word "intrasectional" in different ways. Katri points out that protected classes always require a performance on the part of legal subjects.[131] He reviews how case law deals with cases in which tension exists between appearance, others' perception, and self-definition.

In my view, the notion of intrasectionality cannot be limited to the subjective dimension of an individual's relationship with the law. Nor can it merely link legal categories, because individuals would be able to project themselves in the place of others, which would be akin to a kind of *extra*sectionality not unlike Rawls's veil of ignorance. Intrasectionality, as I understand it, involves analyzing the way in which legal performativity *materially* binds individual destinies together. The resonances among different cases in case law show that each subject of law is an element present in the legal lives of others. In this sense, I agree with physicist Karen Barad's appeal for an epistemology of the *intra* that does not disassociate what is material from what is discursive.[132] The intrasectional point of view I am proposing reinforces and completes the intersectional approach by overcoming the aporias of what I would call *agentivism*—the belief that individual or group agency alone, though important, can transform social norms.[133]

Over the last few decades, there has been a broadening of the grounds for discrimination and a transformation in the relationship of minorities to the law and to jurisprudence.[134] Although there is now a tendency to turn to the law more often as the grounds for discrimination become more numerous,[135] this is not always the case. The law can only be used if it is perceived as a legitimate resource. But when the law has long been a source of oppression, invoking it is far from automatic. In this respect, the notion of gender has been profoundly transformative. Rather than rejecting the law outright or sanctifying its authority, gender advocates have used the law's imperfections, inscribed in legal language itself, as a resource for transforming norms and practices.[136]

The concept of gender has thus not only created new legal protections for women and sexual minorities; it has also changed their relationship to the law and its dominant ideas. Gender has contributed to a true epistemic upheaval by deconstructing the patriarchal anchors of a law that was hitherto conceived as the textual transfiguration of male sexual power. According to historian Pierre Legendre, the power of the law was born of a "love of the Text," itself a substitute for the symbolic power of the "Father."[137] He was specific: "To obviate the lack of a body, organizations develop, buoyed by practices of idolatry, thanks to which the subjects of unconscious desire unravel the disorder of things and end up agreeing on this: power speaks to them, too, however bodiless they are. And that is how one becomes the subject of institutions."[138] The concept of gender ushers in a scathing denial to this patriarchal theory of law. Law and social practices enjoy a pragmatic relationship of coproduction in which subjects conceive of themselves just as much as they are conceived by institutions. What links the subject to the law is not a need for dogmatism[139]—a "symbolic order"—but rather analogical work. Jacques Bouveresse saw in this work a postmodernist dead end.[140] Gender reminds us, to the contrary, that analogy can bring about a more generous form of social bonding,[141] precisely because it resists our constant desire for generalization[142] while connecting people to each other. The analogical perspective is expressed through new legal techniques that protect subjects. Rather than considering forms of discrimination in isolation or in combination, these techniques assess discrimination as it structures every individual's life, including those who may not seem to be directly affected. This is how gender has made it possible to protect sexual orientation and also fight against acts of racism and discrimination involving disability, age, and physical appearance, and so on.

In addition to considering the interdependence of minority classes, analogical reasoning allows a more flexible understanding of each class concerned. In European law, for example, the notion of disability, which was initially only a medical consideration, is now also used to cover disabilities with social or environmental causes.[143] The Equal Employment Directive of 2000 required that "appropriate measures should be provided, i.e. effective and practical measures to adapt the workplace to the disability, for example adapting premises and equipment, patterns of working time, the distribution of tasks, or the provision of training or integration resources."[144]

The definition of disability, however, remained limited. European law changed after the ratification of the 2006 United Nations Convention on the Rights of Persons with Disabilities; this was the first ratification by the European Union as an entity independent of its member states (the United States signed the convention but has not ratified it to date). The convention specifies that disability "results from the interaction between persons with impairments and attitudinal and environmental barriers that hinders their full and effective participation in society on an equal basis with others."[145] Disability thus includes circumstances such as depression, chronic illness, and speech impediments.

In addition, the way a disability is measured has itself evolved. The European Court of Justice now takes temporary impediments into consideration: temporary physical damage as the result of an accident, for example.[146] This broadening illustrates how people who are not minorities but encounter temporary difficulties also benefit from the grounds of discrimination that apply to minorities. The European Court of Human Rights has also extended protections against discrimination to people who live with individuals who are discriminated against. In a first step, it expanded the definition of the right to respect for family life as set out in Article 14 of the European Convention on Human Rights. It ruled that the refusal to grant a disability pension to a disabled person had an impact on the organization of family and professional life as well as on the private life of their relatives, since it required them to play a greater role in support and caregiving.[147] Since then, the court has extended the scope of Article 14 by sanctioning discrimination based on the circumstances of a third party, in this case the claimant's son, whose disability was not taken into account in the calculation of the claimant's tax liability.[148] The court thus offers protection by association.[149]

The UN Convention on the Elimination of All Forms of Discrimination against Women (CEDAW), which was adopted on December 18, 1979, and entered into force in twenty countries on September 3, 1981, has also been interpreted using an analogical approach. In 2020, only five countries in the world had not yet signed the convention (the Vatican, Tonga, Iran, Somalia, and Sudan). The United States signed it as early as 1980 but has yet to ratify it. As legal scholar Aline Rivera Maldonado has recalled, the charter explicitly mentions the situation of women facing multiple forms of discrimination, whether occurring separately or together.[150] For example, in its preamble the text states "that the eradication of apartheid, all forms of racism, racial discrimination, colonialism, neo-colonialism, aggression, foreign occupation and domination and interference in the internal affairs of States is essential to the full enjoyment of the rights of men and women."[151] In addition, the committee responsible for monitoring the implementation of the CEDAW—a committee of twenty-three international experts on women's rights—interprets the text in conjunction with other UN conventions (such as the Convention on the Rights of Persons with Disabilities of December 13, 2006), thereby paying particular attention to intersectional discrimination.

It also strives to consider discrimination contextually. Rather than interpreting each member state's situation in the same way, the committee monitors the application of the convention on the basis of field data. In each country, networks of women assess compliance with the charter and thus drive change in matters of political representation, genital mutilation, contraception, access to education, migration, etc.[152] The committee has stressed the importance of giving priority to protecting women who are most vulnerable because of their economic status, skin color, sexuality, faith, and place of residence; it has also issued several general recommendations to that end, if necessary through the use of temporary and derogatory measures,[153] thus demonstrating an assumed minority perspective. Last but not least, the committee even takes an intrasectional approach since it believes that eliminating discrimination against women means simultaneously tackling poverty, violence and restrictive sexual norms, discrimination in employment, restrictions on movement; etc.[154] Every minority struggle can support the others and transforms the law in a structural way.[155] The CEDAW committee shows that intersectional and intrasectional approaches are inextricably linked.

In the United States, the Equal Employment Opportunity Commission, which enforces federal antidiscrimination law in the workplace, considers transgender people to be protected on the basis of "sex," as provided for in Title VII of the Civil Rights Act.[156] In one case, a transgender police employee had a job offer withdrawn after announcing her change of social identity.[157] On June 15, 2020, the US Supreme Court ruled that Title VII of the Civil Rights Act of 1964 did indeed guarantee gay and transgender people protections against discrimination in the workplace (even if the state concerned had no antidiscrimination provisions on sexual orientation and gender identity[158]). Using the Civil Rights Act (whose primary purpose was to end segregation) in three cases of unfair dismissal (one on the basis of sexual orientation;[159] the other two for disclosing sexual orientation[160] and gender identity[161]), the court compared "sex," gender, sexuality, race, skin color, country of origin, and religion. Thus protections against one form of discrimination can serve others.

This chain of protection remains tenuous, however, because it has not been entered into the US Constitution. The change of majority on the US Supreme Court led to a reversal of case law that now allows state laws to prohibit the right to abortion.[162] In his majority opinion, Justice Clarence Thomas left no doubt that all forms of discrimination are linked. Starting with the question of abortion, he called for a review of access to contraception, same-sex marriage, and even the decriminalization of homosexuality.[163] This kind of cascading reasoning shows the extent to which minority destinies are linked, but this applies both to rights and to disenfranchisement. The chain of protection can also become a chain of destruction. Analogical reasoning is therefore not sufficient in itself, since it can turn against the most vulnerable people and subordinate one struggle to another.[164] It can only be effective if it is accompanied by a relational ethic that links the destiny of the majority to that of the minority, well beyond the field of law.[165] Such an ethic requires a conception of community that binds responsibility for oneself and responsibility for others together.[166] This is what I will explore in the next chapter.

8

TOWARD MINORITY UNIVERSALISM

Does pluralism preclude a universal theory of justice? If we take seriously the importance that each individual attributes to social goods, as Michael Walzer does, how can we reach consensus on robust, general, and enduring principles? Can we do without the fundamental aspiration to a shared condition?

"Universalism" refers to any conception of what is human, societal, and living that encompasses the entire planet. It rejects both the isolation of the subject and the separation of cultures.[1] Both a philosophy and a principle of government, its history is especially rich. It runs through Indian cosmogony as well as the Christian gospels and was an integral part of the hope placed in humanism during the Renaissance, as well as the philosophies of reason in the Age of Enlightenment. In legal terms, universalism is contemporaneous with modernity. At the turn of the sixteenth century, technical revolutions fostered commercial exchanges and required stable relations between religious, ethnic, and linguistic groups, hitherto marked by persecution.[2] In a context of growing tolerance,[3] customary law gradually gave way to royal edicts and jurisprudence. The idea of the universality of the rule of law truly took hold during the English, American, and French revolutions, but it still accommodated a strong marginalization of minority cultures, as indicated by the famous words of Stanislas de Clermont-Tonnerre, the first deputy of the nobility at the

Estates General in 1789, when he requested citizenship for Jews: "We must refuse everything to the Jews as a nation and accord everything to the Jews as individuals; . . . they should not be allowed to form in the state either a political body or an order. They must be citizens individually."[4]

During the nineteenth and twentieth centuries, colonial ventures conquered, subjugated, and killed in the name of an ideal based on the emancipation of peoples.[5] Universalism became epistemic imperialism, a universalizing machine.[6] And yet, at the end of World War II, it was in the very name of universalism that various international conventions were adopted to protect the most fundamental human rights. It was also in the name of critical universalist philosophies, including those from Europe, that the nonaligned countries fought against colonialism. Aimé Césaire and Léopold Sédar Senghor drew from Hegel's *Phenomenology of Spirit* the idea that it is in the "deepening of each particular" that the universal is reached.[7] Likewise, Ghanaian philosopher Ato Sekyi-Otu considers that universalism is "indispensable for radical criticism of conditions of existence in postcolonial society and for vindicating visions of social regeneration."[8]

For several decades now, a major theoretical project has also been developing a new philosophy: pluriversalism. While the first traces of it can be found in Zapatista groups, this philosophy points out that most cultures have produced their own version of universalism. As all cultural traditions are intertwined, each universalism is plurivocal.[9] This is a powerful observation, but one that inevitably leads to practical conflicts over how pluriversal values coexist. As Julia Christ explains, when a principle of freedom is affirmed, "the question of what should be understood as 'non-freedom' immediately arises."[10]

In the end, it is through the very debate on the universal that the universal is constituted. Thus, for Marx, the universal is always equivocal because "the universal class" is both the dominated and dominant class.[11] Because minority presence cuts across both, it paves the way for an ethic that rearranges pluralism and universalism. This is the work I undertake in the present chapter on the model of the "lateral universal" proposed by Maurice Merleau-Ponty: a "lateral universal which we acquire through ethnological experience and its incessant testing of the self through the other person and the other person through the self."[12] This universal is lateral or oblique (Monique Wittig describes it as "oblique" in her foreword to

TOWARD MINORITY UNIVERSALISM

Djuna Barnes's *The Passion*)[13] because it breaks with the idea of centers and margins. Cultural values cannot be universalized, whereas experiences of "decentering," "shifting," and "estrangement" can.[14] By analogy, I strive to articulate these different experiences and offer a minority ethic based on learning through interdependence. Pluralism does not mean rejecting abstract principles (since the one and the many are in reality coextensive), but rather inventing critical ways of administering the universal.[15]

Arguing for a minority universalism can only begin with deconstructing the term itself. Souleymane Bachir Diagne has expressed a preference for "the universal" (*l'universel*) used as a noun. "Universal" reflects the fact that what is human is everywhere. In combining descriptive and prescriptive dimensions,[16] the term "universalism" tends toward aporia: since humanity is divided into different linguistic groups, universalism runs the risk of erecting the "particularity of one's language into the universal of the Logos."[17] François Jullien, for his part, opts for the gerund "universalizing" (*l'universalisant*), which he prefers to "universal."[18] He also puts forward an original proposal against the narrowing that threatens universal rights,[19] considering that abstraction makes them more manageable and easier to mobilize.[20] He notes too that "the universalizing" is characterized above all by what it stands against. This "insurrectional function"[21] is essential today; it would be paradoxical, to say the least, to renounce the possibility of universally protective principles in a world where humanity as a whole is threatened by the degradation of its living space. Protecting the environment requires new universalist formulas designed within a "non-hegemonic"[22] framework built on human finiteness rather than on a fantasy of infinite expansion.[23] For this reason, philosopher Corine Pelluchon believes that the anthropocentrism of the Enlightenment did not invalidate the use of reason.[24] The struggle for the universal is also a struggle between different forms of rationality. These rationalities coexist, together or in opposition to each other. While nothing guarantees the normative superiority of majority reason over minority reason and vice versa, the search for "justified decisions" requires learning from those groups who are primarily concerned.[25] Minority universalism is necessary "in its concrete translations."[26]

A multiplicity of cultural traditions does not mean that similar principles of justice cannot be fostered, as long as ontological temptations are overcome.[27] There is no need to sacrifice the need for universalism on the altar of resistance to hegemony.[28] Even if it is impossible to protect oneself completely against domination,[29] it is nonetheless possible to create other paths toward the universal. The first was suggested by Michael Walzer himself. For him, true universalism stems from the infinite work of establishing relationships,[30] the antithesis of any claim to moral superiority.[31] Rather than describing a set of principles defined once and for all, he considers universalism to result from the repeated introduction of rules that eventually stabilize but can also be transformed in this process of repetition:

> Reiterative universalism . . . requires respect for the others, who are just as much moral makers as we are. That does not mean that the moralities we and they make are of equal value (or disvalue). There is no single uniform or eternal standard of value; standards get reiterated too. But at any moment in time, a given morality may prove inadequate to its occasions, or its practice may fail to measure up to its own standards or to a newly developed or dimly made out set of alternative standards for reiteration is a continuous and contentious activity. The largest requirement of morality, then, the core principle of any universalism, is that we find some way of engaging in that activity while living in peace with the other actors.[32]

Another possible path toward universalism is the practice of harmonization. For legal scholar Mireille Delmas-Marty, there are "two ways for national relativism to adapt to globalization and become 'universal': either through hegemonic extension, imposed unilaterally; or through pluralistic, multilateral harmonization, which provides room for adapting in space (national margins) and in time (for example, the grandfather clause, especially in environmental law)."[33] For her, it was not about making the universal "relative," undermining the principles of law, but rather of "relating them" to a diverse and changing reality on the ground.[34] This approach is one of the principal modus operandi of international law, but also of national law in federal or highly decentralized states as is the case in France for its overseas collectivities (*collectivités*) and New Caledonia.

Adapting the rules is never absolute. They must be reasonable and proportionate to the objective assigned to them. The margin of appreciation of states applying the European Convention on Human Rights cannot lessen the scope of the convention itself. It is about considering its implementation in the context of national law. The same applies to the European Union's principle of subsidiarity, enshrined in Article 5 of the Maastricht Treaty of 1992, which encourages decision-making at the national, regional, or local level, when the supranational level cannot be as effective. This principle makes room for case-by-case assessments. Delmas-Marty notes that the "vagueness" of the law is what makes it possible to invent new mechanisms, as long as it is not thought of in terms of uniqueness. The law can harmonize without unifying, hybridize without merging, make compatible without conforming, and bring together without making identical.[35]

There is a third possible justification for universalism. It is more procedural: the political scientist Alain Policar has demonstrated that the idea of universalism is essential to any deliberative process; in a way, it is its driving force. The existence of what he calls "irreconcilable positions" does not mean that we should abandon the idea of the universal:[36] democracy, as I also mentioned in chapters 3 and 6, is neither the manufacturing of consensus nor the reification of shared values. The convergence of opinions may be the result of deliberation, but it cannot be its end, unless we exclude all antagonistic experiences from the scope of democracy, first and foremost minority experiences. Democracy is a normative and institutional system that guarantees everyone the possibility of change, that is, that can accommodate as yet unknown conceptions of the world.

I subscribe to Alain Policar's idea of epistemic hospitality in democracy. To this I would add the question of minority learning. Universalism is, in my view, an aspiration toward the universal that requires deepening the experience of nonsovereignty. It does not imply a suspension of the self to interchange one's social and cultural positions with those of others within a cosmopolitical framework,[37] but rather the incorporation of an epistemic estrangement of which minority experience is the paragon. Unless it betrays itself, universalism can only be a grounded philosophy: not because it sets out to determine a fundamental anthropological truth but because it links what preexists with what could potentially exist.[38] In every social field, worlds coexist: they intermingle, avoid each other, separate, clash, subjugate each other, combine, and in the process invent other worlds.

Finally, there is a fourth path to universalism: considering universalism as hollow rather than as full. This is Ernesto Laclau's approach. For him, "universality" can be defined as an "empty place unifying a set of equivalent claims."[39] Unlike Mireille Delmas-Marty, Laclau thinks in terms of unifying, but unifying around a universal *without content*. For Laclau, "universality" comes about when our fundamental rights are threatened. To stand up for these rights, social struggles need open yet embodied "chains of equivalence" (without which they would be unable to survive the threats).[40] These chains allow each identity-based claim to enter into a "relationship of universalization" that supports it and extends its scope: "If, for instance, feminist claims enter into chains of equivalence with those of Black groups, ethnic minorities, civil rights activists, etc., they acquire a more global perspective than when they remain restricted to their own particularism."[41]

Commenting on Walzer's book, *Thick and Thin*,[42] Laclau asserted that the only way to provide a powerful ethical foundation for a minimal morality devoid of predetermined content is to extend the chains of interdependence. This is because, "although in an equivalence the differential meaning of its components does not entirely collapse, all the terms of the equivalence point, through their differential bodies, to something other than themselves, what we have called an absent fullness."[43] Because equivalence produces correspondences, it has the effect of "impoverish[ing] meaning"; and therefore, the more the chain extends, the less the universal is attached to a specific culture and the more it opens up to new transcultural "links."[44] Equivalence does not distinguish between cultures; uniqueness is the very condition of equivalence. What binds the vernacular to the universal is exchangeable: in Walzerian terms, the meaning of social goods specific to one sphere of distribution can be translated into other spheres of distribution. It is not the social goods that are equivalent, but rather the meaning of their presence.

These four paths to universalism make it possible to avoid the essentialist bias inherent in all universalist aspirations. Norman Ajari has shown this bias with regard to the work of Alain Badiou and Slavoj Žižek on Saint Paul the Apostle. While their starting point was to understand universalism as the word of truth, they both ended up defining the universal as a renunciation or even a denunciation of the particular.[45] This slippage has characterized France's political debates for decades. It consists in confusing universality with generality, that is, aspiring to live beyond oneself and one's erasure in the collective.

The universalism claimed by Emmanuel Macron during Josephine Baker's induction into the Panthéon is symptomatic of this confusion.[46]

TOWARD MINORITY UNIVERSALISM   185

During the ceremony, the president explained that Baker had gone beyond her identity in favor of a unitary conception of humanity, as if it were not precisely the juxtaposition of the two that constitutes universalism. In their quest for recognition, certain minority theories can also fall into this aporia. They set themselves up as a model and erase the traditions of thought that run through them.[47] In the words of Édouard Glissant, "the more the fabric of the Relationship reveals itself, operates and expands to consider all the world's differences, without neglecting any, the more individuals' space is freed up and the more their freedom comes to constrain them. It thus happens that they are abandoned to their social death, to their final destruction, on the sole pretext of this freedom, which is then assumed and imposed upon them."[48]

We are thus faced with a dilemma, since critiques of universalism themselves become universalized when they are successful, thereby undermining their own logic. Therefore, rather than simply rejecting universalism as an ontologically "dubious" project because it is tainted by European history,[49] we must recognize this limitation and transform it. This is what Markus Messling proposes in his study of the concept of world (*monde*) that the francophone literary movement of world literature (*littérature-monde*) has questioned and redefined.[50] Within the framework of the "Beyond Universalism" research network he coordinates from the Saarland University, Marcus Messling explains that a "minor universality" is not only possible but necessary today: with his colleague Jonas Tinius, he shows that by connecting to a human collectivity, individuals can intensify their experience and better retain "the character of an event."[51] They believe that four conditions are necessary: understanding the way in which the social world is embodied in each person; considering that the idea of "world" is never absolute, but shaped by each language; recognizing that a narrative always mediates the universal; and finally, observing the way in which this narrative is inscribed in the material structures of the world (the division of space, architecture, consumer goods, etc.)[52] "Minor universality" is thus a set of "shared experiences and consciousness of the world" conveyed by multidirectional practices of linguistic, social, and cultural translation.[53]

The minority universalism I advocate is also based on the idea of sharing, but not that of a "universal awareness of our humanity,"[54] since the idea of awareness is itself culturally situated. Minority universalism asserts a "pure presence,"[55] since what is shared is not so much what we are as what we are not. We are linked to others not by a third entity—what is common—but by the fact that we are made up of what we are lacking. We should thus think of universalism not as a series of values, but as a possible connection to the universal, a connection that takes many forms.

This idea was already present in the concept of a "democratic horizon" dear to Claude Lefort. It implies a powerful will to craft "a humanity of which there can be no established figure [*infigurable*]."[56] To my mind, universalism is above all an aspiration toward the universal that emerges with the uncertainties created by the very presence of others. That presence confronts us with what limits our capacity to act.[57] This is what ties my conception of universalism so fundamentally to minority experience: minority universalism is both a universalism of learning, which thinks about and engages with the permanent transformation of the subject,[58] and a relational universalism, which makes room for what is unprecedented.[59] It is based on the subjective and objective experiences of one's own limitations and one's actions based on what subjects do *not* have rather than on what they do have. The result is an approach to social relations that favors solidarity. This is not a project, but the ethical consequence of praxis. The universal always emerges when one experiences the "accident" of one's relationship to the other.[60]

A PHILOSOPHY OF NONSOVEREIGNTY

Communitarian theories are based on the link between identity and recognition:[61] The presence of the other carries meaning that circulates in the form of dialogue[62] or struggle.[63] This struggle is not for recognition of an already constituted identity, but for the affirmation of an identity in the very act of recognition, which means that the latter always leads to the unprecedented.[64] For German philosopher Axel Honneth, recognition has one goal: to give each individual an uninjured identity, an identity that he studies based on experiences of failed love, social contempt, or legal inequality.[65] For Honneth, identity is not only prey to external attacks; it comes from a desire for recognition. He borrows this idea from Adam Smith, who linked "the jurisdiction of the man within" to the "desire of praise-worthiness" and "the aversion to blame-worthiness."[66]

For the Frankfurt School philosopher, however, individuals needed to align their inner desires with external constraints. From a reading of Hegel, Honneth develops the idea of a negative freedom (an inalienable *right* not to be impeded in one's physical and moral integrity, one's contractual freedom, or one's access to property); a reflexive freedom (the fact of *morally* assuming the normative consequences of one's actions); and a social freedom (participating in different spheres of life and being recognized for one's *ethic*).[67] He believes that Hegel, in his *Elements of the Philosophy of Right*,[68] links autonomy and self-realization in such a way that social freedom takes precedence over the other two forms of freedom.[69] He stresses the importance of an ethical life in Hegel: When individuals invest themselves only in a struggle for their rights and in the moral justification of their actions, they have to face the "emptiness" of their existence and can only feel the "suffering from indeterminacy."[70] Honneth takes up this argument, arguing that the increased differentiation of social tasks in the context of globalization requires a communication ethic that can pluralize the principles of justice and fight democratic apathy, especially in terms of political participation.[71]

And yet, Honneth's ethical thinking fails to consider the fact that minority and majority subjects do not assign the same functions to freedom; they simply do not have the same uses for it. There is suffering in indeterminacy when the subject is situated within a majority logic, whereas in a minority dynamic, indeterminacy can be synonymous with enjoyment and a capacity to act.[72] Anthropologist Moisés Lino e Silva has shown that minority subjects win their freedom through "disidentification," conferring new meaning on the notion of freedom and thus paving the way for a new form of political liberalism.[73]

In fact, the main theories of recognition require that subjects are not only "recognizable"[74] but also "grateful"[75] to the group that excluded them.[76] They do not abandon the modern conception of power, which associates control and gratification. This is Philip Pettit's starting point in his analysis of the good life. He maintains that "beyond the satisfaction of basic needs, there is nothing more important to having a good life than enjoying the attachment, the virtue, and the respect of our fellows."[77] Created out of domination, minorities can, of course, seek recognition, but they can also break from it because they know they will always lose the game of recognition. They establish their pride without further consideration for their reputation and the immediate benefits they can derive from it. They thus question the highly decontextualized idea of "fellow." Against the logic of recognition, Judith Butler, based on her own reading of Hegel, proposed a completely different way of thinking about the ethics of one's relationship with the other:

[W]e might consider a certain post-Hegelian reading of the scene of recognition in which precisely my own opacity to myself occasions my capacity to confer a certain kind of recognition on others. It would be, perhaps, an ethics based on our shared, invariable, and partial blindness about ourselves. The recognition that one is, at every turn, not quite the same as how one presents oneself in the available discourse might imply, in turn, a certain patience with others that would suspend the demand that they be self-same at every moment.[78]

Judith Butler does not see reciprocity in a communitarian dialogic form, that of the struggle for recognition, but rather in the resonance of the limitations of our reflexivity. A minority ethic is an ethic based on the suspension of claims of identity: it is an ethic of indeterminacy. Such an ethic poses a challenge: how can the circulation of social goods be conceived in terms of indeterminacy?

I propose that Michael Walzer's perspective, based on the ownership of social goods, should be complemented by a reflection on dispossession and nonownership. Walzer wrote: "Men and women take on concrete identities because of the way they conceive and create, and then possess and employ social goods."[79] By addressing the circulation and distribution of social goods from the perspective of ownership, Walzer set aside other types of relationships with social goods that are characteristic of the minority response to social domination: borrowing, sharing, theft, idolatry, disembodiment, and fabrication, and so on. Literature provides a vivid illustration of these minority relationships to social goods, be they affective relationships, objects, or even living spaces. Think, for example, of Jean Genet's *The Thief's Journal*; Toni Morisson's *Beloved*; Maryse Condé's *I, Tituba: Black Witch of Salem*; Sherman Alexie's *The Lone Ranger and Tonto Fistfight in Heaven*; Helena María Viramontes's *Their Dogs Came with Them*; Rachid O's *L'Enfant ébloui* ("The Dazzled Child"); or Annie Ernaux's novels on aging and social poverty, such as *Cleaned Out* and *I Remain in Darkness*. In all these novels, to give just a few examples, the characters demonstrate that social goods can be diverted from their primary function: theft becomes a sacrament, an everyday object such as a radio or television set becomes a transnational symbol, a highway becomes a border, and so on. By resignifying relationships to social goods, minorities also bring their identities into play. They accept that they no longer own them and have lost control of them, letting them float away, as Sethe's voice blends and fades into Beloved's. This is what brings Michael Warner to say that the culture of coming out is a form of nonownership reflecting asymmetry in an individual's relationship to the norm; it is not about retaining an identity but making it available to others.[80] Conversely, majority cultures show deep attachment to the idea of ownership.[81] The privileges enjoyed by white people in the West and beyond stem from their ownership of symbolic capital, to which other capitals are linked: the ownership of one's own body, of land, or even of one's name.[82] This relationship to ownership is rooted in the history of slavery and colonialism and continues to operate through different forms of cultural hegemony, social domination, and territorial segregation.[83]

The nonownership I am highlighting here—to the point of questioning one's sovereignty over oneself—is by no means an attack on the legal subject. I am advocating a minority ethic that sits atop democracy's two existing pillars: fundamental rights, and checks and balances. I do not subscribe to a positivist logic. French philosopher and mathematician Auguste Comte, because he considered individualism to be a sociological impasse, maintained that "the idea of *right* has to disappear from the political, as the idea of *cause* from the philosophical domain."[84] I am trying to offer an approach to democracy that draws on all the lessons of pluralism. Indeed, since Locke and his notion of "continued existence,"[85] it has been known that the individual is both plural and unique because, in a philosophical sense, it is our ways of conceiving identity and grasping it through language that are "one."[86] By emphasizing that the relationship to oneself is a relationship of both ownership and nonownership, I am orienting the democratic attitude toward a practice of learning one's own limitations and, consequently, a greater presence of the other. A democratic ethic must recognize that there is always an element of "absolute non-recognition" in the community, an element that escapes the double reflection of the I in the We and the We in the I.[87]

Similarly, thinking in terms of nonownership is not simply repeating Pierre-Joseph Proudhon's adage that "property is theft!"[88] What I am emphasizing here is that all individual production is the fruit of collective work: Thomas Piketty has shown that, after the eighteenth century, "learning about equitable institutions" stemmed from the continual acceptance of the collective dimension of wealth creation.[89] Should we not question the whole idea of individual ownership? Rawls engaged in this reflection. He considered that the ownership of social goods was arbitrary, and that merit was not a relevant basis for distributing them. He thus emphasized the need to equalize resources so that everyone could acquire social goods.[90] Why not conclude from this that social goods do not belong to anyone?[91] According to Michael Sandel, this would imply a Christian type of community thinking (being the guardians of resources that belong to God) or of a secular type (being the custodians of social goods that belong to the collective).[92]

The minority ethic that I develop here takes a third path. I maintain that it is possible to legitimize preferential treatment without essentializing the categories concerned, since social goods are seen in terms of their circulation rather than in terms of ownership. Thus, it is conceivable to allocate resources without "*judg[ing]* people as more or less worthy in themselves" according to what they own.[93] Nonownership does not mean not owning anything, but rather considering that what one owns is always a collective product. By maintaining that no one owns the resources they enjoy, Rawls left individuals in turmoil. Conversely, thinking in terms of the collective production of social goods involves recognizing the importance of the exclusive enjoyment of certain social goods: certain ties of friendship, love, and family, and certain objects, have a specific value, which are necessary to all. When students interviewed Albert Camus in Stockholm after he received the Nobel Prize in Literature, he famously said: "I believe in justice, but I will defend my mother before I defend justice."[94] Paradoxically, recognizing the collective dimension of social goods forces individuals to intensify their attachments. The "enlarged self," to use Sandel's terms, is "indebted" to its community, which it needs in order to realize itself as having different identities.[95] This requires us to challenge the concatenation of ownership and individual freedom, a concatenation that runs from the physiocrats to Kant,[96]

GLOBAL RESPONSIBILITY

and conceive of universalism as a confrontation with an embodied collective and the nonownership of the self. This work involves decentering and learning about the presence of the other.[97] It is crucial in a globalized world.

GLOBAL RESPONSIBILITY

Multiculturalist theories have had only limited success outside the English-speaking world. While they have been applied here and there to support the legal recognition of indigenous minorities, especially in South America, postcolonial and post-communist governments have mostly remained impervious to them.[98] For Will Kymlicka, multiculturalism comes at a cost. It involves abandoning certain conceptions of identity, transforming different procedures, and rethinking the fundamental principles of law.[99] Consequently, multiculturalism encounters strong resistance when states are in the process of becoming established and tend to sanctify transcendental values. Moreover, most multiculturalist approaches seemed so attached to cultural identities that they struggle to grasp power relations on a more global scale. Minority universalism strives to compensate for this by proposing a different interpretation of the principle of responsibility.

Universalism is a set of relational principles that the law deploys and invokes in different contexts: equality, freedom, dignity, nonviolence, solidarity, etc. They all relate to the same ethical question: to whom are we accountable? This question is all the more fundamental because globalization is characterized by a marked dilution of responsibility. Our lives are determined by all kinds of social interactions so far removed from us that we fail to perceive their impact, just as we only have a dim awareness of the consequences of our actions on others.

The sociologist Norbert Elias analyzed this phenomenon. He wrote of the lengthening and densification of "chains of interdependence" through the division of labor, the financialization of trade, and the distance between places of production and places of consumption[100]— elements to which are now added the tangle of physical and virtual communication.[101] Elias demonstrated that this globalized and mostly unconscious interdependence was not necessarily a factor of civilization.[102]

Today, the increasing interconnectedness of human lives through various computational and algorithmic techniques gives the illusion that there is an expansion of co-presence and responsibility. But nothing is less certain. The logic that dominates this interweaving is one of demarcation. To interconnect, it is first necessary to segment, that is, isolate, exclude, incarcerate, or expel. In a world of hyperclassification in which places are already distributed, there is no real responsibility. The metaworld is the reticular stage of irresponsibility. Conversely, in the words of Achille Mbembe, it is the "exponentially chaotic"[103] nature of life that requires a sense of others.

Beyond grand declarations of principle, this evolution of social organization explains the lack of progress in the fight against global warming despite the existence of data and solutions.[104] The ease with which COVID-19 circulated around the world heightened our awareness of human interdependence and of the complementarity of humans and nonhumans. However, being aware of a phenomenon does not mean having control over it. Today, the "lengthened reach of our deeds" is such that we find ourselves caught in ethical dilemmas whose consequences are beyond our grasp.[105] We live in a "world-totality"[106] from which we are mostly expelled. The dependence of political power on economic and financial power means that responsibility and power are not necessarily exercised in the same place. This dissociation between acting and the ethics of acting, understood as a movement that runs counter to the coordination of interests that Max Weber called "sociation,"[107] calls for a reevaluation of how responsibility is exercised. Some authors have proposed a cosmopolitical philosophy in which global responsibility would be in the hands of new international organizations, such as an International Court of Environmental Rights.[108] Others have emphasized the importance of naming and shaming the political and economic leaders responsible and the effects of their actions on the most vulnerable.[109] Finally, still others urge the creation of checks and balances against a society that substitutes punishment for responsibility.[110]

The path I am proposing complements and extends the previous ones: considering responsibility from the perspective of minority relations. To be responsible means literally to answer for one's actions, that is, to be accountable. "Pushing the other back into his responsibility"

TOWARD MINORITY UNIVERSALISM

means to sustain the relation since some action is expected from "him."[111] This expectation varies depending on the social position of each person, as demonstrated by the COVID-19 pandemic.[112] During a health crisis, social organization shrinks. Ethical choices align with the interests of the majority.[113] France's containment policies in March and April 2020 assumed that household units—the nuclear family space par excellence— were the only legitimate places of refuge, isolating hundreds of thousands of people, friends, neighbors, lovers, as if the risk of contamination depended on the type of bond rather than the number of people in contact.[114] Political discourse became warlike and virile. The movement of people was relocated to predefined spaces: cities, regions, the nation, or supranational organizations such as the European Union. Foreign students were sent home with little consideration for the health situation they would encounter there. And yet minorities were on the front lines of service and in care professions.[115] "Minority universalism" does not address globalization through sovereignty. Responsibility is not an act that establishes a subject's autonomy;[116] rather, it orients an ethical relationship toward a form of learning about embodied interdependence.[117] The fact of being a minority in one's own living space requires engaging in the process of learning one's limitations. This work involves grasping better the extent of one's ability to act; as long as the stage on which we are acting is global, the constitution of the self is that of a consciousness permeated by the world and yet separate from it.

This is the tension that lies at the heart of the ethical relationship. As Hans Jonas succinctly put it, "Only the idea of Man, by telling us *why* they should be men, tells us also *how* they should be."[118] A minority-inspired universalism sets out to answer these two connected questions. Starting with the observation that we incorporate shortcomings, absences, and uncertainties in our relationships with others, it is no longer possible to conceive of responsibility as the expression of sovereignty through knowledge.[119] It must be understood as a process of learning about the limits of what we know.[120] As Hans Jonas also remarked, "The gap between the ability to foretell and the power to act creates a novel moral problem. With the latter so superior to the former, recognition of ignorance becomes the obverse of the duty to know and thus part of the ethics that must govern the evermore necessary self-policing of our outsized might."[121]

What minority experience teaches us is that the self is formed by a set of other lives that we redeploy in the demand for global responsibility.[122] This perspective is already bearing fruit: social science research shows that enabling minorities to vote leads to improved social protection policies for everyone.[123] This is illustrated by a recent example: in April 2024, a senior women's association successfully brought a case against Switzerland for climate inaction before the European Court of Human Rights. The court held that, under Article 8 of the convention, states had a "positive obligation" to take action to guarantee effective protection for their citizens "from the serious adverse effects of climate change on lives, health, well-being and quality of life" (heat waves leave the elderly particularly vulnerable to the deterioration of their living conditions and the risk of death).[124] This decision makes the enjoyment of a healthy environment a fundamental right for all, a right that other citizens in the European area will henceforth be able to exercise.

THE LIMITATIONS OF EMPATHY

Thought about from the minority perspective, responsibility raises the question of limitations of the embodied collective. Both for reasons of proximity (first wanting to protect one's entourage) and available resources (time, energy, cognitive capacity, etc.), it is impossible to give each person the same amount of attention or care. Cosmopolitical models based on empathy therefore encounter the major pitfall of having to distinguish, more or less consciously, between lives that matter and lives that matter less or not at all.[125] The strength of an embodied presence depends on the ability to identify it and identify with it. There is thus a whole biopolitics involved in determining which presences are legitimate and which bodies must be protected from violence. Empathy, therefore, is limited: either one's immediate community has priority over the rest of the world, or one treats strangers with greater respect.[126] Philosopher Kwame Anthony Appiah has proposed a third way, "rooted cosmopolitanism,"[127] in which moral obligations are not governed by a sense of communion with all of humanity but rather "equitable self-interest."[128] He explains that the negation of others is part of the process of affirming one's identity. It is therefore important to develop ways of thinking about

TOWARD MINORITY UNIVERSALISM

ethical relationships in which care for others does not result from an uncertain altruistic inclination but from a clearly understood mechanism of self-care (since we are constituted by others): "Ethical obligation . . . is internal to the identity. Who you are is constituted, in part, by what you care about."[129]

The hypothesis of minority universalism that I am advocating goes even further. It involves considering the ways in which subjects are constituted not just by what they care about, but also by what they do not pay attention to, and indeed by what they deny, but whose presence is unavoidable.[130] What we do not know and do not dedicate care to nevertheless dwells within us. Minorities demonstrate that the ethical relationship stems from relinquishing the desire to control the relationship with others from others, not from some predisposition to good feelings. It is not a passion for association but a dissociative responsibility. Caring about others is a way of creating conditions of possibility for one's own freedom.[131] As a result, to mistreat others is to mistreat oneself, not out of any moral attachment but because, in social interdependence, association and dissociation are two sides of the same presence. Structural inequalities have to be considered in terms of these two dimensions: the appropriation of social goods stems from being deprived of self-ownership (a phenomenon that Marx and Engels identified in their consideration of labor power as an externality[132]) and from denying self-dissociation (which, minority cultures demonstrate, is a form of hospitality through the maximization of one's own freedom).

Minority universalism is therefore not an ethic of care. Berenice Fisher and Joan Tronto defined "care" in the following terms: "On the most general level, we suggest that caring can be viewed as a *species activity that includes everything that we do to maintain, continue, and repair our "world" so that we can live there as well as possible.* That world includes our bodies, ourselves, and our environment, all of which we seek to interweave in a complex life-sustaining web."[133] Theories of care place a double bet: mitigating the shortcomings of theories of justice, which minimize the way in which everyday gestures organize our social worlds; and valuing the contribution of women, either directly, as when certain theories of care are based on the experience of motherhood at the risk of objectifying it,[134] or indirectly, as when others demonstrate the importance of "values traditionally associated with women."[135] Theories of care demonstrate that the development of commercialism has reduced the role of solicitude, which was at the heart of small living communities until the nineteenth century. This solicitude was cardinal in the work of philosophers such as Hutcheson, Hume, and Smith, and gave way to the lengthening of the chains of interdependence. The vulnerability of others became less perceptible, and immediate interactions lost their collective aspect. In the words of Estelle Ferrarese, "our [capitalistic] form of life . . . compartmentalizes attention to others."[136] Conversely, care seeks to socialize various acts of solicitude[137] by showing that individual autonomy is possible because of a whole chain of human labor, especially on the part of women.

Theories of care, however, tend to substantialize the idea of vulnerability; their main proponents associate weakness with compassion, as if this were a moral configuration that preceded the relationship. Patricia Paperman admits that "the Good Samaritan's compassion is not very different from the gesture of 'care.'"[138] Because many philosophies of care do not discuss how care relationships develop, they end up depoliticizing what they designate. They refer to the "texture" of care, the "lifestyles" that need to be protected, or the "background" of care,[139] but they do not question the type of power over others that is exercised in providing care, in particular the "desire for power" in relation to another.[140] In neglecting or at least minimizing this aspect of violence in care, theories of care trap people in a destiny of vulnerability that is the very antithesis of policies of minority subjectivation.[141] Even more, in failing to truly situate care,[142] the founders of this field tend to rely somewhat paradoxically on a kind of veil of vulnerability, which is reminiscent of Rawlsian analyses. Joan Tronto wrote:

Where the notion, 'I made it on my own, you should make it on your own,' appears to have the formal quality of a morally correct and universalizable judgment, it can also serve to disguise the inequality of resources, powers, and privileges that have made it possible for some to "make it" while others have not. These problems are difficult ones to solve. One way to think about them is to acknowledge that, throughout their lives, all people need care; so the inequality that emerges when some are care-givers and others are care-receivers should not be so morally significant.[143]

Once subjects are identified as vulnerable, what is really left to them in the power dynamic? This is why Judith Butler speaks instead of a "constellation of vulnerability" to disassociate responsibility for others from the idea of passivity.[144] The capacity to act does not mean emerging from one's own vulnerability, but affirming one's very life, that of a persevering and diversely vulnerable bodily presence.[145] "We do not have to love one another to engage in meaningful solidarity," Judith Butler summarizes, because "our 'sentiments' navigate the ambivalence by which they are constituted."[146] This form of presence has materialist roots; the presence of the other contains me, that is, blocks me and simultaneously gives me my strength.

ANTHROPOCENIC KNOWLEDGE

Responsibility for others is both an outcome and a source of concern.[147] Educated in repressive institutions,[148] subjects stand before others as before a small tribunal (a conception that leads institutions to transform any ethical relationship into a technique of government). In the Anthropocene, a paradigm shift is needed in order to understand existence as an ecosystem in which multiple presences are connected. This conception of the subject as both a zone of contact and a zone of emotion is what Stefano Harney and Fred Moten called "hapticality."[149] Hapticality resists the immune reflex,[150] which is the most immediate response to pollution, viral diseases, and climate change. Some members of a community, using their economic and social capital, seek to withdraw and save themselves but not others. Minority experience shatters this illusion of salvation through status and wealth: whatever our degree of privilege, it reminds us that our relationships with others always remain uninterrupted, even in their most extreme forms, such as the Holocaust.[151]

Characterized by the radical transformation of ecosystems caused by human action, the idea of the Anthropocene induces a certain "despecification."[152] The human species is unique but not specific. This shift cannot fail to leave humans in a state of turmoil. How should one act when the scope of one's actions is uncertain? We are living in a paradoxical situation, where the chains of interdependence are getting longer, but the effects of rising seas, aridity in many areas, and increasing temperatures are shrinking our living space ever more quickly.[153] Much environmental degradation is hidden from us on a day-to-day basis: reduced biodiversity, water pollutants, ozone, endocrine disruptors, etc. The fight to preserve a healthy environment thus forces us to rely on authorities, especially scientists, without being able to imagine the consequences of our actions more directly; this is particularly true given that the environment's response time to human activities is exponential—that is, slow at first, before entering a phase of considerable acceleration.[154]

Although the consequences of climate change, pollution, and the depletion of vital resources affect all humanity, each person's position on the climate spectrum is different. Despite pollution and global warming, some individuals can protect themselves a little better and for a little longer than others. Traditional representative government, however, is organized to preserve the interests of specific groups within limited areas, namely today's nation states. Dominique Bourg and Kerry Whiteside have pointed out that "in recent years, we have seen the US Senate refuse to ratify the Kyoto Protocol and the Japanese Parliament defend the right to fish for whales, but we must admit that these representatives marvelously fulfill their functions."[155] We therefore need new modes of democratic action.

To meet this challenge, Bruno Latour has proposed new ways of including environmental issues in politics, based on increasing the number of human and nonhuman actors[156] and using the creation of a parliament of things as a paradigmatic example.[157] Dominique Bourg and Kerry Whiteside also argue in favor of various forms of participatory democracy, for example forums inspired by the functioning of some organizations: environmental NGOs; organizations that represent the interests of the future; or popular juries, that is, oversight bodies whose members are drawn by lot.[158]

I also stand behind another option: the destruction of the environment means that humanity is entering a zone of "nonsovereignty," which minorities have experienced for a long time.[159] The extraction of fossil fuels, for example, is directly linked to the removal of Black bodies in the history of industrialization and global trade.[160] The poorest minorities are already the most exposed to deteriorating living spaces.[161] The fires that routinely devastate California overexpose workers in intensive agriculture who are often undocumented or residence permit holders primarily from Mexico and South America. Already exposed to pesticides, they harvest and distribute basic foodstuffs in often unbreathable air.[162] This is why environmental policy must be minority-based. Environmental degradation impacts minorities more heavily owing to lower average economic resources than the rest of the population; forced mobility (migration, flight to the city, etc.); and settlement in interstitial spaces and temporalities (living on the outskirts; cramped living spaces; night work; etc.).[163] Public authorities tend to minimize or ignore the specific costs of environmental degradation for minorities,[164] and public opinion instead portrays minorities as polluters.[165] The overexposure of racial minorities, combined with the denial of this overexposure, has led several sociologists to speak of "environmental racism."[166] Minorities form micropublics whose existence provides evidence of deficient, albeit shared, understandings of ecological issues. In doing so, they challenge the majority macro-audiences to revise their ways of thinking.

This expertise is not enough to make minorities actors in the drive to transform environmental protection. There are very strong class, gender, and racial dynamics that lead some minorities to exploit others.[167] A practical question also arises: how to be engaged in the world's future when one is or has long been considered as belonging to another world, a third world, or even a subworld?[168] W. E. B. Du Bois highlighted this question in a 1910 essay, corrected and republished in 1920 in *Darkwater*. He described "whiteness" as the "ownership of the world forever and ever."[169] Because minorities make their way through spaces and times that are not made for them, they are highly dependent on external factors. In this respect, minority relationships can serve as a starting point for a better understanding of human fragility in the Anthropocene. It is no coincidence that Serge Moscovici, author of a pioneering study on engaged minorities,[170] also analyzed this dual relationship of production and dependence on the environment.[171]

In France, ecofeminist and ecoqueer currents also defend this standpoint in the wake of Françoise d'Eaubonne's work.[172] For d'Eaubonne, minority relationships are an opportunity for learning that counters the patriarchal fantasies of omnipotence—fantasies that lead to an "unlimited" vision of the world (whether in terms of ownership, production, or social dominance).[173] All the same, she cautioned against lapsing into "antihumanism" by reducing human beings to enemy figures and by projecting a purely friendly imaginary onto animals.[174] The "becoming animal" is the counterprojection of an idealized human becoming (human beings are the ones inventing the animalistic metaphors).

Beyond the metaphorical illusion, animal and human copresences are part of minority thinking on the limitations of the self. Donna Haraway speaks of "becoming-with" to describe how living beings are "opportunists" who occupy spaces at the expense of others while bonding over unavoidable communal activities such as "eating together."[175] It is even possible to think of all living beings as a single body. Because we leave genetic traces of our presence everywhere, we fossilize and digest the traces of others.[176] The paradox of all ecology lies in the radical contradiction of the limitations of the self; although human beings are caught up in a considerable biomass on which they depend and of which they are merely a negligible quantity, they are the only ones capable of thinking and speaking about it. However vast it may be, the biomass is deteriorating without being able to say a word about its own demise. Ecology cannot therefore do without humanism.

This is Bruno Latour's meaning when he underlines the importance of being "down to earth": the earth possesses human beings, but it is humans who radically transform it.[177] What would humanism look like in the Anthropocene?[178] Is human justice, centered on a combination of speech and proof, still effective in the Anthropocene, when we must defend nature, which is voiceless? The mirage of abundance may have its roots in capitalist modernity,[179] but is it not also the hidden face of the discourse of emancipation?[180] We must simultaneously affirm our autonomy and our contiguity to the world. The First National People of Color Environmental Leadership Summit, which took place in Washington, DC, in 1991, put forward proposals in this spirit on issues of habitability, sustainability, nonstandardization, participation, and integrity.[181]

In the collective work *Latinx Environmentalisms*, poet Lucha Corpi describes our relationship to the space in which we live: "Justice has a lot to do with a sense of self, in a group, in culture, in your environment. Sometimes you want justice, which is not the same as a system of law. Justice is separate from a system of law. You have personal justice, your own sense of yourself around others and others around you."[182] In this chapter, I have advocated for a minority conception of universalism by revisiting the notions of ownership, responsibility, and globalization. This has enabled me to address the main objection to any minority theorization of democracy: what should be done about disagreements between minority groups? Several years after publishing *Spheres of Justice*, Michael Walzer suggested a possibly important avenue: differentiating between the state and politics.[183] Thinking in terms of spheres of injustice makes it possible to pursue this avenue without sacrificing anything to relativism. A minority ethic then takes precedence over the search for consensus, a search that does not in itself build a good society. A good society—what Avishai Margalit has called a "decent society" or "moral society"—is one that allows for conflict while working to eliminate the mechanisms that create humiliation.[184] This search for morality is not meant to replace rights; it actualizes them within a logic of reciprocity. Consequently, rather than rejecting the state as a whole, it is better to act on the manufacturing of its moral illusions, including the autonomy of the subject, the free market, and individual merit.[185]

There is, of course, no reason to attribute to minorities a heightened ontological sense of morality or a desire for mutual assistance and care. The death of Tyre Nichols, a Black US citizen arrested and brutalized by the police in Memphis, Tennessee, on January 7, 2023, is a tragic illustration. The members of the police patrol who beat him up and left him to die were themselves Black men serving in a structurally racist institution. However, we have no choice but to create the conditions for developing a minority ethic, as Black churches,[186] Maroon geographies,[187] labor unions,[188] low-income parents of color against the prison pipeline,[189] gay HIV groups[190] and crip art,[191] to give but a few examples, have done throughout history, often with no external help. Indeed, no institutional mechanism and no system for sharing resources can completely eradicate injustices, even the most distributive models.[192] This ethic is based on the minority dimension that is within every individual, which can steer them toward discovering their limitations. This is a double challenge of the strange and the foreign, at once inside and outside oneself. This challenge is the very locus of politics, that is, a process in which the presence of the other becomes an event.

Some may object that this minority dimension lives in us to varying degrees, and that they can be denied, exploited, or turned against minorities themselves. Such criticism is entirely valid. The risk of "reducing the other" (that is, of capturing the other in a specular logic[193]) is inherent in all ethical work. Rethinking social bonds is not enough to transform them. Transforming standards always leads to the production of new ones. Nevertheless, it is a risk that must be taken, because there is also a cumulative effect of minority theorizations[194] that allows the logic of domination to be partially reversed. Minority presence conveys a dissociative conception of the relationship to the other; it creates a "spatial fracturing" that unfolds in multiple spaces and in unique ways.[195] It forces us to negotiate the universal in relationships.[196]

Today, this negotiation is an essential civic virtue because it enables the connection between public policies designed in isolation. Novelist Édouard Louis has demonstrated that it was homophobia that made an invalid of his father, a working-class, heterosexual, racist, white man.[197] The gender roles assigned to boys led him to take up "manly" work that wore out his body. The fight against homophobia is therefore a social policy. The same thing could be said of abortion, contraception, and women's education around the world: women's freedom to do as they wish with their bodies and their level of education has a direct impact on birth rates and levels of human development. In a context of diminishing resources, the fight against sexism is an ecological policy. When public places are adapted for people with disabilities, young children and the elderly also benefit. Accessibility policies are intergenerational policies. When life expectancy in good health is taken into account for calculating retirement rights, pressure on the health care system decreases, which benefits people living in areas with poor access to medical services first and foremost. Retirement policies are spatial planning policies. When income redistribution makes it possible to improve medical services for the poorest, it also protects the most privileged, who may be affected by contagious diseases that could have been contained. Tax policies are also health policies.

By linking minority knowledge, social action, and environmental protection, these public policies enhance the democratic ideal around a powerful and simple question: who am I minoritizing when I act? They articulate a wide range of situations based on the resonances generated by experiences of injustice. They conceive of presence in the world in terms of the limitations of self and others. Universalism is either a minority concept, or it is not.

CONCLUSION: AN ETHIC OF INTERDEPENDENCE

Is might always right? Minority movements that defend minorities not only demand respect for fundamental rights and a better distribution of resources; they also raise questions about the values implicit in majority democracy. Although democracy responds to movements' demands through various mechanisms of recognition, redistribution, and compensation, majority citizenry remains the standard of reference. This centrality is now being challenged.

In this book, I have pursued on a theoretical level the question that underpins the great contemporary struggles for emancipation—what would a democracy be if social bonds were founded on the minority dimension that runs through each one of us to varying degrees? Today, the notion of minority designates individuals linked by common physical, cultural, or social characteristics (language, history, place of residence, gender, sexuality, skin color, disability, religious beliefs, profession, etc.) that distinguish them from the rest of the population and expose them to discrimination. It is on this basis that the law establishes classes of protected persons. *Spheres of Injustice* shows that this approach is not entirely satisfactory because it does not pay sufficient attention to context. In South Africa, the Black population is a majority in number, yet it is nonetheless dominated. A gay man may be at a disadvantage in one sphere of his life but not in another. A person with a motor disability may prefer not to be identified as disabled so as not to be reduced to a physical trait.

A white, heterosexual, affluent man may be minoritized in other aspects of his life, based on his age, appearance, or health, for example. Being a minority is not an immutable status; it means being dominated in a composite and shifting power relationship. Conversely, majority identity is not defined by what it is, but by what it is not; to be white is, among other things, to be neither Black, nor mixed race, nor Arab, nor Asian, etc. It is through this mechanism that majority is equated to universal and contextual inequalities become structural.

In *Spheres of Justice*, Michael Walzer analyzed the different spheres (family, friends, work, etc.) in which power relations are exercised. He considered these spheres to be governed by different principles of justice. Inequality can therefore only be tackled by understanding the complex interactions that take place between these spheres. For my part, I have shown that what organizes each sphere is less an agreement about what justice is than a confrontation with injustice, an experience constitutive of the minority relationship. On this basis, I have put forward a minority ethic of responsibility toward others. This ethic consists in conceiving our connection to others through the experiences of injustice that constitute us, whether it be the suffering of an injustice, its possibility, or its spectacle. It calls for the creation of new institutional mechanisms that go beyond the issues of representation and reparation. Arthur Dénouveaux and Antoine Garapon sum this up well: "Representation . . . brings out the irreplaceable; the truth established by the judicial narrative leaves an unutterable part; recognition indicates that there remains something incommunicable; and judicial redress brings out the experience of irreparability."[1]

To develop this ethical work, I have investigated the intricacies of antidiscrimination law, discourses on identity, activism, and public policies that promote equality, both in France and in the United States. Based on a critical rereading of *Spheres of Justice* and its reception in France, the first chapter has explained how the experience of injustice could open up new ethical perspectives drawn from the minority relationship that develops between dissimilar subjects. To deepen this approach, I have examined the four major challenges confronting the idea of minority today. The second chapter has shown the complexity of legal categories and the way in which they have become a management issue. The third chapter has studied the transformation of the notion of majority under the effect of political polarization and algorithmic methods that favor averages—and

CONCLUSION

not without consequences for minorities. The fourth chapter has investigated the appropriation of the notion of minority by various reactionary groups who, in the media, in the streets, and in the courts, challenge minority rights. Finally, the fifth chapter has questioned competition between minority groups with regard to affirmative action.

In the second part of the book, I have then proposed several paths out of these impasses. The sixth chapter has mobilized the notion of "co-appearance" and demonstrated that all subjectivity bears a minority presence that I have studied in the context of social movements, state violence, and collective memory. The seventh chapter has shed light on the power of analogies between gender, sex, race, disability, age, and sexual orientation in legal casuistry. It introduces the notion of intrasectionality to qualify these resonances and to compensate for the difficulties encountered in applying intersectional conceptions of identity. Finally, the eighth chapter has established that minority universalism is not only possible but necessary for thinking about interdependence down to its economic and environmental dimensions. These last three chapters make up three strands of a single minority theory of justice: social, legal, and political.

In *La Folie du jour*, Maurice Blanchot wrote: "To me, each person was an entire people. That vast other person made me much more than I would have liked."[2] *Spheres of Injustice* questions minority resonances in contemporary French and US societies and beyond. The resulting ethical relationship is not an ontology but the fruit of coexistence. As Maurice Blanchot reminds us, the self overflows with what composes it. The will is nothing without the presence of the embodied collective. No ethical provision born of a dominated position can guarantee in itself the transformation of the social world. An ethic is a potentiality. It requires work in the physical sense of the term, a movement that resists what Gilles Deleuze and Félix Guattari call the "submission of the line to the point,"[3] because "there is no history but of the majority or of minorities as defined in relation to the majority."[4] The strength of a minority ethic lies in its ability to establish a critical dynamic. *Spheres of Injustice* has undertaken this task around three main axes: the co-appearance of the subject, analogical reasoning, and justice as dispossession.

If the minority point of view reveals its ethical force, it is because it apprehends interdependence based on experiences of injustice. This is the meaning behind New York artist Zoe Leonard's powerful manifesto:

I want a dyke for president. I want a person with aids for president and I want a fag for vice president and I want someone with no health insurance and I want someone who grew up in a place where the earth is so saturated with toxic waste that they didn't have a choice about getting leukemia. I want a president who had an abortion at sixteen and I want a candidate who isn't the lesser of two evils and I want a president who lost their last lover to aids, who still sees that in their eyes every time they lay down to rest, who held their lover in their arms and knew they were dying. I want a president with no air conditioning, a president who has stood on line at the clinic, at the DMV, at the welfare office. . . . I want a Black woman for president. I want someone with bad teeth ~~and an attitude~~, someone who has eaten ~~that nasty~~ hospital food, someone who crossdresses and has done drugs and been in therapy. I want someone who has committed civil disobedience. And I want to know why this isn't possible.[5]

Zoe Leonard does not attribute any moral superiority to minorities, but believes that their position in relations of domination can transform the exercise of political power. If this position can be transformative, it is not because it is distinct from that of the majority, or even because it is marginal, dominated, or vulnerable. Theories that essentialize "positionality" lead to dead ends. They give free rein to the moral relativism on which the extreme right feeds. What motivates the minority perspective I am defending here is multipositionality. Because they are raised and/or evolve in majority cultures, minorities speak several languages, circulate between several social backgrounds, and learn to constantly wear and disavow their identities.[6] This dynamic *can* be the starting point for an ethic of presence that pluralizes the relationship to social space and political time. It is not based on any intrinsic quality but arises from the decentering of identity.[7]

So I want to be very clear. A minority ethic is not the prerogative of minorities alone. Being part of a minority group does not even guarantee the emergence of such an ethic. It does encourage it, although some people will perfectly well resist it. I have spoken of the participation of minority personalities in political movements that challenge their own rights. There are many possible explanations for this, including a paradoxical strategy of self-protection that comes from adhering to the values of those who threaten us[8] or a disconnect between several contradictory allegiances.[9] *Spheres of Injustice* therefore never postulates moral coherence. Each minority position is the product of a complex trajectory that does not always point toward a minority ethic. Conversely, people who

CONCLUSION

are not considered minorities and do not define themselves as such can promote a minority ethic by paying close attention to experiences of injustice, even if they themselves have little or no exposure to them. They are disposed to embrace a minority presence, translate it into their own experience, and champion its voice.[10] A minority ethic considers the social world from the point of view of minoritized people but is not the exclusive prerogative of minorities. It is in this sense that it can be described as a heterotopic work: it consists in exploring its own interstices, modalities of self-dispossession, and the events that make us strangers to ourselves, and thus connect us to others. The ethic that I call for here is, therefore, concerned with overcoming the dissension between majorities and minorities, not in communion (celebrating what we have in common) but in interdependence (a "shared incompleteness"[11]). This is what I call "hollow universalism." It challenges moral equivalence but is not founded on absolute values whose cultural anchoring would necessarily exclude. Minority universalism is relational, not relative. It stems from the possibility of transforming our incompleteness into empowerment.

Envisioning which public policies may result from this minority universalism is an almost impossible task, and not one that belongs to me alone. The impact of a social theory on the practices it analyzes (what sociologists call a "loop effect") is very difficult to predict.[12] Similarly, any theoretical elaboration can be criticized for its irenics, its normativism, or even its insensitivity.[13] I accept this. Still, even though the complexities of the social world necessarily overwhelm any critical work, it is no less necessary. When the conditions for reception are right,[14] a theory can help—and this is already a considerable contribution—to open up new ways of thinking and in doing so participate in the construction of new public problems.[15]

In what follows, I will therefore outline some possible measures without providing detailed content. The notion of minority is corrosive only in specific contexts and on the basis of ad hoc situations. There is no single model of minority democracy but rather a set of unique measures specific to each legal tradition. This plurality is essential to avoid amplifying the hegemony that certain legal systems already exercise over others.[16] Moreover, no institutional reform is ever complete; structures adapt and shift but never disappear altogether.[17] Civil servants continue their mission beyond constitutional changes.[18] We must not mystify institutions' capacity for change,[19] as they are often constrained by divergent interests.[20] The recent majority shift to the right on the US Supreme Court reminds us that the law is a battlefield run through with contradictions. Although it has its own characteristics, it is nonetheless intertwined with other social spheres on which it partly depends.[21] The whole paradox of minority policies stems from this tension. Discourses of pure opposition to policies of recognition, whether local, national, or international, overlook people's most concrete needs for protection. They also undermine the capacity for democratic institutions to innovate and learn.[22] Minority struggles, however, must also challenge the very policies that protect them because they both exclude and recognize at the same time. Any minority approach must therefore play along with institutions.

From a committed minority perspective, affirmative action could be better adapted to applications received. A more incremental system would be more flexible and retain the fundamental principles of providing outreach, guaranteeing places, and enabling alternative recruitment procedures. Based on criteria defined upstream and downstream, recruitment procedures would be more inclusive, particularly from the point of view of social class. It is also possible to systematically design, implement, and evaluate public policies based on their impact on minorities. Claire Hédon, France's current Defender of Rights, has called for such an effort, which would make it possible to bind together the objective interests of the majority and those of minorities. Environmental protection policies would certainly be enriched if they were developed from the perspective of the situation of Indigenous populations and their expertise. Similarly, measures aimed at making public spaces more accessible would benefit from being systematically designed by and for people with disabilities. Today, this kind of monitoring work is confined to policies that concern minorities. Yet minorities' relationship to space, whether in terms of perception or use, is a precious resource for enriching everyone's experiences.[23] Finally, more complex forms of participation could be put in place. Many political scientists have been investigating new methods of calculating electoral votes, redrawing constituencies, and appointing senior public officials so that the executive, legislative, and judicial branches better reflect the real composition of the population.[24]

CONCLUSION

Like legal scholar Lani Guinier, I suggest going further by questioning the geographical basis of political representation.[25] When minority populations are highly concentrated in one area, they are represented by just a small number of elected officials; others then have no interest in voicing their demands. When minority populations are spread more widely over an area (as a result of professional mobility, for example), then their interests dissolve. Specific representation of minority interests is necessary. This representation could take the form of a transformation of the second chamber of parliament, the creation of a third, and introducing qualified majority voting when minority interests are at stake (a reflection of Walzer's complex equality in decision-making[26]). Similarly, the courts could systematically be made up of a larger number of minority individuals and people invested in the fight against exclusion when cases of discrimination are heard. It has been proven, in the case of gender, that the perception of less obvious discrimination does not differ according to the number of women on a jury.[27] Might there not nonetheless be a much more powerful dissuasive effect while a justice system based on punishment and compensation may paradoxically result in less responsibility or even a feeling of impunity? The jury model could be explored beyond the judicial sphere. Indeed, it does not require its members to abstract themselves from their own condition to come to a decision, but, on the contrary, to lean on their experiences and produce situated knowledge.[28]

As important as it may be, an institutional transformation is of little use if it is not accompanied by a transformation in ways of thinking. The situation of women in Western countries attests to this every single day. Reforms in favor of equal pay, equal political representation, or less stereotyped education have had significant effects. Although essential, these measures have not succeeded in dismantling a culture that continues to endorse the exchange of women.[29] Transforming our ways of thinking requires deconstructing our relationship with institutions, be it the police, the welfare system, prisons, the judiciary, etc.

This is the essence of the concept of "transformative justice" advocated by Canadian legal reformer Ruth Morris, which is very present in contemporary abolitionist movements:[30] She proposed focusing less on the violation of the law than on the harm caused (its origins and consequences) as well as the possibilities of redress by involving the guilty party.[31] Inspired by her Quaker beliefs, Ruth Morris's approach offers an alternative to the punitive legal system by conceiving of justice on a longer time scale.[32] But it has several important limitations. It expects injustices and facts of violence to be regulated by the goodwill of the community, itself the result of a great "spiritual appetite."[33] Morris's philosophy of reparations is therefore highly unpredictable as it does not take into consideration the size of the community (empathy is not equally distributed) or the importance of the symbolic externality of the law for minorities who are victims of violence. Moreover, it idealizes a return to equilibrium, "as if the situation in which we live were already desirable."[34]

Last but not least, no alternative practice exists entirely outside of institutions. Movements for transformative justice are no exception. To challenge a norm is also to acknowledge its importance. It also means producing other norms in the very act of resistance. The seeming spontaneity of some street mobilizations and ways of interacting online can appear less institutional. However, this is not the case: not only do these spaces establish other norms, such as that of the "function of spokesperson"[35] or "participatory censorship,"[36] but they also act as institutions insofar as they are purveyors of "identity."[37] A minority ethic involves questioning one's own power, however subordinate. This is why it is not an alternative to democratic institutions but rather a third pillar: in addition to fundamental rights and the balanced organization of public powers, it offers a critical dimension based on minority multipositionality. In the words of Claude Lefort: "Democracy is instituted and sustained by the *dissolution of the markers of certainty*. It inaugurates a history in which people experience a fundamental indeterminacy as to the basis of power, law and knowledge, and as to the basis of relations between *self and other*, at every level of social life."[38]

This is the democratic ideal I pursue in *Spheres of Injustice*. By casting a new eye on the experience of injustice, I have defended a minority ethic based on interdependence. This ethic does not stem from transcendental values but from a learning dynamic in an unfavorable power relationship. It thus questions the normative assumptions of contemporary politics with regard to authority, merit, obedience, and representation. It argues for a more demanding democracy, in which equality requires minority presence, and freedom calls for vicarious responsibility.

NOTES

ACKNOWLEDGMENTS

1. Bruno Perreau, "L'égalité inavouable. Homosexualité et adoption en France. Une politique jurisprudentielle," *Nouvelles Questions Féministes* 22, no. 3 (2003): 32–46.

2. Daniel Sabbagh, *L'Égalité par le droit: Les paradoxes de la discrimination positive aux États-Unis* (Paris: Economica, 2003).

3. Bruno Perreau, "L'invention républicaine. Éléments d'une herméneutique minoritaires," *Pouvoirs* 111 (2004): 41–53.

INTRODUCTION

1. "About Black Lives Matter," BlackLivesMatter, June 2019, https:/blacklivesmatter.com/what-we-believe/.

2. See William Julius Wilson, *More than Just Race: Being Black and Poor in the Inner City* (New York: W. W. Norton, 2009); Richard Rochstein, *The Color of Law: A Forgotten History of How Our Government Segregated America* (New York: Liveright Publishing, 2017); Eve L. Ewing, *Ghosts in the Schoolyard: Racism and School Closings on Chicago's South Side* (Chicago: University of Chicago Press, 2018).

3. "What We Believe," BlackLivesMatter .

4. "8 Minutes and 46 Seconds: How George Floyd Was Killed in Police Custody," *New York Times*, May 31, 2020.

5. Tony Romm and Allyson Chiu, "Twitter Flags Trump, White House for 'Glorifying Violence' after Tweeting Minneapolis Looting Will Lead to 'Shooting,'" *Washington Post*, May 29, 2020.

6. "Federal Agents in Unmarked Cars Snatch Black Lives Matter Protesters from Portland Streets," Democracy Now, June 17, 2020, www.democracynow.org.

7. Meg Kelly, Joyce Sohyun Lee, and Jon Swaine, "Partially Blinded by Police," *Washington Post*, July 14, 2020.

8. "Cord Whitaker on the Roots of Today's Anti-Racism Protests," Institute for Advanced Study, June 9, 2020, www.ias.edu/ideas/whitaker-medieval-roots.

9. See, e.g., "White Women in Louisville Line Up to Form Human Shield to Protect Black Protesters," *Chicago Crusader*, June 1, 2020.

10. Assa Traoré and Geoffroy de Lagasnerie, *Le Combat Adama* (Paris: Stock, 2019).

11. Charles Delouche-Bertolasi, "Comité Adama: 'Ce n'est pas une petite victoire que nous voulons,'" *Libération*, June 9, 2020.

12. See, e.g., Michel Wieviorka, "Floyd–Traoré: La France n'est pas les États-Unis," *Ouest France*, June 12, 2020.

13. Kofi Yamgnane, "Racisme: Regarder la réalité en face," *Libération*, June 17, 2020.

14. To analyze this perspective, see Mame-Fatou Niang, "Des particularités françaises de la négrophobie," in *Racismes de France*, ed. Olivier Le Cour Grandmaison and Omar Slaouti (Paris: La Découverte, 2020), 151–169.

15. Michèle Lamont, "Comparaison du racisme aux États-Unis et en France," in *La Dignité des travailleurs: Exclusion, race, classe et immigration en France et aux États-Unis*, ed. Michèle Lamont (Paris: Presses de Sciences Po, 2002), 225–281.

16. See chapter 6.

17. Didier Fassin, "L'écho transatlantique des violences policières," *L'Obs*, June 7, 2020.

18. See Emmanuel Blanchard, "La colonialité des polices françaises," in *Police: Questions sensibles*, ed. Jérémie Gauthier and Fabien Jobard (Paris: Presses universitaires de France, 2018), 37–50.

19. To evoke police abuse, Ta-Nehisi Coates repeats "I knew" in *Between the World and Me* (New York: Spiegel & Grau, 2015), 75–76.

20. Garnette Cadogan, "Walking While Black," *Literary Hub*, July 8, 2016, https://lithub.com/walking-while-black.

21. Jean Beaman, *Citizen Outsider: Children of North African Immigrants in France* (Berkeley: University of California Press, 2017), 86–87.

22. Claire Jean Kim, *Asian Americans in an Anti-Black World* (Cambridge: Cambridge University Press, 2023), 1.

23. Frantz Fanon, *Black Skin, White Masks* (1952), trans. Charles Lam Markmann (London: Pluto Press, 1986), 109.

24. See Pierre Jacquemain, "Pas de convergence des luttes sans alternative politique," *Regards*, December 11, 2019.

25. Yves Citton and Dominique Quessada, "Du commun au comme-un," *Multitudes* 45 (2011): 12–22. *Le comme-un* and *le commun* are homophones.

26. Bruno Perreau, "L'ombre de la loi: Blanchot, Duras, Foucault," *Multitudes* 45 (2011): 95–98.

NOTES TO INTRODUCTION

27. Louis Wirth, "The Problem of Minority Groups," in *The Science of Man in the World Crisis*, ed. Ralph Linton (New York: Columbia University Press, 1945), 347.

28. See also Michel Prum, "Introduction," in *Minorités et Minoritaires*, ed. Florence Binard and Michel Prum (Paris: L'Harmattan, 2018), 7–8.

29. For a more detailed review of the French and American criteria, see chapter 2.

30. Michel Foucault, *The History of Sexuality 1: An Introduction* (1976), trans. Robert Hurley (London: Vintage, 1990), 47.

31. Denise Riley, *Am I That Name? Feminism and the Category of Women in History* (Basingstoke: Macmillan, 1988), 6–7.

32. Daniel Borrillo, "Droit et homosexualité: Une réconciliation fragile," *Droits et Cultures* 56, no. 2 (2008): 35–47.

33. See Janine Mossuz-Lavau, *Les Lois de l'amour: Les politiques de la sexualité en France, de 1950 à nos jours* (1991) (Paris: Payot, 2002) and Marie Bergström, *Les Nouvelles Lois de l'amour. Sexualité, couple et rencontres au temps du numérique* (Paris: La Découverte, 2019).

34. Guillaume Calafat, "Topographies de 'minorités': Notes sur Livourne, Marseille et Tunis au XVIIe siècle," *Liame* 24 (2012), http://journals.openedition.org/liame/271.

35. Colette Guillaumin, "Sur la notion de minorité," *L'Homme et la Société*, 77–78 (1985): 105.

36. Marylène Lieber, *Genre, Violences et Espaces publics: La vulnérabilité des femmes en question* (Paris: Presses de Sciences Po, 2008).

37. Sirma Bilge, "Le dilemme genre/culture ou comment penser la citoyenneté des femmes minoritaires au-delà de la doxa féminisme/multiculturalisme?" in Conseil du statut de la femme, *Diversité de foi, Égalité de droit*, proceedings of the conference of the same name held on March 23–24, 2006 (Quebec City: Éditions numériques du Conseil du statut de la femme, 2006), 89–98.

38. Nicolas de Condorcet, "An Essay on the Application of Probability Theory to Plurality Decision-Making" (1785), in *Foundations of Social Choice and Political Theory*, trans. and ed. Iain McLean and Fiona Hewitt (Aldershot: Edward Elgar, 1994), 120–130.

39. Guillaumin, "Sur la notion de minorité," 107.

40. Iris Marion Young, *Justice and the Politics of Difference* (Princeton, NJ: Princeton University Press, 1990).

41. Jean-Claude Charles, *Le Corps noir* (1980) (Paris: Mémoire d'encrier, 2017), 16.

42. Gilles Deleuze and Félix Guattari, *A Thousand Plateaus* (1980), trans. Brian Massumi (Minneapolis: University of Minnesota Press, 1987), 291–293.

43. Jean-Paul Sartre, *Being and Nothingness* (1943), trans. Hazel. E. Barnes (London: Routledge, 1989), 107–108.

44. Joan W. Scott, *Only Paradoxes to Offer: French Feminists and the Rights of Man* (Cambridge, MA: Harvard University Press, 1996).

45. In chapter 6, I analyze Maurice Blanchot's and Jean-Luc Nancy's arguments on being and belonging: Maurice Blanchot, *The Unavowable Community* (1983), trans. Pierre Joris (Barrytown, NY: Station Hill Press, 1988) and Jean-Luc Nancy, *The Inoperative Community* (1986), trans. Peter Connor, Lisa Garbus, Michael Holland, and Simona Sawhney (Minneapolis: University of Minnesota Press, 1991).

46. Michael Walzer, *Spheres of Justice: A Defense of Pluralism and Equality* (New York: Basic Books, 1983).

47. John Rawls, *A Theory of Justice* (1971) (Cambridge, MA: Harvard University Press, 1999).

48. Rawls, *A Theory of Justice*, 549.

49. Albert Camus, *The Just Assassins* (1949) in *Caligula & Three Other Plays*, trans. Stuart Gilbert (New York: Knopf, 1958), 273.

50. Michael Walzer in Michael Walzer and Astrid von Busekist, *Justice Is Steady Work: A Conversation on Political Theory* (2020), trans. Astrid von Busekist (Cambridge: Polity Press, 2020), 141.

51. René Schérer in René Schérer and Geoffroy de Lagasnerie, *Après tout: Entretiens sur une vie intellectuelle* (Paris: Cartouche, 2007), 53.

52. This is the case of the judicial system in the United States. See Didier Mineur, *Le Pouvoir de la majorité: Fondements et limites* (Paris: Classiques Garnier, 2017), 17.

53. Paula M. Y. Moya, *Learning from Experience: Minority Identities, Multicultural Struggles* (Berkeley: University of California Press, 2001), 136.

54. See Pierre Serna, ed., *Républiques sœurs: Le Directoire et la Révolution atlantique* (Rennes: Presses universitaires de Rennes, 2009).

55. Alexis de Tocqueville, *Democracy in America* (1835), trans. James T. Schleifer (Minneapolis: Liberty Fun, 2012), 384.

56. On the ubiquity of comparatist work and the logic of criss-crossed history, see Sheldon Pollock, "Comparison without Hegemony," in *The Benefit of Broad Horizons: Intellectual and Institutional Preconditions for a Global Social Science*, ed. Hans Joas and Barbro Klein (Leiden: Brill, 2010), 189–190.

57. See Antoine Garapon and Ioannis Papadopoulos, *Juger en Amérique et en France* (Paris: Odile Jacob, 2003), 302–305.

58. Katrina Forrester, *In the Shadow of Justice: Postwar Liberalism and the Remaking of Political Philosophy* (Princeton, NJ: Princeton University Press, 2019).

59. Mathieu Hauchecorne, *La Gauche américaine en France: La réception de John Rawls et des théories de la justice* (Paris: CNRS Éditions, 2019).

60. Michael Omi and Howard Winant, *Racial Formations in the United States* (London: Routledge, 1994), 70.

61. Didier Eribon, *D'une révolution conservatrice et de ses effets sur la gauche française* (Paris: Léo Scheer, 2007).

62. See Igor Martinache and Frédéric Sawicki, eds., *La Fin des partis?* (Paris: Presses universitaires de France, 2020).

NOTES TO INTRODUCTION

63. Loïc Wacquant, *Punishing the Poor: The Neoliberal Government of Social Insecurity* (Durham, NC: Duke University Press, 2009).

64. "Cancel culture" designates the fact of being, actually or supposedly, vilified for an act or word that conflicts with a minority culture. Glenn Greenwald, "How 'Cancel Culture' Repeatedly Emerged in My Attempt to Make a Film about Tennis Legend Martina Navratilova," *The Intercept*, July 14, 2020, https://theintercept.com /2020/07/14/cancel-culture-martina-navratilova-documentary/.

65. This chapter is born of an early contribution on the topic: Bruno Perreau, "Reflections on a New Ethnonational Counterrevolution," in *On the Subject of Ethnonationalism*, ed. Joshua Branciforte and Ramsey McGlazer (New York: Fordham University Press, 2023), 263–296.

66. Bruno Perreau, *Queer Theory: The French Response* (Stanford, CA: Stanford University Press, 2018), 148–157.

67. Supreme Court of the United States, *Students for Fair Admissions Inc. v. President & Fellows of Harvard College*, 600 U.S., 20-1199, June 29, 2023 and *Students for Fair Admissions, Inc. v. University of North Carolina*, 600 U.S., 21-707, June 29, 2023.

68. Sara Rimer and Karen W. Arenson, "Top Colleges Take More Blacks, but Which Ones?" *New York Times*, June 24, 2004.

69. William Julius Wilson, *The Truly Disadvantaged* (Chicago: University of Chicago Press, 1990).

70. Jeannie Suk Gersen, "The Uncomfortable Truth about Affirmative Action and Asian-Americans," *New Yorker*, August 10, 2017.

71. See Catherine Koerner and Soma Pillay, "Conceptualising Cultural Identity: The Great Divide," in *Governance and Multiculturalism: The White Elephant of Social Construction and Cultural Identities*, ed. Catherine Koerner and Soma Pillay (London: Palgrave Macmillan, 2020), 121–180.

72. Jean-Luc Nancy, "The Compearance: From the Existence of 'Communism' to the Community of 'Existence,'" trans. Tracy B. Strong, *Political Theory* 20, no. 3 (August 1992): 371–398.

73. A first version of this chapter was published in an edited volume: Bruno Perreau, "Les analogies du genre: Différance, intrasectionnalité et droit," in *Genre, Droit et Politique*, ed. Charles Bosvieux-Onyekwelu and Véronique Mottier (Paris: LGDJ, 2022), 191–214.

74. Kimberlé Crenshaw, "Mapping the Margins: Intersectionality, Identity Politics, and Violence against Women of Color," *Stanford Law Review* 43, no. 6 (July 1991): 1241–1299.

75. Dominique Bourg and Jean-Louis Schlegel, *Parer aux risques de demain: Le principe de précaution* (Paris: Seuil, 2001), 33.

CHAPTER 1

1. Michael Walzer, *Just and Unjust Wars: A Moral Argument with Historical Illustrations* (New York: Basic Books, 1977).

2. Walzer, *Spheres of Justice.*

3. Robert Nozick, *Anarchy, State and Utopia* (New York: Harper & Row, 1974).

4. Michael Walzer, "In Defense of Equality," in *Twenty-Five Years of Dissent* (London: Routledge, 2021), 297–313.

5. Developed in Canada starting in the mid-1980s, "reasonable accommodation" refers to the compromise measures that the legislature has and judges use when the protection of one social group infringes on that of another. I devote several paragraphs to it in this chapter.

6. Walzer, *Spheres of Justice*, 3.

7. Walzer, 279.

8. Walzer, 239.

9. Walzer, 238.

10. Walzer, xv.

11. Walzer, 11.

12. Walzer, 311.

13. Walzer, 3.

14. Walzer, 4.

15. Walzer, 4.

16. Walzer, 5.

17. Walzer, 11.

18. Rawls, *Theory of Justice*, 17–22.

19. That is what Bertrand Guillarme is after: Bertrand Guillarme, *Rawls et l'égalité démocratique* (Paris: Presses universitaires de France, 1999), 93ff.

20. Rawls, *Theory of Justice*, 80.

21. Walzer, *Spheres of Justice*, 29.

22. Michael Walzer, "The Communitarian Critique of Liberalism," in Michael Walzer, *Thinking Politically: Essays in Political Theory*, ed. David Miller (New Haven, CT: Yale University Press, 2007), 112.

23. Walzer, *Spheres of Justice*, 7–8.

24. Walzer, 8.

25. Walzer, 29.

26. Walzer, 259–262.

27. Walzer, 17.

28. Susan Moller Okin, *Justice, Gender, and the Family* (New York: Basic Books, 1989), 111–117.

NOTES TO CHAPTER 1

29. Walzer, *Spheres of Justice*, 318.

30. Michael Walzer, "Préface à l'édition française," *Sphères de justice*, iv.

31. Walzer, *Spheres of Justice*, v.

32. Michael Walzer, *The Struggle for a Decent Politics: On "Liberal" as an Adjective* (New Haven, CT: Yale University Press, 2023), 3–4.

33. Walzer, *The Struggle for a Decent Politics*, 4.

34. Walzer, 98.

35. Walzer, 148.

36. He defined his political agenda in "Which Socialism?" *Dissent* (Summer 2010), https://www.dissentmagazine.org/issue/winter-2010.

37. See Jacques Delors's former advisor's work: Justine Lacroix, *Michael Walzer: Le pluralisme et l'universel* (Paris: Michalon, 2001).

38. Olivier Mongin, "Paul Ricœur et la revue *Esprit*," *La Revue des revues* 66, no. 2 (2021): 98–113.

39. Quoted by Hauchecorne in *La Gauche américaine en France*, 158.

40. Michael Walzer, *Pluralisme et Démocratie*, ed. Joël Roman, collective trans. (Paris: Éditions Esprit, 1997).

41. Hauchecorne, *La Gauche américaine en France*, 155.

42. Michael Walzer, *Exodus and Revolution* (New York: Basic Books, 1985).

43. Michael Walzer, *The Revolution of the Saints: A Study in the Origins of Radical Politics* (Cambridge, MA: Harvard University Press, 1965).

44. Michael Walzer, *Regicide and Revolution: Speeches at the Trial of Louis XVI* (Cambridge: Cambridge University Press, 1974).

45. Michael Walzer, *Interpretation and Social Criticism* (Cambridge, MA: Harvard University Press, 1987).

46. Michael Walzer, *The Company of Critics: Social Criticism and Political Commitment in the Twentieth Century* (New York: Basic Books, 1988).

47. See, e.g., Christian Delacampagne, "Quelle justice voulons-nous?" *Le Monde*, November 28, 1997.

48. Michael Walzer, *On Toleration* (New Haven, CT: Yale University Press, 1997).

49. Joël Roman, "Un multiculturalisme à la française?" *Esprit* 212, no. 6 (June 1995): 145–160.

50. For a synthesis, see Francesco Fistetti, *Théories du multiculturalisme: Un parcours entre philosophie et sciences sociales*, trans. Philippe Chanial and Marilisa Preziosi (Paris: La Découverte, 2009).

51. Philippe Mangeot "Petite histoire du 'politiquement correct,'" *Vacarme* 1 (1997): 57–59.

52. See Marie-Christine Granjon "Le regard en biais: Attitudes françaises et multiculturalisme américain (1990–1993)," *Vingtième Siècle* 43 (1994): 18–29.

53. Irène Théry, "Le CUS en question," *Notes de la Fondation Saint Simon* (October 1997): 26.

54. See, e.g., the contributions of Alain Finkielkraut, Irène Théry, Catherine Labrusse-Riou, and Caroline Eliacheff in *Esprit* special issues, "Malaise dans la filiation" (1996) and "L'un et l'autre sexe" (2001), as well as the retranscription of Irène Théry's report to Fondation Saint-Simon. For a complete analysis, see Camille Robcis, *The Law of Kinship: Anthropology, Psychoanalysis, and the Family in France* (Ithaca, NY: Cornell University Press, 2013).

55. Alain Minc, "Égalité ou équité?" *Le Monde*, January 5, 1995; Jean-François Théry and François Stasse, *Sur le principe d'égalité: Rapport au Conseil d'État* (Paris: La Documentation française, 1997).

56. Axel Honneth took over Walzer's analysis in terms of spheres. *Freedom's Right: The Social Foundations of Democratic Life*, trans. Joseph Ganahl (New York: Columbia University Press, 2014).

57. See in particular Ernst Cassirer, *The Philosophy of Symbolic Forms*, vol. 3: *Phenomenology of Knowledge* (1929), trans. Ralph Manheim (New Haven, CT: Yale University Press, 1957) and Pierre Bourdieu, "The Market of Symbolic Goods" (1971) in Pierre Bourdieu, *The Field of Cultural Production: Essays on Art and Literature*, ed. Randal Johnson, trans. Rupert Swyer (New York: Columbia University Press, 1993), 112–141.

58. Hauchecorne, *La Gauche américaine en France*, 157.

59. Luc Boltanski, *Love and Justice as Competences: Three Essays on the Sociology of Action*, trans. Catherine Porter (Cambridge: Polity, 2012), 110–113.

60. Pierre Bourdieu and Loïc Wacquant, "On the Cunning of Imperialist Reason" (1988), *Theory, Culture & Society* 16, no. 1 (1999): 51.

61. Hans O. Staub, "The Tyranny of Minorities," *Daedalus* 109, no. 3 (summer 1980): 159–168.

62. See Éric Fassin, "Sexual Event: From Clarence Thomas to Monica Lewinsky, *differences: A Journal of Feminist Cultural Studies* 13, no. 2 (2002): 127–158.

63. Philippe Raynaud, "De la tyrannie de la majorité à la tyrannie des minorités," *Le Débat* 69, no. 2 (1992): 56.

64. Raynaud, "De la tyrannie," 55 (emphasis added).

65. Raynaud, 56.

66. Tocqueville, *Democracy in America*, 413–414.

67. "Federalist no. 10. The Same Subject Continued (The Union as a Safeguard against Domestic Faction and Insurrection). November 22, 1787," in Alexander Hamilton, James Madison and John Jay, *The Federalist Papers*, ed. Michael A. Genovese (New York: Palgrave MacMillan, 2009), 49.

68. Donald J. Maletz, "Tocqueville's Tyranny of the Majority Reconsidered," *Journal of Politics* 64, no. 3 (2002): 755–756.

69. Tocqueville, *Democracy in America*, 418.

NOTES TO CHAPTER 1

70. Tocqueville does not apply his reasoning to Indigenous populations whose unhappy but programmed disappearance he simply describes as an effect of the yoke and territorial conquest of European colonizers. Tocqueville, *Democracy in America*, 540.

71. Tocqueville, 25.

72. Walzer, *Spheres of Justice*, 28.

73. Walzer, 62.

74. Walzer, 331.

75. Walzer, 316.

76. Walzer, 321.

77. For example, Michael Walzer, "La façon juste de dire non à la guerre," *Le Monde*, January 29, 2003, and "Pour une sanction par les urnes," *Le Monde*, May 17, 2004.

78. Florent Guénard, "L'universalisme démocratique selon Walzer," *Revue internationale de philosophie* 274, no. 4 (2015): 399–414.

79. Simon Wuhl, *Michael Walzer et l'Empreinte du judaïsme* (Lormont: Le Bord de l'eau, 2017).

80. Walzer and von Busekist, *Justice Is Steady Work*, 116–133.

81. Walzer and von Busekist, 146–165.

82. Bruno Latour, *An Inquiry into Modes of Existence: An Anthropology of the Moderns*, trans. Catherine Porter (Cambridge, MA: Harvard University Press, 2013), 63–64.

83. Walzer, "Préface à l'édition française," in *Sphères de justice*, iv.

84. Walzer, *Spheres of Justice*, 292.

85. Benjamin Boudou, *Politique de l'hospitalité* (Paris: CNRS éditions, 2017), 217.

86. Walzer and von Busekist, *Justice Is Steady Work*, 124–125.

87. Paul May, *Philosophies du multiculturalisme* (Paris: Presses de Sciences Po, 2016), 20–23.

88. Chandran Kukathas, *The Liberal Archipelago: A Theory of Diversity and Freedom* (Oxford: Oxford University Press, 2003).

89. Walzer, *Spheres of Justice*, 28, 29.

90. Supreme Court of Canada, *Ontario Human Rights Commission and O'Malley v. Simpsons-Sears Ltd.*, 2 SCR, 1985.

91. See Léopold Vanbellingen, "L'accommodement raisonnable de la religion dans le secteur public: Analyse du cadre juridique belge au regard de l'expérience canadienne," *Revue interdisciplinaire d'études juridiques* 75, no. 2 (2015): 228.

92. Ariane Le Moing, "La crise des accommodements raisonnables au Québec: Quel impact sur l'identité collective," *Mémoire(s), identité(s), marginalité(s) dans le monde occidental contemporain* 16 (2016), https://doi.org/10.4000/mimmoc.2458.

93. Supreme Court of Canada, *Multani v. Commission scolaire Marguerite-Bourgeoys*, 1 SCR. 256, 2006.

94. Hérouxville Municipality, "Standards," 2007, quoted in Khadiyatoulah Fall and Georges Vignaux, *Images de l'autre et de soi: Les accommodements raisonnables entre préjugés et réalité* (Quebec City: Presses de l'Université Laval, 2008), 4.

95. For a detailed analysis see Éléonore Lépinard, "Écriture juridique et régulation du religieux minoritaire en France et au Canada," *Revue française de science politique* 64, no. 4 (2014): 669–688.

96. Howard Adelman and Pierre Anctil, eds., *Religion, Culture, and the State: Reflections on the Bouchard-Taylor Report* (Toronto: University of Toronto Press, 2011).

97. Tatiana Gründler, "La théorie des accommodements raisonnables et sa réception en France," *Délibérée* 2 (2017): 60–64.

98. Amélie Barras, Jennifer A. Selby, and Lori G. Beaman, "Rethinking Canadian Discourses of 'Reasonable Accommodation,'" *Social Inclusion* 6, no. 2 (2018): 162–172.

99. Janie Pélabay, "Gouvernance de la diversité et valeurs communes: Une analyse à partir du rapport Bouchard-Taylor," presented at the 12e Congrès de l'Association française de science politique, thematic section 65, July 2013, https://hal-sciencespo .archives-ouvertes.fr/hal-00972736/document.

100. Sarah Song, "Majority, Norms, Multiculturalism, and Gender Equality," *American Political Science Review* 99, no. 4 (2005): 473–489.

101. Supreme Court of the United States, *Santa Clara Pueblo v. Martinez*, 436 U.S. 49, May 15, 1978.

102. New York County Supreme Court, *People v. Chen*, no. 87–7774, December 2, 1988.

103. *People v. Chen*, 476–484.

104. Susan Moller Okin, "Feminism and Multiculturalism: Some Tensions," *Ethics* 108, no. 4 (July 1998): 661–684.

105. Moller Okin, "Feminism," 670.

106. Will Kymlicka, *Liberalism, Community, and Culture* (Oxford: Clarendon Press, 1989), 196.

107. Patrick Savidan analyzes this argument in "Multiculturalisme libéral et monoculturalisme pluriel," *Raisons politiques* 35, no. 3 (2009): 16.

108. Will Kymlicka, *Multicultural Citizenship: A Liberal Theory of Minority Rights* (Oxford: Oxford University Press, 1995), 8.

109. See Olivier Nay, *Histoire des idées politiques: La pensée politique occidentale de l'Antiquité à nos jours* (Paris: Armand Colin, 2016), 877–878.

110. Walzer, *Spheres of Justice*, 313.

111. Walzer, 314.

112. Walzer, 312.

113. Walzer, 312.

114. Walzer, 21–25.

115. Walzer, 313.

NOTES TO CHAPTER 1

116. Walzer, 313–314.

117. Astrid von Busekist, "Territorial Pluralism and Language Communities," in *Forms of Pluralism and Democratic Constitutionalism*, ed. Andrew Arato, Jean L. Cohen, and Astrid von Busekist (New York: Columbia University Press, 2018), 348.

118. Savidan, "Multiculturalisme libéral et monoculturalisme pluriel," 27–29.

119. Françoise Gaspard and Farhad Khosrokhavar, *Le Foulard et la République* (Paris: La Découverte, 1995).

120. Nilüfer Göle, *Musulmans au quotidien: Une enquête européenne sur les controverses autour de l'islam* (Paris: La Découverte, 2015).

121. See Ahmed Djouder's novel, *Désintégration* (Paris: Stock, 2006).

122. See Elise Voguet and Anne Troadec, eds., *Minorités en Islam, islam en minorité* (Paris: Diacritiques éditions, 2021).

123. Christine Delphy, *L'Ennemi principal. 1. Économie politique du patriarcat* (Paris: Syllepse, 2001), 53.

124. Walzer, *Exodus and Revolution*, 40.

125. James Bohman, "Domination, Global Harms, and the Problem of Silent Citizenship: Toward a Republican Theory of Global Justice," *Citizenship Studies* 19, no. 5 (September 2025): 3.

126. Plato, *The Republic* (365 BCE), book II, trans. Tom Griffith, ed. G. R. F. Ferrari (Cambridge: Cambridge University Press, 2000), 38–40.

127. Niccolò Machiavelli, *The Florence History* (1532), book II, chapters XI–XIV, trans. Ninian Hill Thomson (London: Constable, 1906), 93–100.

128. John Stuart Mill, "On the Connexion between Justice and Utility" (1861), in John Stuart Mill, *Utilitarianism and On Liberty*, ed. Mary Warnock (Malden, MA: Blackwell, 2003), 216–234.

129. Céline Spector, *Éloges de l'injustice: La philosophie face à la déraison* (Paris: Seuil, 2016), 12.

130. Spector, *Éloges de l'injustice*, 224.

131. Emmanuel Renault, *The Experience of Injustice: A Theory of Recognition* (2004), trans. Richard A. Lynch (New York: Columbia University Press, 2019), 21–23.

132. Judith Shklar, *Legalism: An Essay on Law, Morals and Politics* (Cambridge, MA: Harvard University Press, 1964), 116–117.

133. Renault, *The Experience of Injustice*, 6.

134. Amartya Sen, *The Idea of Justice* (Cambridge, MA: Harvard University Press, 2009), vii.

135. Miranda Fricker, *Epistemic Injustice: Power and the Ethics of Knowledge* (Oxford: Oxford University Press), 2007, 90.

136. Judith Butler, *Antigone's Claim: Kinship between Life and Death* (New York: Columbia University Press, 2000), 13–14.

137. Marla Brettschneider, *Democratic Theorizing from the Margins* (Philadelphia: Temple University Press, 2002), 159–172.

138. Jean-François Lyotard, in Jean-François Lyotard and Jean-Loup Thébaud, *Just Gaming* (1979), trans. Brian Massumi (Minneapolis: University of Minnesota Press, 1985), 20.

139. Philip Pettit, *Just Freedom: A Moral Compass for a Complex World* (New York: W. W. Norton, 2014), xvii–xxi.

140. Nancy Fraser, *Fortunes of Feminism: From State-Managed Capitalism to Neoliberal Crisis* (London: Verso, 2020), 255.

141. Renault, *The Experience of Injustice*, 92–93.

142. Nancy Fraser, *Scales of Justice: Reimagining Political Space in a Globalized World* (New York: Columbia University Press, 2010), 146.

143. Jacob Bor, Atheendar S. Venkataramani, David R. Williams, and Alexander C. Tsai, "Police Killings and Their Spillover Effects on the Mental Health of Black Americans: A Population-Based, Quasi-Experimental Study," *Lancet* 392, no. 10144 (July 2018), https://www.thelancet.com/journals/lancet/article/PIIS0140 -6736(18)31130-9.

144. Meredith Warden, "'Sitting in the Room with History': Lynchings, Police Brutality, and Spectacle," *On Second Thought* 17 (2020): https://digitalcommons.oberlin .edu/ost/17.

145. Sandy Alexandre, *The Properties of Violence: Claims to Ownership in Representations of Lynching* (Jackson: University Press of Mississippi, 2012): 101.

146. Pablo Oyarzún, *Doing Justice: Three Essays on Walter Benjamin*, trans. Stephen Gingerich (Cambridge: Polity Press, 2020), 79–80.

147. Joan W. Scott, "The Evidence of Experience," *Critical Inquiry* 17, no. 4 (July 1, 1991): 790.

148. Caroline S. Hau, "On Representing Others. Intellectuals, Pedagogy, and the Uses of Errors," in *Reclaiming Identity*, ed. Paula M. L. Moya and Michael R. Hames-García (Berkeley: University of California Press, 2000), 156.

149. Iris Marion Young, *Responsibility for Justice* (Oxford: Oxford University Press, 2011), 44.

150. Young, *Responsibility*, 100, 93.

151. Judith Shklar, *The Faces of Injustice* (New Haven, CT: Yale University Press, 1990), 121–122.

152. I am extracting these five elements from the five faces of oppression that Iris Marion Young highlights in *Justice and the Politics of Difference*, 48, 53, 56, 58, 61.

153. Danielle Allen, Yochai Benkler, Leah Downey, Rebecca Henderson, and Josh Simons, eds., *A Political Economy of Justice* (Chicago: University of Chicago Press, 2022), 7–12.

154. Alain Bihr and Roland Pfefferkorn, *Le Système des inégalités* (Paris: La Découverte, 2021), 50–56.

NOTES TO CHAPTER 2

155. Michael Walzer, *Arguing about War* (New Haven, CT: Yale University Press, 2004), 188.

156. Walzer, *Spheres of Justice*, 315.

157. Michael Walzer, *Obligations: Essays on Disobedience, War, and Citizenship* (Cambridge, MA: Harvard University Press, 1970), 205.

158. Here Michael Walzer is referring to sex, class, religion, race, and political beliefs. Michael Walzer, "The Communitarian Critique of Liberalism," *Political Theory* 18, no. 1 (February 1990): 15.

159. Walzer, "Communitarian," 17.

160. On the conditions of critical citizenship in France, see Janie Pélabay and Réjane Sénac, "French Critical Citizenship: Between Philosophical Enthusiasm and Political Uncertainty," *French Politics* 17 (2019): 407–432.

161. Geoffroy de Lagasnerie, *Juger: L'État pénal face à la sociologie* (Paris: Fayard, 2016), 105.

162. De Lagasnerie, *Juger*, 105.

163. Walzer, *The Struggle for a Decent Politics*, 151.

CHAPTER 2

1. Romain Telliez, *Les Institutions de la France médiévale: XIe–XVe siècle* (Paris: Armand Colin, 2009), 72.

2. *Oxford English Dictionary*, s.v. "minority (n. & adj.)," July 2023.

3. For example see Ethan Putterman, "Rousseau on Agenda-Setting and Majority Rule," *American Political Science Review*, 97, no. 3 (2003): 459–469.

4. Jon Elster, "Nested Majorities," in *Majority Decisions: Principles and Practices*, ed. Stéphanie Novak and Jon Elster (Cambridge: Cambridge University Press, 2014), 34–42.

5. Nancy Hartsock, "Rethinking Modernism: Minority vs. Majority Theories," *Cultural Critique* 7 (1987): 187–206.

6. See Françoise Lionnet and Shu-mei Shih, "Thinking through the Minor, Transnationally," in *Minor Transnationalism*, ed. Françoise Lionnet and Shu-mei Shih (Durham, NC: Duke University Press, 2005), 7.

7. Michel Foucault, "La naissance d'un monde" (1969), in *Dits et Écrits I, 1954–1975* (Paris: Gallimard, 2001), 814.

8. Ernesto Laclau, *Emancipation(s)* (London: Verso, 1996), 43.

9. Robin Medard Inghilterra, "L'intelligibilité par l'harmonisation des définitions de la discrimination en droit interne," in *La Lutte contre les discriminations à l'épreuve de son effectivité. Rapport de la Fédération interdisciplinaire de Nanterre en droit au Défenseur des droits: Annexes*, ed. Tatiana Gründler and Jean-Marc Thouvenin (Nanterre: Publications du Défenseur des droits, 2016), 165–188.

10. "Loi 1972–546 du 1er juillet 1972 relative à la lutte contre le racisme," *Journal Officiel de la République française*, July 2, 1972.

11. Directive 76/207/EEC, February 9, 1976.

12. For a complete critical review, see Robin Medard Inghilterra, *La Réalisation du droit de la non-discrimination* (Paris: LGDJ, 2022).

13. The *Défenseur des droits* is an independent administrative authority created by the constitutional revision of July 23, 2008. Defined in Article 71–1 of the French Constitution, the *Défenseur des droits* ensures respect for rights and freedoms. Daniel Borrillo and Vincent-Arnaud Chappe, "La Haute Autorité de Lutte contre les Discriminations et pour l'Égalité: Un laboratoire juridique éphémère?" *Revue française d'administration publique* 139, no. 3 (2011): 369–380.

14. Loi 2008–496 du 27 mai 2008 portant diverses dispositions d'adaptation au droit communautaire dans le domaine de la lutte contre les discriminations, *Journal Officiel de la République française*, May 28, 2008.

15. Jo Freeman, "How 'Sex' Got into Title VII: Persistent Opportunism as a Maker of Public Policy," *Law and Inequality: A Journal of Theory and Practice* 9, no. 2 (March 1991): 163–184.

16. Supreme Court of the United States, *Bostock v. Clayton County*, 590 U.S., June 17, 2020. For more details, see chapter 7.

17. U.S. District Court for the Southern District of New York, *Rogers v. American Airlines, Inc.*, 527 F. Supp. 229, December 1, 1981.

18. Iyiola Solanke, "The Anti-Stigma Principle-Centralising Intersectionality in the Theory of Anti-Discrimination Law," in *Multiplication des critères de discrimination: Enjeux, effets et perspectives: Actes du colloque des 18 et 19 janvier 2018* (Paris: Publications du Défenseur des droits, 2018), 145.

19. European Court of Justice, *Tadao Maruko v. Versorgungsanstalt der deutschen Bühnen*, C-267/06, January 1, 2008.

20. European Court of Human Rights, *Clift v. United Kingdom*, July 13, 2010, sections 56–58.

21. Supreme Court of the United States, *Griggs v. Duke Power Co.*, 401 U.S. 424, March 8, 1971.

22. Supreme Court of the United States, *Washington v. Davis*, 426 U.S. 229, June 7, 1976.

23. Supreme Court of the United States, *Wards Cove Packing v. Atonio*, 490 U.S. 642, June 5, 1989.

24. Tarunabh Khaitan, *A Theory of Discrimination Law* (Oxford: Oxford University Press, 2015), 73–76.

25. Loi 2008–496, May 27, 2008.

26. European Court of Human Rights, *Opuz v. Turkey*, June 9, 2009.

27. European Court of Human Rights, *D.H. and Others v. Czech Republic*, November 13, 2007, section 175.

28. European Court of Human Rights, *Nachova and Others v. Bulgaria*, July 6, 2005, section 168.

NOTES TO CHAPTER 2

29. Article L1132–1 refers directly to the law of May 27, 2008.

30. Robin Medard Inghilterra, "Le droit à la non-discrimination fait peau neuve: Brèves considérations sur les incidences de la loi de modernisation de la justice du XXIe siècle," *Revue des droits et libertés fondamentaux*, chronique no. 27 (2016): 4 and 5.

31. Serge Slama, "La disparité des régimes de lutte contre les discriminations: Un frein à leur efficacité?" *La Revue des droits de l'homme* 9 (2016), https://doi.org/10.4000/revdh.2061.

32. Robin Medard Inghilterra, "Fragmentation et défragmentation du droit antidiscriminatoire," *La Revue des droits de l'homme* 15 (2018), https://doi.org/10.4000/revdh.5148.

33. Robin Medard Inghilterra, "Les écueils du contentieux antidiscriminatoire au prisme de la jurisprudence canadienne," in Gründler and Thouvenin, eds., *La Lutte contre les discriminations à l'épreuve de son effectivité*, 17.

34. Jules Deschênes, "Qu'est-ce qu'une minorité?" *Les Cahiers de droit* 27, no. 1 (March 1986): 255–291.

35. Helen Mayer Hacker, "Women as Minority Group," *Social Forces* 30, no. 1 (1951): 60–69.

36. Baruch Spinoza, *The Ethics* (1677), trans. William Hale White, revised by Amelia Hutchinson Sterling (London: Macmillan, 1949), 136.

37. The law 2016-832 of June 24, 2016 (aimed at combating discrimination based on social insecurity) introduced the motif of "economic vulnerability" into French criminal and labor law.

38. See Wilson, *The Truly Disadvantaged*, 112–118.

39. Nathalie Bajos and Stéphanie Hennette-Vauchez, "L'essor du droit de la non-discrimination en France: Regards croisés entre droit et sciences sociales," in *Multiplication des critères de discrimination*, 15–19.

40. Daniel Borrillo, *Droit d'asile et homosexualité: Comment prouver l'intime?* (Paris: LGDJ, 2021).

41. Abdellatif Chaouite, Toriki Lehartel and Nathalie Bessard, "L'accompagnement juridique des personnes homosexuelles en demande d'asile," *Rhizome* 60, no. 2 (2016): 7.

42. Jane Elliott, *A Collar in My Pocket: Blue Eyes/Brown Eyes Exercise* (New York: CreateSpace Independent Publishing, 2016).

43. Nella Larsen, *Passing* (New York: Alfred A. Knopf, 1929).

44. That is what Eve Sedgwick called the "glass closet" in *Epistemology of the Closet* (Berkeley: University of California Press, 1990).

45. In 2002, she sued Howard University, which had turned her down for a scholarship, claiming discrimination against her as a white person. Rachel Dolezal also maintained that she was raised in a teepee owing to her Native American origins.

46. Asad Haider, *Mistaken Identity: Race and Class in the Age of Trump* (London: Verso, 2022), 81.

47. Annie Linskey and Amy Gardner, "Elizabeth Warren Apologizes for Calling Herself Native American," *Washington Post*, February 5, 2019.

48. Joshua Jamerson, "Elizabeth Warren Apologizes for DNA Test, Identifying as Native American," *Wall Street Journal*, August 19, 2019.

49. Xavier Bioy, "L'ambiguïté du concept de non-discrimination," in *Le Droit à la non-discrimination au sens de la Convention européenne des droits de l'homme*, ed. Frédéric Sudre and Hélène Surrel (Brussels: Bruylant, 2008), 51–84.

50. Thomas Piketty, *Mesurer le racisme, vaincre les discriminations* (Paris: Seuil, 2022), 43–44.

51. Piketty, *Mesurer le racisme*, 46.

52. Tanya Katerí Hernández, "Latino Anti-Black Bias and the Census Categorization of Latinos: Race, Ethnicity, or Other?" in *Critical Dialogues in Latinx Studies: A Reader*, ed. Ana Y. Ramos-Zayas and Mérida M. Rúa (Durham, NC: Duke University Press, 2021), 361–372.

53. The term comes from the theories of German anatomist Johann Blumenbach in the late eighteenth century; it arrived with nineteenth-century racialist pseudoscience and helped justify racial segregation and sort migration. Nell Irvin Painter, "Why White People Are Called 'Caucasians,'" paper presented at the Fifth Annual Gilder Lehrman Center International Conference at Yale University, November 7–8, 2003; Yolanda Moses, "Why Do We Keep Using the Word 'Caucasian'?" *Sapiens*, February 1, 2017, https://www.sapiens.org/culture/caucasian-terminology-origin/.

54. Moya, *Learning from Experience*, 131.

55. Moya, 131.

56. Éric Fassin, *L'Inversion de la question homosexuelle* (Paris: Éd. Amsterdam, 2005).

57. Opportunity Insights, https://opportunityinsights.org.

58. Raj Chetty, Nathaniel Hendren, Maggie R. Jones, and Sonya R. Porter, "Race and Economic Opportunity in the United States: An Intergenerational Perspective," *Quarterly Journal of Economics* 135, no. 2 (May 2020): 711–783.

59. Brenda Major, Cheryl R. Kaiser, Laurie T. O'Brien, and Shannon K. McCoy, "Perceived Discrimination as Worldview Threat or Worldview Confirmation: Implications for Self-Esteem," *Journal of Personality and Social Psychology* 92, no. 6 (2007): 1068–1086.

60. Donald P. Haidel-Marker and Kenneth J. Meier, "The Politics of Gay and Lesbian Rights: Expanding the Scope of Conflict," *Journal of Politics* 58 (1996): 332–349.

61. Aron Rodrigue, "The Jew as the Original 'Other': Difference, Antisemitism and Race," in *Doing Race: 21 Essays for the 21st Century*, ed. Hazel Rose Markus and Paula Moya (New York: W. W. Norton, 2010), 187.

62. Historian Florence Tamagne spoke of "ersatz tolerance" regarding the treatment of gay men and lesbians in the UK between the wars in her *Histoire de l'homosexualité en Europe: Berlin, Londres, Paris: 1919–1939* (Paris: Seuil, 2000), 453–531.

63. Serge Moscovici, *Social Influence and Social Change* (New York: Academic Press, 1976); *Psychologie des minorités actives* (Paris: Presses universitaires de France, 1979).

NOTES TO CHAPTER 2

64. Solomon E. Asch, "Effects of Group Pressure upon the Modification and Distortion of Judgment," in *Groups, Leadership and Men*, ed. Harold Guetzkow (Pittsburgh: Carnegie Press, 1951), 177–190.

65. Serge Moscovici and Marisa Zavalloni, "The Group as a Polarizer of Attitudes," *Journal of Personality and Social Psychology* 12 (1969): 125–135.

66. Moscovici, *Social Influence and Social Change*, 75–77.

67. Moscovici, 98.

68. Moscovici, *Psychologie des minorités actives*, 255.

69. Gabriel Mugny and Stamos Papastamou, "When Rigidity Does Not Fail: Individualization and Psychologization as Resistances to the Diffusion of Minority Innovations," *European Journal of Social Psychology* 10, no. 1 (1980): 43–61.

70. Christine M. Smith, R. Scott Tindale, and Bernard L. Dugoni, "Minority and Majority Influence in Freely Interacting Groups: Qualitative versus Quantitative Differences," *British Journal of Social Psychology* 35 (1996): 137–149.

71. Charlan J. Nemeth, "The Differential Contributions of Majority and Minority Influence," *Psychological Review* 93 (1986): 23–32.

72. Valerie Purdie-Vaughns and Richard P. Eibach, "Intersectional Invisibility: The Distinctive Advantages and Disadvantages of Multiple Subordinate-Group Identities," *Sex Roles* 59, no 5–6 (2008): 377–391.

73. Clarissa I. Cortland, Maureen A. Craig, Jenessa R. Shapiro, Jennifer A. Richeson, Rebecca Neel, and Noah J. Goldstein, "Solidarity through Shared Disadvantage: Highlighting Shared Experiences of Discrimination Improves Relations between Stigmatized Groups," *Journal of Personality and Social Psychology* 113, no. 4 (2017): 547–567.

74. Natalie M. Daumeyer, Ivuoma N. Onyeador, and Jennifer A. Richeson, "Does Shared Gender Group Membership Mitigate the Effect of Implicit Bias Attributions on Accountability for Gender-Based Discrimination?" *Personality and Social Psychology Bulletin* 47, no. 9 (September 2021): 1343–1357.

75. Melanie Trost, Anne Maass, and Douglas Kenrick, "Minority Influence: Personal Relevance Biases Cognitive Processes and Reverses Private Acceptance," *Journal of Experimental Social Psychology* 28, no. 3 (1992): 234–254.

76. Elisabeth Noelle-Neumann, "The Spiral of Silence: A Theory of Public Opinion," *Journal of Communication* 24, no. 2 (June 1974): 43–51.

77. Katherine Miller, *Communication Theories: Perspectives, Processes, and Contexts* (New York: McGraw-Hill, 2005), 235, 279.

78. Michael Lipsky, "Protest as Political Resource," *American Political Science Review* 62, no. 4 (December 1968): 1150.

79. Michael W. Kraus and Jacinth X. Tan, "Americans Overestimate Social Class Mobility," *Journal of Experimental Social Psychology* 58 (May 2015): 101–111.

80. Michael W. Kraus, Ivuoma N. Onyeador, Natalie M. Daumeyer, Julian M. Rucker, and Jennifer A. Richeson, "The Misperception of Racial Economic Inequality," *Perspectives on Psychological Science* 14, no. 6 (2019): 899–921.

81. Entung Enya Kuo, Michael W. Kraus, and Jennifer A. Richeson, "High-Status Exemplars and the Misperception of the Asian-White Wealth Gap," *Social Psychological and Personality Science* 11, no. 3 (April 2020): 397–405.

82. Mesmin Destin, Michelle Rheinschmidt-Same, and Jennifer A. Richeson, "Status-Based Identity: A Conceptual Approach Integrating the Social Psychological Study of Socioeconomic Status and Identity," *Perspectives on Psychological Science* 12, no. 2 (March 2017): 270–289.

83. See Patrice Mann, *L'Action collective: Mobilisation et organisation des minorités actives* (Paris: Armand Colin, 1991), 133.

84. Elmie Nekmat and William J. Gonzenbach, "Multiple Opinion Climates in Online Forums: Role of Website Source Reference and Within-Forum Opinion Congruency," *Journalism & Mass Communication Quarterly* 90, no. 4 (2013): 736–756.

85. Maureen A. Craig, Julian M. Rucker, and Jennifer A. Richeson, "Racial and Political Dynamics of an Approaching 'Majority-Minority' United States," *Annals of the American Academy of Political and Social Science* 677, no. 1 (April 2018): 204–214.

86. See chapters 4 and 5.

87. For a synthesis of the arguments, see Alex Mahoudeau, *La Panique woke: Anatomie d'une offensive réactionnaire* (Paris: Textuel, 2022).

88. Supreme Court of the United States, *Grutter v. Bollinger et al.*, 539 U.S. 306, June 23, 2003.

89. See Nathan Glazer, *We Are All Multiculturalists Now* (Cambridge, MA: Harvard University Press, 1997).

90. Supreme Court of the United States, *Brown v. Board of Education of Topeka*, 347 U.S. 483, May 17, 1954.

91. Michel Berbrier, "Why Are There So Many 'Minorities?'" *Contexts* 3, no. 1 (Winter 2004): 38–44.

92. Mitch Berbrier, "Making Minorities: Cultural Space, Stigma Transformation Frames, and the Categorical Status Claims of Deaf, Gay, and White Supremacist Activists in Late Twentieth Century America," *Sociological Forum* 17, no. 4 (2002): 553–591.

93. John D. Skrentny, *The Minority Rights Revolution* (Cambridge, MA: Harvard University Press, 2004), 87.

94. Supreme Court of the United States, *Regents of the University of California v. Bakke*, 438 U.S. 265, June 28, 1978.

95. Justice Powell, majority opinion, June 28, 1978, 317.

96. Laure Bereni, "La diversité, ruse ou dévoiement de l'égalité?" *L'Observatoire: La revue des politiques culturelles* 56 (summer 2020), https://doi.org/10.3917/lobs.056 .0030.

97. E. John Gregory, "Diversity Is a Value in American Higher Education, but It Is Not a Legal Justification for Affirmative Action," *Florida Law Review* 52 (December 2000): 930–955.

NOTES TO CHAPTER 2

98. Walter Benn Michaels, *The Trouble with Diversity: How We Learned to Love Identity and Ignore Inequality* (New York: Metropolitan Books, 2006).

99. Daniel Sabbagh, "Les ravages de la pensée moniste: À propos de *La Diversité contre l'égalité* de Walter Benn Michaels, Raisons d'agir, 2009," *Mouvements* 61, no. 1 (2010): 172–180.

100. Réjane Sénac, *L'Invention de la diversité* (Paris: Presses universitaires de France, 2012), 253.

101. Vincent-Arnaud Chappe, *La Genèse de la HALDE: Un consensus a minima* (Saarbrücken: Éditions universitaires européennes, 2010).

102. Laure Bereni and Alexandre Jaunait, "Usages de la diversité," *Raisons politiques* 35, no. 3 (2009): 9.

103. Sara Ahmed, *On Being Included: Racism and Diversity in Institutional Life* (Durham, NC: Duke University Press, 2012), 65–67.

104. Education Amendments, 92-318, 86 Stat. 235, June 23, 1972.

105. Supreme Court of the United States, *Gebser v. Lago Vista Independent School District*, 524 U.S. 274, June 22, 1998, and *Davis v. Monroe County Board of Education*, 526 U.S. 629, May 24, 1999.

106. Department of Education, "Dear Colleague Letter," April 4, 2011, https://www2.ed.gov/about/offices/list/ocr/letters/colleague-201104.html.

107. Laura Kipnis, "Sexual Paranoia Strikes Academe," *Chronicle of Higher Education* 61, no. 25 (February 27, 2015), https://www.chronicle.com/article/sexual-paranoia-strikes-academe/.

108. Kipnis, "Sexual Paranoia Strikes Academe."

109. Katherine Mangan, "Laura Kipnis Is Sued over Portrayal of Graduate Student in Book on Campus 'Sexual Paranoia,'" *Chronicle of Higher Education* 63, no. 37 (May 18, 2017), https://www.chronicle.com/article/laura-kipnis-is-sued-over-portrayal-of-graduate-student-in-book-on-campus-sexual-paranoia/.

110. Morton Schapiro, "The New Face of Campus Unrest," *Wall Street Journal*, March 18, 2015.

111. Laura Kipnis, "My Title IX Inquisition," *Chronicle of Higher Education* 61, no. 38 (May 29, 2015), https://www.chronicle.com/article/my-title-ix-inquisition/.

112. Laura Kipnis, "Eyewitness to a Title IX Witch Trial (the Dismissal Hearing of Peter Ludlow)," *Chronicle of Higher Education* 63, no. 31 (April 2, 2017), https://www.chronicle.com/article/eyewitness-to-a-title-ix-witch-trial/.

113. Laura Kipnis, *Unwanted Advances: Sexual Paranoia Comes to Campus* (New York: Harper, 1997), 131–147.

114. Supreme Court of the United States, *Dobbs v. Jackson Women's Health Organization*, 597 U.S., June 24, 2022.

115. Benjamin Ginsberg, *The Fall of the Faculty. The Rise of the All-Administrative University and Why It Matters* (Oxford: Oxford University Press, 2011), 38–39.

116. Ashley Brown Burns and William Darity Jr., "The Diversity Defense for Affirmative Action in the U.S.," *Du Bois Review: Social Science Research on Race* 16, no. 2 (2019): 348.

117. Brown Burns and Darity Jr., "Diversity Defense," 151.

118. See, e.g., Eleanor Bowes, *Leadership in Diversity and Inclusion: Ultimate Management Guide to Challenging Bias, Creating Organizational Change, and Building an Effective Diversity and Inclusion Strategy* (New York: Deeper Reads, 2021). In France, see Isabelle Barth, *Manager la diversité: De la lutte contre les discriminations au leadership inclusif* (Paris: Dunod, 2018).

119. Aja Romano, "A History of 'Wokeness,'" *Vox*, October 9, 2020, https://www.vox.com/culture/21437879/stay-woke-wokeness-history-origin-evolution-controversy.

120. Francis Dupuis-Déri, *Panique à l'université: Rectitude politique, wokes et autres menaces imaginaires* (Montreal: Lux éditeur, 2022), 18–20; Adrian Daub, *The Cancel Culture Panic: How an American Obsession Went Global* (Stanford, CA: Stanford University Press, 2024).

121. On the differences between the two terms, see Alain Policar, *Le "wokisme" n'existe pas: La fabrication d'un mythe* (Lormont: Le Bord de l'eau, 2024).

122. Caroline Fourest, *Génération offensée: De la police de la culture à la police de la pensée* (Paris: Grasset, 2020).

123. See, e.g., Brice Couturier, *OK millennials! Puritanisme, victimisation, identitarisme, censure, l'enquête d'un baby-boomer sur les mythes de la génération woke* (Paris: Éditions de l'Observatoire, 2021).

124. Laure Murat, *Qui annule quoi?* (Paris: Seuil, 2022), 10.

125. Simon Piel and Nicolas Chapuis, "Une pluie de coups et des mensonges: Retour sur le passage à tabac du producteur de musique Michel Zecler par trois policiers," *Le Monde*, November 27, 2020.

126. Murat, *Qui annule quoi?* 36.

127. Hilary Silver, "Cancel Culture as Social Exclusion," *The Hill*, August 29, 2020, https://thehill.com/opinion/campaign/514231-cancel-culture-as-social-exclusion/.

128. Sally Haslanger, "Focus on the Fire, Not the Spark," *DailyNous*, May 4, 2017, https://dailynous.com/2017/05/04/focus-fire-not-spark-guest-post-sally-haslanger/.

129. Jacob E. Gersen and Jeannie Suk Gersen, "The Sex Bureaucracy," *California Law Review* 104 (March 18, 2016): 881–948.

130. Gersen and Gersen, "Sex Bureaucracy," 918–923.

131. Gersen and Gersen, 924.

132. Gersen and Gersen, 225–226.

133. Katie Dupere, "'Safe Spaces' for LGBTQ People Are a Myth—and Always Have Been," *Mashable*, June 18, 2016, https://mashable.com/article/lgbtq-safe-spaces.

134. Bari Weiss, "When the Left Turned on Its Own," *New York Times*, June 1, 2017.

NOTES TO CHAPTER 3

135. Adrian Daub, *Cancel Culture Transfer: Wie eine moralische Panik die Welt erfasst* (Berlin: Suhrkamp, 2022).

136. See the special issue of *Raison présente* 199, no. 3 (2016).

137. Jan G. Janmaat and Avril Keating, "Are Today's Youth More Tolerant? Trends in Tolerance among Young People in Britain," *Ethnicities* 19, no. 1 (2019): 44–65.

138. William H. Frey, "Diversity Defines the Millennial Generation," *Brookings*, June 28, 2016, https://www.brookings.edu/blog/the-avenue/2016/06/28/diversity-defines -the-millennial-generation.

139. Cathy J. Cohen, "Millennials and the Myth of the Post-Racial Society: Black Youth, Intra-Generational Divisions & the Continuing Racial Divide in American Politics," *Daedalus* 140, no. 2 (2011): 197–205.

140. Rob Cover, "The Corporeal Ethics of Gaming Vulnerability, Mobility, and Social Gaming," in *Woke Gaming: Digital Challenges to Oppression and Social Injustice*, ed. Kishonna L. Gray and David J. Leonard (Seattle: University of Washington Press, 2018), 42.

141. Ellen Berrey, *The Enigma of Diversity: The Language of Race and the Limits of Racial Justice* (Chicago: University of Chicago Press, 2015), 268–272.

142. Roderick A. Ferguson, *The Reorder of Things: The University and Its Pedagogies of Minority Difference* (Minneapolis: University of Minnesota Press, 2012), 62–63.

143. Laure Bereni, "Les stigmates de la vertu: Légitimer la diversité en entreprise, à New York et à Paris," *Actes de la recherche en sciences sociales* 241, no. 1 (2022): 36–55.

144. Ferguson, *The Reorder of Things*, 232.

CHAPTER 3

1. Muriel Reus, "PPDA [Patrick Poivre d'Arvor]: La chute d'un intouchable," *Complètement d'enquête*, video aired on France 2 on May 10, 2022, https://www .francetvinfo.fr.

2. Jonathan Vespa, Lauren Medina, and David M. Armstrong, "Demographic Turn-ing Points for the United States: Population Projections for 2020 to 2060," *US Census Bureau*, February 2020, https://www.census.gov/library/publications/2020/demo/p25 -1144.html.

3. Vespa, Medina, and Armstrong, "Demographic Turning Points. "

4. For an account of the arguments and controversies, see Joan W. Scott, *Parité! Sexual Equality and the Crisis of French Universalism* (Chicago: University of Chicago Press, 2005), 89–126.

5. Conseil constitutionnel, *Quotas par sexe I*, 82–146, November 18, 1982.

6. Joan W. Scott, "French Universalism in the Nineties," *differences: A Journal of Feminist Cultural Studies* 15, no. 2 (2004): 36–40.

7. Just as Évelyne Pisier warned about: Évelyne Pisier, "Sexes et sexualités: Bonnes et mauvaises différences," *Les Temps modernes* 609 (2000): 156–175.

8. Maureen A. Craig and Jennifer A. Richeson, "Hispanic Population Growth Engenders Conservative Shift among Non-Hispanic Racial Minorities," *Social Psychological and Personality Science* 9, no. 4 (May 2018): 383–392.

9. Ariane Chebel d'Appollonia, *Violent America: The Dynamics of Identity Politics in a Multiracial Society* (Ithaca, NY: Cornell University Press, 2023), 122.

10. Deleuze and Guattari, *A Thousand Plateaus*, 291–294.

11. Gilles Deleuze, "Control and Becoming," (1990) in *Negotiations, 1972–1990* (New York: Columbia University Press, 1995), 173–174.

12. Nadia Urbinati, *Democracy Disfigured: Opinion, Truth, and the People* (Cambridge, MA: Harvard University Press, 2014), 169–170.

13. *L'Abécédaire de Gilles Deleuze* (1988), produced by Pierre-André Boutang (Paris: Éditions Montparnasse, 2004), DVD.

14. Linda Martín Alcoff, "Cultural Feminism versus Post-Structuralism: The Identity Crisis in Feminist Theory," *Signs* 13, no. 3 (1988): 432.

15. Yves Citton, *Faire avec: Conflits, coalitions, contagions* (Paris: Les liens qui libèrent, 2021), 82. Yves Citton uses the term "minor" (*mineur* in French) in a Deleuzian sense to emphasize the different relationship to the world that this position implies. The term does not refer to underage people as such.

16. Michael Bitzer, "We Are Witnessing Tyranny of the Minority," WFAE, Charlotte's NPR News Source, October 2, 2013, https://www.wfae.org/politics/2013-10 -02/we-are-witnessing-tyranny-of-the-minority.

17. Arnaud Coutant, "Les Présidents minoritaires aux États-Unis," *Revue française de droit constitutionnel* 90, no. 2 (2012), 35–55.

18. Steven Levitsky and Daniel Ziblatt, "End Minority Rule," *New York Times*, October 23, 2020.

19. David Snyder, "The Tyranny of the Minority: A Post Charlottesville Theory of the First Amendment," *The Hill*, January 19, 2018, https://thehill.com/opinion/civil-rights /369628-the-tyranny-of-the-minority-a-post-charlottesville-theory-of-the-first/.

20. See Lilliana Mason, *Uncivil Agreement: How Politics Became Our Identity* (Chicago: University of Chicago Press, 2018) and Ezra Klein, *Why We're Polarized* (New York: Avid Reader Press, 2020).

21. Benjamin Bishin, *Tyranny of the Minority: The Subconstituency Politics Theory of Representation* (Philadelphia: Temple University Press, 2009), 122.

22. Hélène Landemore, "Deliberation, Cognitive Diversity, and Democratic Inclusiveness: An Epistemic Argument for the Random Selection of Representatives," *Synthese* 190 (2013): 1209–1231.

23. Benjamin I. Page and Martin Gilens, *Democracy in America: What Has Gone Wrong and What We Can Do about It* (Chicago: University of Chicago Press, 2018), 173–174.

24. See John Rawls, "The Idea of an Overlapping Consensus," *Oxford Journal of Legal Studies* 7, no. 1 (spring 1987): 1–25.

NOTES TO CHAPTER 3

25. "America in One Room," Deliberative Democracy Lab, Stanford University, Center on Democracy, Development, and the Rule of Law, https://deliberation.stanford.edu/news/america-one-room-0.

26. James Fishkin and Larry Diamond, "What If There's a Better Way to Handle Our Democratic Debate?" *New York Times*, August 29, 2019.

27. "Online Deliberation Platform," Deliberative Democracy Lab, Stanford University, Center on Democracy, Development, and the Rule of Law, https://deliberation.stanford.edu/tools-and-resources/online-deliberation-platform.

28. Philippe Urfalino, *Décider ensemble* (Paris: Seuil, 2021), 239.

29. Seyla Benhabib, "Deliberative Rationality and Models of Democratic Legitimacy," *Constellations* 1, no. 1 (1994): 32–33.

30. Kathryn Abrams, "Relationships of Representation in Voting Rights Act Jurisprudence," *Texas Law Review* 71, no. 7 (June 1993): 1418.

31. Virginie Dutoya and Samuel Hayat, "Prétendre représenter: La construction sociale de la représentation politique," *Revue française de science politique* 66, no. 1 (2016): 20.

32. Zachary Kramer, *Outsiders: Why Difference Is the Future of Civil Rights* (Oxford: Oxford University Press, 2019), 177–178.

33. Charles Girard, *Délibérer entre égaux: Enquête sur l'idéal démocratique* (Paris: Vrin, 2019), 122.

34. Monique Deveaux, *Gender and Justice in Multicultural Liberal States* (Oxford: Oxford University Press, 2006), 218.

35. Monique Deveaux, *Cultural Pluralism and Dilemmas of Justice* (Ithaca, NY: Cornell University Press, 2000), 168–170.

36. Hélène Landemore and Scott E. Page, "Deliberation and Disagreement: Problem Solving, Prediction, and Positive Dissensus," *Politics, Philosophy, & Economics* 14, no. 3 (2015): 229–254.

37. See chapter 4.

38. Chantal Mouffe, *On the Political* (London: Routledge, 2005), 99.

39. Mouffe, *On the Political*, 126.

40. Mouffe, 17.

41. See chapter 6.

42. Pierre Salmon and Alain Wolfelsperger, "De l'équilibre au chaos et retour: Bilan méthodologique des recherches sur la règle de majorité," *Revue française de science politique* 51, no. 3 (June 2001): 334–336.

43. A consistent choice on a simple basis can be reversed as soon as new elements are considered. Edward H. Simpson, "The Interpretation of Interaction in Contingency Tables," *Journal of the Royal Statistical Society* 13, no. 2 (1951): 238–241.

44. Jean-Charles de Borda, *Mémoire sur les élections au scrutin dans Histoire de l'académie royale des sciences*, 1781.

45. Condorcet, "An Essay on the Application of Probability Theory to Plurality Decision-Making."

46. Kenneth Arrow, *Social Choice and Individual Values* (New Haven, CT: Yale University Press, 2012).

47. Mineur, *Le Pouvoir de la majorité*, 27–162.

48. Albert O. Hirschman, *The Passions and the Interests: Political Arguments for Capitalism before Its Triumph* (Princeton, NJ: Princeton University Press, 1977), 51–52.

49. John Rawls, *Political Liberalism* (1993) (New York: Columbia University Press, 2005), 219–222.

50. Jürgen Habermas, *Between Facts and Norms: Contributions to a Discourse Theory of Law and Democracy* (1992), trans. William Rehg (Cambridge, MA: MIT Press, 1996), 199.

51. Joshua Cohen, "An Epistemic Conception of Democracy," *Ethics* 97, no. 1 (October 1986): 35.

52. Hélène Landemore, *Democratic Reason: Politics, Collective Intelligence, and the Rule of the Many* (Princeton, NJ: Princeton University Press, 2013), 3–6.

53. The social world is not a labyrinth everyone aspires to leave. Landemore, *Democratic Reason*, 234–237.

54. Hélène Landemore, "Pourquoi le grand nombre est plus intelligent que le petit nombre, et pourquoi il faut en tenir compte," *Philosophiques* 40, no. 2 (2013): 283–299.

55. Landemore, *Democratic Reason*, 160–163.

56. Chantal Jaquet, *Transclasses: A Theory of Social Non-Reproduction* (2014), trans. Gregory Elliott (London: Verso, 2023), 28.

57. Landemore, *Democratic Reason*, 239.

58. Yves Citton and Jacopo Rasmi, *Générations collapsonautes: Naviguer par temps d'effondrements* (Paris: Seuil, 2020), 235.

59. Albert Camus, *Notebooks III: 1951–1959*, trans. Ryan Bloom, note dated November 7, 1958 (Chicago: Ivan R. Dee, 1962), 260.

60. Nicolas de Condorcet, "The Sketch (*Esquisse d'un tableau historique des progrès humains*)" (1795), in *Condorcet: Political Writings*, ed. Steven Lukes and Nadia Urbinati, trans. June Barraclough (Cambridge: Cambridge University Press, 2012), 92.

61. Jean-Jacques Rousseau, *The Social Contract* (1762), trans. Henry John Tozer (Ware: Wordsworth, 1998), 77.

62. Yves Sintomer, "La représentation-incarnation: Idéaltype et configurations historiques," *Raisons politiques* 72 (November 2018): 47–49.

63. Melissa Schwartzberg, *Counting the Many: The Origins and Limits of Supermajority Rule* (Cambridge: Cambridge University Press, 2014), 141–144.

64. Dominique Cardon, *À quoi rêvent les algorithmes: Nos vies à l'heure des big data* (Paris: Seuil, 2015), 51.

NOTES TO CHAPTER 3

65. Gilles Deleuze, "Postscript on the Society of Control" (1990), *October* 59 (1992): 5.

66. Cardon, *À quoi rêvent les algorithmes*, 71.

67. Marilyn Strathern, *The Gender of the Gift: Problems with Women and Problems with Society* (Berkeley: University of California Press, 1988), 13.

68. Kurt Iveson and Sophia Maalsen, "Social Control in the Networked City: Datafied Dividuals, Disciplined Individuals and Powers of Assembly," *Environment and Planning D: Society and Space* 37, no. 2 (2019): 331–349.

69. Sanaz Talaifar and Brian S. Lowery, "Freedom and Constraint in Digital Environments: Implications for the Self," *Perspectives on Psychological Science: A Journal for the Association for Psychological Science* 18, no. 3 (September 2022): 544–575.

70. See Sasha Costanza-Chock, *Design Justice: Community Led Practices to Build the World We Need* (Cambridge, MA: MIT Press, 2020).

71. Romain Badouard and Charles Girard, "Internet en mal de démocratie," *Esprit* 479, no. 11 (2021): 33–37.

72. Esther Bruno, Emmanuel Didier, and Julien Prévieux, "Pour un statactivisme," in *Statactivisme: Comment lutter avec des nombres*, ed. Esther Bruno, Emmanuel Didier and Julien Prévieux (Paris: La Découverte, 2014), 22–23.

73. Antoine Garapon and Jean Lassègue, *Justice digitale* (Paris: Presses universitaires de France, 2018), 252.

74. Lucy Bernholz, Hélène Landemore, and Bob Reich, "Introduction," in *Digital Technology and Democratic Theory*, ed. Lucy Bernholz, Hélène Landemore, and Rob Reich (Chicago: University of Chicago Press, 2021), 5.

75. Adrian Daub, *What Tech Calls Thinking: An Inquiry into the Intellectual Bedrock of Silicon Valley* (New York: FSG Originals x Logic, 2020), 25.

76. Brian Christian, *The Alignment Problem: Machine Learning and Human Values* (New York: W. W. Norton, 2020), 213ff.

77. See Lesley Gourlay, *Posthumanism and the Digital University: Texts, Bodies and Materialities* (London: Bloomsbury Publishing, 2020).

78. Citton, *Faire avec*, 21–22.

79. Pat O'Malley, "Simulated Justice: Risk, Money and Telemetric Policing," *British Journal of Criminology* 50, no. 5 (2010): 795–807.

80. Cathy O'Neil, *Weapons of Math Destruction: How Big Data Increases Inequality and Threatens Democracy* (New York: Crown, 2016), 74–75.

81. Julia Angwin, Jeff Larson, Surya Mattu and Lauren Kirchner, "Machine Bias: There's Software Used across the Country to Predict Future Criminals—and It's Biased against Blacks," *ProPublica*, May 23, 2016, https://www.propublica.org/article/machine-bias-risk-assessments-in-criminal-sentencing.

82. Ulrich Beck, *Risk Society: Towards a New Modernity* (1986), trans. Mark Ritter (London: Sage, 1992), 136–137.

83. Moritz Hardt, Eric Price and Nathan Srebro, "Equality of Opportunity in Supervised Learning," *ArXiv*, October 11, 2016, https://arxiv.org/abs/1610.02413.

84. Pradyumna Chari, Yunhao Ba, Shreeram Athreya and Achuta Kadambi, "MIME: Minority Inclusion for Majority Group Enhancement of AI Performance," *ArXiv*, September 1, 2022, https://arxiv.org/abs/2209.00746.

85. Adam Zewen, "A Technique to Improve both Fairness and Accuracy in Artificial Intelligence," *MIT News*, July 20, 2022, https://news.mit.edu/2022/fairness-accuracy-ai-models-0720.

86. See Catherine D'Ignazio and Lauren F. Klein, *Data Feminism* (Cambridge, MA: MIT Press, 2020).

87. Francesca Bisiani, "Les 'minorités' en Italie et en France: L'impact de la traduction automatique sur la détermination des concepts juridiques," *Traduire* 246 (2022): 65–76.

88. Will Knight, "How to Fix Silicon Valley's Sexist Algorithms," *MIT Technological Review*, November 23, 2017, https://www.technologyreview.com/2016/11/23/155858/how-to-fix-silicon-valleys-sexist-algorithms/.

89. Janie Pélabay, "Le communautarisme," in *Questions d'éthique contemporaine*, ed. Ludivine Thiaw-Po-Une (Paris: Stock, 2006), 262–275.

90. Fabrice Dhume-Sonzogni, *Communautarisme: Enquête sur une chimère du nationalisme français* (Paris: Demopolis, 2016), 78–83.

91. Richard Sennett deconstructed the idea of group endogamy by conjuring that "community only exists through a continual hyping up of emotions." Richard Sennett, *The Fall of Public Man: On the Social Psychology of Capitalism* (1974) (New York: Vintage Books, 1978), 308.

92. André Reszler, *Le Pluralisme: Aspects historiques et théoriques dans les sociétés pluralistes* (Paris, La Table Ronde, 2001), 148–151.

93. Esther Benbassa, *La République face à ses minorités: Les Juifs hier, les Musulmans aujourd'hui* (Paris: Mille et une nuits, 2004), 40.

94. See Laurence Roulleau-Berger, "Femmes de Chine à Belleville: Épreuves de captivité économique et invisibilité sociale," in *Belleville: Un quartier populaire entre mythe et réalités*, ed. Roselyne de Villanova et Agnès Deboulet (Ivry-sur-Seine: Éditions Créaphis, 2011), 43–51.

95. Félix Wu, "La communauté asiatique en France, une image à redéfinir," *Revue internationale et stratégique* 73, no. 1 (2009): 113–116.

96. Simeng Wang, Yong Li, Johann Cailhol, Miyako Hayakawa, Youngbin Kim and Sophie Haas, *L'Expérience du racisme et des discriminations des personnes originaires d'Asie de l'Est et du Sud-Est en France (REACTAsie)*, Archives ouvertes. HAL Open Science, March 16, 2023, https://hal.science/hal-04031732/document.

97. Fabien Truong, *Loyautés radicales: L'islam et les "mauvais garçons" de la Nation* (Paris: La Découverte, 2017).

98. Homi K. Bhabha, *The Location of Culture* (1994) (London: Routledge, 2004), 212–214.

NOTES TO CHAPTER 4

99. Kimberly McNair, "Black Twitter and Building Solidarity across Borders," in *#Identity: Hashtagging Race, Gender, Sexuality, and Nation*, ed. Abigail De Kosnik and Keith P. Feldman (Ann Arbor: University of Michigan Press, 2019), 296.

100. See the counterstrategic usage, for example, of the idea of "white innocence." Gloria Wekker, *White Innocence: Paradoxes of Colonialism and Race* (Durham, NC: Duke University Press, 2016), 153.

101. Mancur Olson, *The Logic of Collective Action: Public Goods and the Theory of Groups* (Cambridge, MA: Harvard University Press, 1965).

102. Judith Butler and Athena Athanasiou, *Dispossession: The Performative in the Political* (Cambridge: Polity Press, 2013), 187.

103. Citton and Rasmi, *Générations collapsonautes*, 238–239.

104. Didier Eribon, *Insult and the Making of the Gay Self* (1999), trans. Michael Lucey (Durham, NC: Duke University Press, 1994), 106.

105. Jean-Paul Sartre, *Critique of Dialectical Reason*, vol. 1 (1960), trans. Alan Sheridan-Smith (London: Verso, 2004), 318ff.

106. Sartre, *Critique of Dialectical Reason*, 345–350.

107. Perreau, "L'ombre de la loi: Blanchot, Duras, Foucault."

108. Pap Ndiaye, *La Condition noire: Essai sur une minorité française* (2008) (Paris: Gallimard, 2022), 46–56.

109. Léonora Miano, *Afropea: Utopie post-occidentale et post-raciste* (Paris: Grasset, 2020), 10.

110. Miano, *Afropea*, 10.

111. Miano, 45.

112. Miano, 12.

113. Miano, 13.

114. Miano, 18.

115. Miano, 14–15.

116. Clarence Walker, *We Can't Go Home Again: An Argument about Afrocentrism Attribution* (Oxford: Oxford University Press, 2001).

CHAPTER 4

1. In her typology, Gisèle Sapiro distinguishes essayists (Éric Zemmour, Alain Finkielkraut, and Pascal Bruckner) from writers (Philippe Muray, Michel Houellebecq, Renaud Camus, and Richard Millet). Gisèle Sapiro, "Notables, esthètes et polémistes: Manières d'être un écrivain 'réactionnaire' des années 30 à nos jours," in *Le Discours "néo-réactionnaire": Transgressions conservatrices*, ed. Pascal Durand and Sarah Sindaco (Paris: CNRS Éditions, 2015), 23–46.

2. Yves de Kerdel, "L'insupportable tyrannie des minorités," *Valeurs Actuelles*, September 2, 2016.

3. Mathieu Bock-Côté, "Tyrannie des minorités, majorité silencieuse," *FigaroVox*, July 24, 2020, https://www.lefigaro.fr/vox/societe/mathieu-bock-cote-tyrannie-des-minorites-majorite-silencieuse-20200724.

4. Gérald Bronner, "L'institution doit résister à la 'tyrannie des minorités,'" *La Croix*, October 28, 2019.

5. Alain Finkielkraut, "Finkielkraut: Tyrannie des minorités," posted June 17, 2020, YouTube (video removed).

6. Jean-Yves Le Gallou, "La radicalité contre la dictature des minorités," *Polemia*, April, 14, 2013, http://www.polemia.com/la-radicalite-contre-la-dictature-des-minorites. See also "Les minorités agissantes expliquées par Alain Soral," posted July 2, 2013, YouTube (video removed).

7. Éric Zemmour, *Le Premier Sexe* (Paris: J'ai Lu, 2007).

8. Laurent Bouvet, *L'Insécurité culturelle* (Paris: Fayard, 2015); Laurent Bouvet, *Le Péril identitaire* (Paris: Éditions de l'Observatoire, 2020).

9. Julien Talpin, "La gauche française devrait-elle se détourner davantage de minorités qu'elle n'a jamais choyées?" *Libération*, October 12, 2018.

10. Ludivine Bénard, "Comment le Parti socialiste a abandonné les classes populaires pour les 'minorités,'" *Vice*, April 6, 2017, https://www.vice.com/fr/article/d7qbzy/parti-socialiste-abandon-classes-populaires-minorites.

11. "Patrick Mennucci: 'Le mariage pour tous nous a coûté des voix,'" *Le Monde*, April 1, 2014.

12. Mark Lilla, *The Once and Future Liberal: After Identity Politics* (New York: HarperCollins, 2017).

13. Laurent Dubreuil, *La Dictature des identités* (Paris: Gallimard, 2019), 25.

14. In ancient times Aristotle sought a solution to the risk of losing political power: he proposed the concept of *politeia*, which identifies any political regime that combines the opinion of the majority and the wisdom of a minority of the most virtuous citizens. Aristote, *Politics* (350 BCE) and *The Constitution of Athens* (328–322 BCE), trans. Jonathan Barnes (Cambridge: Cambridge University Press, 1996), book 4, section 9, 104–105.

15. Pablo Stefanoni, *La Rébellion est-elle passée à droite? Dans le laboratoire mondial des contre-cultures néoréactionnaires* (2021), trans. Marc Saint-Upéry (Paris: La Découverte, 2022).

16. Pippa Norris, *Radical Right: Voters and Parties in the Electoral Market* (Cambridge: Cambridge University Press, 2005), 11–19.

17. Daniel Martinez Hosang and Joseph E. Lowndes, *Producers, Parasites, Patriots: Race and the New Right-Wing Politics of Precarity* (Minneapolis: University of Minnesota Press, 2019), 107–111.

18. Charles Tilly, "The Analysis of a Counter-Revolution," *History and Theory* 3, no. 1 (1963): 7–58.

19. Gilles Houle, "L'idéologie: Un mode de connaissance," *Sociologie et Sociétés* 11, no. 1 (1979): 123–145.

NOTES TO CHAPTER 4

20. Norris, *Radical Right*, 3–25.

21. Michel Foucault, "La naissance d'un monde," in *Dits et Écrits I, 1954–1975* (Paris: Gallimard, 2001), 814.

22. Supreme Court of the United States, *Davis v. Massachusetts*, 167 U.S. 43, May 10, 1897.

23. Supreme Court of the United States, *Hague v. Committee for Industrial Organization*, 307 U.S. 496, June 5, 1939.

24. David Kairys, "Freedom of Speech," in *The Politics of Law: A Progressive Critique*, ed. David Kairys (New York: Basic Books, 1998), 197–199.

25. TX SB17, 86th legislature, *Legiscan.com*, 2019–2020.

26. Hannah Denham, "Texas Governor Signs 'Save Chick-Fil-A' Bill into Law," *Washington Post*, July 19, 2019.

27. Max Brantley, "Hutchinson Signs Another Bill Aimed at Discriminating against LGBT People and Women's Medical Rights," *Arkansas Times*, March 26, 2021.

28. Supreme Court of the United States, *Masterpiece Cakeshop v. Colorado Civil Rights Commission*, 584 U.S., June 4, 2018.

29. Adam Liptak, "In Narrow Decision, Supreme Court Sides with Baker Who Turned Away Gay Couple," *New York Times*, June 4, 2018.

30. Arizona Court of Appeals, *Brush & Nib Studio v. Phoenix*, 16–0602, June 7, 2018; Washington Supreme Court, *State of Washington v. Arlene's Flowers*, 91615-2, June 6, 2019.

31. Supreme Court of the United States *Trump v. Hawaii*, 585 U.S., June 26, 2018.

32. Wendy Brown, *In the Ruins of Neoliberalism: The Rise of Antidemocratic Politics in the West* (New York: Columbia University Press, 2019), 147.

33. Brown, *In the Ruins of Neoliberalism*, 143.

34. Supreme Court of the United States, *National Institute of Family and Life Advocates v. Becerra*, 585 U.S., June 26, 2018.

35. Supreme Court of the United States, *National Institute of Family*.

36. Supreme Court of the United States, *National Institute of Family*, "Kennedy, J. Concurring," 1.

37. Brown, *In the Ruins of Neoliberalism*, 157–160.

38. *Sharonell Fulton et al. v. City of Philadelphia et al., Petition for a Writ of Certiorari Granted*, 1.

39. Supreme Court of the United States, *Fulton and al. v. City of Philadelphia*, 593 U.S., June 17, 2021.

40. Supreme Court of the United States, *Employment Division, Department of Human Resources of Oregon v. Smith*, 494 US 872, April 17, 1990.

41. James Esseks, "At End of SCOTUS term, Where Are We on LGBT+ Rights?" *American Civil Liberties Union*, July 12, 2021, https://www.aclu.org/news/lgbtq-rights /at-end-of-scotus-term-where-are-we-on-lgbtq-rights.

42. Court of Appeals, *Otto v. City of Boca Raton*, 11th circuit, 19–10604, November 20, 2020.

43. Court of Appeals, 11th circuit, 39.

44. Andrew Chung, "U.S. Top Court Rejects 'Gay Conversion' Therapy Ban Challenge," Reuters, May 1, 2017, https://www.reuters.com/article/us-usa-court-gayconversion/u-s -top-court-rejects-gay-conversion-therapy-ban-challenge-idUSKBN17X1SJ.

45. Court of Appeals, 4th Circuit, *Grimm v. Gloucester County School Board*, 19–1952, August 26, 2020.

46. Trudy Ring, "Why Gavin Grimm May Be Back in Court," *The Advocate*, February 19, 2021, https://www.advocate.com/transgender/2021/2/19/virginia-school-board -seeks-scotus-hearing-trans-restroom-access.

47. Alex Cooper, "SCOTUS Decision on Trans Youth Gavin Grimm Is Major LGBTQ+ Victory," *The Advocate*, June 28, 2021, https://www.advocate.com/transgender/2021 /6/28/scotus-decision-trans-youth-gavin-grimm-major-lgbtq-victory.

48. Amy Howe, "Today's Orders: Same-Sex Marriage Petitions Denied (updated)," *SCOTUS* (blog), October 6, 2014, https://www.scotusblog.com/2014/10/todays-orders -same-sex-marriage-petitins-denied/.

49. Supreme Court of the United States, *Obergefell v. Hodges*, 576 U.S., June 26, 2015.

50. Sarah Swisher, "Amy Coney Barrett's Rise Is a Threat to Families Like Mine," *New York Times*, October 24, 2020.

51. Supreme Court of the United States, *Dobbs*.

52. Supreme Court of the United States, *Dobbs*, 118.

53. Supreme Court of the United States, *Arlene's Flowers v. Washington et al.*, 19–333, July 2, 2021.

54. Washington State Supreme Court, *Arlene's Flowers*.

55. Supreme Court of the United States, *Loving v. Virginia*, 388 U.S. 1, June 12, 1967.

56. Annie Karni, "Same-Sex Marriage Bill Passes Senate after Bipartisan Breakthrough," *New York Times*, November 29, 2022.

57. Michael D. Shear, "Biden Signs Bill to Protect Same-Sex Marriage Rights," *New York Times*, December 13, 2022.

58. Supreme Court of the United States, *303 Creative LLC and al. v. Elenis and al.*, 21–476, June 30, 2023.

59. "Statement from President Joe Biden on Supreme Court Decision in *303 Creative LLC v. Elenis*," The White House, June 30, 2023, https://www.whitehouse.gov /briefing-room/statements-releases/2023/06/30.

60. Ian Millhiser, "Obamacare Is under Attack by Republican Judges Again. Here's What's at Stake," *Vox*, September 7, 2022, https://www.vox.com/policy-and-politics /2022/9/7/23341076/obamacare-reed-oconnor-prep-supreme-court-braidwood -becerra-affordable-care-act

NOTES TO CHAPTER 4

61. United States District Court Northern District of Texas, Fort Worth Division, *Braidwood Management Incorporated v. Xavier Becerra et al.*, no. 4:20-cv-00283-O, September 7, 2022.

62. The HIV prevalence rate in the United States among gay men is over 25 percent in many major cities and several southern states; in comparison, this rate is 0.1 percent among heterosexuals. Donald G. McNeil Jr., "H.I.V. Rates among Gay Men Are Higher in South, Study Finds," *New York Times*, May 18, 2016. The Black and Latinx population are also disproportionately affected; see Amy Lansky et al., "Estimating the Number of Heterosexual Persons in the United States to Calculate National Rates of HIV Infection," *PLOS One* 10, no. 7 (2015), https://www.ncbi.nlm.nih.gov/pmc/articles/PMC4516312.

63. Supreme Court of the United States, *Burwell v. Hubby Lobby Stores et al.*, 573 U.S. 682, June 30, 2014.

64. Supreme Court of the United States, *Bostock v. Clayton County.*

65. Jeannine Bell, "Pour faire barrage à ceux qui n'ont pas de cœur: Expressions racistes et droits des minorités," in *La Liberté d'expression aux États-Unis et en Europe*, ed. Élizabeth Zoller (Paris: Dalloz, 2008), 56–65.

66. Caroline Winterer, *American Enlightenments: Pursuing Happiness in the Age of Reason* (New Haven, CT: Yale University Press, 2016), 171–195.

67. See Kenneth L. Karst, *Visions of Power in the Politics of Race, Gender, and Religion* (New Haven, CT: Yale University Press, 1993), 59–60.

68. Amandine Barb, "Une laïcité ouverte aux religions? Le modèle américain," *Études*, no.1 (January 2016): 19–34.

69. On the complexity of the interpretation of facts, see Jean-Yves Monfort, "Le racisme, le sexisme et l'homophobie ne sont pas des 'opinions,'" *Legicom*, 54, no. 1 (2015): 77–81.

70. European Court of Human Rights, *Eweida and Others v. the United Kingdom*, 36516/10, January 15, 2013.

71. Joan W. Scott, *Sex and Secularism* (Princeton, NJ: Princeton University Press, 2017), 15.

72. I have shown that prospective adopters were enjoined to self-discipline given the majority expectations of institutions. Bruno Perreau, "What Approval Means," in *The Politics of Adoption: Gender and the Making of French Citizenship*, trans. Deke Dusinberre (Cambridge, MA: MIT Press, 2014), 97–110.

73. For greater detail see Perreau, *Queer Theory*, 40–43.

74. Printemps français, "On ne lâche rien! Manifeste," quoted in Perreau, *Queer Theory*, 67. As minister of justice, Christiane Taubira presented the law on marriage equality before the Parliament.

75. See Sara Garbagnoli and Massimo Prearo, *La Croisade "anti-genre": Du Vatican aux manifs pour tous* (Paris: Textuel, 2017), 96.

76. Henrik Lindell, *Les Veilleurs: Enquête sur une résistance* (Paris: Salvator, 2014), 39.

77. Danièle Kergoat, "Dynamique et consubstantialité des rapports sociaux," in *Sexe, Race, Classe: Pour une épistémologie de la domination*, ed. Elsa Dorlin (Paris: Presses universitaires de France, 2009), 111–125.

78. Sirma Bilge, "Théorisations féministes de l'intersectionnalité," *Diogène* 225, no. 1 (2009): 70–88.

79. Jérôme Garcin, "Emmanuel Macron sur la Manif pour tous: 'On a humilié cette France-là,'" *L'Obs*, February 16, 2017. See Bruno Perreau, *Qui a peur de la théorie queer?* (2016) (Paris: Presses de Sciences Po, 2018), 106–107, 243–245.

80. Amy Chua, *Political Tribes: Group Instinct and the Fate of Nations* (New York: Penguin Books, 2018), 197–204.

81. "Executive Order on Combating Race and Sex Stereotyping," Federal Register, September 22, 2020, https://www.federalregister.gov/documents/2020/09/28/2020 -21534/combating-race-and-sex-stereotyping. For further historical analysis of this rhetoric, especially the Southern Manifesto's fight against school integration in the name of the Constitution, see Carol Anderson, *White Rage: The Unspoken Truth of Our Racial Divide* (London: Bloomsbury Publishing, 2016), 80.

82. "Executive Order on Combating Race and Sex Stereotyping," section 10(a) and 10(b), 85 FR 60683, September 22, 2020.

83. For synthesis of this phenomenon in Europe see the special issue edited and introduced by Mieke Verloo and David Paternotte: "The Feminist Project under Threat in Europe," *Politics and Governance* 6, no. 3, 2018.

84. Sophie Rétif, "Ringards, hypocrites et frustrés? Les militants des associations familiales catholiques face à la réprobation," *Politix* 106 (2014): 85–108.

85. See James Aho, *Far-Right Fantasy: A Sociology of American Religion and Politics* (London: Routledge, 2016), 43.

86. Lars Rensmann, "The Noisy Counter-Revolution: Understanding the Cultural Conditions and Dynamics of Populist Politics in Europe in the Digital Age," *Politics and Governance* 5, no. 4 (2017): 123–135.

87. Ashley Jardina, "Celebrating Whiteness," in *White Identity Politics* (Cambridge: Cambridge University Press, 2019), 136–144.

88. This is what Kathleen Belew shows about paramilitary supremacist groups: the lone wolf is a myth since every supremacist is connected to others through all sorts of references and exchange forums, both real and virtual. Kathleen Belew, *Bringing the War Home: The White Power Movement and Paramilitary America* (Cambridge, MA: Harvard University Press, 2018), 55–76.

89. Susan Faludi, *Backlash: The Undeclared War against American Women* (New York: Three Rivers Press, 2006).

90. See Sylvie Laurent, *La Couleur du marché: Racisme et néolibéralisme aux États-Unis* (Paris: Seuil, 2016).

91. Carmen DeNavas-Walt and Bernadette D. Proctor, *Income and Poverty in the US, Census 2014*, United States Census Bureau, September 2015, 44–55, https://www .census.gov/content/dam/Census/library/publications/2015/demo/p60-252.pdf.

NOTES TO CHAPTER 4   243

92. Sylvie Laurent, *Pauvre Petit Blanc* (Paris: Éditions de la Maison des Sciences de l'Homme, 2020).

93. See James Rosenbaum and Leonard S. Rubinowitz, *Crossing the Class and Color Lines: From Public Housing to White Suburbia* (Chicago: University of Chicago Press, 2000).

94. Eduardo Bonilla-Silva, *Racism without Racists: Color-Blind Racism and the Persistence of Racial Inequality in the United States* (Oxford: Rowman & Littlefield, 2018), 44–49.

95. "Carburants: Macron 'assume parfaitement' la hausse de la taxation," *Capital*, November 4, 2018.

96. Nadia Urbinati, "The Populist Phenomenon," *Raisons Politiques* 51, no. 3 (2013): 138–140.

97. "Gilets jaunes: La Manif pour tous truste la consultation," *L'Express*, January 5, 2019.

98. After a gay couple and a lesbian couple filed claims, California refused to implement Proposition 8. Opponents of same-sex marriage then seized the Court of the District of Northern California. The court held that Proposition 8 was unconstitutional. In its *Hollingsworth v. Perry* decision, the US Supreme Court upheld this decision; it considered that the applicants had no cause of action, Proposition 8 having no impact on their lives. Supreme Court of the United States, *Hollingsworth v. Perry*, 570 U.S. 693, June 26, 2013.

99. Bojan Bugaric, "The Two Faces of Populism: Between Authoritarian and Democratic Populism," *German Law Journal* 20, no. 3 (2019): 390–400.

100. Ernesto Laclau, *On Populist Reason* (London: Verso, 2005), 96–98.

101. Yves Mény and Jan Kermer, *Imperfect Democracies: The Rise of Popular Protest and Democratic Dissent* (London: Rowman & Littlefield, 2021).

102. Danielle Tartakowsky, *Les Droites et la Rue: Histoire d'une ambivalence, de 1880 à nos jours* (Paris: La Découverte, 2014), 166.

103. On authoritarianism see Pippa Norris and Ronald Inglehart, *Cultural Backlash. Trump, Brexit, and Authoritarian Populism* (Cambridge: Cambridge University Press, 2019), 7.

104. Gilles Ivaldi and Joël Gombin, "The Rassemblement National and the New Politics of the Rural in France," in *Rural Protest Groups and Populist Political Parties*, ed. Dirk Strijker, Gerrit Voerman, and Ida J. Terluin (Wageningen: Wageningen Academic Publishers, 2015), 243–264.

105. Nonna Mayer, "From Jean-Marie to Marine Le Pen: Electoral Change on the Far Right," *Parliamentary Affairs* 66, no. 1 (2013): 160–78.

106. Michel Feher, "Solidarité mélancolique: La gauche et les 'gilets jaunes,'" *Analyse Opinion Critique*, January 21, 2019, https://aoc.media/opinion/2019/01/21/solidarite-melancolique-gauche-gilets-jaunes/.

107. Jean-Marie Le Pen founded the National Front (*le Front national*) in 1972 and led it until 2011, when his daughter, Marine Le Pen, succeeded him. She renamed the party the National Rally (*le Rassemblement national*) in 2018.

108. Yoram Hazony, *The Virtue of Nationalism* (New York: Basic Books, 2018).

109. "Les droites radicales cherchent à s'unir autour d'un corpus idéologique," *La Chronique de . . . Jean-Marc Four*, France Inter, February 3, 2020, https://www.radiofrance.fr/franceinter/podcasts/le-monde-a-l-envers/les-droites-radicales-cherchent-a-s-unir-autour-d-un-corpus-ideologique-1182408.

110. On this point see Clarence Y. H. Lo, "Astroturf v. Grassroots. Scenes from Early Tea Party Mobilization," in *Steep: The Precipitous Rise of the Tea Party*, ed. Lawrence Rosenthal and Christine Trost (Berkeley: University of California Press, 2012), 98–130.

111. Ami Pedahzur and Avraham Brichta, "The Institutionalization of Extreme Right-Wing Charismatic Parties: A Paradox?" *Party Politics* 8, no. 1 (2002): 31–49.

112. Cécile Alduy and Stéphane Wahnich, *Marine Le Pen prise aux mots: Décryptage du nouveau discours frontiste* (Paris: Seuil, 2015), 149.

113. Perreau, *Queer Theory*, 117–118.

114. Her entire speech was available in French and in English on the extreme right website *Boulevard Voltaire*. Marion Maréchal, "Discours de Rome," *Boulevard Voltaire*, February 4, 2020 (document removed).

115. Eric J. Hobsbawm, *Nations and Nationalism since 1780: Programme, Myth, Reality* (Cambridge: Cambridge University Press, 1990).

116. Walter Connor, "Self-Determination. The New Phase," *World Politics* 20, no. 1 (1967): 20–53.

117. See also Vernon Van Dyke, "Self-Determination and Minority Rights," *International Studies Quarterly* 13, no. 3 (September 1969): 223–253.

118. Maréchal, "Discours de Rome."

119. "Le 'décolonialisme,' une stratégie hégémonique: L'appel de 80 intellectuels," *Le Point*, November 28, 2018.

120. "L'offensive des obsédés de la race, du sexe, du genre, de l'identité . . ." *Marianne*, April 11, 2019; "Terrorisme intellectuel. Après Sartre, Foucault, Bourdieu, l'idéologie indigéniste entre à l'université," *La Revue des Deux Mondes*, April 18, 2019; "La nouvelle terreur féministe," *Valeurs actuelles*, May 25, 2019; Ariane Nicolas, "Coffin, Lagasnerie . . . Vers un nouveau 'séparatisme" idéologique?'" *Philosophie magazine*, October 14, 2020; "La révolution anti-woke a commencé," *Valeurs actuelles*, December 8, 2022.

121. Such as Jean-Michel Blanquer, who attributed responsibility for the Islamist attacks in October 2020, to "Islamo-leftist" academics, when he was minister of national education. See Soazig Le Nevé, "Polémique après les propos de Jean-Michel Blanquer sur 'l'islamo-gauchisme' à l'université," *Le Monde*, October 23, 2020.

122. Maréchal, "Discours de Rome."

123. Maréchal.

124. Ivan Valerio, "Pour Marine Le Pen, la théorie du 'grand remplacement' relève du 'complotisme,'" *Le Figaro*, November 2, 2014.

NOTES TO CHAPTER 5

125. "Éric Zemmour définitivement condamné pour provocation à la haine raciale," *Le Monde*, September 20, 2019; "Éric Zemmour, condamné à 10 000 euros d'amende pour provocation à la haine raciale, va faire appel," *Le Monde*, January 17, 2022.

126. Jean Raspail, *The Camp of the Saints* (1973), trans. Norman Shapiro (New York: Scribner, 1975).

127. For a full analysis, see Christy Wampole, *Degenerative Realism* (New York: Columbia University Press, 2020), 121–157.

128. Pascal Bruckner, *The Tears of a White Man: Compassion as Contempt* (1983), trans. William Beer (New York: Free Press, 1986).

129. Michel Houellebecq, *Submission: A Novel* (2015), trans. Lorin Stein (New York: Farrar, Straus and Giroux, 2015).

130. See, e.g., "La théorie du genre par Belkacem (arabe ou juive?) des africains et LGBT," posted February 3, 2014, YouTube (video removed).

131. Edmund Burke, *Reflections on the Revolution in France and on the Proceedings in Certain Societies in London Relative to That Event* (London: Dodsley, 1790), 127–28.

132. Walker Connor, "The Politics of Ethnonationalism," *Journal of International Affairs* 27, no. 1 (1973): 4.

133. "The spectacle thus unites what is separate, but it unites it only *in its separateness*," Debord wrote in Guy Debord, *Society of the Spectacle* (1967), trans. Donald Nicholson-Smith (New York: Zone Books, 2019), section 29.

134. Philippe Roger, *The American Enemy: The History of French Anti-Americanism* (Chicago: University of Chicago Press, 2006), 405–409.

135. Alexandra Minna Stern, *Proud Boys and the White Ethnostate: How the Alt-Right Is Warping the American Imagination* (Boston: Beacon Press, 2019).

136. Sabine Hark and Paula-Irene Villa, eds., *(Anti-)Genderismus. Sexualität und Geschlecht als Schauplätze aktueller politischer Auseinandersetzungen* (Bielefield: Transcript, 2015).

137. Sarah Bracke and David Paternotte, "Unpacking the Sin of Gender," *Religion and Gender* 6, no. 2 (2016): 143–154.

138. Monique de Saint Martin, "Extrémisme politique et extrémisme religieux évangélique au Brésil," *Raison Présente* 212 (December 2019): 23–32.

139. Michel Feher and Aurélie Windels, "Une politique aux antipodes du discours," *Plein droit* 83, no. 4 (2009): 12–15.

CHAPTER 5

1. Daniel N. Lipson, "Where's the Justice? Affirmative Action's Severed Civil Rights Roots in the Age of Diversity," *Perspectives on Politics* 6, no. 4 (2008): 691–706.

2. Supreme Court of the United States, *Students for Fair Admissions Inc. v. President & Fellows of Harvard College*, and *Students for Fair Admissions Inc. v. University of North Carolina*.

NOTES TO CHAPTER 5

3. Philip F. Rubio, *A History of Affirmative Action: 1619–2000* (Jackson: University Press of Mississippi, 2001).

4. Supreme Court of the United States, *Dred Scott v. Sandford*, 60 U.S. 393, May 6, 1857.

5. The "Jim Crow" laws got their name from the Black character performed on stage and in the streets by black-faced white actors, among them Thomas D. Rice. These blackface performances were danced and sung to 1928 music that so violently mocked Black Americans that "Jim Crow" became synonymous with "Negro."

6. Supreme Court of the United States, *Plessy v. Ferguson*, 163 U.S. 537, May 18, 1896.

7. Supreme Court of the United States, *Brown v. Board of Education*.

8. United States Court of Appeals for the Third Circuit, *Piscataway Township Board of Education v. Taxman*, 91 F.3d 1547, August 8, 1996.

9. Supreme Court of the United States, *Adarand v. Pena*, 515 U.S. 200, June 12, 1995.

10. Supreme Court of the United States, *Regents of the University of California*.

11. Supreme Court of the United States, *Grutter v. Bollinger et al.*

12. Supreme Court of the United States, *Gratz et al. v. Bollinger et al.*, 539 U.S. 244, June 23, 2003.

13. Randall Kennedy, *For Discrimination. Race, Affirmative Action, and the Law* (New York: Vintage Books, 2015), 214.

14. Keith J. Bybee, *Mistaken Identity. The Supreme Court and the Politics of Minority Representation* (Princeton, NJ: Princeton University Press, 1998), 128–129.

15. Supreme Court of the United States, *Shaw v. Reno*, 509 U.S. 630, June 28, 1993.

16. Supreme Court of the United States, *Hunt v. Cromartie*, 526 U.S. 541, May 17, 1999.

17. On the entire case law, see Pierre Bouretz, "L'affirmative action ou les infortunes de l'égalité," *Pouvoirs* 59 (1991): 115–128, and Daniel Sabbagh, *Equality and Transparency: A Strategic Perspective on Affirmative Action in American Law* (2003) (London: Palgrave, 2006), 137–139.

18. Supreme Court of the United States, *Allen v. Milligan*, 509 U.S., June 8, 2023.

19. Supreme Court of the United States, *Students for Fair Admissions Inc.*, 8.

20. Supreme Court of the United States, *Students for Fair Admissions Inc.*: "Dissenting opinions," Supreme Court, June 29, 2023, supremecourt.gov/opinions/22pdf/20-1199_hgdj.pdf.

21. Joe R. Feagin, "Mythes et réalités de l'Affirmative Action aux États-Unis," *Hommes et Migrations* 1245 (September-October 2003): 29–41.

22. Denis Lacorne, *La Crise de l'identité américaine* (Paris: Fayard, 1997), 335.

23. This expands an article written nearly twenty years ago: Perreau, "L'invention républicaine."

24. Anemona Hartocollis, "He Took on the Voting Rights Act and Won. Now He's Taking on Harvard," *New York Times*, November 19, 2017.

NOTES TO CHAPTER 5

25. Anemona Hartocollis, "Harvard Rated Asian-American Applicants Lower on Personality Traits, Suit Says," *New York Times*, June 15, 2018.

26. United States District Court, District of Massachusetts, *Students for Fair Admissions Inc. v. President & Fellows of Harvard College*, 14–14176–ADB, September 30, 2019, and United States Court of Appeals for the First Circuit, *Students for Fair Admissions Inc. v. President & Fellows of Harvard College*, 19–2005, November 12, 2020.

27. Charlie Savage, "Justice Dept. to Take on Affirmative Action in College Admissions," *New York Times*, August 1, 2017.

28. Anemona Hartocollis, "Justice Dept. Accuses Yale of Discrimination in Application Process," *New York Times*, August 13, 2020.

29. Supreme Court of the United States, *Dobbs v. Jackson Women's Health Organization*.

30. Supreme Court of the United States, *New York State Rifle & Pistol Association v. Bruen*, 597 U.S., June 23, 2022.

31. Supreme Court of the United States, *West Virginia v. Environmental Protection Agency*, 597 U.S., June 30, 2022.

32. Supreme Court of the United States, *Kennedy v. Bremerton School District*, 597 U.S., June 27, 2022.

33. Supreme Court of the United States, *Carson v. Makin*, 596 U.S., June 21, 2022.

34. Supreme Court of the United States, *Fisher v. University of Texas*, 579 U.S. 365, June 23, 2016.

35. "Black, Hispanic and Asian American Adults More Likely than White Adults to Say Race or Ethnicity, Legacy, First-Generation Status Should Be Factors in College Admissions," Pew Research Center, April 22, 2022, https://www.pewresearch.org/short-reads/2022/04/26/u-s-public-continues-to-view-grades-test-scores-as-top-factors-in-college-admissions/.

36. Mary Churchill, "The SAT and ACT Are Less Important Than You Might Think," *Inside Higher Ed*, January 29, 2023, https://www.insidehighered.com/blogs/higher-ed-policy/sat-and-act-are-less-important-you-might-think.

37. Jessica Gourdon, "Sciences Po Paris à l'heure de l'hypersélection," *Le Monde*, November 25, 2021.

38. Jason Xu, president of the *Silicon Valley Chinese Association Foundation*, thus testified against Harvard's admissions practices whereas *Asian Americans Advancing Justice* took the opposite position. See Adam Hiptak and Anemona Hartocollis, "Supreme Court Will Hear Challenge to Affirmative Action at Harvard and U. N. C.," *New York Times*, January 24, 2022.

39. Gersen, "The Uncomfortable Truth about Affirmative Action and Asian-Americans."

40. Tyler Austin Harper, "I Teach at an Elite College. Here's a Look Inside the Racial Gaming of Admissions," *New York Times*, June 19, 2023.

41. Daniel Golden, "An Analytic Survey of Legacy Preferences," in *Affirmative-Action for the Rich: Legacy Preferences in College Admissions*, ed. Richard D. Kahlenberg (New York: Century Foundation Press, 2010), 74–76.

42. It should be noted that Peter Arcidiacono testified in favor of the *Students for Fair Admissions* against Harvard. Peter Arcidiacono, Josh Kinsler, and Tyler Ransom, "Legacy and Athlete Preferences at Harvard," public documents from the Economics Department at Duke University, December 22, 2020, http://public.econ.duke.edu/~psarcidi/legacyathlete.pdf.

43. Arcidiacono, Kinsler, and Ransom, "Legacy," 3.

44. Ira Katznelson, *When Affirmative Action Was White: An Untold History of Racial Inequalities in Twentieth-Century America* (New York: W. W. Norton, 2006).

45. Stephanie Saul, "Elite Colleges' Quiet Fight to Favor Alumni Children," *New York Times*, July 13, 2022.

46. Thomas Sowell, *Affirmative Action around the World: An Empirical Study* (New Haven, CT: Yale University Press, 2004).

47. Adnan Farooqui, "Political Representation of a Minority: Muslim Representation in Contemporary India," *India Review* 19, no. 2 (2020): 153–175.

48. Terry Martin, *The Affirmative Action Empire: Nations and Nationalism in the Soviet Union, 1923–1939* (Ithaca, NY: Cornell University Press, 2001).

49. See Laure Blévis, "Les avatars de la citoyenneté en Algérie coloniale ou les paradoxes d'une catégorisation," *Droit et société* 48, no. 2 (2001): 557–581.

50. Georges Nael, "Minorités et liberté religieuse dans les Constitutions des États de l'Orient arabe," *Égypte/Monde arabe* 10 (2013), https://doi.org/10.4000/ema.3206.

51. Katia Boustany, "Minorités et organisation institutionnelle au Liban: Architecture de l'État et dispositifs juridiques," in *Minorités et organisation de l'État*, ed. Nicolas Levrat (Brussels: Bruylant, 1998), 389–411.

52. Nael, "Minorités et liberté religieuse dans les Constitutions des États de l'Orient arabe."

53. Todd Shepard, "La promotion exceptionnelle de citoyens français musulmans d'Algérie (1956–1962): Une politique d'affirmative action à la française?" Paper presentation, *Institut d'Histoire du Temps Présent*, "Répression, contrôle et encadrement dans le monde colonial au XXe siècle," Paris, March 23, 2004.

54. Sophie Body-Gendrot, "L'universalisme français à l'épreuve des discriminations," *Hommes et migrations* 1245 (September-October 2003): 18.

55. Robert C. Lieberman, "A Tale of Two Countries: The Politics of Color Blindness in France and the United States," *French Politics, Culture and Society* 19, no. 3 (Fall 2001): 32–59.

56. https://avalon.law.yale.edu/18th_century/rightsof.asp.

57. In 1971 the Constitutional Council censured a law for the first time: Conseil constitutionnel, *Loi complétant les dispositions des articles 5 et 7 de la loi du 1er juillet 1901 relative au contrat d'association*, 71–44, July 16, 1971.

NOTES TO CHAPTER 5   249

58. François Stasse, *Rapport public au Conseil d'État* (Paris: La Documentation Française, 1996).

59. Conseil constitutionnel, *Loi de finance rectificative pour 1984*, 84–186, December 29, 1984.

60. Conseil constitutionnel, *Loi portant statut du territoire de la Nouvelle-Calédonie et dépendances, et notamment ses articles 12, 131 et 137*, 84–178, August 30, 1984.

61. Conseil constitutionnel, *Quotas par sexe I*.

62. Conseil constitutionnel, *Loi portant statut de la collectivité territoriale de Corse*, 91-290, May 9, 1991.

63. Conseil constitutionnel, *Charte européenne des langues régionales ou minoritaires*, 99-412, June 15, 1999.

64. Conseil constitutionnel, *Loi complétant le statut d'autonomie de la Polynésie française*, 2004-491, February 12, 2004.

65. According to Article 74 of the Constitution, these *collectivités* have the option of adapting the law as defined by "organic" laws. They are the islands of Saint Barthélemy, Saint Martin, Saint-Pierre-et-Miquelon, French Polynesia, and Wallis and Futuna. New Caledonia has options for constitutionally regulated legislative adaptation (Title VIII of the Constitution). The French Southern and Antarctic Lands are not considered overseas *collectivités*. Owing to the lack of a permanent population, they are administered directly from Paris.

66. This is in reference to the islands of Guadeloupe and Reunion (each of which is both a *département* and an overseas *région*) as well as Martinique, Guyana, and Mayotte (each of which individually forms a unique territorial community following a change made by local referendum to their institutional organization).

67. Conseil constitutionnel, *Loi relative à la Corse*, 2001–454, January 17, 2002.

68. Howard Green, Hichem Trache, and Danielle Blanchard, "An Experiment in French Urban Policy: Evaluation and Reflection on the Implementation of the Zones Franches Urbaines," *Planning Theory & Practice* 2, no. 1 (2001): 53–66.

69. The council thus specified that the Constitution recognizes "overseas populations," even though the title that mentioned it (a title that was about the "French community" and that named the colonial empire) was deleted from the Constitution in 1995. Conseil constitutionnel, *Loi organisant une consultation de la population de Mayotte*, 2000–428, May 4, 2000. See Robin Médard, *La République face aux droits des minorités: Lire l'ordre juridique français à partir de la théorie libérale de Will Kymlicka* (Paris: L'Harmattan, 2015), 59–60.

70. Piketty, *Mesurer le racisme*, 14.

71. Piketty, 16.

72. Perreau, *Queer Theory*, 48–49.

73. Frédérique Matonti, "Classes populaires versus minorité: Une fausse opposition," in *Comment sommes-nous devenus réacs?* (Paris: Fayard, 2021), chapter 3, I-books.

74. Melinda Cooper, *Family Values: Between Neoliberalism and the New Social Conservatism* (New York: Zone Books, 2017).

75. Saad Gulzar, Nicholas Haas, and Benjamin Pasquale, "Does Political Affirmative Action Work, and for Whom?" *American Political Science Review* 14, no. 4 (November 2020): 1230–1246.

76. Libby Adler, *Gay Priori: A Queer Critical Legal Studies Approach to Law Reform* (Durham, NC: Duke University Press, 2018), 175–179.

77. Albert Ogien distinguishes among social minorities, civic minorities, and epistemic minorities. Albert Ogien, *Émancipations: Luttes minoritaires, luttes universelles?* (Paris: Textuel, 2023).

78. See Cyril Delhay, *Promotion ZEP: Des quartiers à Sciences Po* (Paris: Hachette, 2006). See also Bénédicte Robert, *Les Politiques d'éducation prioritaire: Les défis de la réforme* (Paris: Presses universitaires de France, 2001).

79. Zaïr Kedadouche, "Sciences-Politiquement correct," *Libération*, March 8, 2001; "Sciences-Po à l'heure de la 'discrimination justifiée,'" *Le Monde*, April 26, 2001.

80. "Nicolas Sarkozy relance le débat sur la 'discrimination positive,'" *Le Monde*, November 21, 2003.

81. For a summary of these discussions, see Éric Keslassy, *De la discrimination positive* (Paris: Bréal, 2004).

82. "Nicolas Sarkozy relance le débat sur la 'discrimination positive.'"

83. The Law of June 6, 2000, favored the equal representation of women and men in elective office.

84. Anne Le Gall, Françoise Gaspard, and Claude Servan-Schreiber, *Au Pouvoir citoyennes! Liberté, égalité, parité* (Paris: Seuil, 1992).

85. Laure Bereni, *La Bataille de la parité: Mobilisations pour la féminisation du pouvoir* (Paris: Economica, 2015).

86. For an analysis of these questions see Éric Fassin and Michel Feher, "Parité et PaCS: anatomie politique d'un rapport," in *Au-delà du PaCS: L'expertise familiale à l'épreuve de l'homosexualité*, ed. Daniel Borrillo, Éric Fassin, and Marcela Iacub (Paris: Presses universitaires de France, 1999), 13–43.

87. Réjane Sénac, *L'Égalité sous conditions: Genre, parité, diversité* (Paris: Presses de Sciences Po, 2015).

88. Constitute Project, https://www.constituteproject.org/constitution/France_2008.

89. Denis Cosnard, "La ville de Paris mise à l'amende pour avoir nommé trop de directrices," *Le Monde*, December 11, 2020.

90. Constitute Project.

91. Conseil constitutionnel, *Loi relative à la maîtrise de l'immigration, à l'intégration et à l'asile*, 2007–557, November 17, 2007.

92. In any case, the revision of the Constitution would not have been effective, according to the terms of Article 89, without a vote of the Senate followed by referendum or a three-fifth majority vote of the Congress (that is to say, by the National

NOTES TO CHAPTER 5

Assembly and the Senate together), depending on the president of the republic's choice.

93. Benoît Le Floc'h, "Amélie de Montchalin: 'La haute fonction publique a perdu en diversité sociale,'" *Le Monde*, October 7, 2020.

94. Gwénaële Calvès, *La Discrimination positive* (Paris, Presses universitaires de France, 2016), 63.

95. Conseil constitutionnel, *Loi portant diverses dispositions d'ordre social*, 94–357, January 25, 1995.

96. Cour européenne des droits de l'homme, *Stec et al. v. United Kingdom*, April 12, 2006, sections 51,61.

97. Hélène Surrel, "La sanction des discriminations par la Cour européenne des droits de l'homme," *Titre VII* 4 (2020): https://www.conseil-constitutionnel.fr /publications/titre-vii/la-sanction-des-discriminations-par-la-cour-europeenne-des -droits-de-l-homme.

98. Which is why Daniel Sabbagh uses the expression "positive discrimination" in the French version of *Equality and Transparency: L'Égalité par le droit*, 3–5.

99. Daniel Sabbagh, "Groups and Affirmative Action," in *How Groups Matter: Challenges of Toleration in Pluralistic Societies*, ed. Gideon Calder, Magali Bessone, and Federico Zuolo (London: Routledge, 2014), 118–119.

100. Suzy Killmister, "Resolving the Dilemma of Group Membership," in Calder, Bessone, and Zuolo, *How Groups Matter*, 89–108.

101. I mention only a part of my educational path here. I address the modalities of "cleft habitus" in a text currently being written, provisionally entitled "*De l'université en Amérique*" (On the University in America). Pierre Bourdieu outlined academic self-analysis in Pierre Bourdieu, *Sketch for a Self-Analysis* (2004), trans. Richard Nice (Cambridge: Polity Press, 2007), 84–103.

102. The French puns by using the very similar pronunciation of "l'essence" and "les sens."

103. Historian Joan Scott thus developed the concept of "fantasy echo" based on a student's miscomprehension of a German-accented utterance of "*fin-de-siècle*" that made it into his paper. Joan W. Scott, "Fantasy Echo: History and the Construction of Identity," *Critical Theory* 7, no. 2 (winter 2001): 284–304.

104. Richard Descoings, *Sciences Po: De La Courneuve à Shanghai* (Paris: Presses de Sciences Po, 2007).

105. Didier Eribon, *La Société comme verdict* (Paris: Fayard, 2013), 187–190.

106. Paul Pasquali, *Passer les frontières sociales: Comment les "filières d'élite" entrouvrent leurs portes* (Paris: Fayard, 2014), 315.

107. See Abdelilah Laloui, *Les Baskets et le Costume* (Paris: JC Lattès, 2020).

108. On the history of this adaptation in France, see Paul Pasquali, *Héritocratie: Les élites, les grandes écoles et les mésaventures du mérite (1870–2020)* (Paris: La Découverte, 2021).

109. Thomas Fraser Pettigrew and Linda R. Tropp, "A Meta-Analytic Test of Intergroup Contact Theory," *Journal of Personality and Social Psychology* 90, no. 5 (May 2006): 766.

110. For a summary of "The Future of Minority Studies Research Project": Linda Martín Alcoff, Michael R. Hames-García, Satya P. Mohanty, and Paula M. Y. Moya, eds., *Identity Politics Reconsidered* (London: Palgrave MacMillan, 2006).

111. Conseil d'État, *Fédération CFTC de l'agriculture et alii.*, May 7, 2013.

112. European Court of Justice, *Reinhard Prigge and others v. Deutsche Lufthansa AG*, C-447/09, September 13, 2011.

113. Court of Justice of the European Union, *Colin Wolf v. Stadt Frankfurt am Main*, C-229/08, January 12, 2010.

114. Simon Wuhl, *Discrimination positive et justice sociale* (Paris: Presses universitaires de France, 2007), 85–86.

115. For an analysis of the cultural turn in the law, see Patricia Ewick and Susan Silbey, "The Structure of Legality: The Cultural Contradictions of Social Institutions," in *Legality and Community: On the Intellectual Legacy of Philip Selznick*, ed. Robert A. Kagan, Martin Krygier, and Kenneth Winston (Oxford: Rowman & Littlefield, 2002), 149–165.

116. Valérie Amiraux and Virginie Guiraudon, "Discrimination in Comparative Perspective: Policies and Practices," *American Behavioral Scientist*, 53, no. 12 (2010): 1691–1714.

117. That is the title given to the English-language translation of his historical study of conflicts between customary law and colonial law: Jean-Loup Amselle, *Affirmative Exclusion: Cultural Pluralism and the Rule of Custom in France* (1996), trans. Jane Marie Todd (Ithaca, NY: Cornell University Press, 2003).

118. Vincent-Arnaud Chappe, "La preuve par la comparaison: Méthode des panels et droit de la non-discrimination," *Sociologies pratiques* 23, no. 2 (2011): 45–55.

119. See www.antidiscriminations.fr.

120. Lani Guinier, *The Tyranny of the Majority: Fundamental Fairness in Representative Democracy* (New York: Free Press, 1995), 5.

121. Daniel Sabbagh, "L'itinéraire contemporain de la 'diversité' aux États-Unis: de l'instrumentalisation à l'institutionnalisation?" *Raisons politiques* 35, no. 3 (2009): 34.

122. Karen Zivi, *Making Rights Claims: A Practice of Democratic Citizenship* (Oxford: Oxford University Press, 2012), 51.

123. European Court of Justice, *Asociația Accept v. Consiliul Național pentru Combaterea Discriminării*, C-81/12, April 25, 2013, and European Court of Justice, *Centrum voor gelijkheid van kansen en voor racismebestrijding v. Firma Feryn NV*, C-54/07, July 10, 2018.

124. See Kristin Henrard, "The Effective Protection against Discrimination and the Burden of Proof: Evaluating the CJEU's Guidance through the Lens of Race," in *EU*

Anti-Discrimination Law Beyond Gender, ed. Uladzislau Belavusau and Kristin Henrard (Oxford: Hart Publishing, 2020), 106–115

125. She thus takes a punny "de-liber[al]-ative" look at democracy as she emphasizes the importance of the interdependence of moral points of view in deliberative contexts. Astrid von Busekist, *La Religion au tribunal: Essai sur le délibéralisme* (Paris: Albin Michel, 2023), 268–270.

126. Étienne Balibar, *Equaliberty: Political Essays* (2010), trans. James Ingram (Durham, NC: Duke University Press, 2014).

127. Balibar, *Equaliberty*, 276.

128. Conseil d'État, *Denoyez et Chorques*, May 10, 1974.

129. Conseil constitutionnel, *Loi relative à certains ouvrages reliant les voies nationales ou départementales*, 79–107, July 12, 1979.

130. Matthew Frye Jacobson, *Roots Too: White Ethnic Revival in Post-Civil Rights America* (Cambridge, MA: Harvard University Press, 2006), 33–34.

131. Michel Feher, "Empowerment Hazards: Affirmative Action, Recovery Psychology, and Identity Politics," *Representations* 55 (summer 1996): 84–91.

132. For more detail, see Nadia Urbinati, *Representative Democracy: Principles & Genealogy* (Chicago: University of Chicago Press, 2006), 176–221.

CHAPTER 6

1. "Tuerie d'Orlando: Géométries variables," *La Revue de Presse*, France Culture, June 23, 2016, https://www.radiofrance.fr/franceculture/podcasts/la-revue-de-presse/tuerie-d-orlando-geometries-variables-9044477.

2. Melissa Chan, "This Couple Killed in the Orlando Shooting Hoped to Get Married: Now They Will Have a Joint Funeral," *Time*, June 13, 2016.

3. "Orlando Nightclub Shooting. Obama. Full Speech," posted June 12, 2016, YouTube, https://www.youtube.com/watch?v=ArkIHIyAkdY.

4. Adam Goldman, "FBI Has Found No Evidence That Orlando Shooter Targeted Pulse Because It Was a Gay Club," *Washington Post*, July 16, 2016.

5. Marc Fisher, Michelle Boorstein, and Molly Hennessy-Fiske, "How the Colorado Mass Shooting Unfolded—and Ended—Inside Club Q," *Washington Post*, November 21, 2022.

6. Dave Philipps, Simon Romero, and Shawn Hubler, "It Was Never Easy to Be Club Q in Colorado Springs," *New York Times*, November 21, 2022.

7. See, e.g., "Fusillade dans une discothèque LGBTQ aux États-Unis: au moins 5 morts, le tireur arrêté par des 'héros,'" *Le Parisien*, November 20, 2022; Julien Gester, "Avant la tuerie de Colorado Springs, des mois de surenchère homophobe aux États-Unis," *Libération*, November 21, 2022; "Tuerie dans le Colorado: Le tireur devrait répondre de meurtres aggravés d'homophobie," *Le Figaro*, November 21, 2022.

8. Maurice Merleau-Ponty, *Phenomenology of Perception* (1945), trans. Colin Smith (London: Routledge, 2002), 346–347.

9. Ashley Nellis, "The Color of Justice: Racial and Ethnic Disparities in State Prisons," The Sentencing Project, October 13, 2021, https://www.sentencingproject.org/reports/the-color-of-justice-racial-and-ethnic-disparity-in-state-prisons-the-sentencing-project/. See also Ruth Wilson Gilmore, *Golden Gulag: Prisons, Surplus, Crisis, and Opposition in Globalizing California* (Berkeley: University of California Press, 2007).

10. Marion Manier, "Cause des femmes *vs* cause des minorités: Tensions autour de la question des 'femmes de l'immigration' dans l'action publique française," *Revue européenne des migrations internationales* 29, no. 4 (2013): 89–110.

11. Vincent-Arnaud Chappe, "La qualification juridique est-elle soluble dans le militantisme? Tensions et paradoxes au sein de la permanence juridique d'une association antiraciste," *Droit et société* 76, no. 3 (2010): 543–567.

12. That is what Sunmin Kim showed regarding people of Korean heritage living in Los Angeles: Sunmin Kim, "Rethinking Models of Minority Representation: Inter- and Intra-Group Variation in Political 'Styles,'" *Du Bois Review* 16, no. 2 (2019): 489–510.

13. Hans Mayer, *Outsiders: A Study in Life and Letters* (1975), trans. Denis M. Sweet (Cambridge, MA: MIT Press, 1982), 361.

14. James Baldwin, "Go the Way Your Blood Beats: An Interview with James Balwin, by Richard Goldstein" (1984), in *James Baldwin: The Last Interview and Other Conversations* (New York: Melville House, 2014), 68.

15. Isaiah Berlin, "Two Concepts of Liberty" (1958), in *Liberty*, ed. Henry Hardy (Oxford: Oxford University Press, 2002), 166–217.

16. Geoffroy de Lagasnerie, *3: Une aspiration au dehors* (Paris: Flammarion, 2023), 87–95.

17. Norman Ajari, *Dignity or Death: Ethics and Politics of Race* (2019), trans. Matthew B. Smith (Cambridge: Polity, 2023), 200.

18. Michel Foucault, *History of Sexuality*, vol. 1: *An Introduction* (1976), trans. Robert Hurley (New York: Pantheon Books, 1978), 138–140.

19. See Salena Tramel, "Convergence as Political Strategy: Social Justice Movements, Natural Resources and Climate Change," *Third World Quarterly* 39, no. 7 (2018): 1290–1307.

20. See Les Engraineurs (Facebook page), January 5, 2023, https://www.facebook.com/CollectifCitoyenParis; *Fakir*, January 5, 2023, https://fakirpresse.info. See also Benjamin Sourice, *La Démocratie des places: Des Indignados à Nuit debout, vers un nouvel horizon politique* (Paris: Charles Léopold Mayer, 2017), 111–114.

21. Guy Groux and Richard Robert, "Le spectre de la convergence des luttes," *Télos*, April 1, 2020, https://www.telos-eu.com/fr/politique-francaise-et-internationale/le-spectre-de-la-convergence-des-luttes.html.

22. Béligh Nabli, "'Convergence des luttes': théorie et pratique," *Libération* (blog), May 25, 2018, https://www.liberation.fr/debats/2018/05/25/convergence-des-luttes-theorie-et-pratique_1816101.

NOTES TO CHAPTER 6

23. Roderick A. Ferguson, *One-Dimensional Queer* (Cambridge: Polity Press, 2018).

24. James Baldwin, *Notes of a Native Son* (1955) (Boston: Beacon Press, 1963), 109–113.

25. Baldwin, "Go the Way Your Blood Beats," 66–67.

26. Christine Delphy, Irène Jami, and Catherine Achin, "'Partir de ce que les gens vivent': Théorie de l'exploitation, imbrication des rapports sociaux et difficulté de la convergence des luttes," *Mouvements* 100, no. 4 (2019): 127–134.

27. Kehinde Andrews, *Back to Black. Retelling Black Radicalism for the 21st Century* (London: Zed Books, 2018), 175–176.

28. Norman Ajari, *Darkening Blackness. Race, Gender, Class and Pessimism in 21st Century Black Thought* (2022), trans. Matthew B. Smith (Cambridge: Polity Press, 2024), 96.

29. In his introduction to the French edition of *Dignity or Death*, Norman Ajari rejoices in the fact that Hungarian philosopher Gábor Tverdota used his theory of dignity in a study devoted to Belgian social institutions' creation of poverty: Norman Ajari, *La Dignité ou la Mort: Éthique et politique de la race* (Paris: La Découverte, "Les Empêcheurs de penser en rond," 2019), 35.

30. Ajari, *La Dignité ou la Mort*, 35–36.

31. Cedric Robinson, *Black Marxism: The Making of the Black Radical Tradition* (Chapel Hill, NC: University of North Carolina Press, 2021).

32. bell hooks, *Yearning: Race, Gender, and Cultural Politics* (London: Routledge, 2015), 63.

33. Frank B. Wilderson III, *Afropessimism* (New York: W. W. Norton, 2000), 41.

34. Martin Luther King, "The Other America," Civil Rights Movement Archive, April 4, 1967, https://www.crmvet.org/docs/otheram.htm.

35. Jakobi Williams, *From the Bullet to the Ballot: The Illinois Chapter of the Black Panther Party and Racial Coalition Politics in Chicago* (Chapel Hill: University of North Carolina Press, 2013), 125ff.

36. "Jesse Jackson on the Rainbow Coalition" (1984), The American Yawp Reader, January 5, 2023, https://www.americanyawp.com/reader/29-the-triumph-of-the-right/jesse-jackson-on-e-rainbow-coalition-1984/.

37. See Danny Glover and Bill Fletcher, "The Case for a Neo-Rainbow Electoral Strategy," in *Barack Obama and African American Empowerment*, ed. Manning Marable and Kristen Clarke (New York: Palgrave Macmillan, 2009), 91–103. See also Edward Mcclelland, "How Fred Hampton Gave Way to Obama," *Chicago Mag*, February 18, 2021, https://www.chicagomag.com/news/judas-black-messiah-fred-hampton/.

38. "Manifeste. Nous sommes la gauche," *Libération*, May 6, 1997.

39. "Manifeste. Nous sommes la gauche."

40. See, e.g., the appeal made by queer and feminist collectives, by Strass (an organization of sex workers), and Act Up Paris in 2003: "Trahisons socialistes: Solidarité des minorités," *Archives nationales: fonds Act Up-Paris*, repertoire 20140474.

41. Louis-Georges Tin, "Le Pacte pour l'égalité et la diversité: Passons aux actes!" in *Le Pacte. Pour en finir avec les discriminations: Sexisme, Homophobie, Handicap, Âge, Origine*, ed. Louis-Georges Tin (Paris: Autrement, 2012), ch. 1.

42. See the interviews with Réjane Sénac in *Radicales et fluides: Les mobilisations contemporaines* (Paris: Presses de Sciences Po, 2022).

43. Dara Z. Strolovitch, *Affirmative Advocacy: Race, Class and Gender in Interest Group Politics* (Chicago: University of Chicago Press, 2007), 191–205.

44. BlackLivesMatter, "What We Believe."

45. Traoré and de Lagasnerie, *Le Combat Adama*, 302–351.

46. A movement for environmental justice and investment in a massive plan to support the ecological transition in the wake of the European, Australian, and US green parties. US Representative Alexandria Ocasio-Cortez and Senator Edward Markey introduced an ambitious resolution, the "Green New Deal," in Congress in 2019. The phrase "Green New Deal" is attributed to journalist Thomas Friedman: "A Warning From the Garden," *New York Times*, January 19, 2007.

47. Mathieu Magnaudeix, *Génération Ocasio-Cortez: Les nouveaux activistes américains* (Paris: La Découverte, 2020), 232.

48. Magnaudeix, *Génération*, 119.

49. Tommie Shelby, "Foundations of Black Solidarity: Collective Identity or Common Oppression?" *Ethics* 112, no. 2 (2002): 231–66.

50. Nitasha Tamar Sharma, *Hip Hop Desis: South Asian Americans, Blackness, and a Global Race Consciousness* (Durham, NC: Duke University Press, 2010).

51. Beaman, *Citizen Outsider*, 88.

52. On the history of ties between nonprofit organizations and the state and of the empowerment of cooperatives and mutuals to delegating public services, see Jean-Louis Laville, "Les raisons d'être des associations," in *Association, Démocratie et Société civile*, ed. Jean-Louis Laville, Alain Caillé, Philippe Chanial et al. (Paris: La Découverte, 2001), 84–103.

53. Julien Talpin, *Community Organizing: De l'émeute à l'alliance des classes populaires aux États-Unis* (Paris: Raisons d'agir, 2016), 185–186.

54. INCITE! *The Revolution Will Not Be Funded: Beyond the Non-Profit Industrial Complex* (Durham, NC: Duke University Press, 2017).

55. Talpin, *Community Organizing*, 198–202.

56. See Caroline Rolland-Diamond, *Black America: Une histoire des luttes pour l'égalité et pour la justice (XIXe–XXIe siècle)* (Paris: La Découverte, 2016), 480–481.

57. Chayma Drira and Henry Shah, "#SaintDenisSouthSide, ép. 2: De la délicate convergence des luttes à gauche," BondyBlog, June 13, 2020, https://www.bondyblog.fr/international/saintdenissouthside-ep-2-de-la-delicate-convergence-des-luttes-a-gauche/.

58. Michael R. Hames-García, "'Who Are Our Own People?' Challenges for a Theory of Social Identity," in *Reclaiming Identity: Realist Theory and the Predicament*

NOTES TO CHAPTER 6

of Postmodernism, ed. Paula M. L. Moya and Michael R. Hames-García (Berkeley: University of California Press, 2000), 121.

59. See Alban Jacquemart, *Les Hommes dans les mouvements féministes: Socio-histoire d'un engagement improbable* (Rennes: Presses universitaires de Rennes, 2014).

60. "Blessés, participation, coût . . . Un an de gilets jaunes en chiffre," *L'Express*, November 2, 2019.

61. Cécile Bouanchaud, "'Je porte cette défiance dans ma chair': L'amertume des 'gilets jaunes' placés en garde à vue préventive," *Le Monde*, November 16, 2019.

62. Frédéric Veaux, "Techniques d'intervention," Direction Générale de la police nationale, Cab, n°20, 01526D, June 15, 2020.

63. Défenseur des droits, "Maintien de l'ordre: Les recommandations générales du défenseur des droits," Défenseur des droits, July 10, 2020, https://juridique .defenseurdesdroits.fr/index.php?lvl=notice_display&id=23735; Défenseur des droits, "Le maintien de l'ordre au regard des règles de déontologie," Assemblée nationale, December 2017, https://www.defenseurdesdroits.fr/fr/rapports/2018/01/le-maintien -de-lordre-au-regard-des-regles-de-deontologie.

64. Geoffroy de Lagasnerie, *La Conscience politique* (Paris: Fayard, 2019), 119–124, 127–133.

65. Défenseur des droits, "Enquête sur l'accès aux droits. Volume 1: relation police / population: le cas des contrôles d'identité," Défenseur des droits, January 20, 2017, https://www.defenseurdesdroits.fr/enquete-sur-lacces-aux-droits-volume-1-relations -police-population-le-cas-des-controles-didentite.

66. Clément Parrot, "Le récit de l'arrestation d'Adama Traoré, mort dans une gendarmerie du Val-d'Oise le 19 juillet," *France Info TV*, August 1, 2016, https:// www.francetvinfo.fr/faits-divers/adama-traore/enquete-francetv-info-le-recit-de -l-arrestation-d-adama-traore-mort-dans-une-gendarmerie-du-val-d-oise-le-19 -juillet_1562663.html.

67. Paul Butler, *Chokehold: Policing Black Men* (New York: New Press, 2017), 22.

68. Michelle Alexander, *The New Jim Crow: Mass Incarceration in the Age of Colorblindness* (New York: New Press, 2010), 173ff.

69. Chebel d'Appollonia, *Violent America*, 3.

70. Chebel d'Appollonia, 32.

71. Ilham Maad, "Gardiens de la paix," *Arte Radio*, posted June 4, 2020, YouTube, https://www.youtube.com/watch?v=HDrvPpxR_1g.

72. Défenseur des droits, "Discriminations et origines: l'urgence d'agir," June 2020, 4–5, https://www.defenseurdesdroits.fr/fr/rapports/2020/06/discriminations-et-origi nes-lurgence-dagir.

73. Daniel Sabbagh, "Le 'racisme systémique': Un conglomérat problématique," *Mouvements* special issue, no. 2 (September 2022): 63.

74. Daniel N. Maroun, "Agency, Culpability, and Police Brutality: French Reports of Death during *les Contrôles Policiers*," *Contemporary French Civilization* 47, no. 4 (December 2022): 385–401.

75. Pascale Pascariello, "Trois des gendarmes mis en cause dans le décès d'Adama Traoré ont été décorés pour l'avoir interpelé," *Mediapart*, July 16, 2021, https://www .mediapart.fr/journal/france/160721/trois-des-gendarmes-mis-en-cause-dans-le -deces-d-adama-traore-ont-ete-decores-pour-l-avoir-interpelle.

76. Ludovic Seré, "Affaire Adama Traoré: Une nouvelle expertise médicale confirme le rôle des gendarmes et d'un 'coup de chaleur' dans la mort," *Libération*, November 9, 2022.

77. "End of Mission Statement by the United Nations Special Rapporteur on the Rights of Persons with Disabilities, Ms. Catalina Devandas-Aguilar, on Her Visit to France," Office of the High Commissioner to the United Nations, October 16, 2017, https://www.ohchr.org/fr/statements/2017/10/end-mission-statement-united -nations-special-rapporteur-rights-persons.

78. Défenseur des droits, "La mise en œuvre de la Convention relative aux droits des personnes handicapées (CIDPH)," Défenseur des droits, July 2, 2020, https:// www.defenseurdesdroits.fr/fr/rapports/2020/07/la-mise-en-oeuvre-de-la-convention -relative-aux-droits-des-personnes-handicapees.

79. See Joël Zaffran, ed., *Accessibilité et Handicap* (Grenoble: Presses universitaires de Grenoble, 2015).

80. Anne Revillard, *Des droits vulnérables: Handicap, action publique et changement social* (Paris: Presses de Sciences Po, 2020), 119.

81. Jean-François Ravaud, Isabelle Ville, and Annie Jolivet, "Le chômage des personnes handicapées: L'apport d'une explication en termes de discrimination à l'embauche," *Archives des maladies professionnelles et de l'environnement* 56, no. 6 (1995): 445–456.

82. Romuald Bodin, *L'Institution du handicap: Esquisse pour une théorie sociologique du handicap* (Paris: La Dispute, 2018), 106.

83. Council of Europe, European Committee of Social Rights, *European Disability Forum (EDF) and Inclusion Europe v. France*, complaint no.168/2018, April 17, 2023.

84. For a summary, see the Senate report edited by Jean-Marc Juilhard and Paul Blanc: *Maltraitance envers les personnes handicapées: Briser la loi du silence*, Commission of Inquiry Report no. 339, June 10, 2003, and the book based on Myriam Lagraula-Fabre's thesis, *La Violence institutionnelle: Une violence commise sur des personnes vulnérables par des personnes ayant autorité* (Paris: L'Harmattan, 2005).

85. Pierre-Yves Baudot and Emmanuelle Fillion, *Le Handicap cause politique* (Paris: Presses universitaires de France, 2021), 18.

86. Baudot and Fillion, *Handicap*, 14–15, 16–17.

87. Baudot and Fillion, 13. See also Tom Shakespeare, "Disabled People's Self Organisation: A New Social Movement?" *Disability & Society* 8, no. 3 (1993): 249–264.

88. Charlotte Puiseux, *De chair et de fer: Vivre et lutter dans une société validiste* (Paris: La Découverte, 2022), 137–138.

89. Victoria Ann Lewis, "Crip," in *Keywords for Disability Studies*, ed. Rachel Adams, Benjamin Reiss, and David Serlin (New York: New York University Press, 2015), 46–48.

NOTES TO CHAPTER 6

90. See Robert McRuer, *Crip Theory. Cultural Signs of Queerness and Disability* (New York: New York University Press, 2016).

91. Speech given in the National Assembly, February 5, 2013, https://www.assemblee-nationale.fr/14/cri/2012-2013/20130135.asp.

92. Léon-Gontran Damas, *Black-Label* (Paris: Gallimard, 1956), 50–51.

93. Achille Mbembe, *Politique de l'inimitié* (Paris: La Découverte, 2016), chapter 3, I-books.

94. Hanna Fenichel Pitkin, *The Concept of Representation* (Berkeley: University of California Press, 1972), 145–146.

95. Camille Hamidi, "Les minorités doivent-elles être représentées par des minorités? Une *color line* dans les représentations ordinaires de la représentation en France," *Participations* 30, no. 2 (2021): 65–96.

96. Gayatri Spivak, "Can the Subaltern Speak?" (1988), in *Marxism and the Interpretation of Culture*, ed. Cary Nelson and Lawrence Grossberg (Urbana: University of Illinois Press, 1988), 279.

97. Danielle Allen and Jennifer Light, "Introduction," in *From Voice to Influence: Understanding Citizenship in a Digital Age*, ed. Danielle Allen and Jennifer Light (Chicago: University of Chicago Press, 2015), 6.

98. Mathieu Magnaudeix, "Le premier ministre est gay, mais pas trop," *Mediapart*, posted January 10, 2024, https://www.mediapart.fr/journal/politique/100124/le-premier-ministre-est-gay-mais-pas-trop/.

99. "Liberté pour l'histoire," *Libération*, December 12, 2005.

100. Pierre Nora and Françoise Chandernagor, *Liberté pour l'histoire* (Paris: Éditions du CNRS, 2008).

101. Bernard Accoyer, "Rapport d'information au nom de la Mission d'information sur les questions mémorielles," Assemblée nationale, November 18, 2008, https://www.assemblee-nationale.fr/13/rap-info/i1262.asp.

102. Christiane Taubira, *Égalité pour les exclus: Le politique face à l'histoire et à la mémoire coloniales* (Paris: Temps Présent Éditions, 2009), 66–67.

103. On this point see Dipesh Chakrabarty, *Provincializing Europe: Postcolonial Thought and Historical Difference* (Princeton, NJ: Princeton University Press, 2000), 106–111.

104. Ann Cvetkovich, *An Archive of Feelings: Trauma, Sexuality, and Lesbian Public Cultures* (Durham, NC: Duke University Press, 2003), 15.

105. About intergenerational justice see Magali Bessone, *Faire justice de l'irréparable: Esclavage colonial et responsabilités contemporaines* (Paris: Vrin, 2019), 35.

106. Daniel Butt, *Rectifying Historical Injustices: Principles of Compensation and Restitution between Nations* (Oxford: Oxford University Press, 2009).

107. Bessone, *Faire justice de l'irréparable*, 209–210.

108. Judith Jarvis Thomson, *Rights, Restitution, and Risk: Essays in Moral Theory* (Cambridge, MA: Harvard University Press, 1986), 144–151.

109. Bessone, *Faire justice de l'irréparable*, 54.

110. See Michael Rothberg, *Multidirectional Memory: Remembering the Holocaust in the Age of Decolonization* (Stanford, CA: Stanford University Press, 2009).

111. Didier Eribon, "Vies hantées: Subjectivité, sexualité, créativité," *Principes d'une pensée critique* (Paris: Fayard, 2016), 191–222.

112. Judith Butler, "Vulnerability, Precarity, Coalition," in *Politics of Coalition: Thinking Collective Action with Judith Butler*, ed. Delphine Gardey and Cynthia Kraus (Geneva: Seismo, 2016), 261.

113. James Baldwin, *Tell Me How Long the Train's Been Gone* (New York: Dell Publishing, 1968), 216.

114. William James, *The Principles of Psychology* (New York: H. Holt, 1890).

115. Luca Greco and Lorenza Mondada, "Identités en interactions: Une approche multidimensionnelle," in *Identités en interaction*, ed. Luca Greco, Lorenza Mondada, and Patrick Renaud (Limoges: Lambert Lucas, 2014), 7–25.

116. François Laplantine, *Je, Nous et les Autres* (Paris: Le Pommier, 2010), 70.

117. Philip Gleason, "Identifying Identity: A Semantic History," *Journal of American History* 69, no. 4 (March 1983): 910–931.

118. Thomas Pradeu, *The Limits of the Self. Immunology and Biological Identity* (2009), trans. Elizabeth Vitanza (Oxford: Oxford University Press, 2012), 136ff.

119. Thomas Pradeu, *L'Identité. La part de l'autre: Immunologie et philosophie* (Paris: Odile Jacob, 2010), 163.

120. François Jullien, *Altérités: De l'altérité personnelle à l'altérité culturelle* (Paris: Gallimard, Folio, 2021), 27.

121. Jullien, *Altérités*, 80.

122. Didier Eribon analyzes how the narrator of *Journal du voleur* (*The Thief's Journal*) is transformed by the spectacle of the procession of the Carolines in Barcelona, a procession of "fags" who came to pay homage to a urinal, a place of flirtation and gay sociability, which the city had just removed. Didier Eribon, *Une morale du minoritaire: Variations sur un thème de Jean Genet* (Paris: Fayard, 2001), 9–11.

123. Jacques Derrida, *Writing and Difference* (1967), trans. Alan Bass (Chicago: University of Chicago Press, 1967), 133.

124. François Hartog, *Regimes of Historicity: Presentism and Experiences of Time* (2003), trans. Saskia Brown (New York: Columbia University Press, 2016), 193ff.

125. Mathieu Potte-Bonneville, commenting on Beckett, emphasizes that only the presence of "nothing" is continuous. Mathieu Potte-Bonneville, *Recommencer* (Paris: Verdier, 2018), 41.

126. Zaki Laïdi, *Le Sacre du présent* (Paris: Flammarion, 2000), 106.

127. "Laurence Rossignol: 'Le droit des familles est colonisé par la PMA,'" *L'Express*, May 6, 2014.

128. Monique Wittig, "The Trojan Horse" (1984), in *The Straight Mind and Other Essays* (Boston: Beacon Press, 1992), 68–75.

NOTES TO CHAPTER 6

129. Hans Ulrich Gumbrecht, *Production of Presence: What Meaning Cannot Convey* (Stanford, CA: Stanford University Press, 2004), 17.

130. Butler, "Vulnerability, Precarity, Coalition," 265.

131. Jean-Luc Nancy, *Being Singular Plural* (1996), trans. Robert Richardson and Anne O'Byrne (Stanford, CA: Stanford University Press, 2000), 56–65.

132. Maurice Merleau-Ponty, *Signs. Studies in Phenomenology and Existential Philosophy* (1960), trans. Richard C. McCleary (Evanston, IL: Northwestern University Press, 1964), 97.

133. François Jullien, *Si près, tout autre: De l'écart et de la rencontre* (Paris: Grasset, 2018), 199.

134. Nancy, *Being Singular Plural*, 60–62.

135. Magali Bessone, "Du 'je' au 'nous': Désagréger l'identité," in *L'Identité pour quoi faire?* ed. Jean Birnbaum (Paris: Gallimard, 2020), 63.

136. Jean-Paul Sartre, *Antisemite and Jew: An Exploration of the Etiology of Hate* (1946), trans. George J. Becker (New York: Schocken Books, 1948), 40–41.

137. E. Patrick Johnson, *Appropriating Blackness: Performance and the Politics of Authenticity* (Durham, NC: Duke University Press, 2003), 3–7.

138. Nancy, *Being Singular Plural*, 42.

139. Martin Buber, *I and Thou* (1923), trans Ronald Gregor (New York: Touchstone, 1996), 69–70.

140. David Berliner, *Becoming Other. Heterogeneity and Plasticity of the Self* (2022), trans. Stephen Muecke (New York: Berghahn, 2024), 18, 23–24.

141. Hartmut Rosa, *Resonance: A Sociology of Our Relationship to the World* (2016), trans. James Wagner (London: John Wiley and Sons, 2019), 163.

142. Rosa, *Resonance*, 168.

143. Rosa, 184ff.

144. Rosa, 195–201.

145. Nicole Lapierre, *Faut-il se ressembler pour s'assembler?* (Paris: Seuil, 2020), 201.

146. Nicole Lapierre, *Causes communes: Des Juifs et des Noirs* (Paris: Stock, 2011), 295–300.

147. For a critical view of recognition of others as a performance of self, see Patchen Markell, *Bound by Recognition* (Princeton, NJ: Princeton University Press, 2003), 180–181.

148. See Daniel Butt, "On Benefiting from Injustice," *Canadian Journal of Philosophy* 37, no. 1 (March 2007): 129–152.

149. See Rachel Knaebel, "Entre gilets jaunes et syndicats, une convergence possible, 'mais pas sur n'importe quoi,'" *Basta!*, December 7, 2018. See also Matthieu Foucher, "Avec les militants queers qui ont rejoint les 'gilets jaunes,'" *Vice*, December 10, 2018, https://www.vice.com/fr/article/vbap9m/avec-les-militants-queers-qui-ont-rejoint-les -gilets-jaunes.

150. Nina Kirmizi, "Comité Adama, cheminots, étudiants . . . et Gilets Jaunes: l'autre cortège de la manifestation parisienne," *Révolution Permanente*, December 1, 2018, https://www.revolutionpermanente.fr/Comite-Adama-cheminots-etudiants-et -Gilets-Jaunes-l-autre-cortege-de-la-manifestation-parisienne.

151. Souleymane Bachir Diagne, *De langue à langue: L'hospitalité de la traduction* (Paris: Albin Michel, 2022), 13.

152. Judith Butler, *The Psychic Life of Power: Theories in Subjection* (Stanford, CA: Stanford University Press, 1997), 139.

153. Christian List and Philip Pettit, *Group Agency. The Possibility, Design, and Status of Corporate Agents* (Oxford: Oxford University Press, 2011), 201.

154. Judith Butler, *Notes toward a Performative Theory of Assembly* (Cambridge, MA: Harvard University Press, 2015), 150.

CHAPTER 7

1. Conseil d'État, *Denoyez et Chorques*, May 10, 1974.

2. Conseil constitutionnel, *Conseil des prud'hommes*, 78–101, January 17, 1979.

3. European Court of Human Rights, *Abdulaziz, Cabales and Balkandali v. United-Kingdom*, May 28, 1985.

4. Refusal confirmed on appeal: Conseil d'État, *Département de Paris*, October 9, 1996.

5. European Court of Human Rights, *Fretté v. France*, February 26, 2002.

6. See Perreau, *The Politics of Adoption*, 65–66.

7. European Court of Human Rights, *E. B. v. France*, January 22, 2008.

8. European Court of Human Rights, *Konstantin Markin v. Russia*, March 22, 2012, section 127.

9. European Court of Human Rights, *Opuz v. Turkey*, June 9, 2009.

10. European Court of Human Rights, *Volodina v. Russia*, July 9, 2019.

11. Évelyne Pisier, "Sexes et sexualités."

12. John Money, "Hermaphrodism, Gender and Precocity in Hyperadrenocorticism: Psychologic Findings," *Bulletin of the Johns Hopkins Hospital* 96, no. 6 (1955): 253–264.

13. Robert J. Stoller, *Sex and Gender: On the Development of Masculinity and Femininity* (New York: Science House, 1968).

14. Ann Oakley, *Sex, Gender and Society* (London: Maurice Temple Smith), 1972.

15. Joan W. Scott, "Gender: A Useful Category of Historical Analysis," *American Historical Review* 91, no. 5 (1986): 1053–1075.

16. Denise Riley, *Am I That Name? Feminism and the Category of Women in History* (Basingstoke: Macmillan, 1988).

17. See Ilana Eloit, "American Lesbians Are Not French Women: Heterosexual French Feminism and the Americanisation of Lesbianism in the 1970s," *Feminist Theory* 20, no. 4 (2019): 381–404.

NOTES TO CHAPTER 7 263

18. Joan W. Scott, "Genre: Une catégorie utile d'analyse historique," trans. Eleni Varikas, *Les Cahiers du GRIF*, no. 37–38 (1988): 25–153.

19. Among those present were Christine Delphy, Évelyne Peyre, Joëlle Wiels, Nicole-Claude Mathieu, Anne-Marie Devreux, Christine Planté, and Patricia Mercader. See Marie-Claude Hurtig, Michèle Kail, and Hélène Rouch, eds., *Sexe et Genre: De la hiérarchie entre les sexes* (Paris: Éditions du CNRS, 2002).

20. Nicole-Claude Mathieu, *L'Anatomie politique: Catégorisations et idéologies du sexe* (Paris: Côté-Femmes, 1991).

21. Colette Guillaumin, *Racism, Sexism, Power and Ideology* (1972–1988), trans. Andrew Rothwell and Max Silverman (London: Routledge, 1995).

22. See Ilana Löwy and Hélène Rouch, "Genèse et développement du genre: Les sciences et l'origine de la distinction entre sexe et genre," *Cahiers du genre* 34 (2003): 5–16.

23. Éric Fassin, "The Purloined Gender: American Feminism in a French Mirror," *French Historical Studies* 22, no. 1 (1999): 113–138, and "L'empire du genre: L'histoire politique ambiguë d'un outil conceptuel," *L'Homme*, no. 187–188 (2008): 375–392.

24. Judith Butler's *Gender Trouble: Feminism and the Subversion of Identity* was translated into French by Cynthia Kraus: *Trouble dans le genre: Le féminisme et la subversion de l'identité* (1990) (Paris: La Découverte, 2005).

25. Réjane Sénac-Slawinski, "Le gender mainstreaming à l'épreuve de sa genèse et de sa traduction dans l'action publique en France," *Politique européenne*, no. 20 (2006): 9–33.

26. Sonia Mazey, "L'Union européenne et les droits des femmes: De l'européanisation des agendas nationaux à la nationalisation d'un agenda européen?" in *L'Action collective en Europe*, ed. Richard Balme, Didier Chabanet, and Vincent Wright (Paris: Presses de Sciences Po, 2002), 405–432.

27. See Elsa Fondimare, "Le genre, un concept utile pour repenser le droit de la non-discrimination," *La Revue des droits de l'Homme* 5, no. 6 (2014): https://doi.org/10 .4000/revdh.755.

28. Loi 2016–1547 du 18 novembre 2016 de modernisation de la justice du XXIe siècle, *Journal Officiel de la République française*, 0269, November 19, 2016.

29. Commission nationale consultative des droits de l'homme, plenary assembly, *Avis sur l'identité de genre et sur le changement de la mention de sexe à l'état civil*, June 27, 2013, 3.

30. Thomas Hammarberg, "Human Rights and Gender Identity," *Council of l'Europe*, CommDH/IssuePaper, July 29, 2009, https://rm.coe.int/human-rights-and-gender -identity-issue-paper-commissioned-and-publishe/16806da753.

31. Council of Europe, "Discrimination against Transgender People in Europe," Res. 2048, April 22, 2015.

32. See Article 10 of Directive 2011/95/EU on standards for the qualification of third-country nationals or stateless persons as beneficiaries of international protection, for

a uniform status for refugees, or for persons eligible for subsidiary protection, and for the content of the protection granted, December 13, 2011.

33. See Directive 2012/29/EU establishing minimum standards on the rights, support, and protection of victims of crime, and replacing Council Framework Decision 2001/220/JHA, October 25, 2012.

34. Jacques Lagroye, "La légitimation," in *Traité de science politique*, volume 1, ed. Jean Leca and Madeleine Grawitz (Paris: Presses universitaires de France, 1985), 395–467.

35. Diane Roman, "Les stéréotypes de genre, 'vieilles lunes' ou nouvelles perspectives pour le droit," in *Ce que le genre fait au droit*, ed. Stéphanie Hennette-Vauchez, Mathias Möschel, and Diane Roman (Paris: Dalloz, 2013), 93–121.

36. Marie Mesnil, "La démédicalisation du changement de sexe à l'état civil: Une conception renouvelée du sexe et du genre," *Journal de droit de la santé et de l'assurance maladie*, no. 6 (2017): 61–69.

37. Benjamin Moron-Puech, "L'arrêt *A. P., Nicot et Garçon c. France* ou la protection insuffisante par le juge européen des droits fondamentaux des personnes transsexuées," *La Revue des droits de l'Homme* (May 2017): https://doi.org/10.4000/revdh.3049.

38. European Court of Human Rights, *Y. v. France*, January 31, 2023.

39. Marie-Xavière Catto et al., "Questions d'épistémologie: Les études sur le genre en terrain juridique," in Hennette-Vauchez, Möschel, and Roman, *Ce que le genre fait au droit*, 3–24.

40. Several legal scholars, such as Daniel Borrillo, proposed this solution. Although it was never part of the Taubira law, it was broadly weaponized by movements that opposed the law. See Daniel Borrillo, "Biologie et filiation: Les habits neufs de l'ordre naturel," *Contemporary French Civilization* 39, no. 3 (2014): 303–319. The *Conseil constitutionnel* did not rule on this possibility either when it examined the law on modernizing justice in the twenty-first century. See Benjamin Moron-Puech, "L'homme enceint et le Conseil constitutionnel: une rencontre manquée," *Revue des droits et libertés fondamentaux*, chron. no. 28 (2016), https://revuedlf.com/droit-constitutionnel /lhomme-enceint-et-le-conseil-constitutionnel-une-rencontre-manquee-cons-const -17-nov-2016-n-2016-739-dc-loi-de-modernisation-de-la-justice-du-xxie-siecle/.

41. Benjamin Moron-Puech, "Femme-père et homme-mère, quand les minorités de genre interrogent nos catégories juridiques," *Revue des droits et libertés fondamentaux*, chron. no. 26 (2018), https://revuedlf.com/personnes-famille/femme-pere-et -homme-mere-quand-les-minorites-de-genre-interrogent-nos-categories-juridiques/.

42. Tribunal de grande instance de Montpellier, July 22, 2016.

43. Cour d'appel de Montpellier, November 14, 2018.

44. Assemblée nationale, bill of law "École de la confiance," amendement 834 submitted on February 7, 2019; February 12, 2019, https://www.assemblee-nationale.fr /dyn/15/amendements/1629/AN/834.

45. See, e.g., Ludovine de la Rochère and Albéric Dumont, "Parent 1, parent 2: Le déni de la réalité père-mère conduit à l'absurde," *FigaroVox*, February 14, 2019,

NOTES TO CHAPTER 7

https://www.lefigaro.fr/vox/societe/2019/02/14/31003-20190214ARTFIG00262
-parent-1-parent-2-le-deni-de-la-realite-pere-mere-conduit-a-l-absurde.php.

46. Daniel Borrillo, *Disposer de son corps: un droit encore à conquérir* (Paris: Textuel, 2019), 96.

47. Benjamin Moron-Puech, "Intersexuation et binarité, un état des lieux du droit français," in *Droits de l'Homme et sexualité: vers la notion de droits sexuels?* ed. Alain Giami and Bruno Py (Paris: Éditions des archives contemporaines, 2019), 193–216.

48. Tribunal de grande instance de Tours, August 20, 2015.

49. Cour de cassation, 1st Civil Chamber, May 4, 2017.

50. Benjamin Moron-Puech, "Rejet du sexe neutre: Une 'mutilation juridique'?" *Recueil Dalloz*, no. 246 (July 2017): 1404–1408.

51. Council of Europe, *Human Rights and Intersex People*, thematic document published by the Commissioner for Human Rights of the Council of Europe, Strasbourg, 2015, 17, https://rm.coe.int/16806da5d4.

52. Sénat, Délégation aux droits des femmes et à l'égalité des chances entre les hommes et les femmes, *Rapport d'information sur les variations du développement sexuel: lever un tabou, lutter contre la stigmatisation et les exclusions*, no. 441, February 23, 2017, https://www.senat.fr/rap/r16-441/r16-441.html.

53. Défenseur des droits, *Avis relatif au respect des droits des personnes intersexes*, no. 17–04, February 20, 2017, https://juridique.defenseurdesdroits.fr/index.php ?lvl=notice_display&id=21115.

54. Benjamin Moron-Puech, "Le droit des personnes intersexuées," *Socio*, no. 9 (2017): 215–237, https://doi.org/10.4000/socio.2983.

55. Parliamentary Assembly, Council of Europe, "*Discrimination against Transgender People in Europe*," Res. 2048, 2015, https://pace.coe.int/en/files/21736/html.

56. Borrillo, *Disposer de son corps*, 94–99.

57. Borrillo, 103.

58. Emmanuelle Bribosia and Isabelle Rovive, "Why a Global Approach to Non-Discrimination Law Matters: Struggling with the 'Conscience' of Companies," in *Human Rights Tectonics. Global Dynamics of Integration and Fragmentation* (Cambridge: Intersentia, 2018), 111–140.

59. Wendy Brown, "Suffering the Paradoxes of Rights," in *Left Legalism/Left Critique*, ed. Wendy Brown and Janet Halley (Durham, NC: Duke University Press, 2002), 423.

60. Eleni Varikas, "Le paria ou la difficile reconnaissance de la pluralité humaine," *Revue des deux mondes*, no. 11–12 (1999): 362.

61. Joan W. Scott, *Gender and the Politics of History* (New York: Columbia University Press, 1988), 172.

62. Françoise Collin, *Le Différend des sexes* (Paris: Agone, 1999), 56.

63. Andrée Lajoie, *Quand les minorités font la loi* (Paris: Presses universitaires de France, 2002), 27.

64. Réjane Sénac, *Les Non-Frères au pays de l'égalité* (Paris: Presses de Sciences Po, 2017), 91. On the commercial exploitation of minority trajectories also see Miranda Joseph, *Against the Romance of Community* (Minneapolis: University of Minnesota Press, 2002), 50–55.

65. Jacques Derrida, *Speech and Phenomena: Introduction to the Problem of the Sign in Husserl's Phenomenology* (1967), trans. Leonard Lawlord (Evanston, IL: Northwestern University Press, 2011), 79.

66. Jacques Derrida and Élisabeth Roudinesco, *For What Tomorrow . . . A Dialog* (2001), trans. Jeff Fort (Stanford, CA: Stanford University Press, 2004), 21.

67. Jacques Derrida, *Who's Afraid of Philosophy? Right to Philosophy I* (1990), trans. Jan Plug (Stanford, CA: Stanford University, 2002), 5.

68. Scott Brewer, "Exemplary Reasoning: Semantics, Pragmatics, and the Rational Force of Legal Argument by Analogy," *Harvard Law Review* 109, no. 5 (1996): 923–1028.

69. That is the Supreme Court of Ottawa's interpretation of section 15 (1) of the Canadian Charter of Rights and Freedoms. See Robin Medard Inghilterra, "Les écueils du contentieux antidiscriminatoire au prisme de la jurisprudence canadienne," in Gründler and Thouvenin, *La Lutte contre les discriminations à l'épreuve de son effectivité*, 5-6.

70. Grant Lamond distinguishes analogies of classification (the same right questioned in different cases), analogies of proximity (different cases and rights within the same branch), and distant analogies (cases thought through from other cases in other branches of law). Grant Lamond, "Analogical Reasoning in the Common Law," *Oxford Journal of Legal Studies* 34, no. 3 (fall 2014): 567–588.

71. Franklin Edward Kameny, *Petition for a Writ of Certiorari to the United States Court of Appeals for the District of Columbia Circuit*, 1961.

72. See Andrew Koppelman, "The Miscegenation Analogy: Sodomy Law as Sex Discrimination," *Yale Law Journal* 98, no. 1 (1988): 145–164.

73. Supreme Court of the United States, *Hoyt v. Florida*, 368 U.S. 57, November 20, 1961.

74. Supreme Court of the United States, *Reed v. Reed*, 404 U.S. 71, November 22, 1971.

75. See Holly J. McCammon, Brittany N. Hearne, Allison R. McGrath and Minyoung Moon, "Legal Mobilization and Analogical Legal Framing: Feminist Litigators' Use of Race–Gender Analogies," *Law & Policy* 40, no. 1 (2018): 57–78.

76. Craig J. Konnoth, "Created in Its Image: The Race Analogy, Gay Identity, and Gay Litigation in the 1950s-1970s," *Yale Law Journal* 119, no. 2 (2009): 370–371.

77. Janet E. Halley, "'Like Race' Arguments," in *What's Left of Theory? New Work on the Politics of Literary Theory*, ed. Judith Butler, John Guillory, and Kendall Thomas (London: Routledge, 2000), 46.

78. Halley, "'Like Race' Arguments," 60. L. Camille Herbert also agrees with this, taking as an example the use of the category of harassment, which ends up limiting recourse in matters of racist discrimination. L. Camille Herbert, "Analogizing Race

NOTES TO CHAPTER 7 267

and Sex in Workplace Harassment Claims," *Ohio State Law Journal* 58, no. 3 (1997): 820–821.

79. Alan David Freeman, "Legitimizing Racial Discrimination through Antidiscrimination Law: A Critical Review of Supreme Court Doctrine," in *Critical Race Theory*, ed. Kimberlé Crenshaw, Neil Gotanda, Gary Peller, and Kendall Thomas (New York: New Press, 1995), 29–46.

80. Court of Justice of the European Communities, *P. v. S. and Cornwall County Council*, April 30, 1996.

81. Court of Justice of the European Communities, *Grant v. South West Trains Ltd*, February 17, 1998. See "Grant v. South West Trains," *American Journal of International Law* 93, no. 1 (1999): 200–205.

82. Thus the court considers that a company discriminates on the basis of sexual orientation if it grants its married employees benefits (bonus and leave) that it does not grant to its *PaCS* employees (marriage-for-all was not in place at the time of the disclosure of facts). European Court of Justice, *Frédéric Hay v. Crédit agricole mutuel de Charente-Maritime et des Deux-Sèvres*, December 12, 2013.

83. European Court of Human Rights, *D.H. v. Czech Republic*, November 13, 2007.

84. European Court of Human Rights, *Tadeucci and McCall v. Italy*, June 30, 2016, section 85.

85. Robin Medard Inghilterra, "Les écueils du contentieux antidiscriminatoire au prisme de la jurisprudence canadienne," in Gründler and Thouvenin, *La Lutte contre les discriminations*, 6–7.

86. Medard Inghilterra, "Les écueils," 7.

87. Medard Inghilterra, 5.

88. Medard Inghilterra, 8.

89. Gwénaële Calvès, "L'inflation législative des motifs illicites de discrimination: essai d'analyse fonctionnelle," in *Multiplication des critères de discrimination*, 156.

90. Supreme Court of the United States, *Price Waterhouse v. Hopkins*, 490 U.S. 228, May 1, 1989.

91. European Court of Human Rights, *B.S. v. Spain*, July 27, 2012.

92. European Court of Human Rights, *Carvalho Pinto de Sousa Morais v. Portugal*, July 25, 2017.

93. U.S. Court of Appeals, 7th Circuit, *Hively v. Ivy Tech Community College*, 3:14-cv-1791, April 4, 2017.

94. Lisa Carayon and Julie Mattiussi, "Le prix du genre: Note sous CEDH, *Carvalho Pinto De Sousa Morais v. Portugal* (Art. 8 et 14)," *La Revue des droits de l'Homme*, Actualités Droits-Libertés (March 2018): https://doi.org/10.4000/revdh.3787.

95. European Court of Human Rights, *Carvalho Pinto de Sousa Morais v. Portugal*.

96. See Yannick Lécuyer, "L'utilisation 'retenue' de la notion de genre par la Cour européenne des droits de l'homme," *Revue du droit public et de la science politique en France et à l'étranger* 5 (September–October 2015): 1327–1356.

97. Thus by comparing disability and health the Court of Justice of the European Communities concluded that disability was akin to a "long-term illness." Court of Justice of the European Communities, *Sonia Chacón Navas v. Eurest Colectividades SA*, July 11, 2006.

98. Sharon Elizabeth Rush, "Equal Protection Analogies, Identity and Passing: Race and Sexual Orientation," *Harvard Blackletter Law Journal* 65, no. 13 (1997): 70.

99. Darren Rosenblum, "Queer Intersectionality and the Failure of Recent Lesbian and Gay 'Victories,'" *Law & Sexuality* 83, no. 4 (1994): 95.

100. New York Court of Appeal, *Braschi v. Stahl Associates Company*, 543 N.E.2d 49, July 6, 1989.

101. Veronica G. Thomas and Janine A. Jackson, "The Education of African American Girls and Women: Past to Present," *Journal of Negro Education* 16, no. 3 (2007): 357–372.

102. See Serena Mayeri, "Lost Intersections," in *Reasoning from Race: Feminism, Law and the Civil Rights Revolution* (Cambridge, MA: Harvard University Press, 2014), 144–185.

103. Robin Stryker, "Multiplication of Discrimination Criteria: A View from the United States," in *Multiplication des critères de discrimination*, 26.

104. Rachel K. Best, Lauren B. Edelman, Linda Hamilton Krieger, and Scott. R. Eliason, "Multiple Disadvantages: An Empirical Test of Intersectionality Theory in EEO Litigation," *Law & Society Review* 45, no. 4 (2011): 991–1025.

105. Nicholas Pedriana and Robin Stryker, "From Legal Doctrine to Social Transformation? Comparing US Voting Rights, Equal Employment Opportunity and Fair Housing Legislation," *American Journal of Sociology* 123, no. 1 (2017): 86–135.

106. European Court of Justice, *Galina Meister v. Speech Design Carrier Systems*, April 9, 2012.

107. European Court of Justice, *David L. Parris v. Trinity College Dublin, Higher Education Authority et al.*, November 24, 2016.

108. Shreya Atrey, "Illuminating the CJEU's Blind Spot of Intersectional Discrimination in *Parris v. Trinity College Dublin*," *Industrial Law Journal* 47, no. 2 (July 2018): 278–296.

109. See Bernard Bossu, *Les Discriminations dans les relations de travail devant les Cours d'appel. La réalisation contentieuse d'un droit fondamental*, Research Report, Mission de Recherche Droit et Justice de l'Université Lille 2, Droits et perspectives du droit, 2014, https://shs.hal.science/halshs-01157149.

110. Kimberlé Crenshaw, "Demarginalizing the Intersection of Race and Sex: A Black Feminist Critique of Antidiscrimination Doctrine, Feminist Theory and Antiracist Politics," *University of Chicago Legal Forum* 1989, no.1 (1989): 139–167; Crenshaw, "Mapping the Margins."

111. The branches of law that join several legal orders by definition promote a less sectional approach to differences in treatment. See Ivana Isailovic, "Political

NOTES TO CHAPTER 7

Recognition and Transnational Law: Gender Equality and Cultural Diversification in French Courts," in *Private International Law and Global Governance*, ed. Horatia Muir Watt and Diego P. Fernández Arroyo (Oxford: Oxford University Press, 2014), 318–342.

112. Jacques Lagroye, Bastien François, and Frédéric Sawicki, *Sociologie politique* (Paris: Presses de Sciences Po, 2002), 516.

113. Crenshaw, "Mapping the Margins," 1244.

114. Kimberlé Crenshaw, "Les voyages de l'intersectionnalité," in *L'Intersectionnalité: enjeux théoriques et politiques*, ed. Farinaz Fassa, Éléonore Lépinard, and Marta Roca I Escoda (Paris: La Dispute, 2016), 46.

115. Fanon, *Black Skin, White Masks*, 4.

116. Maxime Cervulle, *Dans le blanc des yeux. Diversité, racisme et médias* (Paris: Éd. Amsterdam, 2021), 145–152.

117. Mathieu, *L'Anatomie politique*, 165.

118. Cervulle, *Dans le blanc des yeux*, 198–203.

119. Didier Eribon, *Returning to Reims*, trans. Michael Lucey (New York: Semiotexte, 2013), 225.

120. Kevin Duong, "What Does Queer Theory Teach Us about Intersectionality?" *Politics & Gender* 8, no. 3 (2012): 370–386.

121. Maria Carbin and Sara Edenheim, "The Intersectional Turn in Feminist Theory: A Dream of a Common Language?" *European Journal of Women's Studies* 20, no. 3 (2013): 233–248.

122. Sirma Bilge, "Le blanchissement de l'intersectionnalité," *Recherches féministes* 28, no. 2 (2015): 9–32.

123. Éléonore Lépinard, *Feminist Trouble. Intersectional Politics in Postsecular Times* (Oxford: Oxford University Press, 2020), 7.

124. Jodi Dean, *Solidarity of Strangers. Feminism after Identity Politics* (Berkeley: University of California Press, 1996), 102–107, 179–181.

125. In *Ricci v. DeStefano*, twenty firefighters (one Latinx; nineteen white) passed a job promotion test. The Black candidates got insufficient scores on this test: the city of New Haven rejected the promotion of the other firefighters, believing that the test was biased. The US Supreme Court overturned the city's decision, citing Title VII of the 1964 Civil Rights Act. In her dissenting opinion Justice Ruth Bader Ginsburg held that any discrimination must be examined contextually. Supreme Court of the United States, *Ricci v. DeStefano*, 557 U.S., June 29, 2009.

126. The court sanctioned the decision to refuse granting a Muslim woman her inheritance since she was married to a polygamous man. Constitutional Court of South Africa, *Harksen v. Lane*, 1998 (1) SA 300.

127. For more details see Shreya Atrey, "Comparison in Intersectional Discrimination," *Legal Studies* 38, no. 3 (2018): 390–393.

128. Ruwen Ogien, *L'État nous rend-il meilleur? Essai sur la liberté politique* (Paris: Gallimard, 2013), 248–259.

129. Thus, there is an echo here of the thoughtful work of truth telling that Michel Foucault identifies in the Greek *parrhesia*, a true ethic of the relationship to the presence of others. See Michel Foucault, *Government of Self and Others: Lectures at the Collège de France. 1982–1983*, trans. Graham Burchell (New York: Picador, 2011), 372–374.

130. Ido Katri, "Transgender Intrasectionality: Rethinking Anti-Discrimination Law and Litigation," *University of Pennsylvania Journal of Law and Social Change* 20, no. 1 (2017): 51–79.

131. On the question of performance in antidiscrimination law, see Marie Mercat-Bruns, "Multiple Discrimination and Intersectionality: Issues of Equality and Liberty," *International Social Science Journal*, no. 67 (March-June 2017): 51–52.

132. Karen Barad, "Reconceiving Scientific Literacy as Agential Literacy; Or, Learning How to Intra-Act Responsibly within the World," in *Doing Science + Culture*, ed. Roddey Reid and Sharon Traweek (London: Routledge, 2000), 235–236.

133. On the tensions between critiques and reappropriations of intersectionality, see Shreya Atrey, *Intersectionality and Comparative Discrimination Law: The Tale of Two Citadels* (Leiden: Brill, 2020): 32–43.

134. This is a phenomenon taken up in legal consciousness studies. For an analysis of the tension between law as an "instrument of power and a means of counter-power" at the heart of minority movements, see Jacques Commaille, *À quoi nous sert le droit?* (Paris: Gallimard, 2015), 346–355.

135. Andrew L. Flores and Andrew Park, *Examining the Relationship between Social Acceptance of LGBT People and Inclusion of Sexual Minorities* (Los Angeles: Williams Institute, 2018).

136. On the function of the imperfections in law, see Marianne Constable, *Our Word Is Our Bond: How Legal Speech Acts* (Stanford, CA: Stanford University Press, 2014), 102–106.

137. For a critical analysis, see Sabine Prokhoris, "L'adoration des majuscules," in Borrillo, Fassin, and Iacub, *Au-delà du PaCS*, 145–159.

138. Pierre Legendre, *La Passion d'être un autre: Étude pour la danse* (Paris: Seuil, 2000), 12.

139. Pierre Legendre, *Sur la question dogmatique en Occident: Aspects théoriques* (Paris: Fayard, 1999), 8ff.

140. Jacques Bouveresse, *Prodiges et Vertiges de l'analogie* (Paris: Raisons d'Agir, 1999).

141. Ludwig Wittgenstein, *The Blue and Brown Books* (1958) (New York: HarperCollins, 1965), 53–54.

142. Ludwig Wittgenstein, *Philosophical Investigations* (1953), trans. G. E. M. Anscombe, P. M. S. Hacker, and Joachim Schulte (London: Blackwell, 2009), 39–40.

143. Luísa Lourenço and Pekka Pohjankoski, "Breaking Down Barriers? The Judicial Interpretation of 'Disability' and 'Reasonable Accommodation' in EU

NOTES TO CHAPTER 7 271

Anti-Discrimination Law," in Belavusau and Henrard, *EU Anti-Discrimination Law beyond Gender*, 321–337.

144. Directive 2000/78/EC of the Council of the European Union establishing a general framework for equal treatment in work and employment, November 27, 2000.

145. United Nations, Convention on the Rights of People with Disabilities, December 13, 2006, https://www.ohchr.org/en/instruments-mechanisms/instruments/convention-rights-persons-disabilities.

146. European Court of Justice, *Jette Ring v. Dansk almennyttigt Boligselskab*, C-335/11, April 11, 2013.

147. European Court of Human Rights, *Di Trizio v. Switzerland*, February 2, 2016.

148. European Court of Human Rights, *Guberina v. Croatie*, March 22, 2016.

149. For more details see Hélène Surrel, "La sanction des discriminations par la Cour européenne des droits de l'homme."

150. Aline Rivera Maldonado, "À l'intersection des discriminations structurelles: La Convention et la protection des groupes vulnérables," in *La Convention sur l'élimination de toutes les formes de discrimination à l'égard des femmes*, ed. Diane Roman (Paris: Pédone, 2014), 160.

151. Committee on the Elimination of Discrimination against Women, https://www.ohchr.org/en/treaty-bodies/cedaw.

152. Françoise Gaspard, "Les 'droits de la femme': Construction d'un enjeu en relations internationales," *Revue internationale et stratégique* 47, no. 3 (2002): 51–52.

153. United Nations, Committee on the Elimination of Discrimination against Women, "General Recommendation No. 25, on Article 4, Paragraph 1, of the Convention on the Elimination of All Forms of Discrimination against Women, on Temporary Special Measures," 30th session, 2004, https://www.un.org/womenwatch/daw/cedaw/recommendations/General%20recommendation%2025%20(English).pdf.

154. Committee on the Elimination of Discrimination against Women.

155. Rivera, "À l'intersection des discriminations structurelles," 177–180.

156. "Employment Law. Title VII. EEOC Affirms Protections for Transgender Employees," *Harvard Law Review* 126, no. 6 (April 2013): 1731–1738.

157. Equal Employment Opportunity Commission, *Macy v. Holder*, April 20, 2012.

158. Adam Liptak, "Civil Rights Law Protects Gay and Transgender Workers, Supreme Court Rules," *New York Times*, June 15, 2020.

159. Supreme Court of the United States, *Altitude Express v. Zarda*, 17–1623, June 15, 2020.

160. Supreme Court of the United States, *Bostock v. Clayton County*.

161. Supreme Court of the United States, *R. G & G.R. Harris Funeral Homes v. Equal Employment Opportunity Commission*, 18–107, June 15, 2020.

162. Supreme Court of the United States, *Dobbs*.

163. Supreme Court of the United States, *Dobbs*, 118.

164. Malini Johar Schueller, "Analogy and (White) Feminist Theory: Thinking Race and the Color of the Cyborg Body," *Signs. Journal of Women in Culture and Society* 31, no. 1 (2005): 63–92.

165. On the differences between law and ethics, see Grant Lamond, "Legal Reasoning for Hedgehogs," *Ratio Juris* 30, no. 4 (December 2017): 517–520.

166. Simone de Beauvoir, *The Ethics of Ambiguity* (1944), trans. Bernard Frechtman (New York: Citadel Press, 1976), 137.

CHAPTER 8

1. See Georges Davy's analysis quoted by André Lalande in *Vocabulaire technique et critique de la philosophie* (Paris: Presses universitaires de France, 2002), 1169.

2. David Nirenberg, *Communities of Violence: Persecution of Minorities in the Middle Ages* (Princeton, NJ: Princeton University Press, 2015), 7–13, 142.

3. Joseph Lecler, *Histoire de la tolérance au siècle de la Réforme* (Paris: Albin Michel, 1994).

4. Clermont–Tonnerre, "Speech on Religious Minorities and Questionable Professions (23 December 1789)," Liberty, Equality, Fraternity: Exploring the French Revolution, accessed January 11, 2024, https://revolution.chnm.org/d/284.

5. Hans-Jürgen Lüsebrink, "Universalisme des Lumières et impérialisme colonial: Concepts culturels et positionnements politiques, de G.-T. Raynal à Jules Ferry," in *The Epoch of Universalism 1769–1989*, ed. Franck Hofmann and Markus Messling (Berlin: De Gruyter, 2020), 55–70.

6. See Julien Suaudeau and Mame-Fatou Niang, *Universalisme* (Paris: Anamosa, 2022), 26–31.

7. Marijosé Alie, *Entretiens avec Aimé Césaire* (Bordeaux: Hervé Chopin éditions, 2021), 25.

8. Ato Sekyi-Otu, *Left Universalism: Afrocentric Essays* (London: Routledge, 2018), viii.

9. See, e.g., Dilip Parameshwar Gaonkar, ed., *Alternative Modernities* (Durham, NC: Duke University Press, 2001); Zahra Ali and Sonia Dayan-Herzbrun, eds., "Pluriversalisme décolonial," *Tumultes*, special issue, no. 48 (May 2017); Massimiliano Tomba, *Insurgent Universality: An Alternative Legacy of Modernity* (Oxford: Oxford University Press, 2019).

10. Julia Christ, *L'Oubli de l'universel: Hegel critique du libéralisme* (Paris: Presses universitaires de France, 2021), 15.

11. See Étienne Balibar's analysis in *On Universals: Constructing and Deconstructing Community* (2016), trans. Joshua David Jordan (New York: Fordham University Press, 2020), 31.

NOTES TO CHAPTER 8

12. Merleau-Ponty, *Signs*, 120.

13. Monique Wittig, "The Point of View: Universal or Particular," in *The Straight Mind*, 62.

14. Wittig, "The Point of View," 62.

15. Julia Christ, *L'Oubli de l'universel*, 25ff.

16. Danièle Lochak, *Le Droit et les Paradoxes de l'universalité* (Paris: Presses universitaires de France, 2010), 35.

17. Souleymane Bachir Diagne, "On the Universal and Universalism," in *In Search of Africa(s): Universalism and Decolonial Thought* (2018), ed. Souleymane Bachir Diagne and Jean-Loup Amselle, trans. Andrew Brown (Cambridge: Polity Press, 2020), 22.

18. François Jullien, *On the Universal, the Uniform, the Common and Dialogue Between Cultures*, trans. Michael Richardson and Krzysztof Fijalkowski (Cambridge: Polity, 2014), 100ff.

19. For a complete review of the theoretical critique of human rights, see Justine Lacroix and Jean-Yves Pranchère, *Human Rights on Trial: A Genealogy of the Critique of Human Rights* (2016), trans. Gabrielle Maas (Cambridge: Cambridge University Press, 2018).

20. Jullien, *On the Universal*, 116ff.

21. Jullien, 114.

22. Corine Pelluchon, *Les Lumières à l'âge du vivant* (Paris: Seuil, 2021), 291.

23. Mustapha Kamal Pasha, "After the Deluge: New Universalism and Postcolonial Difference," *International Relations* 34, no. 3 (September 2020): 354–373.

24. Corine Pelluchon speaks of a "tuned in" reason in *Les Lumières à l'âge du vivant*, 60.

25. Girard, *Délibérer entre égaux*, 147.

26. Souleymane Bachir Diagne, *The Ink of the Scholars: Reflections on Philosophy in Africa* (2013), trans. Jonathan Adjemian (Dakar: CODESRIA, 2016), 77.

27. Judith Butler, "Restaging the Universal. Hegemony and the Limits of Formalism," in Judith Butler, Ernesto Laclau, and Slavoj Žižek, *Contingency, Hegemony, Universality: Contemporary Dialogues on the Left* (London: Verso, 2000), 166–167.

28. See Michelle Perrot with Eduardo Castillo, *Le Temps des féminismes* (Paris: Grasset, 2023), 143–148.

29. Sébastien Chauvin, "Pour une critique bienveillante de la notion de 'minorité': Le cas des 'minorités sexuelles,'" *Contretemps* 7 (May 2003): 34–35.

30. See Florent Guénard, *La Démocratie universelle: Philosophie d'un modèle politique* (Paris: Seuil, 2016), 305–308.

31. Walzer, *Spheres of Justice*, 29.

32. Michael Walzer, "Nation and Universe," *The Tanner Lectures on Human Values, Brasenose College*, Oxford University, May 1989, 532, https://tannerlectures.utah.edu /_resources/documents/a-to-z/w/walzer90.pdf.

33. This clause refers to the fact that a reform applies only to new entrants. Mireille Delmas-Marty, *Le Relatif et l'Universel. Les forces imaginantes du droit* (Paris: Seuil, 2004), 405–406.

34. Delmas-Marty, *Le Relatif et l'Universel,* 406.

35. Delmas-Marty, 412–413.

36. Alain Policar, *L'Universalisme en procès* (Lormont: Le Bord de l'eau, 2021), 108.

37. Étienne Tassin, *Un monde commun. Pour une cosmo-politique des conflits* (Paris: Seuil, 2003).

38. Frédéric Fruteau de Laclos, "Pour un universalisme de terrain," ed. Stéphane Dufoix and Alain Policar, *L'Universalisme en débat(s)* (Lormont: Le Bord de l'eau, 2024), 137–147.

39. Laclau, *Emancipation(s),* 56.

40. Laclau, 57.

41. Laclau, 57.

42. Michael Walzer, *Thick and Thin: Moral Argument at Home and Abroad* (Notre Dame, IN: University of Notre Dame Press, 1994).

43. Ernesto Laclau, "The Death and Resurrection of the Theory of Ideology," *Modern Language Notes* 112, no. 3 (1997): 309.

44. Laclau, *Emancipation(s),* 310.

45. Norman Ajari, *Dignity or Death,* 105–106.

46. Trica Keaton, *#You Know You're Black in France When . . . The Fact of Everyday Antiblackness* (Cambridge, MA: MIT Press, 2023), 213.

47. About the hole left by "race" in critical thought on the "Negro" identity, see Achille Mbembe, *Critique of Black Reason* (2013), trans. Laurent Dubois (Durham, NC: Duke University Press, 2017), 89–90.

48. Édouard Glissant, *Philosophie de la relation. Poésie en étendue* (Paris: Gallimard, 2009), 74–75.

49. Naomi Schor, "The Crisis of French Universalism," *Yale French Studies* 100 (2001): 64.

50. Markus Messling, *Universality after Universalism. On Francophone Literatures of the Present,* trans. Michael Thomas Taylor (Berlin: De Gruyter, 2023), 63–64.

51. Markus Messling and Jonas Tinius, "On Minor Universality," in *Minor Universality: Rethinking Humanity after Western Universalism,* ed. Markus Messling and Jonas Tinius, trans. John Angell, Anna Galt, Michael Thomas Taylor, and Liz Carey Libbrecht (Berlin: De Gruyter, 2023), 19.

52. Messling and Tinius, "On Minor Universality," 20–23.

53. Messling and Tinius, 3.

54. Messling and Tinius, 2.

55. Christian Bobin, *La Présence pure et autres textes* (1999) (Paris: Gallimard, 2018).

NOTES TO CHAPTER 8

56. Claude Lefort, *Writing, the Political Test* (1992), trans. David Ames Curtis (Durham, NC: Duke University Press, 2000), 22.

57. Vincent Descombes, *Puzzling Identities* (2013), trans. Stephen Adam Schwartz (Cambridge, MA: Harvard University Press, 2016), 117.

58. Tim Ingold, "Le problème de la symétrie ontologique," in Philippe Descola and Tim Ingold, *Être au monde. Quelle expérience commune?* trans. Benjamin Fau (Lyon: Presses universitaires de Lyon, 2014), 73.

59. Anne Lafont, "De l'universalité de la critique," *Esprit*, no. 461 (January 2020): 77–78.

60. Norman Ajari, *Dignity or Death*, 89ff.

61. For an overview of theses and controversies at the heart of communitarian thought, see Janie Pelabay, "Communitarian Equality: To Each According to Their Contribution to the Group Identity," *International Social Science Journal* 67, no. 223–224 (March-June 2017): 21–30.

62. Charles Taylor, "The Politics of Recognition," in *Multiculturalism: Difference and Democracy*, ed. Amy Gutmann (Princeton, NJ: Princeton University Press, 1994), 25ff.

63. Axel Honneth, *The Struggle for Recognition: The Moral Grammar of Social Conflicts* (1992), trans. Joel Anderson (Cambridge, MA: MIT Press, 1996), 92ff.

64. Jacques Rancière, "Critical Questions on the Theory of Recognition" in *Recognition or Disagreement: A Critical Encounter on the Politics of Freedom, Equality, and Identity. Axel Honneth and Jacques Rancière*, ed. Katia Genel and Jean-Philippe Deranty (New York: Columbia University Press, 2016), 90.

65. Rancière, "Critical Questions on the Theory of Recognition," 113–172.

66. Quoted in Axel Honneth, *Recognition: A Chapter in the History of European Ideas*, trans. Joseph Ganahl (Cambridge: Cambridge University Press, 2021), 79.

67. For a synthesis, see Louis Carré, *Axel Honneth: Le droit de la reconnaissance* (Paris: Michalon, 2013), 93–95.

68. Georg Wilhelm Friedrich Hegel, *Elements of the Philosophy of Right* (1820), trans. T. M. Knox (Oxford: Oxford University Press, 1967).

69. Axel Honneth, *The Pathologies of Individual Freedom: Hegel's Social Theory* (2001), trans. Ladislaus Löb (Princeton, NJ: Princeton University Press, 2010), 49ff.

70. Hegel quoted in Honneth, *Pathologies*, 43, 48.

71. Axel Honneth, "Justice et liberté communicationnelle: Réflexions à partir de Hegel," *La Reconnaissance aujourd'hui*, ed. Alain Caillé and Christian Lazzeri, trans. Marion Schumm (Paris: CNRS Éditions, 2009), 43–64.

72. Fred Moten, *The Universal Machine* (Durham, NC: Duke University Press, 2018), 237.

73. Moisés Lino E Silva, *Minoritarian Liberalism: A Travesti Life in a Brazilian Favela* (Chicago: University of Chicago Press, 2022), 14.

74. Markell, *Bound by Recognition*, 170.

75. Florent Guénard sees in it the permanence of an aristocratic conception of social bonds: *La Passion de l'égalité* (Paris: Seuil, 2022), 247–248.

76. Norman Ajari thinks Axel Honneth has a naive conception of recognition. *Dignity or Death*, 171.

77. Philip Pettit, *The Robust Demands of the Good: Attachment, Virtue, and Respect* (Oxford: Oxford University Press, 2015), 1.

78. Judith Butler, *Giving an Account of Oneself* (New York: Fordham University Press, 2005), 41–42.

79. Walzer, *Spheres of Justice*, 28.

80. Michael Warner, *The Trouble with Normal. Sex, Politics, and the Ethics of Queer Life* (Cambridge, MA: Harvard University Press, 1999), 133.

81. Cheryl Harris, "Whiteness as Property," *Harvard Law Review* 106, no. 8 (1993): 1707–1791.

82. Nicole Lapierre studies the function of name changes in different minority spaces and thus sheds light on the privileges that property grants to majority groups: she studies the question of names for Jews after the Holocaust, for Armenians faced with the memory of the genocide, and for French families of North African descent faced with the desymbolization of the father's name. Nicole Lapierre, *Changer de nom* (Paris: Gallimard, 2006).

83. Stuart Hall, "When Was the 'Post-Colonial'? Thinking at the Limits" (1996), in *Selected Writings on Marxism*, ed. Gregor McLennan (Durham, NC: Duke University Press, 2021), 298–299.

84. Auguste Comte, *The Catechism of Positive Religion, or Summary of the Universal Religion in Thirteen Systematic Conversations between a Woman and a Priest of Humanity* (1891), trans. Richard Congreve (Cambridge: Cambridge University Press, 2009), 230.

85. John Locke, "Of Identity and Diversity" (1694) in *An Essay Concerning Human Understanding*, book 2, chapter 27, section 29, ed. Roger Woolhouse (New York: Penguin Classics, 1999), 313.

86. Stéphane Ferret, *Le Bateau de Thésée: Le problème de l'identité à travers le temps* (Paris: Minuit, 1996), 139.

87. Étienne Balibar, *Citizen Subject: Foundations for Philosophical Anthropology* (2011), trans. Steven Miller (New York: Fordham University Press, 2017), 142.

88. Pierre-Joseph Proudhon, *What Is Property?* (1840), ed. and trans. Donald R. Kelley and Bonnie G. Smith (Cambridge: Cambridge University Press, 1994), 8, 13.

89. Thomas Piketty, *A Brief History of Equality* (2021), trans. Steven Rendall (Cambridge, MA: Harvard University Press, 2022), 9–10.

90. Rawls, *A Theory of Justice*, 465.

91. Michael Sandel, *Liberalism and the Limits of Justice* (1982) (Cambridge: Cambridge University Press, 1988), 95–96.

NOTES TO CHAPTER 8

92. Sandel, *Liberalism*, 97–98.

93. Sandel, 140.

94. Dominique Birmann, "Albert Camus a exposé aux étudiants suédois son attitude devant le problème algérien," *Le Monde*, December 14, 1957.

95. Sandel, *Liberalism*, 144, 142.

96. See Pierre Crétois, *La Part commune: Critique de la propriété privée* (Paris: Éditions Amsterdam, 2020), 120–121.

97. See Edward J. Hughes, *Egalitarian Strangeness. On Class Disturbance and Levelling in Modern and Contemporary French Narrative* (Liverpool: Liverpool University Press, 2021).

98. Will Kymlicka, *Multicultural Odysseys: Navigating the New International Politics of Diversity* (Oxford: Oxford University Press, 2007), 19.

99. Kymlicka, *Multicultural Odysseys*, 21.

100. Norbert Elias, *Involvement and Detachment* (1983), trans. Edmund Jephcott (London: Blackwell, 1987), 10–11.

101. Saskia Sassen, *Territory, Authority, Rights: From Medieval to Global Assemblages* (Princeton, NJ: Princeton University Press, 2006), 340–348.

102. Norbert Elias, *What Is Sociology?* (1970), trans. Stephen Mennell and Grace Morrissey (London: Hutchinson, 1978), 155–157. For Elias, civilization and decivilization can work together: Norbert Elias, *The Germans: Power Struggles and the Development of Habitus in the Nineteenth and Twentieth Centuries* (1989), trans. Eric Dunning and Stephen Mennell (New York: Columbia University Press, 1996), 196ff.

103. Achille Mbembe, *The Earthly Community: Reflections on the Last Utopia*, trans. Steven Corcoran (Rotterdam: V2 Publishing, 2022), 67.

104. François Gemenne, *Géopolitique du climat: Négociations, stratégies, impacts* (Paris: Armand Colin, 2021).

105. Hans Jonas, *The Imperative of Responsibility: In Search of an Ethics for the Technological Age* (1979), trans. Hans Jonas and David Herr (Chicago: University of Chicago Press, 1984), x.

106. The "world-totality" is the notion that Édouard Glissant uses to describe the deployment of the network of human relations as being like a vast rhizome. Édouard Glissant, *Introduction to a Poetry of Diversity* (1995), trans. Celia Britton (Liverpool: Liverpool University Press, 2020), 19–20, 42–45.

107. Max Weber, *Economy and Society* (1921), trans. Keith Tribe (Cambridge, MA: Harvard University Press, 2019), 402ff.

108. Ulrich Beck, *Power in the Global Age: A New Global Political Economy* (2002), trans. Kathleen Cross (Cambridge: Polity, 2005).

109. Édouard Louis, *Who Killed My Father?* (2018), trans. Lorin Stein (New York: New Directions, 2019).

110. de Lagasnerie, *La Conscience politique*, 120.

111. Roland Barthes, *How to Live Together: Novelistic Simulations of Some Everyday Spaces. Notes for a Lecture Course and Seminar at the Collège de France (1976–1977)*, trans. Kate Briggs (New York: Columbia University Press, 2012), 165.

112. Barbara Stiegler, *De la démocratie en pandémie: Santé, recherche, éducation* (Paris: Gallimard, 2021), 50–51.

113. Willy Dunbar and Yves Coppieters, "Le Covid suscite une nouvelle stigmatisation des personnes LGBT+," *The Conversation*, May 14, 2020, https://theconversation.com/le-covid-19-suscite-une-nouvelle-stigmatisation-des-personnes-lgbt-138159.

114. Geoffroy de Lagasnerie, "Les 'impressions dissonantes' de Geoffroy de Lagasnerie sur la crise en cours," *Les Inrockuptibles*, April 1, 2020.

115. Cécile Coudriou, "La crise sanitaire ne fait qu'aggraver les inégalités et les violations des droits des plus vulnérables," *Le Monde*, April 21, 2020.

116. According to Kwame Anthony Appiah total autonomy is impossible and thus creates an impasse of the idea of partial autonomy: "Autonomy as Intolerance," in *The Ethics of Identity* (Princeton, NJ: Princeton University Press, 2005), 41–45.

117. Moya, *Learning from Experience*, 131.

118. Jonas, *The Imperative of Responsibility*, 43.

119. See the critique of responsibility for others as a technique of self-improvement and self-control within a neoliberal framework: Émilie Hache, "La responsabilité: Une technique de gouvernementalité néolibérale?" *Raisons politiques* 28, no. 4 (2007): 49–65.

120. Stefano Harney and Fred Moten, *All Incomplete* (Colchester: Minor Compositions, 2021), 23–24.

121. Jonas, *The Imperative of Responsibility*, 8.

122. I have devoted a more complete analysis to it: Perreau, "L'irréel du présent" and "L'enchaînement du sujet," in *Qui a peur de la théorie queer?*, 273–284.

123. Michael Suk-Young Chwe, "Minority Voting Rights Can Maximize Majority Welfare," *American Political Science Review* 93, no. 1 (1999): 85–97.

124. European Court of Human Rights, *Verein KlimaSeniorinnen Schweiz and Others v. Switzerland*, April 9, 2024.

125. Steven Lukes, *Moral Relativism* (New York: Picador, 2008), 49–50.

126. The Christian basis of the multitude that François Noudelmann criticizes: *Pour en finir avec la généalogie* (Paris: Léo Scheer, 2004), 118–119.

127. Appiah, *The Ethics of Identity*, 213–214.

128. Appiah, 231–232.

129. Appiah, 236.

130. I also have reservations about the metaphor of roots insofar as it refers identity to an infrapolitical foundation, straight out of genealogy. See also Christy Wampole, *Rootedness: The Ramifications of a Metaphor* (Chicago: University of Chicago Press, 2016), 193–195.

NOTES TO CHAPTER 8   279

131. Lauren Berlant, *On the Inconvenience of Other People* (Durham, NC: Duke University Press, 2022), 131.

132. Karl Marx and Fredrick Engels, *The German Ideology, Part One (1845–1846)*, ed. and trans. C. J. Arthur (London: Lawrence & Wishart, 1974), 46–47.

133. Berenice Fisher and Joan Tronto, "Toward a Feminist Theory of Caring," in *Circles of Care: Work and Identity in Women's Lives*, ed. Emily K. Abel and Margaret K. Nelson (Albany, NY: SUNY Press, 1990), 40.

134. Carol Gilligan, *In a Different Voice: Psychological Theory and Women's Development* (Cambridge, MA: Harvard University Press, 1982).

135. Joan Tronto, *Moral Boundaries: A Political Argument for an Ethic of Care* (London: Routledge, 1993), 3.

136. Estelle Ferrarese, *The Fragility of Concern for Others: Adorno and the Ethics of Care* (2018), trans. Steven Corcoran (Edinburgh: Edinburgh University Press, 2021), 5.

137. Pascale Molinier, Sandra Laugier, and Patricia Paperman, *Qu'est-ce que le care? Souci des autres, sensibilité, responsabilité* (Paris: Payot, 2009), 71.

138. Patricia Paperman, "Pour un monde sans pitié," *Revue du MAUSS* 32, no. 2 (2008): 272.

139. For a discussion these unspoken aspects, see Sandra Laugier, "Care et perception. L'éthique comme attention au particulier," in *Le Souci des autres: Éthique et politique du care*, ed. Patricia Paperman and Sandra Laugier (Paris: Presses de l'EHESS, 2011), 359–393.

140. Ferrarese, *The Fragility of Concern for Others*, 97.

141. Judith Butler, *The Force of Nonviolence: An Ethico-Political Bind* (London: Verso, 2020), 186–187.

142. That is Seyla Benhabib's very strong critique of them: *Situating the Self: Gender, Community, and Postmodernism in Contemporary Ethics* (Cambridge: Polity Press, 1992), 180–182.

143. Tronto, *Moral Boundaries*, 147.

144. Butler, *The Force of Nonviolence*, 192.

145. Butler, 194.

146. Butler, 203.

147. Sarah Schulman, *Conflict Is Not Abuse: Overstating Harm, Community Responsibility, and the Duty of Repair* (Vancouver: Arsenal Pulp Press, 2016), 47–50.

148. Charles Fourier, "Principes de l'éducation" (1822), in René Schérer, *Charles Fourier ou la Contestation globale* (Paris: Séguier, 1996), 205–206. See also David Zeldin, *The Educational Ideas of Charles Fourier* (London: Frank Cass, 1969).

149. Stefano Harney and Fred Moten, *The Undercommons: Fugitive Planning & Black Study* (Wivenhoe: Minor Composition, 2013), 98.

150. Roberto Esposito, *Immunitas: The Protection and Negation of Life* (2002), trans. Zakiya Hanafi (Cambridge: Polity Press, 2011), 8–9.

151. As Primo Levi showed, the extermination of deportees is a futile obliteration of everything that linked Jews to their executioners: *If This Is a Man* (1958), trans. Stuart Woolf (New York: Orion Press, 1959).

152. Despecification makes it possible to think about social and economic models with more precision. See Thomas Lemke, *The Government of Things: Foucault and the New Materialisms* (New York: New York University Press, 2021), 186.

153. Dominique Bourg and Kerry Whiteside, *Vers une démocratie écologique: Le citoyen, le savant et le politique* (Paris: Seuil, 2010), 36.

154. Bourg and Whiteside, *Vers une démocratie écologique*, 12, 14.

155. Bourg and Whiteside, 65.

156. Bruno Latour, *Politics of Nature: How to Bring the Sciences into Democracy* (1999), trans. Catherine Porter (Cambridge, MA: Harvard University Press, 2004).

157. Bruno Latour, "Esquisse d'un Parlement des choses," *Écologie & Politique* 56, no. 1 (2018): 47–64. See also Bruno Latour, "The Parliament of Things" in *We Have Never Been Modern* (1991), trans. Catherine Porter (Cambridge, MA: Harvard University Press, 1993), 142–145.

158. Bourg and Whiteside, *Vers une démocratie écologique*, 56–57, 76–78, 79–80.

159. Yves Citton, *Altermodernités des Lumières* (Paris: Seuil, 2022), 363.

160. David McDermott Hughes, "Plantation Slaves. The First Fuel," *Energy without Conscience: Oil, Climate Change, and Complicity* (Durham, NC: Duke University Press, 2017), 29–40.

161. Robert D. Bullard, *Dumping in Dixie. Race, Class, and Environmental Quality* (Boulder, CO: Westview, 1990).

162. Somini Sengupta, "Heat, Smoke and Covid Are Battering the Workers Who Feed America," *New York Times*, August 25, 2020.

163. Michael Gochfeld and Joanna Burger, "Disproportionate Exposures in Environmental Justice and Other Populations: The Importance of Outliers," *American Journal of Public Health* 101, no. 1 (2011): 53–63.

164. Adam R. Pearson, Jonathon P. Schuldt, Rainer Romero-Canyas, Matthew T. Ballew, and Dylan Larson-Konar, "Diverse Segments of the US Public Underestimate the Environmental Concerns of Minority and Low-Income Americans," *Proceedings of the National Academy of Sciences of the United States of America* 115, no. 49 (December 4, 2018): 12429–12434.

165. Jenn Richler, "Beliefs about Minority Groups," *Nature Climate Change*, no. 8 (2018): 1033.

166. Robert Bullard, Paul Mohai, Robin Saha, and Beverly Wright, "Toxic Wastes and Race at Twenty: Why Race Still Matters after All of These Years," *Environmental Law* 38, no. 2 (2007): 371–411.

167. See Malia Davis, "Philosophy Meets Practice: A Critique of Ecofeminism through the Voices of Three Chicana Activists," in *Chicano Culture, Ecology, Politics:*

NOTES TO CHAPTER 8   281

Subversive Kin, ed. Devon G. Peña (Tucson: University of Arizona Press, 2008), 201–231.

168. Travis Holloway, *How to Live at the End of the World? Theory, Art, and Politics for the Anthropocene* (Stanford, CA: Stanford University Press, 2022), 63.

169. W. E. B. DuBois, "The Soul of White Folk" (1920), in *W. E. B. DuBois Writings* (New York: Library of America, 1987), 924.

170. Serge Moscovici, *Social Influence and Social Change*.

171. Serge Moscovici, *Society against Nature: The Emergence of Human Societies* (1972), trans. Sacha Rabinovitch (London: Harvester Press, 1976).

172. See Caroline Goldblum, *Françoise d'Eaubonne et l'écoféminisme* (Paris: Le Passager clandestin, 2019).

173. Françoise d'Eaubonne, *Écologie/Féminisme: Révolution ou mutation?* (Paris: A.T.P., 1978), 79–80.

174. Myriam Bahaffou, *Des paillettes sur le compost: Écoféminismes au quotidien* (Paris: Le Passager clandestin, 2022), 82.

175. Donna Haraway, *When Species Meet* (Minneapolis: University of Minnesota Press, 2008), 315, 310, 307.

176. Emanuele Coccia, *Metamorphoses* (2020), trans. Robin Mackay (Cambridge: Polity, 2021), 3–6.

177. He refers to this in English, not without some irony, as a "wicked universality." Bruno Latour, *Down to Earth: Politics in the New Climatic Regime* (2017), trans. Catherine Porter (Cambridge: Polity, 2018), 43.

178. David Harvey, *Justice, Nature and the Geography of Difference* (Cambridge: Blackwell, 1996), 375.

179. Pierre Charbonnier, *Affluence and Freedom: An Environmental History of Political Ideas* (2020), trans. Andrew Brown (Cambridge: Polity Press, 2021), 242–243.

180. Cy Lecerf Maulpoix, *Écologies déviantes: Voyage en terres queers* (Paris: Cambourakis, 2021).

181. David Schlosberg, *Defining Environmental Justice: Theories, Movements, and Nature* (Oxford: Oxford University Press, 2007), 136–138.

182. Gabriela Nuñez, "'Justice Is a Living Organism': An Interview with Lucha Corpi," in *Latinx Environmentalisms. Place, Justice, and the Decolonial*, ed. Sarah D. Wald, David J. Vázquez, Priscilla Solis Ybarra, and Sarah Jaquette Ray (Philadelphia: Temple University Press, 2019), 194.

183. Michael Walzer, *On Toleration* (New Haven, CT: Yale University Press, 1997).

184. Avishai Margalit, *The Decent Society*, trans. Naomi Goldblum (Cambridge, MA: Harvard University Press, 1996).

185. Bernard Harcourt, *Critique & Praxis: A Critical Philosophy of Illusions, Values, and Action* (New York: Columbia University Press, 2020), 266–267.

186. Henry Louis Gates Jr., *The Black Church: This Is Our Story, This Is Our Song* (New York: Penguin Press, 2021).

187. Celeste Winston, *How to Lose the Hounds: Maroon Geographies and a World beyond Policing* (Durham, NC: Duke University Press, 2023).

188. Philip Dray, *There Is Power in a Union: The Epic Story of Labor in America* (New York: Anchor Books, 2011).

189. Mark R. Warren, *Willful Defiance: The Movement to Dismantle the School-to-Prison Pipeline* (Oxford: Oxford University Press, 2021).

190. David France, *How to Survive a Plague: The Story of How Activists and Scientists Tamed Aids* (New York: Vintage, 2016).

191. Mara Mills and Rebecca Sanchez, eds., *Crip Authorship: Disability as Method* (New York: NYU Press, 2023).

192. Despite their inventiveness, phalansteries (in which functions and professions switch from one person to another) cannot completely evade the imperative of task specialization and hierarchization. See Charles Fourier, *Théorie des quatre mouvements et des destinées générales (1808) suivi du Nouveau Monde amoureux (1845–1849)* (Dijon: Les Presses du réel, 1998), 123–128.

193. Tiphaine Samoyault, *Traduction et Violence* (Paris: Seuil, 2020), 27–28.

194. Patricia Hill Collins, *Intersectionality as Critical Social Theory* (Durham, NC: Duke University Press, 2019), 116–120.

195. See the French version of *The Earthly Community: La Communauté terrestre* (Paris: La Découverte, 2023), 57–66.

196. Noudelmann, *Pour en finir avec la généalogie*, 160–162.

197. Louis, *Who Killed My Father?* 34–35.

CONCLUSION

1. Arthur Dénouveaux and Antoine Garapon, *Victimes, et après?* (Paris: Gallimard, 2019), 28.

2. Maurice Blanchot, *The Madness of the Day* (1973), trans. Lydia Davis (Barrytown, NY: Station Hill Press, 1981), 9.

3. Deleuze and Guattari, *A Thousand Plateaus*, 293, 292.

4. Deleuze and Guattari, 292.

5. Zoe Leonard, "I Want a President" (1992), Whitney Museum, https://whitney.org/collection/works/62454.

6. Perreau, *Queer Theory*, 169–170, 187–188.

7. Diagne, "On the Universal and Universalism."

8. See Shari Benstock, "Paris Lesbianism and the Politics of the Reaction, 1900–1940," in *Hidden from History. Reclaiming the Gay and Lesbian Past*, ed. Martin Duberman, Martha Vicinius, and George Chauncey (New York: Meridian, 1989), 332–346.

NOTES TO CONCLUSION

9. Didier Eribon, *Hérésies: Essais sur la théorie de la sexualité* (Paris: Fayard, 2003), 169–206.

10. Jacques Derrida, *Monolingualism of the Other, or the Prosthesis of Origin* (1996), trans. Patrick Mensah (Stanford, CA: Stanford University Press, 1998), 39.

11. Fred Moten and Stefano Harney quoted in Citton and Rasmi, *Générations collapsonautes*, 249.

12. Kyung-Man Kim, *Discourses on Liberation: An Anatomy of Critical Theory* (Boulder, CO: Paradigm, 2005), 104.

13. Isaac Ariail Reed, *Interpretation and Social Knowledge: On the Use of Theory in the Human Sciences* (Chicago: University of Chicago Press, 2011), 84–88.

14. See Pascale Casanova, *World Republic of Letters* (1999), trans. M. B. DeBevoise (Cambridge, MA: Harvard University Press, 2004).

15. See Emmanuel Henry, *Amiante: Un scandale improbable. Sociologie d'un problème public* (Rennes: Presses universitaires de Rennes, 2007).

16. This is highlighted in the treatment of migrants, who are caught in several institutional systems. Camilo Pérez-Bustillo and Karla Hernández Mares, *Human Rights, Hegemony and Utopia in Latin America: Poverty, Forced Migration and Resistance in Mexico and Columbia* (Chicago: Haymarket Books, 2017).

17. Kathleen Thelen, "Comment les institutions évoluent: perspectives de l'analyse comparative historique," *L'Année de la régulation*, 7 (2003): 13–43. See also Kathleen Thelen, *How Institutions Evolve: The Political Economy of Skills in Germany, Britain, the United States and Japan* (Cambridge: Cambridge University Press, 2004).

18. Bastien François, *Naissance d'une Constitution: La Cinquième République. 1958–1962* (Paris: Presses de Sciences Po, 1997).

19. Geoffroy de Lagasnerie, *Sortir de notre impuissance politique* (Paris: Fayard, 2020), 46–48.

20. Emmanuel Henry, *La Fabrique des non-problèmes: Ou comment éviter que la politique s'en mêle* (Paris: Presses de Sciences Po, 2021).

21. Pierre Bourdieu, "The Force of Law" (1986), trans. Richard Terdiman, *Hastings Law Journal* 38 (July 1987): 817–826.

22. Melissa Schwartzberg, *Democracy and Legal Change* (Cambridge: Cambridge University Press, 2007), 195–197.

23. Myriam Winance, "L'accessibilité: une question d'accès ou de vivre ensemble?" in Baudot and Fillion, *Le Handicap cause politique*, 55–58.

24. See Andrew Rehfeld and Melissa Schwartzberg, "Designing Electoral Systems. Normative Tradeoffs and Institutional Innovations," in *Political Science, Electoral Rules, and Democratic Governance*, ed. Mala Htun and G. Bingham Powell Jr., American Political Science Association, Task Force Report, September 2013, 56–61.

25. Guinier, *The Tyranny of the Majority*, 127.

26. Schwartzberg, *Counting the Many*, 184–185.

27. Daumeyer, Onyeador and Richeson, "Does Shared Gender Group Membership Mitigate the Effect of Implicit Bias Attributions on Accountability for Gender-Based Discrimination?"

28. Schwartzberg, "Democracy, Judgment and Juries," in Novak and Elster, *Majority Decisions*, 215.

29. Paola Tabet, *La Grande Arnaque: Sexualité des femmes et échange économico-sexuel* (1987–2001), trans. Josée Contréras (Paris: L'Harmattan, 2004).

30. Sandrine Lefranc, "Le mouvement pour la justice restauratrice," *Droit et société* 63–64 (2006): 393–409.

31. See Ruth Morris, *Practical Path to Transformative Justice* (Toronto: Rittenhouse, 1994).

32. adrienne maree brown, "Unthinkable Thoughts: Call Out Culture in the Age of COVID-19," July 2021, https://adriennemareebrown.net/2020/07/17/unthinkable-thoughts-call-out-culture-in-the-age-of-covid-19/.

33. Ruth Morris, *Why Transformative Justice?* (Toronto: Rittenhouse, 1999), 11.

34. Emma Bigé, "Interrompre le cycle des violences, transformer la communauté," *Multitudes* 88 (2022): 57.

35. Philippe Juhem, "Le porte-parolat et l'accès asymétrique à l'espace public," in *Agir par la parole: Porte-paroles et asymétries de l'espace public*, ed. Philippe Juhem and Julie Sedem (Rennes: Presses universitaires de Rennes, 2016), 101–129.

36. Romain Badouard, *Les Nouvelles Lois du web: Modération et censure* (Paris: Seuil, 2020), 56.

37. Mary Douglas, "Institutions Do the Classifying," in *How Institutions Think* (Syracuse, NY: Syracuse University Press, 1986).

38. Claude Lefort, "The Question of Democracy" (1983), in *Democracy and Political Theory*, trans. David Macey (Minneapolis: University of Minnesota Press, 1988), 19.

SELECTED BIBLIOGRAPHY

AFFIRMATIVE ACTION

Ahmed, Sara. *On Being Included: Racism and Diversity in Institutional Life*. Durham, NC: Duke University Press, 2012.

Anderson, Terry H. *The Pursuit of Fairness: A History of Affirmative Action*. Oxford: Oxford University Press, 2004.

Bergmann, Barbara R. *In Defense of Affirmative Action*. New York: Basic Books, 1996.

Berrey, Ellen. *The Enigma of Diversity: The Language of Race and the Limits of Racial Justice*. Chicago: University of Chicago Press, 2015.

Cahn, Steven M., ed. *The Affirmative Action Debate*. London: Routledge, 1995.

Calvès, Gwénaële. *La Discrimination positive* (2004). Paris: Presses universitaires de France, 2016.

Deslippe, Dennis. *Protesting Affirmative Action: The Struggle over Equality after the Civil Rights Revolution*. Baltimore: Johns Hopkins University Press, 2012.

Farooqui, Adnan. "Political Representation of a Minority: Muslim Representation in Contemporary India." *India Review* 19, no. 2 (2020): 153–175.

Feher, Michel. "Empowerment Hazards: Affirmative Action, Recovery Psychology, and Identity Politics." *Representations* 55 (summer 1996): 84–91.

Ferguson, Roderick A. *The Reorder of Things: The University and Its Pedagogies of Minority Difference*. Minneapolis: University of Minnesota Press, 2012.

Gerapetritis, George. *Affirmative Action Policies and Judicial Review Worldwide*. New York: Springer, 2016.

Kahlenberg, Richard D., ed. *Affirmative-Action for the Rich: Legacy Preferences in College Admissions*. New York: Century Foundation Press, 2010.

Katznelson, Ira. *When Affirmative Action Was White: An Untold History of Racial Inequalities in Twentieth-Century America*. New York: W. W. Norton, 2006.

Kennedy, Randall. *For Discrimination: Race, Affirmative Action, and the Law*. New York: Vintage Books, 2013.

Le Gall, Anne, Françoise Gaspard, and Claude Servan-Schreiber. *Au pouvoir citoyennes! Liberté, égalité, parité*. Paris: Seuil, 1992.

Martin, Terry. *The Affirmative Action Empire: Nations and Nationalism in the Soviet Union, 1923–1939*. Ithaca, NY: Cornell University Press, 2001.

Mills, Nicolaus, ed. *Debating Affirmative Action: Race, Gender, and the Politics of Inclusion*. New York: Delta, 1994.

Pasquali, Paul. *Passer les frontières sociales: Comment les "filières d'élite" entrouvrent leurs portes*. Paris: Fayard, 2014.

Perreau, Bruno. "L'invention républicaine: Éléments d'une herméneutique minoritaires," *Pouvoirs* 111 (2004): 41–53.

Piketty, Thomas. *Mesurer le racisme, vaincre les discriminations*. Paris: Seuil, 2022.

Rubio, Philip F. *A History of Affirmative Action: 1619–2000*. Jackson: University Press of Mississippi, 2001.

Sabbagh, Daniel. *Equality and Transparency: A Strategic Perspective on Affirmative Action in American Law* (2003). London: Palgrave, 2006.

Sabbagh, Daniel. "Une convergence problématique: Les stratégies de légitimation de la 'discrimination positive' dans l'enseignement supérieur aux États-Unis et en France." *Politix* 73, no. 1 (2006): 211–229.

Sénac, Réjane. *L'Égalité sous conditions: Genre, parité, diversité*. Paris: Presses de Sciences Po, 2015.

Skrentny, John D. *The Minority Rights Revolution*. Cambridge, MA: Belknap Press, 2002.

Sowell, Thomas. *Affirmative Action around the World: An Empirical Study*. New Haven, CT: Yale University Press, 2004.

Strolovitch, Dara Z. *Affirmative Advocacy: Race, Class and Gender in Interest Group Politics*. Chicago: University of Chicago Press, 2007.

Thomas, Kendall. "The Political Economy of Recognition: Affirmative Action Discourse and Constitutional Equality in Germany and the U.S.A." *Columbia Journal of European Law*, no. 329 (1999): 329–364.

Wuhl, Simon. *Discrimination positive et justice sociale*. Paris: Presses universitaires de France, 2007.

COMMUNITIES, ACTIVISM, AND SOCIAL VIOLENCE

Abrams, Kathryn. "Elusive Coalitions: Reconsidering the Politics of Gender and Sexuality." *UCLA Law Review* 57 (2009): 1135–1147.

Alexander, Michelle. *The New Jim Crow. Mass Incarceration in the Age of Colorblindness* (New York: New Press, 2010).

Alexandre, Sandy. *The Properties of Violence: Claims to Ownership in Representations of Lynching* (Jackson: University Press of Mississippi, 2012).

Allavena, Julien. *L'Hypothèse autonome.* Paris: Éd. Amsterdam, 2020.

Allen, Danielle. *Talking to Strangers: Anxieties of Citizenship since Brown v. Board of Education.* Chicago: University of Chicago Press, 2004.

Baudot, Pierre-Yves, and Emmanuelle Fillion. *Le Handicap cause politique.* Paris: Presses universitaires de France, 2021.

Beaman, Jean. *Citizen Outsider: Children of North African Immigrants in France.* Berkeley: University of California Press, 2017.

Bessone, Magali. *Faire justice de l'irréparable: Esclavage colonial et responsabilités contemporaines.* Paris: Vrin, 2019.

Bihr, Alain, and Roland Pfefferkorn. *Le Système des inégalités* (2008). Paris: La Découverte, 2021.

Bodin, Romuald. *L'Institution du handicap: Esquisse pour une théorie sociologique du handicap.* Paris: La Dispute, 2018.

Borrillo, Daniel. *Droit d'asile et homosexualité: Comment prouver l'intime?* Paris: LGDJ, 2021.

Breines, Winifred. *The Trouble between Us: An Uneasy History of White and Black Women in the Feminist Movement.* Oxford: Oxford University Press, 2006.

Butler, Paul. *Chokehold: Policing Black Men.* New York: New Press, 2017.

Butt, Daniel. *Rectifying Historical Injustices: Principles of Compensation and Restitution between Nations.* Oxford: Oxford University Press, 2009.

Cervulle, Maxime. *Dans le blanc des yeux: Diversité, racisme et médias* (2013). Paris: Éd. Amsterdam, 2021.

Chebel d'Appollonia, Ariane. *Violent America: The Dynamics of Identity Politics in a Multiracial Society.* Ithaca, NY: Cornell University Press, 2023.

Dean, Jodi. *Solidarity of Strangers: Feminism after Identity Politics.* Berkeley: University of California Press, 1996.

Dhume-Sonzogni, Fabrice. *Communautarisme: Enquête sur une chimère du nationalisme français.* Paris: Demopolis, 2016.

Dray, Philip. *There Is Power in a Union: The Epic Story of Labor in America*. New York: Anchor Books, 2011.

Eribon, Didier. *La Société comme verdict*. Paris: Fayard, 2013.

Ewing, Eve L. *Ghosts in the Schoolyard: Racism and School Closings on Chicago's South Side*. Chicago: University of Chicago Press, 2018.

Fanon, Frantz. *Black Skin, White Masks* (1952). Translated by Charles Lam Markmann. New York: Grove Press, 1967.

Fassa, Farinaz, Éléonore Lépinard, and Marta Roca i Escoda, eds. *L'Intersectionnalité: Enjeux théoriques et politiques*. Paris: La Dispute, 2016.

France, David. *How to Survive a Plague: The Story of How Activists and Scientists Tamed Aids* (New York: Vintage, 2016).

Gardey, Delphine, and Cynthia Kraus, eds. *Politiques de la coalition: Penser et se mobiliser avec Judith Butler*. Translated by Jean-Michel Landry and Fabienne Boursiquo. Geneva: Seismo, 2016.

Gates, Henry Louis Jr. *The Black Church: This Is Our Story, This Is Our Song*. New York: Penguin Press, 2021.

Hill Collins, Patricia. *Intersectionality as Critical Social Theory*. Durham, NC: Duke University Press, 2019.

Hughes, Edward J. *Egalitarian Strangeness: On Class Disturbance and Levelling in Modern and Contemporary French Narrative*. Liverpool: Liverpool University Press, 2021.

Jaquet, Chantal. *Les Transclasses ou la Non-Reproduction*. Paris: Presses universitaires de France, 2014.

Johnson, E. Patrick. *Appropriating Blackness: Performance and the Politics of Authenticity*. Durham, NC: Duke University Press, 2003.

Joseph-Gabriel, Annette K. *Reimagining Liberation: How Black Women Transformed Citizenship in the French Empire*. Urbana: University of Illinois Press, 2020.

Kim, Claire Jean. *Asian Americans in an Anti-Black World*. Cambridge: Cambridge University Press, 2023.

King, Martin Luther Jr. "The Other America," Civil Rights Movement Archive (website), April 4, 1967.

Kramer, Zachary. *Outsiders: Why Difference Is the Future of Civil Rights*. Oxford: Oxford University Press, 2019.

Lagasnerie, Geoffroy de. *La Conscience politique*. Paris: Fayard, 2019.

Lapierre, Nicole. *Causes communes: Des Juifs et des Noirs*. Paris: Stock, 2011.

Lapierre, Nicole. *Faut-il se ressembler pour s'assembler?* Paris: Seuil, 2020.

Le Cour Grandmaison, Olivier, and Omar Slaouti, eds. *Racismes de France*. Paris: La Découverte, 2020.

SELECTED BIBLIOGRAPHY

Lépinard, Éléonore. *Feminist Trouble: Intersectional Politics in Postsecular Times.* Oxford: Oxford University Press, 2020.

Magnaudeix, Mathieu. *Génération Ocasio Cortez: Les nouveaux activistes américains.* Paris: La Découverte, 2020.

Maroun, Daniel M. "Agency, Culpability, and Police Brutality: French Reports of Death during *les Contrôles Policiers.*" *Contemporary French Civilization* 47, no. 4 (December 2022): 385–401.

Mills, Mara, and Rebecca Sanchez, eds. *Crip Authorship: Disability as Method.* New York: NYU Press, 2023.

Pasquali, Paul. *Passer les frontières sociales: Comment les "filières d'élite" entrouvrent leurs portes.* Paris: Fayard, 2014.

Pavard, Bibia, Florence Rochefort, and Michèle Zancarini-Fournel. *Ne nous libérez pas, on s'en charge: Une histoire des féminismes de 1789 à nos jours.* Paris: La Découverte, 2020.

Revillard, Anne. *Des droits vulnérables: Handicap, action publique et changement social.* Paris: Presses de Sciences Po, 2020.

Rochstein, Richard. *The Color of Law: A Forgotten History of How Our Government Segregated America.* New York: Liveright Publishing, 2017.

Rolland-Diamond, Caroline. *Black America: Une histoire des luttes pour l'égalité et pour la justice (XIXe–XXIe siècle).* Paris: La Découverte, 2016.

Sénac, Réjane. *Les Non-Frères au pays de l'égalité.* Paris: Presses de Sciences Po, 2017.

Sénac, Réjane. *Radicales et fluides: Les mobilisations contemporaines.* Paris: Presses de Sciences Po, 2022.

Sourice, Benjamin. *La Démocratie des places: Des Indignados à Nuit debout, vers un nouvel horizon politique.* Paris: Charles Léopold Mayer, 2017.

Talpin, Julien. *Community Organizing: De l'émeute à l'alliance des classes populaires aux États-Unis.* Paris: Raisons d'agir, 2016.

Truong, Fabien. *Loyautés radicales: L'islam et les "mauvais garçons" de la Nation.* Paris: La Découverte, 2017.

Warren, Mark R. *Willful Defiance: The Movement to Dismantle the School-to-Prison Pipeline.* Oxford: Oxford University Press, 2021.

Washington, Myra S. *Blasian Invasion: Racial Mixing in the Celebrity Industrial Complex.* Jackson: University Press of Mississippi, 2017.

Williams, Jakobi. *From the Bullet to the Ballot: The Illinois Chapter of the Black Panther Party and Racial Coalition Politics in Chicago.* Chapel Hill: University of North Carolina Press, 2013.

Wilson, William Julius. *More Than Just Race: Being Black and Poor in the Inner City*. New York: W. W. Norton, 2009.

Wilson, William Julius. *The Truly Disadvantaged* (1987). Chicago: University of Chicago Press, 1990.

Winston, Celeste. *How to Lose the Hounds: Maroon Geographies and a World beyond Policing*. Durham, NC: Duke University Press, 2023.

DEMOCRACY AND THE MAJORITY RULE

Benbassa, Esther. *Minorités visibles en politique*. Paris: CNRS éditions, 2011.

Bernholz, Lucy, Hélène Landemore, and Rob Reich, eds. *Digital Technology and Democratic Theory*. Chicago: University of Chicago Press, 2021.

Bruno, Esther, Emmanuel Didier, and Julien Previeux, eds. *Statactivisme: Comment lutter avec des nombres*. Paris: La Découverte, 2014.

Bybee, Keith J. *Mistaken Identity: The Supreme Court and the Politics of Minority Representation*. Princeton, NJ: Princeton University Press, 1998.

Christian, Brian. *The Alignment Problem: Machine Learning and Human Values*. New York: W. W. Norton, 2020.

Chwe, Michael Suk-Young. "Minority Voting Rights Can Maximize Majority Welfare." *American Political Science Review* 93, no. 1 (1999): 85–97.

Condorcet, Nicolas de. "An Essay on the Application of Probability Theory to Plurality Decision-Making" (1785). In *Foundations of Social Choice and Political Theory*, edited and translated by Iain McLean and Fiona Hewitt, 120–130. Aldershot: Edward Elgar, 1994.

Fruteau de Laclos, Frédéric. "Pour un universalisme de terrain." In *L'Universalisme en débat(s)*, edited by Stéphane Dufoix and Alain Policar, 137–147. Lormont: Le Bord de l'eau, 2024.

Girard, Charles. "La règle de la majorité en démocratie: Équité ou vérité?" *Raisons politiques* 53, no. 1 (2014): 107–137.

Guinier, Lani. *The Tyranny of the Majority: Fundamental Fairness in Representative Democracy*. New York: Free Press, 1995.

Hartsock, Nancy. "Rethinking Modernism: Minority vs. Majority Theories." *Cultural Critique* 7 (1987): 187–206.

Keating, Michael, and John McGarry. *Minority Nationalism and the Changing International Order*. Oxford: Oxford University Press, 2001.

Kim, Sunmin. "Rethinking Models of Minority Representation. Inter- and Intra-Group Variation in Political 'Styles.'" *Du Bois Review* 16, no. 2 (2019): 489–510.

Kreider, Kyle, and Tomas Baldino. *Minority Voting in the United States*. Westport, CT: Praeger, 2015.

SELECTED BIBLIOGRAPHY

Lajoie, Andrée. *Quand les minorités font la loi*. Paris: Presses universitaires de France, 2002.

"La représentation incarnation." *Raisons politiques* 72, no. 4 (November 2018).

McDonald, Michael D., Ian Budge, and Ribon E. Best. "Electoral Majorities, Political Parties and Collective Representation." *Comparative Political Studies* 45, no. 9 (2012): 1104–1131.

McGann, Anthony. *The Logic of Democracy: Reconciling Equality, Deliberation, and Minority Protection*. Ann Arbor: University of Michigan Press, 2006.

Mineur, Didier. *Archéologie de la représentation politique*. Paris: Presses de Sciences Po, 2010.

Mineur, Didier. *Le Pouvoir de la majorité: Fondements et limites*. Paris: Garnier, 2017.

Mouffe, Chantal. *On the Political*. London: Routledge, 2005.

Novak, Stéphanie, and Jon Elster, eds. *Majority Decisions: Principles and Practices*. Cambridge: Cambridge University Press, 2014.

Ober, Josiah. "The Original Meaning of 'Democracy': Capacity to Do Things, Not Majority Rule." *Constellations: An International Journal of Critical & Democratic Theory* 15, no. 1 (2008): 3–9.

O'Neil, Cathy. *Weapons of Math Destruction: How Big Data Increases Inequality and Threatens Democracy*. New York: Crown, 2016.

Patten, Alan. *Equal Recognition: The Moral Foundations of Minority Rights*. Princeton, NJ: Princeton University Press, 2014.

Policar, Alain. *L'Universalisme en procès*. Lormont: Le Bord de l'eau, 2021.

Rule, Wilma, and Joseph Zimmerman. *United States Electoral Systems: Their Impact on Women and Minorities*. Westport, CT: Praeger, 1992.

Schwartzberg, Melissa. *Counting the Many: The Origins and Limits of Supermajority Rule*. Cambridge: Cambridge University Press, 2014.

Song, Sarah. "Majority, Norms, Multiculturalism, and Gender Equality." *American Political Science Review* 99, no. 4 (2005): 473–489.

Tassin, Étienne. *Un monde commun: Pour une cosmo-politique des conflits*. Paris: Seuil, 2003.

GROUP DYNAMICS, INSTITUTIONS, AND REPRESENTATION

Allen, Danielle, and Jennifer S. Light, eds. *From Voice to Influence: Understanding Citizenship in a Digital Age*. Chicago: University of Chicago Press, 2015.

Althusser, Louis. "Ideology and Ideological State Apparatuses (Notes towards an Investigation)." In *Lenin and Philosophy and Other Essays*, translated by Ben Brewster, 79–87. New York: Monthly Review Press, 1971.

Arrow, Kenneth. *Social Choice and Individual Values*. New Haven, CT: Yale University Press, 2012.

Boudou, Benjamin. *Politique de l'hospitalité*. Paris: CNRS éditions, 2017.

Bourdieu, Pierre. "Two Imperialisms of the Universal." In *French Global: A New Approach to Literary History*, edited by Christie McDonald and Susan Rubin Suleiman, 239–250. New York: Columbia University Press, 2010.

Butler, Judith. *Notes toward a Performative Theory of Assembly*. Cambridge, MA: Harvard University Press, 2015.

Butler, Judith, and Athena Athanasiou. *Dispossession: The Performative in the Political*. Cambridge: Polity Press, 2013.

Calder, Gideon, Magali Bessone, and Federico Zuolo, eds. *How Groups Matter: Challenges of Toleration in Pluralistic Societies*. London: Routledge, 2014.

Citton, Yves, and Dominique Quessada, eds. "Du commun au comme-un." *Multitudes* 45, special issue (2011).

Cohen, Jean Louise. *Regulating Intimacy: A New Legal Paradigm*. Princeton, NJ: Princeton University Press, 2002.

Daub, Adrian. *What Tech Calls Thinking: An Inquiry into the Intellectual Bedrock of Silicon Valley*. New York: FSG Originals x Logic, 2020.

Douglas, Mary. *How Institutions Think*. Syracuse, NY: Syracuse University Press, 1986.

"Entités collectives." *Raisons politiques* 66, no. 2 (May 2017).

François, Bastien. *Naissance d'une Constitution: La Cinquième République, 1958–1962*. Paris: Presses de Sciences Po, 1997.

Girard, Charles. *Délibérer entre égaux: Enquête sur l'idéal démocratique*. Paris: Vrin, 2019.

Greco, Luca, Lorenza Mondada, and Patrick Renaud, eds. *Identités en interaction*. Limoges: Lambert Lucas, 2014.

Gutmann, Amy, and Dennis Thompson. "Why Deliberative Democracy is Different." *Social Philosophy and Policy* 17, no. 1 (2000): 161–180.

Henry, Emmanuel. *La Fabrique des non-problèmes: Ou comment éviter que la politique s'en mêle*. Paris: Presses de Sciences Po, 2021.

Hirschman, Albert O. *The Passions and the Interests: Political Arguments for Capitalism before Its Triumph*. Princeton, NJ: Princeton University Press, 1977.

Joseph, Miranda. *Against the Romance of Community*. Minneapolis: University of Minnesota Press, 2002.

Juhem, Philippe, and Julie Sedem, eds. *Agir par la parole: Porte-paroles et asymétries de l'espace public*. Rennes: Presses universitaires de Rennes, 2016.

Lefort, Claude. *Democracy and Political Theory* (1986). Translated by David Macey. Minneapolis: University of Minnesota Press, 1988.

Lefort, Claude. *Writing: The Political Test* (1992). Translated by David Ames Curtis. Durham, NC: Duke University Press, 2000.

Lewis, Amanda E. "'What Group?' Studying Whites and Whiteness in the Era of 'Color-Blindness.'" *Sociological Theory* 22, no. 4 (December 2004): 623–646.

List, Christian, and Philip Pettit. *Group Agency: The Possibility, Design, and Status of Corporate Agents*. Oxford: Oxford University Press, 2011.

Olson, Mancur. *The Logic of Collective Action: Public Goods and the Theory of Groups*. Cambridge, MA: Harvard University Press, 1965.

Pettigrew, Thomas Fraser, and Linda R. Tropp. "A Meta-Analytic Test of Intergroup Contact Theory." *Journal of Personality and Social Psychology* 90, no. 5 (May 2006): 751–783.

Schwartzberg, Melissa. *Democracy and Legal Change*. Cambridge: Cambridge University Press, 2007.

Thelen, Kathleen. *How Institutions Evolve: The Political Economy of Skills in Germany, Britain, the United States and Japan*. Cambridge: Cambridge University Press, 2004.

Urbinati, Nadia. *Democracy Disfigured: Opinion, Truth, and the People*. Cambridge, MA: Harvard University Press, 2014.

Urfalino, Philippe. *Décider ensemble*. Paris: Seuil, 2021.

Verba, Sidney. *Small Groups and Political Behaviors: A Study of Leadership*. Princeton, NJ: Princeton University Press, 1961.

Weber, Max. *Economy and Society* (1921). Translated by Keith Tribe. Cambridge, MA: Harvard University Press, 2019.

Williams, Jakobi. *From the Bullet to the Ballot: The Illinois Chapter of the Black Panther Party and Racial Coalition Politics in Chicago*. Chapel Hill: University of North Carolina Press, 2013.

Zaffran, Joël, ed. *Accessibilité et Handicap*. Grenoble: Presses universitaires de Grenoble, 2015.

ETHICS AND IDENTITY

Appiah, Kwame Anthony. *The Ethics of Identity*. Princeton, NJ: Princeton University Press, 2005.

Balibar, Étienne. *Citizen Subject: Foundations for Philosophical Anthropology* (2011). Translated by Steven Miller. New York: Fordham University Press, 2017.

Balibar, Étienne. *On Universals: Constructing and Deconstructing Community* (2016). Translated by Joshua David Jordan. New York: Fordham University Press, 2020.

Barad, Karen. "Reconceiving Scientific Literacy as Agential Literacy: Or, Learning How to Intra-Act Responsibly within the World." In *Doing Science + Culture*, edited by Roddey Reid and Sharon Traweek, 221–258. London: Routledge, 2000.

Barthes, Roland. *How to Live Together: Novelistic Simulations of Some Everyday Spaces. Notes for a Lecture Course and Seminar at the Collège de France (1976–1977)*. Translated by Kate Briggs. New York: Columbia University Press, 2012.

Beauvoir, Simone de. *The Ethics of Ambiguity* (1944). Translated by Bernard Frechtman. New York: Citadel Press, 1976.

Benhabib, Seyla. *Situating the Self: Gender, Community, and Postmodernism in Contemporary Ethics*. Cambridge: Polity Press, 1992.

Benhabib, Seyla, Ian Shapiro, and Danilo Petranovic, eds. *Identities, Affiliations, and Allegiances*. Cambridge: Cambridge University Press, 2007.

Berlant, Lauren. *On the Inconvenience of Other People*. Durham, NC: Duke University Press, 2022.

Berliner, David. *Becoming Other. Heterogeneity and Plasticity of the Self* (2022). Translated by Stephen Muecke. New York: Berghahn, 2024.

Birnbaum, Jean, ed. *L'Identité pour quoi faire?* Paris: Gallimard, 2020.

Blanchot, Maurice. *The Unavowable Community* (1983). Translated by Pierre Joris. Barrytown, NY: Station Hill Press, 1988.

Bourdieu, Pierre. *Sketch for a Self-Analysis* (2004). Translated by Richard Nice. Cambridge: Polity Press, 2007.

Buber, Martin. *I and Thou* (1923). Translated by Ronald Gregor. New York: Touchstone, 1996.

Butler, Judith. *Giving an Account of Oneself*. New York: Fordham University Press, 2005.

Butler, Judith. *The Psychic Life of Power: Theories in Subjection*. Stanford, CA: Stanford University Press, 1997.

Collin, Françoise. *Le Différend des sexes*. Paris: Agone, 1999.

Dénouveaux, Arthur, and Antoine Garapon. *Victimes, et après?* Paris: Gallimard, 2019.

Derrida, Jacques. *Monolingualism of the Other, or The Prosthesis of Origin* (1996). Translated by Patrick Mensah. Stanford, CA: Stanford University Press, 1998.

Derrida, Jacques. *Speech and Phenomena: Introduction to the Problem of the Sign in Husserl's Phenomenology* (1967). Translated by Leonard Lawlord. Evanston, IL: Northwestern University Press, 2011.

Derrida, Jacques. *Who's Afraid of Philosophy? Right to Philosophy I* (1990). Translated by Jan Plug. Stanford, CA: Stanford University, 2002.

SELECTED BIBLIOGRAPHY

Derrida, Jacques. *Writing and Difference* (1967). Translated by Alan Bass. Chicago: University of Chicago Press, 1967.

Descola, Philippe, and Tim Ingold. *Être au monde: Quelle expérience commune?* Translated by Benjamin Fau. Lyon: Presses universitaires de Lyon, 2014.

Descombes, Vincent. *Puzzling Identities* (2013). Translated by Stephen Adam Schwartz. Cambridge, MA: Harvard University Press, 2016.

Diagne, Souleymane Bachir. *De langue à langue: L'hospitalité de la traduction.* Paris: Albin Michel, 2022.

Esposito, Roberto. *Immunitas: The Protection and Negation of Life* (2002). Translated by Zakiya Hanafi. Cambridge: Polity Press, 2011.

Ferrarese, Estelle. *The Fragility of Concern for Others: Adorno and the Ethics of Care* (2018). Translated by Steven Corcoran. Edinburgh: Edinburgh University Press, 2021.

Ferret, Stéphane. *Le Bateau de Thésée: Le problème de l'identité à travers le temps.* Paris: Éditions de Minuit, 1996.

Gilligan, Carol. *In a Different Voice: Psychological Theory and Women's Development.* Cambridge, MA: Harvard University Press, 1982.

Glissant, Édouard. *Introduction to a Poetry of Diversity* (1995). Translated by Celia Britton. Liverpool: Liverpool University Press, 2020.

Glissant, Édouard. *Philosophie de la relation: Poésie en étendue.* Paris: Gallimard, 2009.

Gumbrecht, Hans Ulrich. *Production of Presence: What Meaning Cannot Convey.* Stanford, CA: Stanford University Press, 2004.

Hall, Stuart. *Identités et Cultures: Politiques des cultural studies.* Edited by Maxime Cervulle, translated by Christophe Jaquet. Paris: Éd. Amsterdam, 2007.

Hartog, François. *Regimes of Historicity: Presentism and Experiences of Time* (2003). Translated by Saskia Brown. New York: Columbia University Press, 2016.

Honneth, Axel. *Recognition: A Chapter in the History of European Ideas* (2018). Translated by Joseph Ganahl. Cambridge: Cambridge University Press, 2021.

Honneth, Axel. *The Struggle for Recognition: The Moral Grammar of Social Conflicts* (1992). Translated by Joel Anderson. Cambridge, MA: MIT Press, 1996.

Jullien, François. *Altérités: De l'altérité personnelle à l'altérité culturelle* (2010). Paris: Gallimard, Folio, 2021.

Jullien, François. *Si près, tout autre: De l'écart et de la rencontre.* Paris: Grasset, 2018.

Laclau, Ernesto. "The Death and Resurrection of the Theory of Ideology." *Modern Language Notes* 112, no. 3 (1997): 297–321.

Laclau, Ernesto. *Emancipation(s).* London: Verso, 1996.

Laidi, Zaïki. *Le Sacre du présent*. Paris: Flammarion, 2000.

Laplantine, François. *Je, Nous et les Autres* (1999). Paris: Le Pommier, 2010.

Levi, Primo. *If This Is a Man* (1958). Translated by Stuart Woolf. New York: Orion Press, 1959.

Locke, John. "Of Identity and Diversity" (1694). In *An Essay Concerning Human Understanding*, edited by Roger Woolhouse, 296–313. New York: Penguin Classics, 1999.

Lukes, Steven. *Moral Relativism*. New York: Picador, 2008.

Markell, Patchen. *Bound by Recognition*. Princeton, NJ: Princeton University Press, 2003.

Martín Alcoff, Linda, Michael R. Hames-García, Satya P. Mohanty, and Paula M. Y. Moya, eds. *Identity Politics Reconsidered*. London: Palgrave MacMillan, 2006.

Merleau-Ponty, Maurice. *Phenomenology of Perception* (1945). Translated by Colin Smith. London: Routledge, 2002.

Merleau-Ponty, Maurice. *Signs: Studies in Phenomenology and Existential Philosophy* (1960). Translated by Richard C. McCleary. Evanston, IL: Northwestern University Press, 1964.

Nancy, Jean-Luc. *Being Singular Plural* (1996). Translated by Robert Richardson and Anne O'Byrne. Stanford, CA: Stanford University Press, 2000.

Nancy, Jean-Luc. "The Compearance: From the Existence of 'Communism' to the Community of 'Existence.'" Translated by Tracy B. Strong. *Political Theory* 20, no. 3 (August 1992): 371–398.

Noudelmann, François. *Pour en finir avec la généalogie*. Paris: Leo Scheer, 2004.

Paperman, Patricia, and Sandra Laugier, eds. *Le Souci des autres. Éthique et politique du care*. Paris: Presses de l'EHESS, 2011.

Phillips, Anne. *The Politics of Presence*. Oxford: Oxford University Press, 1995.

Potte-Bonneville, Mathieu. *Recommencer*. Paris: Verdier, 2018.

Pradeu, Thomas. *The Limits of the Self: Immunology and Biological Identity* (2009). Translated by Elizabeth Vitanza. Oxford: Oxford University Press, 2012.

Reszler, André. *Le Pluralisme: Aspects historiques et théoriques dans les sociétés pluralistes*. Paris: Table Ronde, 2001.

Riley, Denise, *Am I That Name? Feminism and the Category of Women in History*. Basingstoke: Macmillan, 1988.

Rosa, Hartmut. *Resonance: A Sociology of Our Relationship to the World* (2016). Translated by James Wagner. London: John Wiley and Sons, 2019.

Rothberg, Michael. *Multidirectional Memory: Remembering the Holocaust in the Age of Decolonization*. Stanford, CA: Stanford University Press, 2009.

SELECTED BIBLIOGRAPHY 297

Sartre, Jean-Paul. *Being and Nothingness* (1943). Translated by Hazel. E. Barnes. London: Routledge, 1989.

Sartre, Jean-Paul. *Critique of Dialectical Reason*, volume 1 (1960). Translated by Alan Sheridan-Smith. London: Verso, 2004.

Sennett, Richard. *The Fall of Public Man: On the Social Psychology of Capitalism* (1974). New York: Vintage Books, 1978.

Spinoza, Baruch. *The Ethics* (1677). Translated by William Hale White, revised by Amelia Hutchinson Sterling. London: Macmillan, 1949.

Thomson, Judith Jarvis. *Rights, Restitution, and Risk: Essays in Moral Theory*. Cambridge, MA: Harvard University Press, 1986.

Tronto, Joan. *Moral Boundaries: A Political Argument for an Ethic of Care*. London: Routledge, 1993.

JUSTICE AND DEMOCRACY

Allen, Danielle, Yochai Benkler, Leah Downey, Rebecca Henderson, and Josh Simons, eds. *A Political Economy of Justice*. Chicago: University of Chicago Press, 2022.

Arato, Andrew, Jean L. Cohen, and Astrid von Busekist, eds. *Forms of Pluralism and Democratic Constitutionalism*. New York: Columbia University Press, 2018.

Balibar, Étienne. *Equaliberty: Political Essays* (2010). Translated by James Ingram. Durham, NC: Duke University Press, 2014.

Benhabib, Seyla. *The Rights of Others: Aliens, Residents, and Citizens*. Cambridge: Cambridge University Press, 2004.

Berlin, Isaiah. "Two Concepts of Liberty." (1958) In *Liberty*, edited by Henry Hardy, 166–217. Oxford: Oxford University Press, 2002.

Boudou, Benjamin. *Politique de l'hospitalité*. Paris: CNRS éditions, 2017.

Brown, Wendy. *Undoing the Demos: Neoliberalism's Stealth Revolution*. New York: Zone Books, 2015.

Busekist, Astrid von. *La Religion au tribunal: Essai sur le délibéralisme*. Paris: Albin Michel, 2023.

Christ, Julia. *L'Oubli de l'universel: Hegel critique du libéralisme*. Paris: Presses universitaires de France, 2021.

Citton, Yves. *Altermodernités des Lumières*. Paris: Seuil, 2022.

Cohen, Jean L. *Globalization and Sovereignty: Rethinking Legality, Legitimacy, and Constitutionalism*. Cambridge: Cambridge University Press, 2012.

Cohen, Joshua. "An Epistemic Conception of Democracy." *Ethics* 97, no. 1 (October 1986): 26–38.

Condorcet, Nicolas de. "The Sketch (*Esquisse d'un tableau historique des progrès humains*)" (1795). In *Condorcet: Political Writings*, edited by Steven Lukes and Nadia Urbinati, translated by June Barraclough, 1–147. Cambridge: Cambridge University Press, 2012.

Deveaux, Monique. *Cultural Pluralism and Dilemmas of Justice*. Ithaca, NY: Cornell University Press, 2000.

Deveaux, Monique. *Gender and Justice in Multicultural Liberal States*. Oxford: Oxford University Press, 2006.

Dworkin, Ronald. "Liberal Community." *California Law Review* 77, no. 3 (May 1989): 479–504.

Eisenberg, Avigail, and Jeff Spinner-Halev, eds. *Minorities within Minorities: Equality, Rights and Diversity*. Cambridge: Cambridge University Press, 2005.

Fourier, Charles. *Théorie des quatre mouvements et des destinées générales (1808) suivi du Nouveau Monde amoureux (1845–1849)*. Dijon: Les Presses du réel, 1998.

Fricker, Miranda. *Epistemic Injustice: Power and the Ethics of Knowledge*. Oxford: Oxford University Press, 2007.

Garapon Antoine, and Jean Lassègue. *Justice digitale*. Paris: Presses universitaires de France, 2018.

Guénard, Florent. *La Démocratie universelle: Philosophie d'un modèle politique*. Paris: Seuil, 2016.

Guénard, Florent. *La Passion de l'égalité*. Paris: Seuil, 2022.

Guillarme, Bertrand. *Rawls et l'égalité démocratique*. Paris: Presses universitaires de France, 1999.

Hamilton, Alexander, James Madison, and John Jay. *The Federalist Papers (1787–1788)*. Mineola, NY: Dover, 2014.

Hauchecorne, Mathieu. *La Gauche américaine en France: La réception de John Rawls et des théories de la justice*. Paris: CNRS Éditions, 2019.

Hegel, Georg Wilhelm Friedrich. *Elements of the Philosophy of Right* (1820). Translated by T. M. Knox. Oxford: Oxford University Press, 1967.

Honneth, Axel. "Justice et liberté communicationnelle: Réflexions à partir de Hegel." In *La Reconnaissance aujourd'hui*, edited by Alain Caillé and Christian Lazzeri, translated by Marion Schumm, 43–64. Paris: CNRS Éditions, 2009.

Honneth, Axel. *The Pathologies of Individual Freedom: Hegel's Social Theory* (2001). Translated by Ladislaus Löb. Princeton, NJ: Princeton University Press, 2010.

Kymlicka, Will. *Liberalism, Community, and Culture*. Oxford: Clarendon Press, 1989.

Laborde, Cécile, and John Maynor. *Republicanism and Political Theory*. Malden, MA: Blackwell Publishing, 2008.

SELECTED BIBLIOGRAPHY

Lacroix, Justine, and Jean-Yves Pranchère. *Human Rights on Trial: A Genealogy of the Critique of Human Rights* (2016). Translated by Gabrielle Maas. Cambridge: Cambridge University Press, 2018.

Lafont, Anne. "De l'universalité de la critique." *Esprit*, no. 461 (January 2020): 71–78.

Lagasnerie, Geoffroy de. *Juger: L'État pénal face à la sociologie*. Paris: Fayard, 2016.

Landemore, Hélène. *Democratic Reason: Politics, Collective Intelligence, and the Rule of the Many*. Princeton, NJ: Princeton University Press, 2013.

Lefranc, Sandrine. "Le mouvement pour la justice restauratrice." *Droit et société* 63–64 (2006): 393–409.

Lyotard, Jean-François, and Jean-Loup Thébaud. *Just Gaming* (1979). Translated by Brian Massumi. Minneapolis: University of Minnesota Press, 1985.

Macedo, Stephen. *Liberal Virtues: Citizenship, Virtue and Community in Liberal Constitutionalism*. Oxford: Oxford University Press, 1990.

Marx, Karl, and Fredrick Engels, *The German Ideology: Part One (1845–1846)*. Edited and translated by C. J. Arthur. London: Lawrence & Wishart, 1974.

May, Paul. *Philosophie du multiculturalisme*. Paris: Presses de Sciences Po, 2016.

Messling, Markus. *Universality after Universalism: On Francophone Literatures of the Present*. Translated by Michael Thomas Taylor. Berlin: De Gruyter, 2023.

Messling, Markus, and Jonas Tinius, eds. *Minor Universality: Rethinking Humanity after Western Universalism*. Translated by John Angell, Anna Galt, Michael Thomas Taylor, and Liz Carey Libbrecht. Berlin: De Gruyter, 2023.

Mill, John Stuart. "On the Connexion between Justice and Utility" (1861). In John Stuart Mill, *Utilitarianism and On Liberty*, edited by Mary Warnock, 216–234. Malden, MA: Blackwell, 2003.

Moller Okin, Susan. *Justice, Gender, and the Family*. New York: Basic Books, 1989.

Morris, Ruth. *Why Transformative Justice?* Toronto: Rittenhouse, 1999.

Nirenberg, David. *Communities of Violence: Persecution of Minorities in the Middle Ages*. Princeton, NJ: Princeton University Press, 1996.

Nozick, Robert. *Anarchy, State and Utopia*. New York: Harper & Row, 1974.

O'Malley, Pat. "Simulated Justice: Risk, Money and Telemetric Policing." *British Journal of Criminology* 50, no. 5 (2010): 795–807.

Oyarzún, Pablo. *Doing Justice: Three Essays on Walter Benjamin* (1999). Translated by Stephen Gingerich. Cambridge: Polity Press, 2020.

Pélabay, Janie. "Communitarian Equality: To Each According to Their Contribution to the Group Identity." *International Social Science Journal* 67 (2017): 21–30.

Pettit, Philip. *Just Freedom: A Moral Compass for a Complex World*. New York: W. W. Norton, 2014.

Pettit, Philip. *The Robust Demands of the Good: Attachment, Virtue, and Respect*. Oxford: Oxford University Press, 2015.

Piketty, Thomas. *A Brief History of Equality* (2021). Translated by Steven Rendall. Cambridge, MA: Harvard University Press, 2022.

Pitkin, Hanna Fenichel. *The Concept of Representation*. Berkeley: University of California Press, 1967.

Proudhon, Pierre-Joseph. *What Is Property?* (1840). Edited and translated by Donald R. Kelley and Bonnie G. Smith. Cambridge: Cambridge University Press, 1994.

Rawls, John. *Political Liberalism* (1993). New York: Columbia University Press, 2005.

Rawls, John. *A Theory of Justice* (1971). Cambridge, MA: Harvard University Press, 1999.

Renault, Emmanuel. *The Experience of Injustice: A Theory of Recognition* (2004). Translated by Richard A. Lynch. New York: Columbia University Press, 2019.

Rousseau, Jean-Jacques. *The Social Contract* (1762). Translated by Henry John Tozer. Ware: Wordsworth, 1998.

Sandel, Michael. *Liberalism and the Limits of Justice* (1982). Cambridge: Cambridge University Press, 1988.

Savidan, Patrick. "Multiculturalisme libéral et monoculturalisme pluriel." *Raisons politiques* 35, no. 3 (2009): 11–29.

Sen, Armatya. *The Idea of Justice*. Cambridge, MA: Harvard University Press, 2009.

Shklar, Judith. *The Faces of Injustice*. New Haven, CT: Yale University Press, 1990.

Song, Sarah. *Justice, Gender, and the Politics of Multiculturalism*. Cambridge: Cambridge University Press, 2007.

Spector, Céline. *Éloges de l'injustice: La philosophie face à la déraison*. Paris: Seuil, 2016.

Suau, Julien, and Mame-Fatou Niang. *Universalisme*. Paris: Anamosa, 2022.

Taylor, Charles. *Multiculturalism: Difference and Democracy*. Edited by Amy Gutmann. Princeton, NJ: Princeton University Press, 1994.

Tilly, Charles. *Democracy*. Cambridge: Cambridge University Press, 2007.

Tocqueville, Alexis de. *Democracy in America* (1835). Translated by James T. Schleifer. Minneapolis: Liberty Fun, 2012.

Tomba, Massimiliano. *Insurgent Universality: An Alternative Legacy of Modernity*. Oxford: Oxford University Press, 2019.

Tully, James. *Strange Multiplicity: Pluralism in an Age of Diversity*. Cambridge: Cambridge University Press, 1995.

SELECTED BIBLIOGRAPHY

Urbinati. Nadia, *Representative Democracy: Principles and Genealogy*. Chicago: University of Chicago Press, 2006.

Walzer, Michael. "The Communitarian Critique of Liberalism." *Political Theory* 18, no. 1 (February 1990): 6–23.

Walzer, Michael. *Interpretation and Social Criticism*. Cambridge, MA: Harvard University Press, 1987.

Walzer, Michael. *Just and Unjust Wars: A Moral Argument with Historical Illustrations*. New York: Basic Books, 1977.

Walzer, Michael. *Obligations: Essays on Disobedience, War, and Citizenship*. Cambridge, MA: Harvard University Press, 1970.

Walzer, Michael. *The Paradox of Liberation: Secular Revolutions and Religious Counterrevolutions*. New Haven, CT: Yale University Press, 2015.

Walzer, Michael. *Spheres of Justice: A Defense of Pluralism and Equality*. New York: Basic Books, 1983.

Walzer, Michael. *The Struggle for a Decent Politics: On "Liberal" as an Adjective*. New Haven, CT: Yale University Press, 2023.

Walzer, Michael. *Thick and Thin: Moral Argument at Home and Abroad*. Notre Dame, IN: University of Notre Dame Press, 1994.

Walzer, Michael. *Thinking Politically: Essays in Political Theory*. New Haven, CT: Yale University Press, 2007.

Walzer, Michael, and Astrid von Busekist. *Justice Is Steady Work: A Conversation on Political Theory* (2020). Translated by Astrid von Busekist. Cambridge: Polity Press, 2020.

Young, Iris Marion. *Justice and the Politics of Difference*. Princeton, NJ: Princeton University Press, 1990.

Young, Iris Marion. *Responsibility for Justice*. Oxford: Oxford University Press, 2011.

POPULISM AND NEOLIBERALISM

Aho, James. *Far-Right Fantasy: A Sociology of American Religion and Politics*. New York: Routledge, 2016.

Alduy, Cécile, and Stéphane Wahnich. *Marine Le Pen prise aux mots: Décryptage du nouveau discours frontiste*. Paris: Seuil, 2015.

Bonilla-Silva, Eduardo. *Racism without Racists: Color-Blind Racism and the Persistence of Racial Inequality in the United States* (2003). Oxford: Rowman & Littlefield, 2018.

Branciforte, Josha, and Ramsey McGlazer, eds. *On the Subject of Ethnonationalism*. New York: Fordham University Press, 2023.

Brown, Wendy. *In the Ruins of Neoliberalism: The Rise of Antidemocratic Politics in the West*. New York: Columbia University Press, 2019.

Connor, Walker. "The Politics of Ethnonationalism." *Journal of International Affairs* 27, no. 1 (1973): 1–21.

Connor, Walker. "Self-Determination. The New Phase." *World Politics* 20, no. 1 (1967): 20–53.

Cooper, Melinda. *Family Values: Between Neoliberalism and the New Social Conservatism*. New York: Zone Books, 2017.

Eribon, Didier. *D'une révolution conservatrice et de ses effets sur la gauche française*. Paris: Léo Scheer, 2007.

Faludi, Susan. *Backlash: The Undeclared War against American Women*. New York: Three Rivers Press, 2006.

Fassin, Éric. "Sexual Event: From Clarence Thomas to Monica Lewinsky." *differences: A Journal of Feminist Cultural Studies* 13, no. 2 (2002): 127–158.

Garbagnoli, Sara, and Massimo Prearo, *La Croisade "anti-genre": Du Vatican aux manifs pour tous*. Paris: Textuel, 2017.

Haider, Asad. *Mistaken Identity: Race and Class in the Age of Trump* (2018). London: Verso, 2018.

Harcourt, Bernard E. *The Counterrevolution: How Our Government Went to War against Its Own Citizens*. New York: Basic Books, 2018.

Hobsbawm, Eric J. *Nations and Nationalism since 1780: Programme, Myth, Reality*. Cambridge: Cambridge University Press, 1990.

Hosang Martinez, Daniel, and Joseph E. Lowndes. *Producers, Parasites, Patriots: Race and the New Right-Wing Politics of Precarity*. Minneapolis: University of Minnesota Press, 2019.

Jardina, Ashley. *White Identity Politics*. Cambridge: Cambridge University Press, 2019.

Laclau, Ernesto. *On Populist Reason*. London: Verso, 2005.

Lacorne, Denis. *La Crise de l'identité américaine*. Paris: Fayard, 1997.

Laurent, Sylvie. *La Couleur du marché: Racisme et néolibéralisme aux États-Unis*. Paris: Seuil, 2016.

Laurent, Sylvie. *Pauvre Petit Blanc*. Paris: Éditions de la Maison des Sciences de l'Homme, 2020.

Mahoudeau, Alex. *La Panique woke: Anatomie d'une offensive réactionnaire*. Paris: Textuel, 2022.

Matonti, Frédérique. *Comment sommes-nous devenus réacs?* Paris: Fayard, 2021.

SELECTED BIBLIOGRAPHY

Mény, Yves, and Jan Kermer. *Imperfect Democracies: The Rise of Popular Protest and Democratic Dissent.* London: Rowman & Littlefield, 2021.

Norris, Pippa. *Radical Right: Voters and Parties in the Electoral Market.* Cambridge: Cambridge University Press, 2005.

Norris, Pippa, and Ronald Inglehart. *Cultural Backlash: Trump, Brexit, and Authoritarian Populism.* Cambridge: Cambridge University Press, 2019.

Page, Benjamin I., and Martin Gilens. *Democracy in America? What Has Gone Wrong and What We Can Do about It.* Chicago: University of Chicago Press, 2018.

Rensmann, Lars. "The Noisy Counter-Revolution: Understanding the Cultural Conditions and Dynamics of Populist Politics in Europe in the Digital Age." *Politics and Governance* 5, no. 4 (2017): 123–135.

Sapiro, Gisèle. "'Notables, esthètes et polémistes: Manières d'être un écrivain 'réactionnaire' des années 30 à nos jours." In *Le Discours "néo-réactionnaire": Transgressions conservatrices,* edited by Pascal Durand and Sarah Sindaco, 23–46. Paris: CNRS Éditions, 2015.

Scott, Joan W. *Sex and Secularism.* Princeton, NJ: Princeton University Press, 2017.

Stefanoni, Pablo. *La Rébellion est-elle passée à droite? Dans le laboratoire mondial des contre-cultures néoréactionnaires* (2021). Translated by Marc Saint-Upéry. Paris: La Découverte, 2022.

Stern, Alexandra Minna. *Proud Boys and the White Ethnostate: How the Alt-Right Is Warping the American Imagination.* Boston: Beacon Press, 2019.

Tartakowsky, Danielle. *Les Droites et la Rue: Histoire d'une ambivalence, de 1880 à nos jours.* Paris: La Découverte, 2014.

Urbinati, Nadia. "The Populist Phenomenon." *Raisons Politiques* 51, no. 3 (2013): 137–154.

Verloo, Mieke, and David Paternotte, eds. "The Feminist Project under Threat in Europe." *Politics and Governance* 6, no. 3, special issue, 2018.

Wampole, Christy. *Degenerative Realism.* New York: Columbia University Press, 2020.

LEGAL REASONING AND THE RULE OF LAW

Adler, Libby. *Gay Priori: A Queer Critical Legal Studies Approach to Law Reform.* Durham, NC: Duke University Press, 2018.

Atrey, Shreya. "Illuminating the CJEU's Blind Spot of Intersectional Discrimination in *Parris v. Trinity College Dublin.*" *Industrial Law Journal* 47, no. 2 (July 2018): 278–296.

Atrey, Shreya. *Intersectionality and Comparative Discrimination Law: The Tale of Two Citadels.* Leiden: Brill, 2020.

Bell, David A. *Lawyers & Citizens: The Making of a Political Elite in Old Regime France.* Oxford: Oxford University Press, 1994.

Borrillo, Daniel. *Disposer de son corps: Un droit encore à conquérir.* Paris: Textuel, 2019.

Borrillo, Daniel, and Vincent-Arnaud Chappe. "La Haute Autorité de Lutte contre les Discriminations et pour l'Égalité: Un laboratoire juridique éphémère?" *Revue française d'administration publique* 139, no. 3 (2011): 369–380.

Bosvieux-Onyekwelu, Charles, and Véronique Mottier, eds. *Genre, Droit et Politique.* Paris: LGDJ, 2022.

Bourdieu, Pierre. "The Force of Law" (1986). Translated by Richard Terdiman. *Hastings Law Journal* 38 (July 1987): 817–853.

Bouveresse, Jacques. *Prodiges et Vertiges de l'analogie.* Paris: Raisons d'Agir, 1999.

Brewer, Scott. "Exemplary Reasoning: Semantics, Pragmatics, and the Rational Force of Legal Argument by Analogy." *Harvard Law Review* 109, no. 5 (1996): 923–1028.

Brown, Wendy, and Janet Halley, eds. *Left Legalism/Left Critique.* Durham, NC: Duke University Press, 2002.

Cassirer, Ernst. *The Philosophy of Symbolic Forms*, volume 3: *Phenomenology of Knowledge* (1929). Translated by Ralph Manheim. New Haven, CT: Yale University Press, 1957.

Commaille, Jacques. *À quoi nous sert le droit?* Paris: Gallimard, 2015.

Constable, Marianne. *Our Word Is Our Bond: How Legal Speech Acts.* Stanford, CA: Stanford University Press, 2014.

Crenshaw, Kimberlé. "Mapping the Margins: Intersectionality, Identity Politics, and Violence against Women of Color." *Stanford Law Review* 43, no. 6 (July 1991): 1241–1299.

Delmas-Marty, Mireille. *Le Relatif et l'Universel: Les forces imaginantes du droit.* Paris: Seuil, 2004.

Ewick, Patricia, and Susan S. Silbey. *The Common Place of Law: Stories from Everyday Life.* Chicago: University of Chicago Press, 1998.

Freeman, Jo. "How 'Sex' Got into Title VII: Persistent Opportunism as a Maker of Public Policy." *Law and Inequality: A Journal of Theory and Practice* 9, no. 2 (March 1991): 163–184.

Freshman, Clark. "Beyond Atomized Discrimination: Use of Acts of Discrimination against 'Other' Minorities to Prove Discriminatory Motivation under Federal Employment Law." *Stanford Law Review* 43, no. 1 (November 1990): 241–73.

Gründler, Tatiana, and Jean-Marc Thouvenin, eds. *La Lutte contre les discriminations à l'épreuve de son effectivité: Rapport de la Fédération interdisciplinaire de Nanterre en droit au Défenseur des droits. Annexes.* Nanterre: Publications du Défenseur des droits, 2016.

SELECTED BIBLIOGRAPHY

Habermas, Jürgen. *Between Facts and Norms: Contributions to a Discourse Theory of Law and Democracy* (1992). Translated by William Rehg. Cambridge, MA: MIT Press, 1996.

Halley, Janet. "Like Race Arguments." In *What's Left of Theory? New Work on the Politics of Literary Theory*, edited by Judith Butler, John Guillory and Kendall Thomas, 40–74. New York: Routledge, 2000.

Hennette-Vauchez, Stéphanie, Mathias Möschel, and Diane Roman, eds. *Ce que le genre fait au droit*. Paris: Dalloz, 2013.

Hennette-Vauchez, Stéphanie, Marc Picard, and Diane Roman, eds. *La Loi et le Genre: Études critiques de droit français*. Paris: CNRS éditions, 2014.

Isailovic, Ivana. "Political Recognition and Transnational Law: Gender Equality and Cultural Diversification in French Courts." In *Private International Law and Global Governance*, edited by Horatia Muir Watt and Diego P. Fernández Arroyo, 318–342. Oxford: Oxford University Press, 2014.

Johar Schueller, Malini. "Analogy and (White) Feminist Theory: Thinking Race and the Color of the Cyborg Body." *Signs: Journal of Women in Culture and Society* 31, no. 1 (2005): 63–92.

Kairys, David, ed. *The Politics of Law: A Progressive Critique* (1982). New York: Basic Books, 1998.

Karst, Kenneth L. *Law's Promise, Law's Expression: Visions of Power in the Politics of Race, Gender, and Religion*. New Haven, CT: Yale University Press, 1993,

Katri, Ido. "Transgender Intrasectionality: Rethinking Anti-Discrimination Law and Litigation." *University of Pennsylvania Journal of Law and Social Change* 20, no. 1 (2017): 51–79.

Khaitan, Tarunabh. *A Theory of Discrimination Law*. Oxford: Oxford University Press, 2015.

Konnoth, Craig J. "Created in Its Image: The Race Analogy, Gay Identity, and Gay Litigation in the 1950–1970s." *Yale Law Journal* 119, no. 2 (November 2009): 316–372.

Lamond, Grant. "Analogical Reasoning in the Common Law." *Oxford Journal of Legal Studies* 34, no. 3 (Fall 2014): 567–588.

Lépinard, Éléonore. "Écriture juridique et régulation du religieux minoritaire en France et au Canada." *Revue française de science politique* 64, no. 4 (2014): 669–688.

Lochak, Danièle. *Le Droit et les Paradoxes de l'universalité*. Paris: Presses universitaires de France, 2010.

Mayeri, Serena. *Reasoning from Race: Feminism, Law, and the Civil Rights Revolution*. Cambridge, MA: Harvard University Press, 2011.

McCammon, Holly J., Brittany N. Hearne, Allison R. McGrath, and Minyoung Moon. "Legal Mobilization and Analogical Legal Framing: Feminist Litigators' Use of Race–Gender Analogies." *Law & Policy* 40, no. 1 (January 2018): 57–78.

Mercat-Bruns, Marie. "Multiple Discrimination and Intersectionality: Issues of Equality and Liberty." *International Social Science Journal*, no. 67 (March–June 2017): 43–54.

Multiplication des critères de discrimination: Enjeux, effets et perspectives. Actes du colloque des 18 et 19 janvier 2018. Paris: Publications du Défenseur des droits, 2018.

Ogien, Ruwen. *L'État nous rend-il meilleur? Essai sur la liberté politique*. Paris: Gallimard, Folio, 2013.

Rush, Sharon Elizabeth. "Equal Protection Analogies—Identity and Passing: Race and Sexual Orientation." *Harvard Blackletter Law Journal* 65, no. 13 (1997): 65–106.

Schulman, Sarah. *Conflict Is Not Abuse: Overstating Harm, Community Responsibility, and the Duty of Repair*. Vancouver: Arsenal Pulp Press, 2016.

Shklar, Judith. *Legalism: An Essay on Law, Morals and Politics*. Cambridge, MA: Harvard University Press, 1964.

Wittgenstein, Ludwig. *The Blue and Brown Books* (1958). New York: HarperCollins, 1965.

Wittgenstein, Ludwig. *Philosophical Investigations* (1953). Translated by G. E. M. Anscombe, P. M. S. Hacker, and Joachim Schulte. London: Blackwell, 2009.

Zivi, Karen. *Making Rights Claims: A Practice of Democratic Citizenship*. Oxford: Oxford University Press, 2012.

MINORITY INFLUENCE AND SOCIAL CHANGE

Abel, Emily K., and Margaret K. Nelson, eds. *Circles of Care: Work and Identity in Women's Lives*. Albany, NY: SUNY Press, 1990.

Ahmed, Sara. *On Being Included: Racism and Diversity in Institutional Life*. Durham, NC: Duke University Press, 2012.

Asch, Solomon E. "Effects of Group Pressure upon the Modification and Distortion of Judgment." In *Groups, Leadership and Men*, edited by Harold Guetzkow, 177–190. Pittsburgh: Carnegie Press, 1951.

Berbrier, Mitch. "Making Minorities: Cultural Space, Stigma Transformation Frames, and the Categorical Status Claims of Deaf, Gay, and White Supremacist Activists in Late Twentieth Century America," *Sociological Forum* 17, no. 4 (2002): 553–591.

Berbrier, Mitch. "Why Are There So Many 'Minorities'?" *Contexts* 3, no. 1 (winter 2004): 38–44.

Bereni, Laure. "Les stigmates de la vertu: Légitimer la diversité en entreprise, à New York et à Paris." *Actes de la recherche en sciences sociales* 241, no. 1 (2022): 36–55.

Berrey, Ellen. *The Enigma of Diversity: The Language of Race and the Limits of Racial Justice*. Chicago: University of Chicago Press, 2015.

Bilge, Sirma. "Le blanchissement de l'intersectionnalité." *Recherches féministes* 28, no. 2 (2015): 9–32.

SELECTED BIBLIOGRAPHY

Cortland, Clarissa I., Maureen A. Craig, Jenessa R. Shapiro, Jennifer A. Richeson, Rebecca Neel, and Noah J. Goldstein. "Solidarity through Shared Disadvantage: Highlighting Shared Experiences of Discrimination Improves Relations between Stigmatized Groups." *Journal of Personality and Social Psychology* 113, no. 4 (2017): 547–567.

Craig, Maureen A., and Jennifer A. Richeson. "Hispanic Population Growth Engenders Conservative Shift among Non-Hispanic Racial Minorities." *Social Psychological and Personality Science* 9, no. 4 (May 2018): 383–392.

Craig, Maureen A., Julian M., Rucker, and Jennifer A. Richeson. "Racial and Political Dynamics of an Approaching 'Majority-Minority' United States." *Annals of the American Academy of Political and Social Science* 677, no. 1 (April 2018): 204–214.

Daumeyer, Natalie M., Ivuoma N. Onyeador, and Jennifer A. Richeson. "Does Shared Gender Group Membership Mitigate the Effect of Implicit Bias Attributions on Accountability for Gender-Based Discrimination?" *Personality and Social Psychology Bulletin* 47, no. 9 (September 2021): 1343–1357.

Destin, Mesmin, Michelle Rheinschmidt-Same, and Jennifer A. Richeson. "Status-Based Identity: A Conceptual Approach Integrating the Social Psychological Study of Socioeconomic Status and Identity." *Perspectives on Psychological Science* 12, no. 2 (March 2017): 270–289.

Gersen, Jacob E., and Jeannie Suk Gersen. "The Sex Bureaucracy." *California Law Review* 104 (March 18, 2016): 881–948.

Glazer, Nathan. *We Are All Multiculturalists Now*. Cambridge, MA: Harvard University Press, 1997.

Hamidi, Camille. "Les minorités doivent-elles être représentées par des minorités? Une *color line* dans les représentations ordinaires de la représentation en France." *Participations* 30, no. 2 (2021): 65–96.

Jacquemart, Alban. *Les Hommes dans les mouvements féministes: Socio-histoire d'un engagement improbable*. Rennes: Presses universitaires de Rennes, 2014.

Kipnis, Laura. *Unwanted Advances: Sexual Paranoia Comes to Campus*. New York: Harper, 1997.

Kraus, Michael W., and Jacinth X. Tan. "Americans Overestimate Social Class Mobility." *Journal of Experimental Social Psychology* 58 (May 2015): 101–111.

Kuo, Entung Enya, Michael W. Kraus, and Jennifer A. Richeson. "High-Status Exemplars and the Misperception of the Asian-White Wealth Gap." *Social Psychological and Personality Science* 11, no. 3 (April 2020): 397–405.

Manier, Marion. "Cause des femmes *vs* cause des minorités: Tensions autour de la question des 'femmes de l'immigration' dans l'action publique française." *Revue européenne des migrations internationales* 29, no. 4 (2013): 89–110.

Mann, Patrice. *L'Action collective: Mobilisation et organisation des minorités actives*. Paris: Armand Colin, 1991.

Moscovici, Serge. *Social Influence and Social Change*. Translated by Carol Sherrard and Greta Heinz. New York: Academic Press, 1976.

Moscovici, Serge, and Marisa Zavalloni. "The Group as a Polarizer of Attitudes." *Journal of Personality and Social Psychology* 12 (1969): 125–135.

Moten, Fred. *The Universal Machine*. Durham, NC: Duke University Press, 2018.

Mugny, Gabriel, and Stamos Papastamou. "When Rigidity Does Not Fail: Individualization and Psychologization as Resistances to the Diffusion of Minority Innovations." *European Journal of Social Psychology* 10, no. 1 (1980): 43–61.

Murat, Laure. *Qui annule quoi?* Paris: Seuil, 2022.

Nekmat, Elmie, and William J. Gonzenbach. "Multiple Opinion Climates in Online Forums: Role of Website Source Reference and Within-Forum Opinion Congruency." *Journalism & Mass Communication Quarterly* 90, no. 4 (2013): 736–756.

Nemeth, Charlan J. "The Differential Contributions of Majority and Minority Influence." *Psychological Review* 93 (1986): 23–32.

Noelle-Neumann, Elisabeth. "The Spiral of Silence: A Theory of Public Opinion." *Journal of Communication* 24, no. 2 (June 1974): 43–51.

Ogien, Albert. *Émancipations: Luttes minoritaires, luttes universelles?* Paris: Textuel, 2023.

Purdie-Vaughns, Valerie, and Richard P. Eibach. "Intersectional Invisibility: The Distinctive Advantages and Disadvantages of Multiple Subordinate-Group Identities." *Sex Roles* 59, no. 5–6, (2008): 377–391.

Smith, Christine M., R. Scott Tindale, and Bernard L. Dugoni. "Minority and Majority Influence in Freely Interacting Groups: Qualitative versus Quantitative Differences." *British Journal of Social Psychology* 35 (1996): 137–149.

Trost, Melanie, Anne Maass, and Douglas Kenrick. "Minority Influence: Personal Relevance Biases Cognitive Processes and Reverses Private Acceptance." *Journal of Experimental Social Psychology* 28, no. 3 (1992): 234–254.

RESPONSIBILITY, GLOBALIZATION, ECOLOGY

Badouard, Romain. *Les Nouvelles Lois du web: Modération et censure*. Paris: Seuil, 2020.

Banting, Keith, and Will Kymlicka, eds. *The Strains of Commitment. The Political Sources of Solidarity in Diverse Societies*. Oxford: Oxford University Press, 2017.

Beck, Ulrich. *Risk Society: Towards a New Modernity* (1986). Translated by Mark Ritter. London: Sage, 1992.

Bhabha, Homi K. *The Location of Culture* (1994). London: Routledge, 2004.

SELECTED BIBLIOGRAPHY

Bourg, Dominique, and Jean-Louis Schlegel. *Parer aux risques de demain: Le principe de précaution.* Paris: Seuil, 2001.

Bourg, Dominique, and Kerry Whiteside. *Vers une démocratie écologique: Le citoyen, le savant et le politique.* Paris: Seuil, 2010.

Brown, Wendy. *Regulating Aversion: Tolerance in the Age of Identity and Empire.* Princeton, NJ: Princeton University Press, 2006.

Bullard, Robert D. *Dumping in Dixie. Race, Class, and Environmental Quality.* Boulder, CO: Westview, 1990.

Bullard, Robert, Paul Mohai, Robin Saha, and Beverly Wright. "Toxic Wastes and Race at Twenty: Why Race Still Matters after All of These Years." *Environmental Law* 38, no. 2 (2007): 371–411.

Butler, Judith, Zeynep Gambetti, and Leticia Sabsay, eds. *Vulnerability in Resistance.* Durham, NC: Duke University Press, 2016.

Butler, Judith, Ernesto Laclau, and Slavoj Žižek. *Contingency, Hegemony, Universality: Contemporary Dialogues on the Left.* London: Verso, 2000.

Cardon, Dominique. *À quoi rêvent les algorithmes: Nos vies à l'heure des big data.* Paris: Seuil, 2015.

Chakrabarty, Dipesh. "Anthropocene Time." *History and Theory* 57, no. 1 (March 2018): 5–32.

Charbonnier, Pierre. *Affluence and Freedom: An Environmental History of Political Ideas* (2020). Translated by Andrew Brown. Cambridge: Polity Press, 2021.

Citton, Yves. *Faire avec: Conflits, coalitions, contagions.* Paris: Les liens qui libèrent, 2021.

Citton, Yves, and Jacopo Rasmi. *Générations collapsonautes: Naviguer par temps d'effondrements.* Paris: Seuil, 2020.

Coccia, Emanuele. *Metamorphoses* (2020). Translated by Robin Mackay. Cambridge: Polity, 2021.

Crétois, Pierre, *La Part commune: Critique de la propriété privée.* Paris: Éd. Amsterdam, 2020.

Diagne, Souleymane Bachir, and Jean-Loup Amselle. *In Search of Africa(s): Universalism and Decolonial Thought* (2018). Translated by Andrew Brown. Cambridge: Polity Press, 2020.

Eaubonne, Françoise d'. *Écologie/Féminisme: Révolution ou mutation?* Paris: A.T.P., 1978.

Elias, Norbert. *Involvement and Detachment* (1983). Translated by Edmund Jephcott. London: Blackwell, 1987.

Fraser, Nancy. *Scales of Justice: Reimagining Political Space in a Globalized World.* New York: Columbia University Press, 2009.

Gemenne, François. *Géopolitique du climat: Négociations, stratégies, impacts* (2009). Paris: Armand Colin, 2021.

Gochfeld, Michael, and Joanna Burger. "Disproportionate Exposures in Environmental Justice and Other Populations: The Importance of Outliers." *American Journal of Public Health* 101, no. 1 (2011): 53–63.

Hache, Émilie. "La responsabilité: Une technique de gouvernementalité néolibérale?" *Raisons Politiques* 28, no. 4 (2007): 49–65.

Haraway, Donna. *When Species Meet.* Minneapolis: University of Minnesota Press, 2008.

Harcourt, Bernard. *Critique and Praxis: A Critical Philosophy of Illusions, Values, and Action.* New York: Columbia University Press, 2020.

Harvey, David. *Justice, Nature and the Geography of Difference.* Cambridge, MA: Blackwell, 1996.

Hofmann, Franck, and Markus Messling, eds. *The Epoch of Universalism, 1769–1989.* Berlin, De Gruyter, 2020.

Holloway, Travis. *How to Live at the End of the World: Theory, Art, and Politics for the Anthropocene.* Stanford, CA: Stanford University Press, 2022.

Jonas, Hans. *The Imperative of Responsibility: In Search of an Ethics for the Technological Age* (1979). Translated by Hans Jonas and David Herr. Chicago: University of Chicago Press, 1984.

Jullien, François. *On the Universal, the Uniform, the Common and Dialogue between Cultures* (2008). Translated by Michael Richardson and Krzysztof Fijalkowski. Cambridge: Polity, 2014.

Kymlicka, Will. *Multicultural Odysseys: Navigating the New International Politics of Diversity.* Oxford: Oxford University Press, 2007.

Latour, Bruno. *Down to Earth: Politics in the New Climatic Regime* (2017). Translated by Catherine Porter. Cambridge: Polity, 2018.

Latour, Bruno. *Politics of Nature: How to Bring the Sciences into Democracy* (1999). Translated by Catherine Porter. Cambridge, MA: Harvard University Press, 2004.

Latour, Bruno. *We Have Never Been Modern* (1991). Translated by Catherine Porter. Cambridge, MA: Harvard University Press, 1993.

Lecerf Maulpoix, Cy. *Écologies déviantes: Voyage en terres queer.* Paris: Cambourakis, 2021.

Margalit, Avishai. *The Decent Society.* Translated by Naomi Goldblum. Cambridge, MA: Harvard University Press, 1996.

Mbembe, Achille. *The Earthly Community: Reflections on the Last Utopia.* Translated by Steven Corcoran. Rotterdam: V2 Publishing, 2022.

SELECTED BIBLIOGRAPHY   311

Mbembe, Achille. *Politique de l'inimitié*. Paris: La Découverte, 2016.

McDermott, Hughes David. *Energy without Conscience: Oil, Climate Change, and Complicity*. Durham, NC: Duke University Press, 2017.

Moscovici, Serge. *Society against Nature: The Emergence of Human Societies* (1972). Translated by Sacha Rabinovitch. London: Harvester Press, 1976.

Pelluchon, Corine. *Les Lumières à l'âge du vivant*. Paris: Seuil, 2021.

Peña, Devon G., ed. *Chicano Culture, Ecology, Politics: Subversive Kin*. Tucson: University of Arizona Press, 2008.

Sassen, Saskia. *Territory, Authority, Rights: From Medieval to Global Assemblages*. Princeton, NJ: Princeton University Press, 2006.

Schlosberg, David. *Defining Environmental Justice: Theories, Movements, and Nature*. Oxford: Oxford University Press, 2007.

Tramel, Salena. "Convergence as Political Strategy: Social Justice Movements, Natural Resources and Climate Change." *Third World Quarterly* 39, no. 7 (2018): 1290–1307.

Wald, Sarah D., David J. Vázquez, Priscilla Solis Ybarra, and Sarah Jaquette, eds. *Latinx Environmentalisms: Place, Justice, and the Decolonial*. Philadelphia: Temple University Press, 2019.

CRITICAL THEORY AND MINORITY STUDIES

Ajari, Norman. *Darkening Blackness. Race, Gender, Class and Pessimism in 21st Century Black Thought* (2022). Translated by Matthew B. Smith, Cambridge: Polity Press, 2024.

Ajari, Norman. *Dignity or Death: Ethics and Politics of Race* (2019). Translated by Matthew B. Smith. Cambridge: Polity, 2023.

Andrews, Kehinde. *Back to Black: Retelling Black Radicalism for the 21st Century*. London: Zed Books, 2018.

Baldwin, James. *Notes of a Native Son* (1955). Boston: Beacon Press, 1963.

Baldwin, James. *Tell Me How Long the Train's Been Gone*. New York: Dell Publishing, 1968.

Bilge, Sirma. "Théorisations féministes de l'intersectionnalité." *Diogène* 225, no. 1 (2009): 70–88.

Brettschneider, Marla. *Democratic Theorizing from the Margins*. Philadelphia: Temple University Press, 2002.

Butler, Judith. *The Force of Nonviolence: An Ethico-Political Bind*. London: Verso, 2020.

Butler, Judith. "Wittig's Material Practice: Universalizing a Minority Point of View." *GLQ: A Journal of Lesbian and Gay Studies* 13, no. 4 (2007): 519–533.

Crenshaw, Kimberlé, Neil Gotanda, Gary Peller, and Kendall Thomas, eds. *Critical Race Theory*. New York: New Press, 1995.

Dean, Jodi. *Solidarity Strangers: Feminism after Identity Politics*. Berkeley: University of California Press, 1996.

Deleuze, Gilles, and Félix Guattari. *A Thousand Plateaus* (1980). Translated by Brian Massumi. Minneapolis: University of Minnesota Press, 1987.

Du Bois, William Edward Burghart. *The Souls of Black Folks* (1903). Oxford: Oxford University Press, 2007.

Eribon, Didier. *Hérésies: Essais sur la théorie de la sexualité*. Paris: Fayard, 2003.

Eribon, Didier. *Insult and the Making of the Gay Self* (1999). Translated by Michael Lucey. Durham, NC: Duke University Press, 1994.

Eribon, Didier. *Une morale du minoritaire: Variations sur un thème de Jean Genet*. Paris: Fayard, 2001.

Eribon, Didier. *Principes d'une pensée critique*. Paris: Fayard, 2016.

Ferguson, Roderick A. *One-Dimensional Queer*. Cambridge: Polity Press, 2018.

Foucault, Michel. *Government of Self and Others: Lectures at the Collège de France. 1982–1983*. Translated by Graham Burchell. New York: Picador, 2011.

Guillaumin, Colette. *Racism, Sexism, Power and Ideology* (1972–1988). Translated by Andrew Rothwell and Max Silverman. London: Routledge, 1995.

Harney, Stefano, and Fred Moten. *The Undercommons: Fugitive Planning & Black Study*. Wivenhoe: Minor Composition, 2013.

hooks, bell. *Yearning. Race, Gender, and Cultural Politics* (1990). London: Routledge, 2015.

Kergoat, Danièle. "Dynamique et consubstantialité des rapports sociaux." In *Sexe, Race, Classe: pour une épistémologie de la domination*, edited by Elsa Dorlin, 111–125. Paris: Presses universitaires de France, 2009.

Lino e Silva, Moisés. *Minoritarian Liberalism: A Travesti Life in a Brazilian Favela*. Chicago: University of Chicago Press, 2022.

Lionnet, Françoise, and Shu-mei Shih, eds. *Minor Transnationalism*. Durham, NC: Duke University Press, 2005.

Mathieu, Nicole-Claude. *L'Anatomie politique: Catégorisations et idéologies du sexe*. Paris: Côté-Femmes, 1991.

Mayer, Hans. *Outsiders: A Study in Life and Letters* (1975). Translated by Denis M. Sweet. Cambridge, MA: MIT Press, 1982.

McRuer, Robert. *Crip Theory: Cultural Signs of Queerness and Disability*. New York: New York University Press, 2006.

SELECTED BIBLIOGRAPHY

Miano, Léonora. *Afropea: Utopie post-occidentale et post-raciste*. Paris: Grasset, 2020.

Moya, Paula M. Y. *Learning from Experience: Minority Identities, Multicultural Struggles*. Berkeley: University of California Press, 2001.

Moya, Paula M. Y., and Michael R. Hames-García, eds. *Reclaiming Identity: Realist Theory and the Predicament of Postmodernism*. Berkeley: University of California Press, 2000.

Ndiaye, Pap. *La Condition noire: Essai sur une minorité française* (2008). Paris: Gallimard, 2022.

Perreau, Bruno. *The Politics of Adoption: Gender and the Making of French Citizenship*. Cambridge, MA: MIT Press, 2014.

Perreau, Bruno. *Queer Theory: The French Response*. Stanford, CA: Stanford University Press, 2016.

Puiseux, Charlotte. *De chair et de fer: Vivre et lutter dans une société validiste*. Paris: La Découverte, 2022.

Robinson, Cedric. *Black Marxism: The Making of the Black Radical Tradition* (1983). Chapel Hill: University of North Carolina Press, 2021.

Samuels, Maurice. *The Right to Difference: French Universalism and the Jews*. Chicago: University of Chicago Press, 2016.

Sekyi-Out, Ato. *Left Universalism: Afrocentric Essays*. London: Routledge, 2018.

Scott, Joan W. "The Evidence of Experience." *Critical Inquiry* 17, no. 4 (July 1, 1991): 773–797.

Sharma, Nitasha Tamar. *Hip Hop Desis: South Asian Americans, Blackness, and a Global Race Consciousness*. Durham, NC: Duke University Press, 2010.

Spivak, Gayatri Chakravorty. "Can the Subaltern Speak?" In *Marxism and the Interpretation of Culture*, edited by Cary Nelson and Lawrence Grossberg, 66–111. Urbana: University of Illinois Press, 1988.

Taubira, Christiane. *Égalité pour les exclus: Le politique face à l'histoire et à la mémoire coloniale*. Paris: Temps Présent, 2009.

Walker, Clarence. *We Can't Go Home Again: An Argument about Afrocentrism Attribution*. Oxford: Oxford University Press, 2001.

Wilderson, Frank B. III. *Afropessimism*. New York: W. W. Norton, 2000.

Wittig, Monique. *The Straight Mind and Other Essays* (1980–1990). Boston: Beacon Press, 1992.

INDEX OF COURT RULINGS

CANADA, SUPREME COURT

Multani v. Commission scolaire Marguerite-Bourgeoys, 30–31, 219n93

Ontario Human Rights Commission and O'Malley v. Simpsons Sears Ltd., 30, 219n90

EUROPEAN COURT OF HUMAN RIGHTS

Abdulaziz, Cabales and Balkandali v. United-Kingdom, 157, 262n3

B.S. v. Spain, 169, 267n91

Carvalho Pinto De Sousa Morais v. Portugal, 169, 267n92, 267n94, 267n95

Clift v. United Kingdom, 46, 224n20

D.H. v. Czech Republic, 47, 168, 224n27, 267n83

E. B. v. France, 158, 262n7

Eweida and Others v. United Kingdom, 95, 241n70

F. v. France, 157–158, 262n5

Konstantin Markin v. Russia, 158, 262n8

Nachova and Others v. Bulgaria, 47, 224n28

Opuz v. Turkey, 47, 158, 224n26, 262n9

Stec et al. v. United Kingdom, 122, 251n96

Tadeucci and McCall v. Italy, 168, 267n84

Verein KlimaSeniorinnen Schweiz and Others v. Switzerland, 194, 278n124

Volodina v. Russia, 158, 262n10

Y. v. France, 264n38

EUROPEAN COURT OF JUSTICE (FORMERLY COURT OF JUSTICE OF THE EUROPEAN COMMUNITIES)

Asociaţia Accept v. Consiliul Naţional pentru Combaterea Discriminării, 127, 252n123

Centrum voor gelijkheid van kansen en voor racismebestrijding v. Firma Feryn NV, 127, 252n123

Colin Wolf v. Stadt Frankfurt am Main, 126, 252n113

David L. Parris v. Trinity College Dublin, Higher Education Authority et al., 170, 268n107

Frédéric Hay v. Crédit agricole mutuel de Charente-Maritime et des Deux-Sèvres, 168, 267n82

INDEX OF COURT RULINGS

Galina Meister v. Speech Design Carrier Systems, 170, 268n106

Grant v. South West Trains Ltd, 168, 267n81

Jette Ring v. Dansk almennyttigt Boligselskab, 176, 271n146

P. v. S. and Cornwall County Council, 167–168, 267n80

Reinhard Prigge and others v. Deutsche Lufthansa AG, 126, 252n112

Sonia Chacón Navas v. Eurest Colectividades SA, 169, 268n97

Tadao Maruko v. Versorgungsanstalt der deutschen Bühnen, 46, 224n19

FRANCE, CONSTITUTIONAL COUNCIL (CONSEIL CONSTITUTIONNEL)

Charte européenne des langues régionales ou minoritaires, 117, 249n63

Conseil des prud'hommes, 157, 262n2

Loi complétant le statut d'autonomie de la Polynésie française, 117, 249n64

Loi complétant les dispositions des articles 5 et 7 de la loi du 1ᵉʳ juillet, 116, 248n57

Loi de finance rectificative pour 1984, 117, 249n59

Loi organisant une consultation de la population de Mayotte, 118, 249n69

Loi portant diverses dispositions d'ordre social, 122, 251n95

Loi portant statut de la collectivité territoriale de Corse, 117, 249n62

Loi portant statut du territoire de la Nouvelle-Calédonie et dépendances, 117, 249n60

Loi relative à certains ouvrages reliant les voies nationales ou départementales, 128, 253n129

Loi relative à la Corse, 118, 249n67

Loi relative à la maîtrise de l'immigration, à l'intégration et à l'asile, 121, 250n91

Quotas par sexe I, 231n5, 117, 249n61

FRANCE, COURT OF CASSATION (COUR DE CASSATION)

1st Civil Chamber, 164, 265n49

FRANCE, COUNCIL OF STATE (CONSEIL D'ÉTAT)

Denoyez et Chorques, 128, 157, 253n128, 262n1

Département de Paris, 157, 262n3

FRANCE, COURT OF APPEALS (COUR D'APPEL)

Montpellier, 163, 264n43

FRANCE, DISTRICT COURTS (TRIBUNAUX JUDICIAIRES, FORMERLY TRIBUNAUX DE GRANDE INSTANCE)

Montpellier, 163, 264n42

Tours, 163–164, 265n48

SOUTH AFRICA, CONSTITUTIONAL COURT

Harksen v. Lane, 71, 173, 269n126

U.S. SUPREME COURT

303 Creative LLC and al. v. Elenis and al., 93–94, 240n58, 240n59

Arlene's Flowers v. Washington et al., 93, 240n53, 240n54

Bostock v. Clayton County, 45, 94, 224n16, 241n64

Brown v. Board of Education of Topeka, 45, 56, 108, 246n7, 228n90.

Burwell v. Hubby Lobby Stores et al., 94, 241n63

Carson v. Makin, 112, 247n33

Davis v. Massachusetts, 87–88, 239n22

Davis v. Monroe County Board of Education, 58, 229n105

Dobbs v. Jackson Women's Health Organization, 60, 93, 112, 178,

229n114, 240n51, 240n52, 247n29, 272n162, 272n163

Dred Scott v. Sandford, 108, 246n4

Employment Division, Department of Human Resources of Oregon v. Smith, 91, 239n40

Fisher v. University of Texas, 112, 247n34

Fulton v. Philadelphia, 91, 239n38, 239n39

Gebser v. Lago Vista Independent School District, 58, 229n105

Gratz et al. v. Bollinger, 109, 246n12

Griggs v. Duke Power Company, 46, 224n21

Grutter v. Bollinger, 56, 109, 228n88, 246n11

Hague v. Committee for Industrial Organization, 88, 239n23

Hollingsworth v. Perry, 100, 243n98

Hoyt v. Florida, 167, 266n73

Hunt v. Cromartie, 109, 246n16

Kennedy v. Bremerton School District, 112, 247n32

Loving v. Virginia, 93, 240n55

Masterpiece Cakeshop v. Colorado Civil Rights Commission, 89, 239n28

National Institute of Family and Life Advocates v. Becerra, 90, 239n34, 239n35, 239n36

New York State Rifle & Pistol Association v. Bruen, 112, 247n30

Obergefell v. Hodges, 93, 240n49

Plessy v. Ferguson, 108, 246n6

Price Waterhouse v. Hopkins, 169, 267n90

R. G & G.R. Harris Funeral Homes v. Equal Employment Opportunity Commission, 178, 272n161

Reed v. Reed, 167, 266n74

Regents of the University of California v. Bakke, 57, 107–109, 228n94, 246n10

Roe v. Wade, 112

Santa Clara Pueblo v. Martinez, 32, 220n101

Shaw v. Reno, 109, 246n15

Students for Fair Admissions, Inc. v. President & Fellows of Harvard College, 110, 111, 113, 215n67, 245n2, 246n19, 246n20

Students for Fair Admissions, Inc. v. University of North Carolina, 110, 111, 113, 215n67, 245n2, 246n19, 246n20

Trump v. Hawaii, 89, 239n31

Wards Cove Packing v. Atonio, 46, 224n23

Washington v. Davis, 46, 224n22

West Virginia v. Environmental Protection Agency, 112, 247n31

U.S. COURTS OF APPEALS

1st Circuit, *Students for Fair Admissions Inc. v. President & Fellows of Harvard College*, 111, 247n26

3rd Circuit, *Piscataway Township Board of Education v. Taxman*, 108, 246n8

4th Circuit, *Grimm v. Gloucester County School Board*, 92, 240n45

7th Circuit, *Hively v. Ivy Tech Community College*, 169, 267n93

11th Circuit, *Otto v. City of Boca Raton*, 92, 240n42, 240n43

U.S. DISTRICT COURTS

District of Massachusetts, *Students for Fair Admissions Inc. v. President & Fellows of Harvard College*, 111, 247n26

Northern District of Texas, Fort Worth Division, *Braidwood Management Incorporated v. Xavier Becerra et al.*, 94, 241n61

Southern District of New York, *Rogers v. American Airlines*, 46, 224n17

STATE SUPREME COURT

Washington State, *State of Washington v. Arlene's Flowers*, 93, 239n30

STATE COURTS OF APPEALS

Arizona Court of Appeals, *Brush & Nib Studio v. Phoenix*, 89, 239n30
New York Court of Appeals, *Braschi v. Stahl Associates* Company, 170, 268n100

COUNTY SUPREME COURT

New York, *People v. Chen*, 32, 220n102, 220n103

INDEX OF INSTITUTIONS, ORGANIZATIONS, AND PLACES

Algeria, 116
"America in One Room," 70
American Academy of Child and
    Adolescent Psychiatry, 92
American Civil War, 108
Arabian Peninsula, 104
Arab Spring, 96
Arizona, 113
Argentina, 164
Arkansas, 89
Australia, 164, 256n46
Austria, 106

Belgium, 25, 162
Brazil, 106

California
  environmental policies, 198
  Proposition 8, 100
  Proposition 209, 113
  Reproductive FACT Act, 90–92
Canada
  Charter of Rights and Freedoms, 168
  House of Commons, 29
  multicultural policies, 25, 30, 32, 216n5

Royal Commission on Bilingualism
    and Biculturalism, 29–30
  Supreme Court, 30–31, 168
Catholic Social Services (CSS), 91
Cherokee Nation, 50
Chicago
  community organizing, 137
  school of sociology, 6
Chick-fil-A, 88
Colorado
  Colorado Civil Rights Commission,
    89, 93–94,
  Club Q (nightclub), 132, 151
Corsica, 41, 116, 117
Council of Europe
  Commissioner, 161
  European Charter for Regional for
    Minority Languages, 117–118
  European Committee of Social Rights,
    146
  European Convention on Human
    Rights, 44, 134, 157, 82–183
  European Court of Human Rights, 44,
    47, 70, 95, 122, 157–158, 161–162,
    168, 169, 176, 194

Council of Europe (cont.)
European Social Charter, 146
Report, 164
Crisis Pregnancy Centers (CPCs), 89–90
Czech Republic, 47, 50

Denmark, 164

Egypt, 51
Estates General, 180
European Network on Independent
Living movement, 146–147
European Union, 76, 160, 161, 176, 193
Amsterdam Treaty, 160
European Court of Justice (previously
Court of Justice of the European
Communities), 126, 127, 163–168,
170–171, 176
Equal Employment Directive, 175
gender directives, 161
law, 47
Maastricht Treaty, 183
qualified majority system, 76
relations with member states, 176
subsidiarity principle, 182
supranationality, 193

First Nations, 47–48
Florida
Affirmative Action, 113
Boca Raton County, 91–92
Palm Beach County, 91–92
Pulse (nightclub), 16, 131, 132
France, Constitution and laws
Civil Code, 162–164
Constitution of 1946, 121
Constitution of 1958, 69, 116–117,
120–121
Copé-Zimmermann law, 121
Declaration of the Rights of Man and
of the Citizen, 116–117
Debré law, 138
ELAN law, 145
Fifth Republic, 69, 101

Freedom of the press law, 95
Gayssot law, 95
Joxe law, 117
Labor code, 47
Pacte civil de solidarité (PaCS) law,
26, 51
Pasqua law, 138
Penal Code, 47
Pleven law, 44, 95
Taubira law of 2001, 149–150
Taubira law of 2013, 96–97
France, institutions
Council of State (Conseil d'État), 116,
157
Constitutional Council (Conseil con-
stitutionnel), 66, 86, 117–118, 121,
157, 248n57
Defender of Rights, France
(Défenseur·e des droits), 45, 127,
143, 145, 164, 208
District Courts (Tribunaux judici-
aires, formely Tribunaux de grande
instance), 161, 163
Economic, Social and Environmen-
tal Council (Conseil économique,
social et environnemental), 100
High Authority for the Fight against
Discrimination and for Equality
(Haute Autorité de Lutte contre les
Discriminations et pour l'Égalité),
44–45
Ministry of Justice, 147
Ministry of the Civil Service, 121
National Assembly, 147, 148, 163
National Police, 143–144
France, political parties
Christian Democrats, 25
Green Party, 120
Marine Blue Rally far right coalition,
104
National Front (Front national), 12,
101, 243n107
National Rally Party (Rassemblement
national), 100, 101, 243n107

INDEX OF INSTITUTIONS, ORGANIZATIONS, AND PLACES

New Left, 25
Socialist Party, 85–86, 120, 139
Sovereignty, Independence, and Liberties Party, 104
France, social movements and non-governmental organizations
Act Up Paris, viii, 138, 139
Adama committee, 3, 140–143
Animafac, 139
Antigones (Les), 97
Association des paralysés de France, 139
Association des Parents et futurs parents Gays et Lesbiens, 139
Autosupport Banlieue, 139
Bus des Femmes, 139
Cabiria, 139
Catho Pride, 97
Charte de la diversité, 139
Comité de Libération et d'Autonomie Queer, 155
Comité Idaho de lutte contre l'homophobie, 139
Commission nationale consultative des droits de l'homme, 161
Conférence "Sexe et genre" of 1989, 160
Conseil Représentatif des Associations Noires, 139
Engraineurs (Les), 135, 254n20
Fédération des aveugles de France, 139
Fédération des Tunisiens pour une Citoyenneté des deux Rives, 139
Femen, 97
French Spring, 96–97
Graines de France, 139
Groupe d'Information et de Soutien des Immigrés, 138
Hommen, 97
Manif pour tous movement, 96, 100
Institut Montaigne, 139
Marie Pas Claire, 139
Mix-Cité, 139

Mouvement français pour le planning familial, 138–139
Nanas Beurs (Les), 139
Nuit Debout movement, 135
Prévention Action Santé auprès des Transsexuels et Travestis, 139
République et Diversité, 139
Sans-Papiers de Saint-Bernard collective, 138
SOS-Homophobie, 139
Sourds en colère (Les), 139
Témoignage chrétien, 139
Touche pas à mon pote, 85
Veilleurs (Les), 97
Yellow Vests (Gilets jaunes), 99–100, 121–122, 143, 155
Frankfurt School, 187
Freedom Drive, 146
French Revolution, 105

Gallimard (publisher), 25
Germany, 106, 164
"God, Honor, Country" movement, 101–102

Hawaii, 89
Higher Education
American Council of Learned Societies, viii
Brandeis University, 160
Center for Advanced Study in the Behavioral Sciences (CASBS), viii, ix
Cornell University, 113
Evergreen State College, 62
Georgia Southern University, 61–62
Grandes Écoles, 113
Harvard University, 57, 109–110, 111, 114
Opportunity Insights project, 52
Institute of Social, Economic, and Political Sciences (ISSEP), 104
Massachusetts Institute of Technology, viii, 79, 113
Data+Feminism Lab, 79

Higher Education (cont.)
National School of Administration (ENA), now National Institute of Public Service (INSP), 116
New York University, 160
Northwestern University, 59
Saarland University, 185
Sciences Po, ix, 15, 110, 113, 114, 119, 122, 123, 124, 125, 127
Conventions Éducation Prioritaire (CEP) or Priority Education Agreements, xviii, 15, 110, 113–114, 119, 121–125
Stanford University, viii, 70
University of California
Berkeley, ix
Davis, 57, 107, 109
Los Angeles (UCLA), 79
University of Michigan, 56, 109
University of North Carolina, 109–110, 111, 114
University of Paris 1 Panthéon-Sorbonne, vii, 124
University of Paris 12 Val de Marne, 124
University of Paris Nanterre, 28
Yale University, 111, 113
Hungary, 101

Idaho, 113
India, viii, 115, 119, 164, 179
Indiana, 93
International Court of Environmental Rights, 192
Iran, 176
Iraq, 132
Islamic State of Iraq and Syria (ISIS), 132
Israel, 101
Italy, 101, 106

Japan, 198
Jordan, 116

Korea, 254n12
Kyoto Protocol, 198

La Découverte (publisher), viii
Lebanon, 115–116

Maghreb, 51
Maine, 112
Malaysia, 164
Massachusetts, 50, 88, 111, 138
Mexico, 104, 198
Michigan, 113
Mississippi, 112
Missouri, 1
Montana, 50

Nebraska, 113
Nepal, 164
Netherlands, 164
New Caledonia, viii, 110, 117, 124, 182, 249n65
New Hampshire, 113
New Jersey, 19, 108
New York, 26, 46, 111–112, 132–133, 136, 205
New York Times, 111, 132
New Zealand, 105, 164

Oklahoma, 93, 113
Oregon, 91
Overseas territories (départements, régions et collectivités d'outre-mer), 182, 249n65, 249n66, 249n69

Paris, city of, 121
Pew Research Center, 113
Poland, 42
Portugal, 169
Philadelphia, Department of Human Services, 91

Quebec, 30–31, 48
Bouchard-Taylor commission, 31–33

INDEX OF INSTITUTIONS, ORGANIZATIONS, AND PLACES

Code of Life, 31
Consultation Commission on Accommodation Practices Related to Cultural Differences, 31, 32–33
Court of Appeals, 30–31
Superior Court, 48
YMCA (Montreal), 31

Rendez-vous de l'Histoire de Blois festival, 149
Russia, 115, 158

Scotland, 42
Second Persian Gulf War, 28
Seuil (publisher), 25
Somalia, 176
South Africa, 7, 48, 71, 164, 173
Sudan, 176
Switzerland, 194
Syria, 132

Tennessee, 201
Texas, 50, 88, 89, 94,
Treaty of Versailles, Article 93, 42
Tonga, 176
Tribal law, 32
Tunisia, 139
Turkey, 51

Ukraine, 97, 141
United Kingdom, 11, 51, 115, 122, 168
United Nations, 160, 161
  Charter, 41
  Convention on the Elimination of All Forms of Discrimination against Women (CEDAW), 176–177
  Convention on the Rights of Persons with Disabilities, 145, 175–176, 177
  Declaration on Sexual Orientation and Gender Identity, 161
  General Assembly, 144–145
  Office of the High Commissioner for Human Rights, 145

  General Assembly, 41, 144
  International Covenant on Civil and Political Rights (ICCPR), 41
  Universal Declaration of Human Rights, 41
  UNESCO, 25
United States, Constitution and laws
  Americans with Disabilities Act, 45
  Affordable Care Act (or "Obamacare"), 94, 240n60
  Age Discrimination in Employment Act, 45
  Civil Rights Act of 1957, 45
  Civil Rights Act of 1964, 45, 56, 57, 94, 108, 177–178
    Title VII, 45, 94, 177–178
  Civil Rights Act of 1991, 47
  Education Act, 57, 58, 92
    Dear Colleague Letter, 58–59
    Title IX, 58, 92
  Equality Act, 94
  First Amendment, 14, 87–91
  Fifth Amendment, 109
  Fourteenth Amendment, 14, 46, 56–57, 92, 103, 108–109
  Genetic Information Nondiscrimination Act, 45
  National Labor Relations Act, 108
  Pregnancy Discrimination Act, 45
  Second Amendment, 112
United States, institutions
  Congress, 42, 47, 93, 108
  Constitutional Convention of 1787, 42
  Court of Appeals for the First Circuit, 111
  Court of Appeals for the Third Circuit, 108
  Court of Appeals for the Fourth Circuit, 92–93
  Court of Appeals for the Ninth Circuit, 90
  Court of Appeals for the Eleventh Circuit, 91–92

United States, institutions (cont.)
Department of Education, 59–60
Department of Justice, Civil Rights Division, 111
Electoral College, 68
Environmental Protection Agency, 112
Equal Employment Opportunity Commission, 177
Federal Bureau of Investigation, 137
House of Representatives, 69–70
Office for Civil Rights (OCR), 57
Senate, 93, 198
Supreme Court, 14, 32, 45, 46–47, 56–57, 60, 70, 87–94, 107, 108–109, 111, 112–113, 177, 178
Trump administration, 59, 111
United States, political parties
Democratic Party, 50, 69, 70, 112, 137, 138, 141
Green Party, 138
Green-Rainbow Party, 138
Rainbow Coalition Party of Massachusetts, 138
Republican Party, 2, 50, 69, 73, 101, 138
Tea Party, 99
United States, social movements and non-governmental organizations
Alliance Defending Freedom, 89
AllLivesMatter, 2
American Civil Liberties Union, 167
American Indian Movement, 137
Asian Americans for Black Lives, 2
Association of Community Organizations for Reform Now (ACORN), 142
Black Lives Matter, 1–2, 3, 11, 60, 81, 140, 211n1, 11n3, 211n6, 256n44
Black Panther Party, 137

Brown Berets, 137
Catholic Charismatic Renewal, 93
Cathy Foundation, 88
Civil Rights movement, 106, 107
Disability Rights Movement, 146
Edmund Burke Foundation, 101
First National People of Color Environmental Leadership Summit, 200
Green New Deal movement, 140, 256n46
INCITE! collective, 141
Lincoln Park Poor People's Coalition, 137
Los Angeles Pride parade, 131
#MeToo movement, 62, 66
National Association for the Advancement of Colored People (NAACP), 50
National Rainbow Coalition, 137–138
Occupy Wall Street movement, 140
Operation PUSH (People United to Save Humanity), 138
Queer Nation, 152
Red Guard Party, 137
Salvation Army, 88
Stonewall uprising, 133–134
Students for a Democratic Society, 137
Students for Fair Admissions, Inc., 111, 113
We Build the Wall organization, 105
White supremacists, 86–87, 99, 104–105, 242n88
Young Lords, 137
Young Patriots Organization, 137
Utah, 93

Vatican, 96
Vermont, 141
Vietnam war, 24, 137
Virginia, 45, 92–93

INDEX OF INSTITUTIONS, ORGANIZATIONS, AND PLACES

Washington (District of Columbia),
200
Washington (state), 112, 113
West Virginia, 112
Wisconsin, 93
World War II, 121, 180,

Yogyakarta principles, 161

Zapatista groups, 180
Zionists, 102

NAME INDEX

Abbott, Greg, 88–89
Abrams, Kathryn, 233n30
Accoyer, Bernard, 258n101
Achin, Catherine, 255n26
Adelman, Howard, 220n96
Adler, Libby, 119, 250n76
Ahmed, Sara, 229n103
Aho, James, 242n85
Ajari, Norman, 134, 136, 184, 254n17, 255n28, 255n29, 255n30, 274n45, 275n60, 276n76
Alcoff, Linda Martín, 232n14, 252n110
Alduy, Cécile, 244n112
Alexander, Michelle, 143–144, 257n68
Alexandre, Sandy, 37–38, 222n145
Alexie, Sherman, 188
Ali, Zahra, 272n9
Alie, Marijosé, 272n7
Allen, Danielle, 259n97
Amiraux, Valérie, 252n116
Amselle, Jean-Loup, 252n117
Anctil, Pierre, 220n96
Anderson, Carol, 242n81
Anderson, Keenan, 4
Andrews, Kehinde, 136, 255n27

Angwin, Julia, 235n81
Apollinaire, Guillaume, 97
Appiah, Kwame Anthony, 194–195, 278n116, 278n127, 278n128, 278n129
Aragon, Louis, 97
Arcidiacono, Peter, 114, 248n42, 248n43
Arenson, Karen W., 215n68
Aristote, 97, 238n14
Armstrong, David M., 231n2, 231n3
Armstrong, Joshua, ix
Arendt, Hannah, 97
Arrow, Kenneth, 72–73, 234n46
Asch, Solomon E., 53, 227n64
Ashley Jardina, 242n87
Athanasiou, Athena, 102
Athreya, Shreeram, 236n84
Atrey, Shreya, 268n108, 269n127, 270n133
Aurélie, Windels, 245n139

Ba, Yunhao, 236n84
Badiou, Alain, 184
Badouard, Romain, 235n71, 284n36

NAME INDEX

Bahaffou, Myriam, 281n174
Bajos, Nathalie, 225n39
Baker, Josephine, 184–185
Bakke, Allan, 57
Baldwin, James, 134, 135–136, 150,
 254n14, 255n24, 255n25, 260n113
Balibar, Étienne, 128, 253n126,
 253n127, 272n11, 276n87
Balladur, Edouard, 120
Ballew, Matthew T., 280n164
Bannon, Steve, 105
Barad, Karen, 174, 270n132
Barb, Amandine, 241n68
Barnes, Djuna, 181
Barras, Amélie, 220n98
Barres, Maurice, 104
Barrett, Amy Coney, 93, 112–113
Barth, Isabelle, 230n118
Barthes, Roland, 278n111
Baudot, Pierre-Yves, 146, 258n85,
 258n86, 258n87
Beaman, Jean, 141, 212n21, 256n51
Beaman, Lori G., 220n98
Beauvoir (de), Simone, 272n166
Beck, Ulrich, 235n82, 277n108
Beckett, 260n125
Belew, Kathleen, 242n88
Bell, Jeannine, 241n65
Bénard, Ludivine, 238n10
Benbassa, Esther, 236n93
Benhabib, Seyla, 233n29, 279n142
Benstock, Shari, 282n8
Berbrier, Michel (Mitch), 228n91,
 228n92
Bereni, Laure, 57, 228n96, 229n102,
 231n143, 250n85
Bergström, Marie, 213n33
Berlant, Lauren, 279n131
Berlin, Isaiah, 134, 254n15
Berliner, David, 261n140
Berner, Christian, 28
Bernholz, Lucy, 235n74
Berrey, Ellen, 231n141

Bertinotti, Dominique, 147
Bessard, Nathalie, 225n41
Bessone, Magali, 150, 258n105,
 258n107, 259n105259n107, 260n109,
 261n135
Best, Rachel K., 268n104
Bhabha, Homi K. 236n98
Biden, Joe, 60, 93–94
Bigé, Emma, 284n34
Bihr, Alain, 39, 222n154
Bilge, Sirma, 97, 213n37, 242n78,
 269n122
Bioy, Xavier, 226n49
Bilge, Sirma, 97, 213n37, 242n78,
 269n122
Binet, Erwann, 147
Birmann, Dominique, 277n94
Bishin, Benjamin, 232n21
Bisiani, Francesca, 236n87
Bitzer, Michael, 232n16
Blanc, Paul 258n84
Blanchard, Danielle, 249n68
Blanchard, Emmanuel, 212n18
Blanchot, Maurice, 205, 214n45, 282n2
Blanquer, Jean-Michel, 163, 244n121
Blévis, Laure, 248n49
Blum, Edward, 111
Blumenbach, Johann, 226n53
Bobin, Christian, 274n55
Bock-Côté, Mathieu, 238n3
Bodin, Romuald, 258n82
Body-Gendrot, Sophie, 248n54
Bohman, James, 221n125
Boltanski, Luc, 26, 218n59
Bonilla-Silva, Eduardo, 243n94
Boorstein, Michelle, 253n5
Bor, Jacob, 222n143
Borda (de), Jean-Charles, 72, 233n44
Borrillo, Daniel, 163, 213n32, 224n13,
 225n40, 264n40, 265n46, 265n56,
 265n57
Bossu, Bernard, 268n109
Bouanchaud, Cécile, 257n61

NAME INDEX

Bouchard, Gérard, 31
Boudou, Benjamin, 29, 219n85
Bourdieu, Pierre, 26–27, 218n57,
 218n60, 251n101, 283n21
Bouretz, Pierre, 246n17
Bourg, Dominique, 198, 215n75,
 280n153, 280n154, 280n158
Boustany, Katia, 248n51
Bouveresse, Jacques, 175, 270n140
Bouvet, Laurent, 238n8
Bowes, Eleanor, 230n118
Bracke, Sarah, 245n137
Brantley, Max, 239n27
Brettschneider, Marla, 222n137
Brewer, Scott, 266n68
Breyer, Stephen, 112–113
Bribosia, Emmanuelle, 265n58
Brichta, Avraham, 244n111
Bronner, Gérald, 238n4
brown, adrienne maree, 284n32
Brown, Michael, 1
Brown, Scott, 50
Brown, Wendy, 90, 239n37, 265n59
Bruckner, Pascal, 25, 105, 237n1,
 245n128
Bruno, Esther, 235n72
Buber, Martin, 261n139
Bugaric, Bojan, 243n99
Bullard, Robert D., 280n161, 280n166
Burger, Joanna, 280n163
Burke, Edmund, 104, 105, 245n131
Burns, Ashley Brown, 230n116,
 230n117
Busekist (von), Astrid, 20, 28, 218n81,
 219n80, 219n86, 221n117, 253n125
Bush, George W., 73
Butler, Judith, ix, 150, 156, 160,
 188, 196–197, 221n136, 237n102,
 260n112, 261n130, 262n152,
 262n154, 263n24, 276n78, 273n27,
 279n141, 279n144, 279n145,
 279n146
Butler, Paul, 257n67

Butt, Daniel, 258n106, 259n106,
 261n148
Bybee, Keith J., 246n14

Cadogan, Garnette, 212n20
Cailhol, Johann, 236n96
Calafat, Guillaume, 213n34
Calvès, Gwénaële, 168–169, 251n94,
 267n89
Camus, Albert, 75, 97, 190, 214n49,
 234n59
Camus, Renaud, 104–105
Carayon, Lisa, 267n94
Carbin, Maria 269n121
Cardon, Dominique, 76, 234n64,
 235n66
Carosella, Edgardo, 151
Carré, Louis, 275n67
Casanova, Pascale, 283n14
Cassirer, Ernst, 26, 218n57
Castillo, Eduardo, 273n28
Cathy, Daniel Truett, 88
Catto, Marie-Xavière, 264n39
Cervulle, Maxime, 172, 269n116,
 269n118
Césaire, Aimé, 180
Chakrabarty, Dipesh, 258n103,
 259n103
Chan, Melissa, 253n2
Chandernagor, Françoise, 149, 259n100
Chaouite, Abdellatif, 225n41
Chappe, Vincent-Arnaud, 224n13,
 229n101, 252n118, 254n11
Chapuis, Nicolas, 230n125
Charbonnier, Pierre, 281n179
Charest, Jean, 31–32
Chari, Pradyumna, 236n84
Charles, Jean-Claude, 213n41
Charles V, King of England, 42
Chauvin, Sébastien, 273n29
Chebel d'Appollonia, Ariane, 66,
 143–144, 232n9, 257n69, 257n70
Chetty, Raj, 226n58

Chirac, Jacques, 119–120
Chiu, Allyson, 211n5
Christ, Julia, 180, 272n10, 273n15
Christian, Brian, 235n76
Chua, Amy, 242n80
Chung, Andrew, 240n44
Churchill, Mary, 247n36
Clinton, Hillary, 73
Citton, Yves, 74, 82, 212n25, 232n15, 234n58, 235n78, 237n103, 280n159
Clermont-Tonnerre (de), Stanislas, 179–180, 272n4
Coates, Ta-Nehisi, 212n19
Coccia, Emanuele, 281n176
Cohen, Cathy J., 231n139
Cohen, Joshua, 74, 234n51
Collin, Françoise, 165, 265n62
Collins, Patricia Hill, 282n194
Commaille, Jacques, 270n134
Comte, Auguste, 189, 276n84
Condé, Maryse, 188
Condorcet (de), Nicolas, 7, 72–73, 75, 128–129, 213n38, 234n45, 234n60
Connor, Walter, 102–103, 105–106, 244n116, 245n132
Constable, Marianne, 270n136
Cooper, Alex, 240n47
Cooper, Melinda, 250n74
Coppieters, Yves, 278n113
Coq, Guy, 26
Corpi, Lucha, 200
Cortland, Clarissa I., 227n73
Costanza-Chock, Sasha, 235n70
Coudriou, Cécile, 278n115
Coutant, Arnaud, 232n17
Couturier, Brice, 230n123
Cover, Rob, 231n140
Craig, Maureen A., 227n73, 228n85, 232n8
Crenshaw, Kimberlé, 16, 171, 215n74, 268n110, 269n113, 269n114
Crétois, Pierre, 277n96
Creton, Pierre, 155

Cullors, Patrisse, 1, 4
Cvetkovich, Ann, 258n104, 259n104

Dale, Susannah, ix
Damas, Léon-Gontran, 147, 258n92, 259n92
Darity, William, Jr., 230n116, 230n117
Daub, Adrian, 230n120, 231n135, 235n75
Daumeyer, Natalie M., 227n74, 227n80, 284n27
Davis, Malia, 280n167
Davy, Georges, 272n1
Dayan-Herzbrun, Sonia, 272n9
Dean, Jodi, 173, 269n124
Debord, Guy, 245n133
Delacampagne, Christian, 25, 217n47
Deleuze, Gilles, 8, 66–67, 76, 205, 213n41, 232n10, 232n11, 235n65, 282n3
Delhay, Cyril, 119, 250n78
Delmas-Marty, Mireille, 182, 274n33, 274n34, 274n35
Delors, Jacques, 217n37
Delphy, Christine, 221n123, 255n26, 263n19
DeNavas-Walt, Carmen, 242n91
Denham, Hannah, 239n26
Dénouveaux, Arthur, 204, 282n1
Derrida, Jacques, 152, 166, 260n123, 266n65, 266n66, 266n67, 283n10
Deschênes, Jules, 48, 225n34
Descoings, Richard, 119, 251n104
Descombes, Vincent, 275n57
Destin, Mesmin, 228n82
Deveaux, Monique, 71, 233n34, 233n35
DeVos, Betsy, 59–60
Devreux, Anne-Marie, 263n19
Dhume-Sonzogni, Fabrice, 236n90
Diagne, Souleymane Bachir, 181, 262n151, 273n17, 273n26, 282n7
Diamond, Larry, 70, 233n26

NAME INDEX

Didier, Emmanuel, 235n72
Djouder, Ahmed, 221n121
Dolezal, Rachel, 50, 225n45
Douglas, Mary, 284n37
Dray, Philip, 282n188
Drira, Chayma, 256n57
DuBois, W. E. B., 155, 199, 281n169
Dubreuil, Laurent, 238n13
Dugoni, Bernard L., 227n70
Dumont, Albéric, 264n45
Dumont, Louis, 77
Dunbar, Willy, 278n113
Duong, Kevin, 269n120
Dupere, Katie, 230n133
Dupuis-Déri, Francis, 230n120
Dupuy, Jean-Pierre, 25
Dutoya, Virginie, 233n31

Edelman, Lauren B., 268n104
Edenheim, Sara, 269n121
Eibach, Richard P., 227n72
Einstein, Albert, 97
Eliacheff, Caroline, 218n54
Elias, Norbert, 191–192, 277n100, 277n102
Eliason, Scott. R., 268n104
Elliott, Gregory, 28
Elliott, Jane, 49, 225n42
Eloit, Ilana, 262n17
Elster, Jon, 223n4
Engels, Fredrick, 195, 279n132
Entung Enya Kuo, 228n81
Eribon, Didier, 82, 152, 172, 214n61, 237n104, 251n105, 260n111, 260n122, 269n119, 283n9
Ernaux, Annie, 188
Esposito, Roberto, 279n150
Esseks, James, 239n41
Ewick, Patricia, 252n115
Ewing, Eve L., 211n2

Fall, Khadiyatoulah, 220n94
Faludi, Susan, 242n89

Fanon, Frantz, 5, 136, 147–148, 171–172, 212n23, 269n115
Farooqui, Adnan, 248n47
Farrelly, Peter, 52
Fassin, Didier, 212n17
Fassin, Éric, 51, 160, 218n62, 226n56, 250n86, 263n23
Feagin, Joe R., 246n21
Feher, Michel, 243n106, 245n139, 250n86, 253n131
Ferguson, Roderick A., 63, 231n142, 231n144, 255n23
Ferrarese, Estelle, 196, 279n136, 279n140
Ferret, Stéphane, 276n86
Ferry, Luc, 25
Fesperman, William, 137
Fillion, Emmanuelle, 146, 258n85, 258n86, 258n87
Finkielkraut, Alain, 25, 218n54, 237n1, 238n5
Fisher, Berenice, 195, 279n133
Fisher, Marc, 253n5
Fishkin, James, 70, 233n26
Fistetti, Francesco, 217n50
Fletcher, Bill, 255n37
Flores, Andrew L., 270n135
Floyd, George, 2, 3, 4, 140
Fondimare, Elsa, 263n27
Forrester, Katrina, 214n58
Foucault, Michel, 29, 213n30, 223n7, 239n21, 254n18, 270n129
Foucher, Matthieu, 261n150
Fourest, Caroline, 230n122
Fourier, Charles, 279n148, 282n192
France, David, 282n190
François, Bastien, 269n112, 283n18
Fraser, Nancy, 222n140, 222n142
Freeman, Alan David, 267n79
Freeman, Jo, 224n15
Frey, William H., 231n138
Fricker, Miranda, 36, 221n135
Friedman, Thomas, 256n46

Fruteau de Laclos, Frédéric, 274n38
Furet, François, 25

Gandhi, Mahatma, 97
Gaonkar, Dilip Parameshwar, 272n9
Garapon, Antoine, 204, 214n57, 235n73, 282n1
Garbagnoli, Sara 241n75
Garcin, Jérôme, 242n79
Gardner, Amy, 226n47
Garner, Eric, 1
Garza, Alicia, 1
Gaspard, Françoise, 221n119, 250n84, 271n152
Gates, Henry Louis, Jr., 282n186
Gavroche (fictional character), 96
Gemenne, François, 277n104
Genet, Jean, 188
Gersen, Jacob E., 61–62, 230n129, 247n39
Gersen, Jeannie Suk, 61–62, 215n70, 230n129, 230n130, 230n131, 230n132
Gilens, Martin, 232n23
Gilligan, Carol, 279n134
Gilmore, Ruth Wilson, 254n9
Gilroy, Paul, 155, 281n169
Gingrich, Newt, 101
Ginsberg, Benjamin, 229n115
Ginsburg, Ruth Bader, 112–113, 167, 269n125
Girard, Charles, 233n33, 235n71, 273n25
Glazer, Nathan, 228n89
Gleason, Philip, 260n116
Glissant, Édouard, 185, 274n48, 277n106
Glover, Danny 255n37
Gochfeld, Michael, 280n163
Goldblum, Caroline, 281n172
Golden, Daniel, 248n41
Goldman, Adam, 253n4
Goldstein, Noah J., 227n73

Göle, Nilüfer, 221n120
Gombin, Joël, 243n104
Gonzenbach, William J., 228n84
Gore, Al, 73
Gorsuch, Neil M., 112
Gourdon, Jessica, 247n37
Gourlay, Lesley, 235n77
Granjon, Marie-Christine, 217n52
Grant, Britt C., 92
Greco, Luca, 260n115
Green, Howard, 249n68
Greenwald, Glenn, 215n64
Gregory, E. John, 228n97
Grimm, Gavin, 92
Groux, Guy, 254n21
Gründler, Tatiana, 220n97
Guattari, Félix, 8, 66–67, 205, 213n41, 232n10, 282n3
Guénard, Florent, 219n78, 273n30, 276n75
Guillarme, Bertrand, 216n19
Guillaumin, Colette, 6–7, 160, 213n35, 213n39, 263n21
Guinier, Lani, 209, 252n120, 283n25
Guiraudon, Virginie, 252n116
Gulzar, Saad, 250n75
Gumbrecht, Hans Ulrich, 261n129
Guru, Gopal, viii

Haas, Nicholas, 250n75
Haas, Sophie, 236n96
Habermas, Jürgen, 74, 234n50
Hache, Émilie, 278n119
Hacker, Helen Mayer, 225n35
Haidel-Marker, Donald P., 226n60
Haider, Asad, 225n46
Hall, Stuart, 276n83
Halley, Janet E., 167, 266n77, 266n78
Hames-García, Michael R., 142, 252n110., 256–257n58
Hamidi, Camille, 259n95
Hamilton, Alexander, 218n67
Hammarberg, Thomas, 161, 263n30

NAME INDEX

Hamon, Benoît, 85
Hampton, Fred, 137, 138
Haraway, Donna, 200, 281n175
Harcourt, Bernard, 281n185
Hardt, Moritz, 236n83
Hark, Sabine, 245n136
Harney, Stefano, 197, 278n120, 279n149, 283n11
Harper, Tyler Austin, 247n40
Harris, Cheryl, 276n81
Hartocollis, Anemona, 246n24, 247n25, 247n28, 247n38
Hartog, François, 260n124
Harvey, David, 281n178
Haslanger, Sally, 230n128
Hau, Caroline S., 38, 222n148
Hauchecorne, Mathieu, 26, 214n59, 217n39, 217n41, 218n58
Hayakawa, Miyako, 236n96
Hayat, Samuel, 233n31
Hazony, Yoram, 101–102, 244n108
Hearne, Brittany N., 266n75
Hédon, Claire, 208
Hegel, Georg Wilhelm Friedrich, 180, 187, 188, 275n68, 275n70
Hendren, Nathaniel, 226n58
Hennessy-Fiske, Molly, 253n5
Hennette-Vauchez, Stéphanie, 225n39
Henrard, Kristin, 252n124
Henry, Emmanuel, 283n15, 283n20
Herbert, L. Camille, 266n78–267n78
Hernández, Tanya Katerí, 226n52
Hiptak, Adam, 247n38
Hirschman, Albert O., 234n48
Hobsbawm, Eric J., 244n115
Hollande, François, 99, 120
Holloway, Travis, 281n168
Honneth, Axel, 26, 186–187, 218n56, 275n63, 275n66, 275n69, 275n70, 275n71, 276n76
hooks, bell, 255n32
Hosang, Daniel Martinez, 238n17

Houellebecq, Michel, 105, 237n1, 245n129
Houle, Gilles, 238n19
Howe, Amy, 240n48
Hubler, Shawn, 253n6
Huckabee, Mike, 88
Hughes, David McDermott, 280n160
Hughes, Edward J., 277n97
Hugo, Victor, 96
Hume, David, 196
Hurtig, Marie-Claude, 263n19
Hutcheson, Frances, 196
Hutchinson, Asa, 89
Husserl, Edmund, 153

Ignazio (d'), Catherine, 236n86
Inglehart, Ronald, 243n103
Ingold, Tim, 275n58
Ivaldi, Gilles, 243n104
Iveson, Kurt, 235n68

Jackson, Janine A., 268n101
Jackson, Jesse, 137–138, 255n36
Jackson, Ketanji Brown, 110
Jacobson, Matthew Frye, 253n128
Jacquemain, Pierre, 212n24
Jacquemart, Alban, 257n59
Jamerson, Joshua, 226n48
James, William, 260n114
Jami, Irène, 255n26
Janmaat, Jan G., 231n137
Jaquet, Chantal, 74, 234n56
Jaunait, Alexandre, 229n102
Jay, John, 218n67
Jiménez, José Cha Cha, 137
John Paul II, Pope, 101, 102
Johnson, E. Patrick, 261n137
Johnson, Lyndon, 108
Jolivet, Annie, 258n81
Jonas, Hans, 193, 277n105, 278n118, 278n121
Jones, Maggie R., 226n58
Juhem, Philippe, 284n35

Juilhard, Jean-Marc 258n84
Jullien, François, 153, 181, 260n120, 260n121, 261n133, 273n20, 273n18, 273n21

Kadambi, Achuta, 236n84
Kagan, Elena, 110
Kail, Michèle, 263n19
Kairys, David, 239n24
Kaiser, Cheryl R., 226n59
Kameny, Franklin Edward, 266n71
Kant, Immanuel, 191
Karni, Annie, 240n56
Karst, Kenneth L., 241n67
Katri, Ido, 173–174, 270n130
Katznelson, Ira, 248n44
Kauffman, L. A., 141
Kavanaugh, Brett M., 112
Keating, Avril, 231n137
Keaton, Trica, 274n46
Kedadouche, Zaïr, 250n79
Kelly, Meg, 212n7
Kennedy, Anthony, 90, 112–133
Kennedy, Randall, 246n13
Kenrick, Douglas, 54, 227n75
Kergoat, Danièle, 242n77
Kermer, Jan, 243n101
Keslassy, Éric, 250n81
Khaitan, Tarunabh, 224n24
Khosrokhavar, Farhad, 221n119
Killmister, Suzy, 251n100
Kim, Claire Jean, 5, 212n22
Kim, Sunmin, 254n12
King, Martin Luther, Jr., 2, 97, 137, 255n34
King, Mel, 137, 138
Kinsler, Josh, 114, 248n42, 248n43
Kipnis, Laura, 59, 229n107, 229n108, 229n111, 229n112, 229n113
Kirchner, Lauren, 235n81
Kirmizi, Nina, 262n150
Klein, Ezra, 232n20
Klein, Lauren F., 236n86

Knaebel, Rachel, 261n149
Knight, Will, 236n88
Koerner, Catherine, 215n71
Koppelman, Andrew, 266n72
Kosofsky Sedgwick, Eve, 225n44
Kramer, Zachary, 233n32
Kraus, Michael W., 227n79, 227n80, 228n81
Krieger, Linda Hamilton, 268n104
Kukathas, Chandran, 219n88
Kymlicka, Will, 32, 42, 191, 220n106, 220n108, 277n98, 277n99
Kyung-Man, Kim, 283n12

Labrusse-Riou, Catherine, 218n54
Laclau, Ernesto, 43–44, 183–184, 223n8, 243n100, 274n39, 274n40, 274n41, 274n43, 274n44
Lacorne, Denis, 246n22
Lacroix, Justine, 20, 28, 217n37, 273n19
Lafont, Anne, 275n59
Lagasnerie (de), Geoffroy, 140, 223n161, 223n162, 254n16, 256n45, 257n64, 277n110, 278n114, 283n19
Lagoa, Barbara, 92
Lagraula-Fabre, Myriam, 258n84
Lagroye, Jacques, 264n34, 269n112
Laïdi, Zaki, 260n126
Lajoie, Andrée, 265n63
Lalande, André, 272n1
Laloui, Abdelilah, 251n107
Lamond, Grant, 266n70, 272n165
Lamont, Michèle, 212n15
Landemore, Hélène, 71, 74, 232n22, 233n36, 234n52, 234n53, 234n54, 234n55, 234n57, 235n74
Lapierre, Nicole, 155, 261n145, 261n146, 276n82
Laplantine, François, 150–151, 260n116
Larsen, Nella, 49–50, 225n43
Larson, Jeff, 235n81
Larson-Konar, Dylan, 280n164

NAME INDEX

Lassègue, Jean, 235n73
Latour, Bruno, 28, 198, 200, 219n82, 280n156, 280n157, 281n177
Laugier, Sandra, 279n137, 279n139
Laurent, Sylvie, 243n92
Laville, Jean-Louis, 256n52
Lazzeri, Christian, 28
Lecler, Joseph, 272n3
Lécuyer, Yannick, 267n96
Lee, Joyce Sohyun, 212n7
Le Floc'h, Benoît, 251n93
Lefort, Claude, 186, 210, 275n56, 284n38
Lefranc, Sandrine, 284n30
Le Gall, Anne, 250n84
Le Gallou, Jean-Yves, 85, 238n6
Legendre, Pierre, 175, 270n138, 270n139
Lehartel, Toriki, 225n41
Lemaitre, Eric, 97
Lemke, Thomas, 280n152
Le Moing, Ariane, 219n92
Leonard, Zoe, 205–206, 282n5
Le Pen, Jean-Marie, 101, 105, 119, 243n107
Le Pen, Marine, 97, 101, 104–105, 243n107
Lépinard, Éléonore, 173, 220n95, 269n123
Levi, Primo, 280n151
Levitsky, Steven, 232n18
Lewis, Victoria Ann, 258n89
Lieber, Marylène, 213n36
Lieberman, Robert C., 248n55
Light, Jennifer, 258n97, 259n97
Lilla, Mark, 238n12
Lindell, Henrik, 241n76
Lino E Silva, Moisés, 187, 275n73
Linskey, Annie, 226n47
Lionnet, Françoise, 223n6
Lipsky, Michael, 227n78
Lipson, Daniel N., 245n1
Liptak, Adam, 239n29

List, Christian 262n153
Lo, Clarence Y. H., 244n110
Lochak, Danièle, 273n16
Locke, John, 189, 276n85
Louis, Édouard, 202, 277n109
Lourenço, Luísa, 270n143
Lowery, Brian S., 235n69
Lowndes, Joseph E., 238n17
Löwy, Ilana, 263n22
Ludlow, Peter, 59
Lukes, Steven, 278n125
Lüsebrink, Hans-Jürgen, 272n5
Lyotard, Jean-François, 222n138

Maad, Ilham, 257n71
Maalsen, Sophia, 235n68
Maass, Anne, 54, 227n75
Machiavelli, Niccolò, 35, 221n127
Macron, Emmanuel, 98–100, 184–185
Madison, James, 27, 218n67
Magnaudeix, Mathieu, 256n47, 256n48, 258n98, 259n98
Mahoudeau, Alex, 228n87
Major, Brenda, 226n59
Maldonado, Aline Rivera, 176, 271n150, 271n155
Maletz, Donald J., 218n68
Manaktala, Gita, ix
Mangan, Katherine, 229n109
Mangeot, Philippe, 217n51
Manier, Marion, 254n10
Mann, Patrice, 228n83
Maréchal (Le Pen), Marion, 101, 102, 103–104, 105, 244n114, 244n118, 244n122, 244n123
Mares, Karla Hernández, 283n16
Margalit, Avishai, 201, 281n184
Markell, Patchen, 261n147, 276n74
Markey, Edward, 256n46
Maroun, Daniel N., 257n74
Martin, Beverly C., 92
Martin, Terry, 248n48
Martin, Trayvon, 1

Martinache, Igor, 214n62
Marx, Karl, 180, 195, 279n132
Mason, Lilliana, 232n20
Mateen, Omar, 131, 132
Mathieu, Nicole-Claude, 263n19, 263n20, 269n117
Matonti, Frédérique, 249n73
Mattiussi, Julie, 267n94
Mattu, Surya, 235n81
Maulpoix, Cy Lecerf, 281n180
May, Paul, 219n87
Mayer, Hans, 134, 254n13
Mayer, Nonna, 243n105
Mayeri, Serena, 268n102
Mazey, Sonia, 263n26
Mbembe, Achille, 147–148, 192, 258–259n93, 274n47, 277n103
McCammon, Holly J., 266n75
Mcclelland, Edward, 255n27
McCoy, Shannon K., 226n59
McGrath, Allison R., 266n75
McNair, Kimberly, 237n99
McNeil, Donald G., Jr., 241n62
McRuer, Robert, 259n90
Medard Inghilterra, Robin, 44, 223n9, 224n12, 225n30, 225n32, 225n33, 266n69, 267n85, 267n86, 267n87, 267n88
Medina, Lauren, 231n2, 231n3
Megret, Félix, 28
Meier, Kenneth J., 226n60
Meloni, Giorgia, 101
Mennucci, Patrick 238n11
Mény, Yves, 243n101
Mercader, Patricia, 263n19
Mercat-Bruns, Marie, 270n131
Merleau-Ponty, Maurice, 153, 180, 253n8, 261n132, 273n12
Mesnil, Marie, 264n36
Messling, Markus, 185, 274n50–54
Miano, Léonora, 83–84, 237n109, 237n110, 237n111, 237n112, 237n113, 237n114, 237n115

Michaels, Walter Benn, 229n98
Mill, John Stuart, 221n128
Miller, Katherine, 227n77
Millet, Richard, 237n1
Millhiser, Ian, 240n60
Mills, Mara, 282n191
Minc, Alain, 218n55
Mineur, Didier, 214n52, 234n47
Mohai, Paul, 280n166
Mohanty, Satya P., 252n110
Moller Okin, Susan, 23–24, 32, 216n28, 220n104, 220n105, 224n28
Molinier, Pascale, 279n137
Mondada, Lorenza, 260n115
Money, John, 159, 262n12
Monfort, Jean-Yves, 241n69
Mongin, Olivier, 25, 217n38
Montchalin (de), Amélie, 122, 251n93
Moon, Minyoung, 266n75
Moron-Puech, Benjamin, 163, 164, 264n37, 264n40, 264n41, 265n47, 265n50, 265n54
Morris, Ruth, 209–210, 284n31, 284n33
Morrison, Toni, 188
Moscovici, Serge, 13, 43, 52–54, 55, 199, 226n63, 227n65, 227n66, 227n68, 281n170, 281n171
Moses, Yolanda, 226n53
Mossuz-Lavau, Janine, 213n33
Moten, Fred, 197, 275n72, 278n120, 279n149, 283n11
Mouffe, Chantal, 71–72, 233n38, 233n40
Mounier, Emmanuel, 26
Moya, Paula M. Y., 51, 214n53, 226n54, 226n55., 252n110, 278n117
Mugny, Gabriel, 227n69
Murat, Laure, 61, 230n124, 230n126
Muray, Philippe, 237n1

Nabli, Béligh, 254n22
Nael, Georges, 248n50, 248n52

NAME INDEX

Nancy, Jean-Luc, 16, 133, 153, 154, 214n45, 215n72, 261n131, 261n134, 261n138
Nay, Olivier, 220n109
Ndiaye, Pap, 237n108
Neel, Rebecca, 227n73
Negri, Antonio, 66–67
Nekmat, Elmie, 228n84
Nellis, Ashley, 254n9
Nemeth, Charlan J., 227n71
Niang, Mame-Fatou, 212n14
Nichols, Tyre, 201
Nirenberg, David, 272n2
Noelle-Neumann, Elisabeth, 54–55, 227n76
Nora, Pierre, 149, 259n100
Norris, Pippa, 238n16, 239n20, 243n103
Noudélmann, François, 278n126, 282n196
Nozick, Robert, 19, 216n3
Nuñez, Gabriela, 281n182

O, Rachid, 188
Oakley, Ann, 262n14
Obama, Barack, 99, 112, 132
O'Brien, Laurie T., 226n59
Ocasio-Cortez, Alexandria, 141, 256n46
O'Connor, Reed, 94
Ogien, Albert, 250n77
Ogien, Ruwen, 270n128
Olson, Mancur, 82, 237n101
O'Malley, Pat, 235n79
Omar, Ilhan, 141
Omi, Michael, 214n60
O'Neil, Cathy, 235n80
Onyeador, Ivuoma N., 227n74, 227n80, 284n27
Orbán, Viktor, 101
Oyarzún, Pablo, 222n146

Page, Benjamin I. 232n23
Page, Scott E., 71, 233n36

Painter, Nell Irvin, 226n53
Papadopoulos, Ioannis, 214n57
Papastamou, Stamos, 227n69
Paperman, Patricia, 196, 279n137, 279n138
Park, Andrew, 270n135
Parrot, Clément, 257n66
Pascal, Blaise, 21
Pascariello, Pascale, 258n75
Pasha, Mustapha Kamal, 273n23
Pasquale, Benjamin, 250n75
Pasquali, Paul, 251n106, 251n108
Paternotte, David, 242n83, 245n137
Patrick, Dan, 88
Paul the Apostle, Saint, 184
Pearson, Adam R., 280n164
Pedahzur, Ami, 244n111
Pedriana, Nicholas, 268n105
Pélabay, Janie, 223n160, 236n89, 275n61
Pelluchon, Corine, 181, 273n22, 273n24
Pérez-Bustillo, Camilo, 283n16
Perreau, Bruno, 211n1, 211n3, 212n26, 215n65, 215n66, 215n73, 237n107, 241n72, 241n73, 241n74, 244n113, 246n22, 249n70, 262n6, 278n122, 282n6
Perrot, Michelle, 273n28
Petit, Valérie, 163
Pettigrew, Thomas Fraser 126, 252n109
Pettit, Philip, 37, 187–188, 222n139, 262n153, 276n77
Peyre, Évelyne, 263n19
Pfefferkorn, Roland, 39, 222n154
Philippot, Florian, 97
Philipps, Dave, 253n6
Piel, Simon 230n125
Piketty, Thomas, 51, 118–119, 190, 226n50, 226n51, 276n89
Pillay, Soma, 215n71
Pisier, Évelyne 231n7, 262n11
Pitkin, Hanna Fenichel, 258n94, 259n94

Planté, Christine, 263n19
Plato, 22, 35, 221n126
Pohjankoski, Pekka, 270n143
Policar, Alain, 183, 230n121, 274n36
Pollack, Martha E., 113
Pollock, Sheldon, 214n56
Porter, Sonya R., 226n58
Potte-Bonneville, Mathieu, 260n125
Powell, Lewis, 57
Pradeu, Thomas, 151, 260n118, 260n119
Pranchère, Jean-Yves, 273n19
Prearo, Massimo, 241n75
Prévieux, Julien, 235n72
Price, Eric, 236n83
Proctor, Bernadette D., 242n91
Prokhoris, Sabine, 270n137
Proudhon, Pierre-Joseph, 190, 276n88
Prum, Michel, 213n28
Purdie-Vaughns, Valerie, 227n72
Putterman, Ethan, 223n3

Quessada, Dominique, 212n25

Raffarin, Jean-Pierre, 120
Rancière, Jacques, 275n64, 275n65
Ransom, Tyler, 114
Rasmi, Jacopo, 74, 234n58, 237n103
Raspail, Jean, 105, 245n126
Ravaud, Jean-François, 258n81
Rawls, John, 9, 22, 74, 174, 190, 196, 214n47, 214n48, 216n16, 216n20, 232n24, 234n49, 276n90
Raynaud, Philippe, 27, 218n63, 218n64, 218n65
Reagan, Ronald, 11–12, 19, 101, 102
Reed, Cynthia, viii
Reed, Isaac Ariail, 283n13
Reed, John, viii
Rehfeld, Andrew, 283n24
Reich, Robert (Bob), 235n74
Renault, Emmanuel, 36, 221n131, 221n133, 222n141

Rensmann, Lars, 242n86
Reszler, André, 236n92
Rétif, Sophie, 242n84
Reus, Muriel, 231n1
Revillard, Anne, 258n80
Rheinschmidt-Same, Michelle, 228n82
Rice, Thomas D., 246n5
Richeson, Jennifer A., 227n73, 227n74, 227n80, 228n81, 228n82, 228n85, 232n8, 284n27
Richler, Jenn, 280n165
Ricœur, Paul, 25
Riley, Denise, 159, 213n31, 262n16
Rimer, Sara, 215n68
Ring, Trudy, 240n46
Robcis, Camille, 218n54
Robert, Richard, 254n21
Roberts, John, 110
Robinson, Cedric, 136, 255n31
Rocard, Michel, 25
Rochère (de la), Ludovine, 264n45
Rochstein, Richard, 211n2
Rodrigue, Aron, 226n61
Roger, Philippe, 245n134
Rolland-Diamond, Caroline, 256n56
Rolnik, Suely, viii
Roman, Diane, 264n35
Roman, Joël, 25, 217n49
Romano, Aja, 230n119
Romero-Canyas, Rainer, 280n164
Romero, Simon, 253n6
Romm, Tony, 211n5
Rosa, Hartmut, 154, 261n141, 261n142, 261n143, 261n144
Rosenbaum, James, 243n93
Rosenblum, Darren, 169, 268n99
Rossignol, Laurence, 152–153
Rothberg, Michael, 260n110
Rouch, Hélène, 263n19, 263n22
Roudinesco, Élisabeth, 266n66
Roulleau-Berger, Laurence, 236n94
Rousseau, Jean-Jacques, 234n61
Rovive, Isabelle, 265n58

NAME INDEX

Rubinowitz, Leonard S., 243n93
Rubio, Philip F., 246n3
Rucker, Julian M., 227n80, 228n85
Rush, Sharon Elizabeth, 169, 268n98

Sabbagh, Daniel, vii, 229n99, 252n121,
 251n98, 251n99, 257n73
Saha, Robin, 280n166
Saint Martin (de), Monique, 245n138
Sallenave, Danièle, 25
Salmon, Pierre 233n42
Samoyault, Tiphaine, 282n193
Sanchez, Rebecca, 282n191
Sandel, Michael, 42, 190–191, 276n91,
 277n92, 277n93, 277n95
Sanders, Bernie, 141
Sapiro, Gisèle, 237n1
Sarkozy, Nicolas, 120, 122, 250n80,
 250n82
Sartre, Jean-Paul, 8, 82, 153–154,
 213n43, 237n105, 237n106, 261n136
Sassen, Saskia, 277n101
Saul, Stephanie, 248n45
Savage, Charlie, 247n27
Savidan, Patrick, 220n107, 221n118
Sawicki, Frédéric, 214n62, 269n112
Scalia, Antonin, 112
Schapiro, Morton, 229n110
Schérer, René, 9, 214n51
Schlegel, Jean-Louis, 215n76
Schlosberg, David, 281n181
Schor, Naomi, 274n49
Schueller, Malini Johar, 272n164
Schuldt, Jonathon P., 280n164
Schulman, Sarah, 279n147
Schwartzberg, Melissa, 234n63, 283n22,
 283n24, 284n28
Scott, Joan W., 38, 159–160, 165,
 213n44, 222n147, 231n4, 231n6,
 241n71, 251n103, 262n15, 263n18,
 265n61
Scott, Tim, 2
Senghor, Léopold Sédar, 180

Sekyi-Otu, Ato, 180, 272n8
Selby, Jennifer A., 220n98
Sen, Amartya, 36, 221n134
Sénac Réjane, 166, 223n160, 229n100,
 250n87, 256n42, 263n25, 266n64
Sengupta, Somini, 280n162
Sennett, Richard, 236n91
Seré, Ludovic, 258n76
Serna, Pierre, 214n54
Servan-Schreiber, Claude, 250n84
Shah, Henry, 256n57
Shakespeare, Tom, 258n87
Shakil, Albeena, viii
Shapiro, Jenessa R., 227n73
Sharma, Nitasha Tamar, 256n50
Shear, Michael D., 240n57
Shelby, Tommie, 256n49
Shepard, Todd, 116, 248n53
Shih, Shu-mei, 223n6
Shirley, Don, 52
Shklar, Judith, 35–36, 221n132,
 222n151
Silbey, Susan, 252n115
Silver, Hilary, 230n127
Simpson, Edward H., 233n43
Sintomer, Yves, 234n62
Skrentny, John D., 228n93
Slama, Serge, 225n31
Smith, Adam, 186, 196
Smith, Christine M., 227n70
Smith, Howard, 45
Snyder, David, 232n19
Solanke, Iyiola, 224n18
Solzhenitsyn, Aleksandr, 53–54
Song, Sarah, 32, 220n100
Sotomayor, Sonia, 89, 110, 112–113
Sourice, Benjamin, 254n20
Sowell, Thomas, 248n46
Spector, Céline, 35, 221n129, 221n130
Spielberg, Steven, 79
Spinoza, Baruch, 48, 225n36
Spivak, Gayatri, 148, 259n96
Srebro, Nathan, 236n83

Stasse, François, 218n55, 249n58
Staub, Hans O., 218n61
Stefanoni, Pablo, 238n15
Stern, Alexandra Minna, 245n135
Stiegler, Barbara, 278n112
Stoller, Robert J., 262n13
Strathern, Marilyn, 77, 235n67
Strolovitch, Dara Z., 140, 256n43
Stryker, Robin, 170, 268n103, 268n105
Suaudeau, Julien 272n6
Suk-Young Chwe, Michael, 278n123
Surrel, Hélène, 122, 251n97, 271n149
Swaine, Jon, 212n7
Swisher, Sarah, 240n50
Sylvie Laurent, 242n90

Tabet, Paola, 284n29
Talaifar, Sanaz, 235n69
Talpin, Julien, 238n9, 256n53, 256n55
Tamagne, Florence, 226n62
Tan, Jacinth X., 227n79
Tartakowsky, Danielle, 243n102
Tassin, Étienne, 274n37
Taubira, Christiane, 147, 148–149, 258n102, 259n102
Taylor, Charles, 31–32, 42, 275n62
Telliez, Romain, 223n1
Thatcher, Margaret, 19
Thelen, Kathleen, 283n17
Théry, Irène, 26, 218n53, 218n54
Théry, Jean-François 218n55
Thomas, Clarence, 27, 93, 178
Thomas, Veronica G. 268n101
Thomson, Judith Jarvis, 259n108
Tilly, Charles, 87, 238n18
Tin, Louis-Georges, 139, 256n41
Tindale, R. Scott, 227n70
Tinius, Jonas, 185, 274n51–274n54
Tocqueville (de), Alexis, 13, 27, 214n55, 218n66, 219n69, 219n70, 219n71
Tomba, Massimiliano, 272n9
Tometi, Opal, 1
Toubon, Jacques, 143, 144, 145, 164

Touraine, Alain, 25
Trache, Hichem, 249n68
Tramel, Salena, 254n19
Traoré, Adama, 2–3, 143, 144, 155, 256n45
Traoré, Assa, 3, 140, 212n10
Traoré, Bagui, 143
Troadec, Anne, 221n122
Tronto, Joan, 195, 196, 279n133, 279n135, 279n143
Tropp, Linda R., 126, 252n109
Trost, Melanie, 54, 227n75
Trudeau, Pierre, 29
Trump, Donald, 2, 59, 69, 73, 89, 92, 93, 98, 99, 105, 112
Truong, Fabien, 81, 236n97
Tsai, Alexander C., 222n143
Tverdota, Gábor, 255n29

Urbinati, Nadia, 232n12, 243n96, 253n132
Urfalino, Philippe, 233n28

Valerio, Ivan, 244n124
Van Dyke, Vernon, 244n117
Vanbellingen, Léopold, 219n91
Varikas, Eleni, 159–160, 165, 265n60
Veaux, Frédéric, 257n62
Venkataramani, Atheendar S., 222n143
Verloo, Mieke, 242n83
Vespa, Jonathan, 231n2, 231n3
Vignaux, Georges, 220n94
Villa, Paula-Irene, 245n136
Ville, Isabelle, 258n81
Villepin (de), Dominique, 120
Viramonte, Helena María, 188
Vischer, Robert, 155
Voguet, Elise, 221n122

Wacquant, Loïc, 26–27, 215n63, 218n60
Wahnich, Stéphane, 244n112
Walker, Clarence, 83–84, 237n116

NAME INDEX

Walzer, Michael, vii, 6–7, 9–10, 12–13, 19, 21–40, 83–84, 115, 179, 182, 184, 188, 201, 204, 214n46, 214n50, 216n1, 216n2, 216n4, 217n29, 217n30, 217n31, 217n32, 217n33, 217n34, 217n35, 217n40, 217n42, 217n43, 217n44, 217n45, 217n46, 217n48, 218n56, 219n72, 219n73, 219n74, 219n75, 219n76, 219n77, 219n80, 219n81, 219n83, 219n84, 219n86, 219n89, 220n110, 220n111, 220n112, 220n113, 220n11, 220n115, 221n116, 221n124, 223n155, 223n156, 223n157, 223n158, 223n15, 223n16, 224n27, 273n31, 273n32, 274n42, 276n79, 281n183
Wampole, Christy, 245n127, 278n130
Wang, Simeng, 236n96
Warden, Meredith, 222n144
Warner, Michael, 189, 276n80
Warren, Elizabeth, 50
Warren, Mark R., 282n189
Weber, Max, 192, 277n107
Weinstein, Bret, 62
Weiss, Bari, 230n134
Wekker, Gloria, 237n100
Whiteside, Kerry, 198, 280n153, 280n154, 280n158
Wiels, Joëlle, 263n19
Wieviorka, Michel, 212n12
Wilderson, Frank B,. III, 136, 255n33
Williams, David R., 222n143
Williams, Jakobi, 255n35
Wilson, William Julius, 49, 211n2, 215n69, 225n38
Winance, Myriam, 283n23
Winant, Howard, 214n60
Winston, Celeste, 282n187
Winterer, Caroline, 241n66
Wirth, Louis, 6, 213n27
Wittgenstein, Ludwig, 270n141, 270n142

Wittig, Monique, 180–181, 260n128, 273n13, 273n14
Wolfelsperger, Alain, 233n42
Wornell, Gregory, 79
Wright, Beverly, 280n166
Wu, Félix, 236n95
Wuhl, Simon, 20, 28, 219n79, 252n114

Xu, Jason, 247n38

Yamgnane, Kofi, 212n13
Yong Li, 236n96
Young, Iris Marion, 38–39, 213n40, 222n149, 222n150, 222n152
Youngbin, Kim, 236n96

Zaffran, Joël, 258n79
Zavalloni, Marisa, 227n65
Zeldin, David, 279n148
Zemmour, Éric, 85, 101, 105, 237n1, 238n7, 245n125
Zewen, Adam, 236n85
Ziblatt, Daniel, 232n18
Zimmerman, George, 1
Zivi, Karen, 252n122
Žižek, Slavoj, 184

SUBJECT INDEX

Abortion
  affirmative action and, 112
  antiminority politics and, 89–90,
    93, 97
  Christians and, 90
  comfort, 97
  diversity and, 56, 60
  ethics and, 206
  legal issues and, 6, 56, 60, 89–90, 93,
    97, 112, 178, 202, 206
  universalism and, 202
Activists
  affirmative action and, 111
  antiminority politics and, 86–87, 93,
    95, 97, 99, 104, 106
  Catholic, 95, 97
  co-appearing and, 135–142, 146, 155
  cohesion and, 82
  community and, 1, 82, 87, 137, 141
  competition and, 86
  cultural issues and, 87, 106, 137
  ethics and, 204
  ethnonational, 104
  influence and, 87
  legal issues and, 159, 163, 167

LGBTQ, 93
  minority concepts and, 1–2
  universalism and, 184
Affirmative action
  abortion and, 112
  activists and, 111
  age and, 107
  Asian Americans and, 111, 114
  Black people and, 108–109, 128
  Christians and, 115–116
  coalitions and, 129
  community and, 116, 118
  competition and, 110–115, 118,
    122–129
  conformity and, 127
  conservatism and, 111–112
  convergence of struggles and, 129
  cultural issues and, 115–119, 129
  differential treatment and, 110, 116
  disabilities and, 122
  distribution and, 108, 110, 115–119,
    126
  domination and, 114
  ecological issues and, 129
  economic issues and, 115–118, 126

Affirmative action (cont.)
education and, 107–110, 114–118, 123–127
egalitarianism and, 119
employment and, 107–108, 115, 126
equality and, 108–110, 115–117, 120–123, 128
equivalence and, 108
exclusion and, 120, 124, 126–127
feminism and, 120
French, 110, 113–114, 118–123, 127, 129
gender and, 107, 122
globalization and, 129
goal of, 107–108
health and, 108, 112, 119
hegemony and, 123, 128
homophobia and, 127
housing and, 122, 125
human rights and, 122
identity and, 117, 128
inequality and, 115–119, 122, 128
interdependence and, 116
intrasectionality and, 129
Jews and, 115
labor and, 108
language and, 116–117
Latinx people and, 110
legal issues and, 110, 113, 116–119, 122, 126–127, 129
liberalism and, 119–120
moral issues and, 107
Muslims and, 115–116, 120
nepotism and, 114, 124
parity and, 120–121
pluralism and, 110, 123
police and, 119
positive discrimination and, 14, 111, 120, 122–123
power and, 112, 115, 120, 123, 128
prejudice and, 126, 128
presence and, 115, 125, 129
quotas and, 107, 116–117, 121

race and, 107–113, 119–123
reciprocity and, 110, 115, 123–129
relational association and, 123, 128–129
religion and, 112, 115–116, 120–121
responsibility and, 121, 126, 129
Sciences Po and, 15, 110, 113–114, 119, 122–127
segregation and, 108, 110, 113, 115–116, 119
sexual issues and, 112, 120–122
sovereignty and, 129
stereotypes and, 109, 111
Trump and, 111–112
United States and, 56, 107–113, 115, 122, 128–129
value and, 126–127, 129
violence and, 122, 127
women and, 112, 115, 117, 120–121
Afropessimism, 136
Age
adoption and, 158
affirmative action and, 107
class and, 62
demographics, 66, 76
disability and, 16, 44–45, 159, 171, 175, 205
discrimination and, 12, 16, 44–46, 107, 158–159, 169, 171, 175
ethics and, 204–205
heterocentrism and, 62
homogeneity of, 62
legal issues and, 45–46, 158–159, 169, 171, 175
royal ascension and, 42
Age of Enlightenment, 179, 181
Algorithms
demographics and, 68, 76–80, 83–84
diversity and, 63
dividual and, 76–80
ethics and, 204
Facebook and, 78, 132
majority systems and, 14

SUBJECT INDEX 345

minority concepts and, 12, 14
universalism and, 192
Analogical reasoning, 166–170, 266n70
Animality, 200
Anthropocene, 197–198
Antiminority politics
abortion and, 89–90, 93, 97
activists and, 86–87, 93, 95, 97, 99, 104, 106
appropriation strategies and, 95–98
Black people and, 86, 99
Christians and, 86, 90, 95, 102
civil rights and, 89, 94, 98, 106
coalitions and, 102–104
community and, 87, 102
competition and, 86, 90, 106
conformity and, 101
conservatism and, 88, 93, 101–102
cultural issues and, 99, 103, 106
democracy and, 100, 102
disabilities and, 95–96
distribution and, 99
domination and, 98
economic issues and, 87, 99–104
education and, 92
egalitarianism and, 103
employment and, 91, 101
equality and, 92, 94–95, 98
equivalence and, 98
ethics and, 92, 104
ethnonationalism and, 101–106
exclusion and, 99
feminism and, 97, 103
freedom of expression and, 87–94
French, 85–86, 95–101, 104, 106
gay people and, 91–94, 96–97
gender and, 86–89, 92, 94, 97–98, 103
globalization and, 87, 104
health and, 89–94, 99
hegemony and, 96
heterosexuals and, 96
homophobia and, 95, 100
human rights and, 95

identity and, 86–87, 92, 98–101
ideologies and, 86–89, 97–98, 102–104
influence and, 14, 87, 90
Jews and, 97
language and, 88, 96
Latinx people and, 99
legal issues and, 86–88, 91, 94, 102, 106
LGBTQ community and, 88, 93–94
liberalism and, 86–88, 98, 102
majority rule and, 86
moral issues and, 86, 89, 94–98, 106
Muslims and, 89
new humanism and, 86, 102–105
parity and, 86, 97
power and, 85–87, 90, 98, 102–103
presence and, 85, 97, 101
protest and, 85, 97–100
race and, 89, 94–95, 98–99
racism and, 85–86, 95–100
religion and, 85–95
same-sex couples and, 88–96, 100
sexual issues and, 7–8, 85–102
slavery and, 89, 97, 103
social media and, 105
sovereignty and, 86, 102, 104
stereotypes and, 98
transgender people and, 89, 92
United States and, 86–87, 93–95, 98–101, 105–106
value and, 87, 94, 96, 100, 102, 104–105
violence and, 88, 96, 99
vulnerability and, 100
women and, 86, 89–90, 94, 96–99, 105
Arabs, 138, 143, 204
Asian Americans
affirmative action and, 111, 114
demographics and, 66, 80–81
diversity and, 55
ethics and, 204
minority concepts and, 2, 15
Asphyxiation, 3

Asylum, 49–50
Authoritarianism, 40, 100–101
Autonomy, 24, 29, 39, 44, 75, 118, 145–151, 187, 193, 196, 201, 278n116
Autopsies, 3

Becoming, 8, 66–67, 200
Belief systems, 20, 87, 102, 210
Biculturalism, 29
Binarism, 75, 165, 264n40
Biological parent, 163
Black people
  affirmative action and, 108–109, 128
  Afropessimism and, 136
  antiminority politics and, 86, 99
  blackness, 1, 4–7, 49–52, 60, 78, 134–137, 141–142, 147, 198, 201, 203–204
  co-appearing and, 133–143, 147
  demographics and, 78, 81, 83
  diversity and, 48–52, 60
  ethics and, 203–206
  French, 2–4, 16, 48, 81, 83, 86
  Jim Crow and, 143, 246n5
  legal issues and, 170–171
  minority concepts and, 1–7, 11, 15–16
  universalism and, 184, 188, 198, 201
Borders, 40, 65, 79, 103, 141
Burkinis, 85

Cancel culture, 13, 61
Capitalism, 19, 24, 136, 141, 166, 196–200
Care theories, 195–196
Catholics, 30, 91, 93, 95, 97, 102, 176
Caucasians, 51
Cherokee Nation, 50
Chicano farmers, 137
China, 48, 137
Christian Democrats, 25

Christians
  abortion and, 90
  affirmative action and, 115–116
  antiminority politics and, 86, 90, 95, 102
  co-appearing and, 139, 147
  evangelical, 102, 106
  experiences and, 26, 40
  Mounier and, 26
  sovereignty and, 86
  universalism and, 179, 190
Civil disobedience, 107, 206
Civil rights
  affirmative action and, 107–108, 111
  antiminority politics and, 89, 94, 98, 106
  co-appearing and, 146
  diversity and, 45–47, 51, 56–58
  experiences and, 24
  legal issues and, 177
  universalism and, 184
Civil unions, 51, 158
Class
  age and, 62
  defectors and, 74
  discrimination and, 12, 15–16, 45, 51, 119, 162, 172, 203
  equality and, 165
  ethics and, 208
  homogeneity of, 62
  interdependence and, 16, 175
  legal issues and, 162, 165–166, 172, 175
  middle, 86, 99, 123
  minority concepts and, 4, 6, 12, 15–16
  protected classes, 6, 15–16, 45, 162, 174, 203
  second-class citizens and, 119
  struggle of, 137
  subordination and, 125
  universalism and, 180, 199, 202
  working, 99, 118, 202

SUBJECT INDEX

Coalitions
affirmative action and, 129
antiminority politics and, 102–104
co-appearing and, 133–142
conscience and, 137
convergence of struggles and, 133–142
legal issues and, 172
parallax and, 133–142
rainbow, 137–138
Co-appearing
activists and, 135–142, 146, 155
Black people and, 133–143, 147
Christians and, 139, 147
civil rights and, 146
coalitions and, 133–142
collective action for, 153–154
commonalities and, 5, 16, 48, 141, 153
communitarianism and, 154
community and, 132, 135, 137, 141–144
conformity and, 135
convergence of struggles and, 133–142, 153, 155
cultural issues and, 132, 137, 149
direct speech and, 15
disabilities and, 134, 144–147
distribution and, 155, 175
economic issues and, 138, 143–144
education and, 135, 142–145, 149
employment and, 144
equality and, 136, 139, 145, 150
equivalence and, 136
ethics and, 152, 155, 205
exclusion and, 133–134, 151
experiences and, 15, 153
feminism and, 139, 142, 146, 155
France and, 138–149, 152
gay people and, 132–133, 138–139, 146, 148
gender and, 135
globalization and, 135
hegemony and, 149–151

heterosexuals and, 135
homophobia and, 131–132, 139–141, 144
housing and, 142–145
humanism and, 155
human rights and, 134, 141, 145
hypertrophy of assimilation and, 136
identity and, 141, 150–153
inequality and, 133, 141, 146, 150
interdependence and, 133, 137, 141
Jews and, 138, 153
language and, 131, 136, 152–153
Latinx people and, 131, 133, 137
legal issues and, 135, 138, 143, 150–152, 156
lesbians and, 133, 138, 146, 152
liberalism and, 139
minorities and, 131–156
mirror representation and, 147–148
moral issues and, 134, 150–151
multiculturalism and, 137
Nancy on, 133, 153–154
parallax and, 133–142
pluralism and, 149
police and, 134–137, 140, 143–144
power and, 135–136, 139, 141, 143, 148–156
presence and, 133, 137, 143, 147–156
protest and, 140, 143
racism and, 135–137, 140, 143–144, 147
relational association and, 142, 154
religion and, 139, 151, 153
resonances and, 133, 136, 150, 154–155
responsibility and, 145, 149, 153
same-sex couples and, 152
sexual issues and, 135–136, 139, 144, 148, 152–153
slavery and, 149–150
social media and, 131
solidarity and, 132, 139, 142, 155
sovereignty and, 153, 155–156

Co-appearing (cont.)
  struggle for visibility, 131–133, 147–156
  translation of term, 16
  United States and, 131, 134, 137, 141, 145, 151
  value and, 134, 136, 140, 154
  violence and, 132–137, 142–147, 151
  voting and, 142, 145, 148
  vulnerability and, 146
  women and, 134, 138, 145
Colonialism
  epistemic imperialism and, 180
  France and, 115–116
  gender and, 62
  postcolonialism, 103, 191
  racism and, 4, 62, 82, 103, 115–116, 176, 180, 189, 191
  slavery and, 189
  social dynamics and, 82
Colonization, 7, 98, 152
Commonalities, 5, 16, 48, 141, 153
Communism, 102, 191
Communitarianism
  anticommunitarian rhetoric and, 81
  co-appearing and, 154
  demographics and, 80–82
  France and, 3, 12, 24–29, 80–81, 154
  pluralism and, 80
  United States, 3
  universalism and, 186, 188
Community
  activists and, 1, 82, 87, 137, 141
  affiliation and, 36
  affirmative action and, 116, 118
  antiminority politics and, 87, 102
  belief systems and, 20, 87, 102, 210
  belonging and, 17, 41, 190
  co-appearing and, 132, 135, 137, 141–144
  commitment to, 9
  cultural issues and, 9, 11, 14, 29–31, 41–42, 84, 87, 118, 137, 144
  demographics and, 78, 82–84

distribution and, 21–24
diversity and, 41–42
ethics and, 210
intercommunity, 2, 29, 144
interpretive, 11
as jointed incompleteness, 14, 82–83, 207
legal issues and, 160, 178
meaning of, 11
moral issues and, 9, 17, 20, 36, 39, 194
organizers and, 1, 141–142
phalansteries, 282n192
political, 10, 30
Rawls on, 22
rules for, 23, 31
seriality and, 80–84
sustainability and, 39
universalism and, 189–190, 194, 197
Competition
  affirmative action and, 110–115, 118, 122–129
  antiminority politics and, 86, 90, 106
  demographics and, 72, 75, 80, 82
  discrimination and, 15, 57, 90, 106, 110, 114
  diversity and, 57
  ethics and, 205
  experiences and, 20
  majority rule and, 72, 75
  minority concepts and, 2, 12, 15, 111–115
  remembrance and, 5
Compliance, 53, 177
Conformity
  affirmative action and, 127
  antiminority politics and, 101
  co-appearing and, 135
  demographics and, 67
  experiences and, 39
  legal issues and, 165, 169
  psychology and, 52
  universalism and, 183
  vs. joining, 53

SUBJECT INDEX

Consciousness, 14, 26, 36, 38, 49, 107, 110–112, 123, 137 153, 172, 178, 185, 191, 193–194, 270n134
Conservatism
affirmative action and, 111–112
antiminority politics and, 88, 93, 101–102
diversity and, 56, 62
experiences and, 27
minority concepts and, 2, 12–13
among minority groups, 201–202, 206–207
Consistency, 13, 33, 53, 98, 142, 167, 233n43
Convergence
affirmative action and, 129
coalition and, 133–142
co-appearing and, 133–142, 153, 155
demographics and, 69–70
experiences and, 27
ideological, 69–70
legal issues and, 171
LGBTQ community and, 133, 135
minority concepts and, 5, 15–16
parallax and, 133–142
of struggles, 129, 133, 135
universalism and, 183
Conversion therapy, 88, 91–92
Corruption, 35, 43, 97, 106
Cosmopolitism, 183, 192, 194
COVID-19 pandemic, 2, 5, 113, 141, 192–193
Creed, 1, 12, 76
Crip theory, 147
Cultural issues
activists, 87, 106, 137
affirmative action, 115–119, 129
antiminority politics, 99, 103, 106
appropriation, 83–84
belief systems, 20, 87, 102, 210
biculturalism, 29
cancel culture, 13, 61
co-appearing, 132, 137, 149

demographics, 65, 71, 79–84
diversity, 42, 48, 54
ethics, 203, 207
experiences, 20, 24–25, 29–33, 38
French, 6
identity, 6, 42, 65, 80, 83, 99, 117, 137, 189, 191, 203
interpretative community, 11
migrants, 15, 66, 118, 137–138, 145, 155
minority concepts, 5–6, 9–14
multiculturalism, 12–13
pluralism, 13, 80, 181
political tools, 14
religion, 13, 29–30, 42, 81, 203
separatism, 5
social goods, 9, 13, 20–21, 23, 33, 84, 184–185, 189
United States, 6
universalism, 180–185, 189, 191
Walzer on, 9
Wirth on, 6
wokeness, 56, 60–62
Cultural Revolution, 137

Decolonization, 62
Defamation, 34, 88, 95
Democracy
antiminority politics and, 100, 102
demographics and, 68–71, 75
diversity and, 42–43
ethics and, 203, 207, 210
experiences and, 25, 27, 33, 37, 40
liberalism and, 57
majority rule and, 72–76
pluralism and, 13, 25–26, 33, 189
universalism and, 183, 189, 198, 201
value of, 11–17
Demographics
age, 66, 76
algorithms and, 68, 76–80, 83–84
Asian Americans and, 66, 80–81
communitarianism and, 80–82

Demographics (cont.)
community and, 78, 82–84
competition and, 72, 75, 80, 82
conformity and, 67
convergence of struggles and, 69–70
cultural issues and, 65, 71, 79–84
democracy and, 68–71, 75
distribution and, 76, 83–84
dividual and, 76–80
domination and, 67, 70–75, 80, 82, 84
economic issues and, 77
education and, 79
employment and, 79
equality and, 66, 71, 73
equivalence and, 71
ethics and, 69
exclusion and, 72
feminism and, 79
French, 66, 69, 80–81
gender, 76
globalization and, 75
Hastert rule and, 69–70
hegemony and, 84
human rights and, 70
identity and, 78, 83
ideologies and, 69–71, 81
impact of number, 65–84
inequality and, 71, 79
influence and, 76, 80
interdependence and, 68, 75
labor and, 66
language and, 65, 73, 82
Latinx people and, 66
legal issues and, 66, 78
lesbians and, 78
liberalism and, 71, 73
limits of consensus, 68–72
majority rule and, 68–69, 72–80
moral issues and, 68, 71, 73, 77
numerical majority and, 66
parity and, 66, 79
pluralism and, 72, 80
police violence, 143

popular vote and, 73
power and, 65–69, 73–74, 77–84
presence and, 71, 82–83
race, 76, 81
religion and, 81
resonances and, 61
segregation and, 66, 79–80
seriality and, 80–84
sexual issues and, 66, 78
social goods and, 76, 84
stereotypes and, 80
United States and, 66, 68–69, 83
value and, 68, 72, 80
violence and, 66, 81
vulnerability and, 72
women and, 66
Despotism, 27, 86
Differance, 159, 162–166
Difference, 5, 7, 14, 23, 31, 39, 58, 63,
67, 89, 96, 102, 151, 162–170, 173,
185
Differential treatment, 6, 36, 48, 55,
110, 116, 120, 150, 157–159, 171
Digital society, 76–80
Disabilities
accessibility issues and, 134
affirmative action and, 122
age and, 16, 44–45, 159, 171, 175, 205
antiminority politics and, 95–96
co-appearing and, 134, 144–147
crip theory and, 147
discrimination and, 15–16, 44–45, 95,
146, 159, 168, 175–177, 203
diversity and, 44–45
ethics and, 203–205, 208
legal issues and, 159, 168, 171,
175–177
race and, 1, 12, 16, 44–45, 95–96, 171,
175, 202, 205
universalism and, 202
Discrimination
age, 12, 16, 44–46, 107, 158–159, 169,
171, 175

SUBJECT INDEX 351

competition and, 15, 57, 90, 106, 110, 114
difference and, 162–166
differential treatment and, 6, 36, 48, 55, 110, 116, 120, 150, 157–159, 171
disabilities and, 15–16, 44–45, 95, 146, 159, 168, 175–177, 203
disparate impact and, 46
equality and, 6, 16, 30, 35, 39, 45, 55–60, 71, 92, 95, 108, 116, 119–123, 139, 146, 150, 157–158, 165, 173, 177, 204, 209
France and, 6, 14, 28, 43–46, 49, 58, 95, 106, 110, 118, 120–123, 127, 138–139, 146, 157–158, 161, 164, 204
gender, 12, 15–16, 44–45, 52, 54, 60, 89, 92, 94, 107, 158–178, 203, 209
health, 12, 37, 44, 52, 89–90, 108, 119
homophobia and, 4, 51, 95, 100, 127, 131–132, 139–141, 144, 202
inequality and, 6, 30, 35, 55, 71, 116, 119, 133, 146, 150, 157
influence and, 7–8, 43, 90
interdependence and, 16, 37
intrasectionality and, 170–178
legal issues and, 162–166
positive, 14, 111, 120, 122–123
skin color and, 4, 15, 45–46, 50, 177–178, 203
stereotypes and, 15, 80, 98, 109, 111, 161, 164, 169, 209
Disparate impact, 46
Dissidence, 5, 15, 53, 55, 61, 70–71, 79, 92, 110, 269n125
Dissociation, 192, 195, 202
Distribution
affirmative action and, 108, 110, 115–119, 126
antiminority politics and, 99
co-appearing and, 155, 175
demographics and, 76, 83–84
ethics and, 203, 210

experiences and, 19–24, 26, 28, 33, 39–40
inequality and, 13, 23, 33, 115–119
social goods and, 10, 13, 20–24, 28, 33, 39–40, 76, 84, 184, 188, 190, 202
society of, 21–24
universalism and, 184, 188, 190, 192, 199–201
value and, 21, 23, 203
Walzer and, 9, 13, 19–28, 33, 39–40, 115, 184, 188
Diversity
abortion and, 56, 60
algorithms and, 63
Asian Americans and, 55
Black people and, 48–52, 60, 78, 81, 83
bureaucratic inflation and, 56–63
civil rights and, 45–47, 51, 56–58
community and, 41–42
competition and, 57
conformity and, 52–55
conservatism and, 56, 62
cultural issues and, 42, 48, 54
democracy and, 42–43
disabilities and, 44–45
domination and, 48, 61
economic issues and, 44, 47, 51–52, 55
education and, 45, 49, 55–60
egalitarianism and, 52, 57
employment and, 44–46, 51, 58
equality and, 44–45, 57–58, 60
equivalence and, 46
exclusion and, 48, 55
France and, 41–49, 58
gay people and, 49, 51
gender and, 44–45, 52, 54, 59–62
globalization and, 42, 61, 63
health and, 44, 52
hegemony and, 44
homophobia and, 51
human rights and, 41, 44, 47
identity and, 43–44, 50, 59–62

Diversity (cont.)
inequality and, 55
influence and, 13, 43, 51–56, 63
labor and, 44, 47, 51
language and, 41–44, 50
legal issues and, 42–52, 63
lesbians and, 49
liberalism and, 57–58
majority rule and, 43
minority concepts and, 41–57
moral issues and, 43, 56
multiculturalism and, 42
neutrality and, 49
police and, 47, 60–61
power and, 43, 46, 49–63
prejudice and, 54
protest and, 62–63
race and, 42, 44–47, 50, 57, 60, 62
relational association and, 43
religion and, 41–47, 56
responsibility and, 54
same-sex couples and, 51
segregation and, 45, 49–50, 56, 60
sexual issues and, 44–46, 49–51, 58–62
skin color and, 45–46, 50
social media and, 43, 61, 63
United States and, 41–46, 50–52, 55, 58, 60, 62
value and, 43, 61–62
violence and, 46–47, 51–52, 59–62
vulnerability and, 41, 44, 59
women and, 44–48, 54, 56, 59–60
Dividual, 76–80
Domination
affirmative action and, 114
antiminority politics and, 98
creation through mimicry, 84
demographics and, 67, 70–75, 80, 82, 84
diversity and, 48, 61
ethics and, 182, 187–189, 202
experiences and, 21–23, 27, 29, 34, 37, 39

legal issues and, 160, 172, 177
minority concepts and, 2, 8, 13, 15
social goods and, 21, 39, 73, 188–189
universalism and, 182, 187–189, 199, 202
Dress codes, 46
Drug addicts, 138

Ecological issues
affirmative action and, 129
experiences and, 37
environmental damage, 100, 141, 197–199
globalization, 129
lynching and, 37
minority concepts and, 17
universalism and, 199–202
whale fishing, 198
Economic issues
affirmative action and, 115–118, 126
antiminority politics and, 87, 99–104
co-appearing and, 138, 143–144
diversity and, 44, 47, 51–52, 55
demographics and, 77
employment, 1
ethics and, 205
experiences and, 20, 39
globalization and, 87
inflation, 141
legal issues and, 160, 177
minority concepts and, 2, 7
universalism and, 192, 197, 199
Education
affirmative action and, 107–110, 114–118, 123–127
campus safety and, 60–62
co-appearing and, 135, 142–145, 149
Dear Colleague Letter, 58–59
demographics and, 79
DeVos and, 59–60
diversity and, 45, 49, 55–60
ethics and, 209
experiences and, 21, 29

SUBJECT INDEX

legal issues and, 58, 92, 163, 170, 177
minority concepts and, 15
nepotism and, 114, 124
Priority Education Agreements and,
15, 110, 113–114, 119, 122–125, 129
quotas and, 57
Sciences Po and, 15, 110, 113–114,
119, 122–127
segregation and, 45, 108, 113, 116
single investigator system and, 58–59
stereotypes and, 15, 209
Trump and, 59–60
universalism and, 202
Egalitarianism
affirmative action and, 119
antiminority politics and, 103
building, 9
diversity and, 52, 57
Opportunity Insights and, 52
societal complexity and, 23
universalism and, 39
Walzer and, 24–25
Emotions, 154, 197, 236n91
Empathy, 17, 20, 155, 194–197, 210
Employment
affirmative action and, 107–108, 115,
126
antiminority politics and, 91, 101
co-appearing and, 144
demographics and, 79
diversity and, 44–46, 51, 58
legal issues and, 175, 177
minority concepts and, 1, 3, 6, 14
retirement and, 3, 20, 119, 202
unemployment, 3, 101, 138
Endocrine system, 159, 198
Environmental damage, 100, 141,
197–199
Equality
affirmative action and, 108–110,
115–117, 120–123, 128
antiminority politics and, 92–95, 98
class and, 165

co-appearing and, 136, 139, 145, 150
complex, 9, 12–13, 19–20, 24, 26, 28,
209
conditional, 120–121
demographics and, 66, 71, 73
discrimination and, 6, 16, 30, 35, 39,
45, 55–60, 71, 92, 95, 108, 116,
119–123, 139, 146, 150, 157–158,
165, 173, 177, 204, 209
diversity and, 44–45, 57–58, 60
ethics and, 204, 209–210
experiences and, 19–28, 31–32, 37,
39–40
gender, 16, 31–32, 40, 98, 158, 160,
164–165, 173, 209
income and, 209
legal issues and, 157–160, 164–166,
173, 175–177
minority concepts and, 9–13, 16
universalism, 182, 191
voting and, 45
Equivalence
affirmative action and, 108
antiminority politics and, 98
co-appearing and, 136
demographics and, 71
diversity and, 46
ethics and, 207
experiences and, 26
legal issues and, 173
universalism and, 183–184
Ethics
abortion and, 206
activists and, 204
age and, 204–205
algorithms and, 204
antiminority politics and, 92, 104
Asian Americans and, 204
Black people and, 11, 203–206
class and, 208
co-appearing and, 152, 155, 205
community and, 210
competition and, 205

SUBJECT INDEX

Ethics (cont.)
cultural issues and, 203, 207
democracy and, 203, 207, 210
disabilities and, 203–205, 208
distribution and, 203, 210
domination and, 182, 187–189, 202
economic issues and, 205
education and, 209
equality and, 204, 209–210
equivalence and, 207
exclusion and, 209
experiences and, 40
France and, 204, 208
gay people and, 203
gender and, 12, 203, 205, 209
health and, 204, 206
hegemony and, 207
heterosexuals and, 202, 204
identity and, 204–206, 210
inequality and, 195, 204
interdependence and, 17, 203–210
intrasectionality and, 205
legal issues and, 173, 178, 205–210
measurement and, 69
minority concepts and, 11–12, 17
police and, 209
power and, 204–210
presence and, 205–207, 210
race and, 12, 204–205
relational association and, 207
relativism and, 206
religion and, 92, 173, 203
responsibility and, 204, 209–210
sexual issues and, 203–205
Genet on, 260n122
skin color and, 203
stereotypes and, 209
transpartisan, 69
United States and, 204
universalism and, 180–197, 201–202
value and, 203, 206–207, 210
violence and, 205, 210

voting and, 209
women and, 209
Ethnonationalism, 80, 86, 101–106
Evangelicals, 102, 106
Exclusion
affirmative action and, 120, 124, 126–127
antiminority politics and, 99
co-appearing and, 133–134, 151
demographics and, 72
diversity and, 48, 55
ethics and, 209
experiences and, 37, 39
minority concepts and, 15
Experiences
anthropocenic knowledge and, 197–202
Canada and, 25, 29–32
Christians and, 26, 40
civil rights and, 24
co-appearing and, 15, 153
competition and, 20
conformity and, 39
conservatism and, 27
convergence of struggles and, 27
cultural issues and, 20, 24–25, 29–33, 38
democracy and, 25, 27, 33, 37, 40
direct, 37
distribution and, 19–24, 26, 28, 33, 39–40
domination and, 21, 23, 27, 29, 34, 37, 39
ecological issues and, 37
economic issues and, 20, 39
education and, 21, 29
equality and, 12–13, 19–28, 31–32, 37, 39–40, 209
equivalence and, 26
ethics and, 40
exclusion and, 37, 39
feminism and, 23–24, 28, 40
French, 20, 24–28, 31–34, 40

SUBJECT INDEX

health and, 37, 39, 139, 141–142, 145
hegemony and, 13, 23, 26, 29, 39
housing and, 38–39
identity and, 38, 40
inequality and, 23, 30, 32–35
of injustice, 13, 20, 29, 34–40, 52, 79, 84, 155, 201–207, 210
interdependence and, 21, 37
Jewish, 24, 30–31, 40
language and, 25, 31
legal issues and, 26, 31, 34–40
LGBTQ community and, 135
liberalism and, 19–22, 24, 27, 30, 32, 39–40
minority, 20–29, 32–34, 38–40
moral issues and, 20, 23–29, 32–36, 39
multiculturalism and, 20, 25, 29–32
Muslims, 30, 34, 40
pluralism and, 19, 22, 25–26, 29–33, 39
power and, 21–22, 27, 29, 38, 40
presence and, 40
as processing information, 38–39
reciprocity, 110
relational association and, 31
religion and, 21, 26, 29–30, 34, 40
resonances and, 38
sexual issues and, 26–27, 33–34
social goods and, 20–24, 33, 39–40
solidarity and, 20, 26, 37
spheres of, 20–40
tyranny and, 13, 27–28, 33, 68–69, 85
United States and, 25, 28, 32, 40
value and, 20–23, 31–32, 39
violent, 26, 37–38
vulnerability and, 24, 27, 35
women and, 21–24, 31–34
Extrasectionality, 174

Facebook, 78, 132
Feminism
affirmative action and, 120
antiminority politics and, 97, 103
co-appearing and, 139, 142, 146, 155

demographics and, 79
experiences and, 23–24, 28, 40
legal issues and, 159, 173
minority concepts and, 2, 7
universalism and, 184, 199
First Nations people, 47–48
France
affirmative action and, 110, 113–114, 118–123, 127, 129
antiminority politics and, 85–86, 95–101, 104, 106
Black people and, 2–4, 16, 48, 81, 86
burkini and, 85
Catholics and, 95
co-appearing and, 138–149, 152
colonialism and, 115–116
communitarianism and, 3, 12, 24–29, 80–81, 154
demographics and, 66, 69, 80–81
differential treatment and, 157–159
discrimination and, 6, 14, 28, 43–46, 49, 58, 95, 106, 110, 118, 120–123, 127, 138–139, 146, 157–158, 161, 164, 204
diversity in, 41–49, 58
ethics and, 204, 208
experiences in, 20, 24–28, 31–34, 40
Left of, 12
legal issues and, 157–164
minority concepts in, 2–6, 11–16
Muslims and, 34, 120
New Left and, 20, 25, 137
positive discrimination and, 14, 111, 120, 122–123
Priority Education Agreements and, 15, 110, 113–114, 119, 122–125, 129
Republic, 3, 116–118
Sciences Po and, 15, 110, 113–114, 119, 122–127
segregation in, 3, 66, 80, 113
seriality and, 80–81
Traoré death and, 2–3, 140, 143–144, 155

France (cont.)
  universalism and, 182, 184, 193, 199
  Yellow Vests and, 99–100, 121, 143,
    155
Frankfurt School, 187
Freedom
  affirmation of, 180
  of belief, 95
  of choice, 97
  of expression, 14, 33–34, 59, 87–94,
    103, 106, 173
  of movement, 7, 37, 144, 147
  of the press, 95
  principles of, 12
  of religion, 34, 86, 91
  restriction of, 27
  social, 187
  of speech, 87, 91

Gay people
  anti-gay rights movement and, 96
  antiminority politics and, 91–94,
    96–97
  asylum and, 49
  co-appearing and, 132–133, 138–139,
    146, 148
  diversity and, 49, 51
  ethics and, 203
  gay marriage and, 96
  Green Book and, 52
  homophobia and, 4, 51, 95, 100, 127,
    131–132, 139–141, 144, 202
  legal issues and, 157–158, 172, 177,
    178
  majority and, 7
  marriage, 96
  PreP HIV-preventive therapy and, 94
  religion and, 93
  same-sex couples and, 51
  sexual issues and, 7, 49, 52, 93, 96–97,
    132–133, 138, 146, 157–158, 172,
    177, 201, 203
  universalism and, 201

Gender
  affirmative action and, 107, 122
  antiminority politics and, 86–89, 92,
    94, 97–98, 103
  co-appearing and, 135
  colonialism and, 62
  demographics and, 76
  discrimination and, 12, 15–16, 44–45,
    52, 54, 60, 89, 92, 94, 107, 158–178,
    203, 209
  diversity and, 44–45, 52, 54, 59–62
  equality and, 16, 31–32, 40, 98, 158,
    160, 164–165, 173, 209
  ethics and, 12, 203, 205, 209
  identity of, 44–45, 59–60, 92,
    160–163, 165, 167, 177–178
  legal issues and, 16, 44, 45, 59–60, 92,
    158–178
  medical interventions and, 161
  #MeToo movement, 62, 66
  policy making and, 159–162
  race and, 16
  stereotypes and, 164–165, 168–169
  universalism and, 199, 202
  violence and, 135, 158, 171, 205
Generation Z, 62
Gerrymandering, 4, 109
Globalization
  affirmative action and, 129
  antiminority politics and, 87, 104
  co-appearing and, 135
  demographics and, 75
  diversity and, 42, 61, 63
  ecology and, 129
  economic issues and, 87
  legal issues and, 171
  moral issues and, 24, 187, 201
  responsibility and, 191–194
  sovereignty and, 104, 193
  universalism and, 182, 187, 191–194,
    201
Goodness, 36
Gynecology, 169

SUBJECT INDEX

Hapticality, 197

Harassment, 27, 46, 58–61, 134, 160, 266n78

Hastert rule, 69–70

Health
abortion and, 6, 56, 60, 89–90, 93, 97, 112, 178, 202, 206
access to care of, 52, 108
affirmative action and, 108, 112, 119
antiminority politics and, 89–94, 99
co-appearing and, 139, 141–142, 145
coverage for, 94, 206
disabilities and, 44, 268n97
discrimination and, 12, 37, 44, 52, 89–90, 108, 119
diversity and, 44, 52
ethics and, 204, 206
experiences and, 37, 39
legal issues and, 6
mental, 37
minority concepts and, 6, 12
private centers for, 89
sick leave and, 3
universalism and, 193–194, 198, 202
women's, 89–90, 99, 112, 145, 194, 202

Hegemony
affirmative action and, 123, 128
antiminority politics and, 96
co-appearing and, 149–151
demographics and, 84
diversity and, 44
ethics and, 207
experiences and, 13, 23, 26, 29, 39
legal issues and, 172
universalism and, 181–182, 189

Heterosexuals
antiminority politics and, 96
co-appearing and, 135
ethics and, 202, 204
legal issues and, 26, 135, 158, 168–169

Hispanics, 66, 138

HIV, 6, 94, 138, 201, 241n62

Holocaust, 89, 150, 197, 276n82, 280n51

Homophobia
affirmative action and, 127
antiminority politics and, 95, 100
co-appearing and, 131–132, 139–141, 144
diversity and, 51
minority concepts and, 4
universalism and, 202

Hospitality, 155, 183, 195

Housing
affirmative action and, 122, 125
co-appearing and, 142–145
experiences and, 38–39
legal issues and, 170
minority concepts and, 6, 14

Humanism
antiminority politics and, 86, 102–105
co-appearing and, 155
conscience and, 26
new, 86, 102–105
universalism and, 179, 199–200

Human rights
affirmative action and, 122
antiminority politics and, 95
co-appearing and, 134, 141, 145
demographics and, 70
diversity and, 41, 44, 47
legal issues and, 157–158, 161, 165, 168–169, 176
universalism and, 180, 182, 194

Hybridization, 183

Identity
affirmative action and, 117, 128
antiminority politics and, 86–87, 92, 98–101
Baldwin on, 134–136
co-appearing and, 141, 150–153
cultural issues and, 6, 42, 65, 80, 83, 99, 117, 137, 189, 191, 203
demographics and, 78, 83

Identity (cont.)
  diversity and, 43–44, 50, 59–62
  driver's licenses, 4
  ethics and, 204–206, 210
  experiences and, 38, 40
  fundamental rights and, 43
  gender and, 44–45, 59–60, 92,
    160–163, 165, 167, 177–178
  legal issues and, 38, 43–48, 151,
    157–167, 171–172, 177–178, 186,
    189, 204–205
  liquidity of, 86
  majority rule and, 74
  police and, 8
  sexual orientation and, 6, 44–46,
    49–50, 60, 92, 94, 158–171, 175,
    177–178, 205
  social labels and, 44
  social position and, 78
  universalism and, 184–191, 194–195
  vector of, 38
Ideologies
  antiminority politics and, 86–89,
    97–98, 102–104
  convergence of struggles and, 69–70,
    70
  Democrat vs. Republican, 69
  demographics and, 69–71, 81
  French Left, 12
  New Left, 20, 25, 137
Imperialism, 26, 38, 180
Incompleteness, 14, 82–83, 207
Inequality
  affirmative action and, 115–119, 122,
    128
  co-appearing and, 133, 141, 146, 150
  demographics and, 71, 79
  discrimination and, 6, 30, 35, 55, 71,
    116, 119, 133, 146, 150, 157
  distribution and, 13, 23, 33, 115–119
  diversity and, 55
  ethics and, 195, 204
  experiences and, 23, 30, 32–35

legal issues and, 165
local, 115–119
minority concepts and, 13
moral issues and, 32, 35, 71, 195–196
second-class citizens and, 119
tyranny and, 13, 27–28, 33, 68–69, 85
universalism and, 186, 195–196
Infantilization, 15, 59
Inflation, 141
Influence
  activists and, 87
  antiminority politics and, 14, 87, 90
  demographics and, 76, 80
  discrimination and, 7–8, 43, 90
  diversity and, 13, 43, 51–56, 63
  legal issues and, 168
  power and, 13–14, 27, 43, 52–53, 56, 90
  tyranny of the majority and, 27
  Walzer and, 28
Injustice
  antiminority politics and, 97, 106
  discrimination and, 36–37
  experiences and, 13, 20, 29, 34–40, 52,
    79, 84, 155, 201–207, 210
  preceding justice, 36
  reciprocity and, 115
  resistance to, 97
  social meaning of, 9–11
  structural nature of, 150
  universalism and, 17
Intercommunity, 2, 29, 144
Interdependence
  affirmative action and, 116
  chains of, 191–192
  class and, 16, 175
  co-appearing and, 133, 137, 141
  demographics and, 68, 75
  discrimination and, 16, 37
  ethics and, 17, 203–210
  experiences and, 21, 37
  legal issues and, 11, 175
  Rawls on, 9
  universalism and, 181, 184, 191–197

Intersectionality, 97
  affirmative action and, 129
  ethics and, 205
  extrasectionality and, 174
  legal issues and, 159, 170–178
  minority concepts and, 12, 16
  self-knowledge and, 173–174
Intrasectionality, 12, 16, 129, 159,
    170–178, 205
Islamophobia, 4, 144

Jews
  affirmative action and, 115
  antiminority politics and, 97
  co-appearing and, 138, 153
  experiences and, 24, 30–31, 40
  minority concepts and, 7
  religious holidays and, 30
  universalism and, 180
  Zionist, 102
Jim Crow, 143

Labor
  affirmative action and, 108
  demographics and, 66
  diversity and, 44, 47, 51
  division of, 21, 191
  employment, 3
  legal issues and, 21, 44, 108, 170
  slavery and, 4, 16, 85, 89, 97, 103,
    149–150, 160, 189
  universalism and, 191, 195–196, 201
Language
  affirmative action and, 116–117
  antiminority politics and, 88, 96
  co-appearing and, 131, 136, 152–153
  demographics and, 65, 73, 82
  diversity and, 41–44, 50
  experiences and, 25, 31
  legal issues and, 166, 174
  minority concepts and, 8, 12
  universalism and, 181, 185, 189
Latinx people

affirmative action and, 110
antiminority politics and, 99
co-appearing and, 131, 133, 137
demographics and, 66
LGBTQ community and, 2, 16,
  131–132
minority concepts and, 2
Orlando nightclub massacre and, 16,
  131–132, 151
universalism and, 200
Legal issues
  abortion, 6, 56, 60, 89–90, 93, 97, 112,
    178, 202, 206
  activists, 159, 163, 167
  affirmative action, 110, 113, 116–119,
    122, 126–127, 129
  age, 45–46, 158–159, 169, 171, 175
  analogical reasoning, 166–170
  antiminority politics, 86–88, 91, 94,
    102, 106
  Black people, 170–171
  class, 162, 165–166, 172, 175
  coalitions, 172
  co-appearing, 135, 138, 143, 150–152,
    156
  community, 160, 178
  conformity, 165, 169
  context, 42, 269n125
  contradictions, 208
  convergence, 171
  demographics, 66, 78
  difference, 162–166
  differential treatment, 6, 36, 48, 55,
    110, 116, 120, 150, 157–159, 171
  disabilities, 159, 168, 171, 175–177
  discrimination, 162–166
  disparate impact, 46
  dissenting opinions, 70
  diversity, 42–52, 63
  domination, 160, 172, 177
  economic issues, 160, 177
  education, 58, 92, 163, 170, 177
  employment, 175, 177

Legal issues (cont.)
  equality, 157–160, 164–166, 173, 175–177
  equivalence, 173
  ethics, 173, 178, 205–210
  experiences, 26, 31, 34–40
  feminism, 159, 173
  freedom of expression, 87–94
  French, 157–164
  gay people, 157–158, 172, 177, 178
  gender, 16, 44, 45, 59–60, 92, 158–178
  globalization, 171
  health, 6
  hegemony, 172
  heterosexuals, 26, 135, 158, 168–169
  housing, 170
  human rights, 157–158, 161, 165, 168–169, 176
  identity, 38, 43–48, 151, 157–167, 171–172, 177–178, 186, 189, 204–205
  inequality, 165
  influence, 168
  interdependence, 11, 175
  international law, 42, 161, 182, 268n111
  intrasectionality, 159, 170–178
  labor, 21, 44, 108, 170
  language, 166, 174
  lesbians, 159, 169
  maternity, 162–163
  minority concepts, 2, 6, 11–12, 16, 43–48, 161, 165–168, 171–178
  moral issues, 169, 172
  neutrality, 89
  orientation, 6
  parity, 166
  police, 2, 12, 119, 143, 177
  power, 166, 171–172, 175
  prejudice, 158, 169
  presence, 173
  race, 165, 167, 170–171, 175–178
  reciprocity, 77

  relational association, 178
  religion, 171, 173, 178
  resonances, 164, 174
  responsibility, 163, 173, 178
  retirement, 3, 20, 119, 202
  same-sex couples, 26, 34, 51, 88, 162–163, 168, 178
  segregation, 45, 108, 167, 178
  sexual issues, 158–178
  skin color, 177–178
  slavery, 160
  solidarity, 173
  stereotypes, 161, 164, 169
  transgender people, 89, 92, 161–164, 174, 177
  United States, 161, 167, 170, 174, 176–177
  universalism, 182, 186, 189, 191
  value, 172–173
  violence, 158, 166, 171, 177
  vulnerability, 169, 177–178
  women, 158–161, 167, 170–177
Lesbians
  antiminority politics and, 93
  asylum and, 49
  co-appearing and, 133, 138, 146, 152
  demographics and, 78
  diversity and, 49
  gay marriage and, 96
  homophobia and, 4, 51, 95, 100, 127, 131–132, 139–141, 144, 202
  legal issues and, 159, 169
  religion and, 93
  same-sex couples and, 51
LGBTQ community
  activists and, 93
  antiminority politics and, 88, 93–94
  Asian Americans for Black Lives and, 2
  Barrett nomination and, 93
  Chick-fil-A and, 88
  Colorado nightclub shooting, 132, 151
  convergence of struggles and, 133, 135

experiences and, 135
external resources and, 135
increased visibility of, 148
Latinx people and, 2, 16, 131–132
Orlando nightclub massacre, 16,
131–132, 151
rainbow flag and, 132
Liberal civicism, 58
Liberalism
affirmative action and, 119–120
antiminority politics and, 86–88, 98,
102
co-appearing and, 139
deliberalism, 253n125
demographics and, 71, 73
diversity and, 57–58
experiences and, 19–22, 24, 27, 30, 32,
39–40
minority concepts and, 9, 13
universalism and, 187
Lynching, 37

Majority privilege, 114, 124
Majority rule
antiminority politics and, 86
competition and, 72, 75
demographics and, 68–69, 72–80
distortion of representation by, 73
diversity and, 43
dividual and, 76–80
justification of, 73–74
moral issues and, 73
normative limitations of, 72–76
qualified-majority system and, 75–76
super-majority system and, 75–76
Maroon geographies, 201
Materialism, 4, 9, 21, 23, 26, 30, 56, 67,
123, 128, 160, 174, 185, 197
Maternity, 3, 162–163
Mediapart newspaper, 144
Memory, 12, 15, 123, 133, 149–150, 205
Migrants, 15, 66, 118, 137–138, 145,
155

Minorities
affirmative action and, 107–129
antiminority politics, 85–106
co-appearing and, 131–156
defining, 1–18
demographics and, 65–84
ethical interdependence and, 203–210
experiences of, 20–29, 32–34, 38–40
invisibilisation of, 5, 51, 80, 161, 165
legal analogy and, 161, 165–168,
171–178
diversity and, 41–57
universalism and, 179–202
Minority concepts
activists and, 1–2
algorithms and, 12, 14
Asian Americans and, 2, 15
Black people and, 1–7, 11, 15–16
bodies, 3, 4, 46, 87, 147–151, 189,
200, 202
class, 4, 6, 12, 15–16
colonialism and, 4, 62, 82, 103, 115–
116, 176, 180, 189, 191
competition and, 2, 12, 15, 111–115
conservatism and, 2, 12–13
constitution, 234n14
convergence of struggles and, 5, 15–16
criteria for, 6
cultural issues and, 5–6, 9–14
diversity, 12–13, 41–43
domination, 2, 8
ecological issues and, 17
economic issues and, 2, 7
education and, 15
employment and, 1, 3, 6, 14
equality and, 9–13, 16
ethics and, 11–12, 17
exclusion and, 15
feminism and, 2, 7
French, 2–6, 11–16
health, 6, 12
homophobia and, 4
housing and, 6, 14

Minority concepts (cont.)
inequality and, 13
intrasectionality and, 12, 16
Jews and, 7
language and, 8, 12
Latinx people and, 2
legal issues and, 2, 6, 11–12, 16, 43–48
liberalism and, 9, 13
moral issues and, 9–10, 17
multiculturalism and, 12–13
police and, 1–4, 12, 16
power and, 1, 5, 7–10, 13–15, 51–56
presence and, 4–5, 8–11, 15–16
protest and, 1–2
racism, 4
relational association and, 5, 7, 65, 72
religion and, 13
resonances, 5–8
segregation and, 1–4
sexual issues and, 1, 4, 6, 12, 15–16
social goods, 9–13
solidarity and, 139
United States and, 1–6, 11–14
value, 2, 9, 11–17
violence and, 2–7, 16
vulnerability, 17
women and, 5–7, 13
Moral issues
affirmative action and, 107
antiminority politics and, 86, 89,
94–98, 106
co-appearing and, 134, 150–151
community and, 9, 17, 20, 36, 39,
194
conscience, 26, 36, 137
demographics and, 68, 71, 73, 77
diversity and, 43, 56
experiences and, 20, 23–29, 32–36, 39
globalization and, 24, 187, 201
inequality, 32, 35, 71, 195–196
legal issues and, 169, 172
majority rule and, 73
minimal morality, 20, 24, 28, 68, 184

minority concepts and, 9–10, 17
relativism and, 24, 34, 95, 201, 206
religion and, 26, 34, 56, 86, 89,
94–95
social goods and, 9, 20, 39, 95, 184,
195
universalism and, 182, 184, 187,
193–196, 201
Multiculturalism
co-appearing and, 137
diversity and, 42
experiences and, 20, 25, 29–32
minority concepts and, 12–13
universalism and, 191
Muslims
affirmative action and, 115–116, 120
antiminority politics and, 89
burkini and, 85
experiences of, 30, 34, 40
Islamophobia and, 4, 144
religious holidays and, 30
visas and, 89
Mutual aid, 2, 82

Neoliberalism, 13, 19–20, 119
Nepotism, 114, 124
Neutrality, 29, 49, 80, 89
New Left, 20, 25, 137
New York Times, 111, 132
Nuclear family, 2, 193

Ontology, 181, 185, 201, 205
Ozone, 198

Parity
affirmative action and, 120–121
antiminority politics and, 86, 97
demographics and, 66, 79
legal issues and, 166
Passing, 48–50
Performativity, 29, 34, 37, 82, 110,
119–123, 149, 156, 174, 246n5,
270n131

SUBJECT INDEX 363

Pluralism
  affirmative action and, 110, 123
  Canada and, 29–31
  co-appearing and, 149
  communitarianism and, 80
  democracy and, 13, 25–26, 33, 189
  demographics and, 72, 80
  experiences and, 19, 22, 25–26,
    29–33, 39
  neutrality and, 29
  relativism and, 72, 183
  test of, 29–33
  universalism and, 179–182, 189
  Walzer on, 12–13, 19, 25–26, 33, 39,
    179
Pluriversalism, 180
Polarization, political, 63, 68, 69, 204
Police
  affirmative action and, 119
  Arte Radio and, 144
  co-appearing and, 134–137, 140,
    143–144
  diversity and, 47, 60–61
  ethics and, 209
  journalists and, 143
  kettling and, 143
  legal issues and, 2, 12, 119, 143,
    177
  minority concepts and, 1–4, 12, 16
  preventive arrests and, 143
  taser and, 4
  universalism and, 201
  violence and, 1–2, 16, 47, 60–61,
    132–137, 142–147
  WhatsApp group, 144
Pollution, 100, 141, 197–199
Popular vote, 73
Populism
  creative minority and, 67
  new, 40
  redemptive, 98–101
  tyranny and, 85
Positioning, 7–8, 26, 68

Positive discrimination, 14, 111, 120,
    122–123, 251n98
Poverty, 99, 119, 137, 177, 188
Power
  affirmative action and, 112, 115, 120,
    123, 128
  antiminority politics and, 85–87, 90,
    98, 102–103
  co-appearing and, 135–136, 139, 141,
    143, 148–156
  demographics and, 65–69, 73–74,
    77–84
  diversity and, 43, 46, 49, 51–56, 58–63
  ethics and, 204–210
  experiences and, 21–22, 27, 29, 38, 40
  influence and, 13–14, 27, 43, 52–53,
    56, 90
  legal issues and, 166, 171–172, 175
  minority concepts and, 1, 5, 7–10,
    13–15, 51–56
  philosophy of, 206
  universalism and, 180, 184, 186–187,
    191–196, 202
Prejudice
  affirmative action and, 126, 128
  conversational ideal and, 71
  diversity and, 54
  epistemic injustice and, 36
  legal issues and, 158, 169
  normative lines and, 126
  stereotypes and, 15, 80, 98, 109, 111,
    161, 164, 169, 209
PreP HIV-preventive treatment, 94
Presence
  affirmative action and, 115, 125, 129
  antiminority politics and, 85, 97,
    101
  co-appearing and, 133, 137, 143,
    147–156
  demographics and, 71, 82–83
  ethics and, 205–207, 210
  experiences and, 40
  incitement of, 150–156

Presence (cont.)
  legal issues and, 173
  minority concepts and, 4–5, 8–11, 15–16
  reciprocity and, 15
  struggle for visibility, 131–133, 147–156
  universalism and, 180, 184, 186, 189, 191–197, 200–202
Preventive arrests, 143
Priority Educational Agreements (Conventions Éducation Prioritaire)
  affirmative action and, 15, 110, 113–114, 119, 122–125, 129
  establishment of, 119
  reciprocity and, 123–125
Protected classes, 6, 15–16, 45, 162, 174, 203
Protest
  Adama committee and, 3
  antiminority politics and, 85, 97–100
  Black Lives Matter and, 1–2
  co-appearing and, 140, 143
  diversity and, 62–63
  minority concepts and, 1–2
  race and, 2
  Trump and, 2
  violence and, 2
  Yellow Vests and, 99–100, 121, 143, 155
Public good, 35, 95, 116–117
Public opinion, 199

Quakers, 210
Qualified-majority system, 75–76
Queer Nation, 152
Quotas
  affirmative action and, 107, 116–117, 121
  education and, 57
  women and, 66

Race
  affirmative action and, 107–113, 119–123
  antiminority politics, 89, 94–95, 98–99
  categorization and, 11
  co-appearing and, 135
  demographics and, 76
  disabilities and, 1, 12, 16, 44–45, 95–96, 171, 175, 202, 205
  diversity and, 42, 44–45, 50, 57, 62
  ethics and, 12, 204–205
  gender and, 16
  identity, 134–136, 274n47
  legal issues and, 165, 167, 170–171, 178
  majority and, 7
  migrants and, 15, 66, 118, 137–138, 145, 155
  mixed, 2, 4, 135, 171, 204
  movements for, 137
  passing, 48–50
  prejudice and, 36, 54, 71, 126, 128, 158, 169
  protest and, 2
  quotas and, 57, 107, 116–117, 121
  skin color and, 4, 15, 45–46, 50, 177–178, 203
  stereotypes and, 15, 80, 98, 109, 111, 161, 164, 169, 209
  violence and, 2, 4, 47, 60, 81, 99, 135, 137, 143–144, 171, 205
Racism
  affirmative action and, 121
  antiminority politics and, 85–86, 95–100
  co-appearing and, 135–137, 140, 143–144, 147
  colonialism and, 4, 62, 82, 103, 115–116, 176, 180, 189, 191
  demographics and, 81
  diversity and, 47, 50, 60, 62
  legal issues and, 167, 175–176

SUBJECT INDEX

minority concepts and, 4
universalism and, 199–202
Reasonable accommodation, 20,
  30–31, 45
Reciprocity
  affirmative action and, 110, 115,
    123–129
  Butler on, 188
  experiences and, 110
  ideal of, 115
  legal issues and, 77
  pedagogy of, 123–129
  presence and, 15
  universalism and, 188, 201
Recognition
  policies, 7, 10, 29, 108–110, 191, 203,
    208
  theories, 17, 52, 55, 86, 96, 99, 117,
    128, 132–133, 162–163, 165, 167,
    173, 185–194
Relational association
  affirmative action and, 123, 128–129
  co-appearing and, 142, 154
  diversity and, 43
  ethics and, 207
  experiences and, 31
  legal issues and, 178
  minority concepts and, 5, 7, 65, 72
  universalism and, 186, 191
Relationality, 154
Relativism
  ethics and, 206
  idea of justice and, 35
  majority voting and, 73
  moral issues and, 24, 34, 95, 201, 206
  pluralism and, 72, 183
  universalism and, 182, 201
  value creation and, 104
  Walzer and, 9, 24, 26, 33
Religion
  activists and, 95, 97
  affirmative action and, 112, 115–116,
    120–121

antiminority politics and, 85–95
Catholics, 30, 91, 93, 95, 97, 102
co-appearing and, 139, 151, 153
creed and, 1, 12, 76
cultural issues and, 13, 29–30, 42, 81,
  203
demographics and, 81
diversity and, 41–47, 56
ethics and, 92, 173, 203
experiences and, 21, 26, 29–30, 34,
  40
First Nations people and, 47–48
freedom of, 34, 86, 91
gay people and, 93
Islamophobia and, 4, 144
legal issues and, 171, 173, 178
lesbians and, 93
minority concepts and, 13
moral issues and, 26, 34, 56, 86, 89,
  94–95
Muslims, 30, 34, 40, 85, 89, 115–116,
  120
Quakers, 210
Sikhs, 30, 115
universalism and, 179
Representation, 15, 27, 34, 57, 69–75,
  83, 115–116, 120–123, 148, 154,
  177, 204, 209–210
Republicanism, 58, 81
Republicans
  Black Lives Matter and, 2
  Blum, 101
  Brown, 50
  Bush, 73
  demographics and, 69
  Gingrich, 101
Resonances
  co-appearing and, 133, 136, 150,
    154–155
  demographics and, 61
  experiences and, 38
  global media and, 61
  legal issues and, 164, 174

366 SUBJECT INDEX

Resonances (cont.)
  minority concepts and, 5–8
  universalism and, 188
Responsibility
  affirmative action and, 121, 126, 129
  anthropocenic knowledge and,
    197–202
  co-appearing and, 145, 149, 153
  collective, 17
  dissociative, 195, 197
  diversity and, 54
  ethics and, 204, 209–210
  global, 191–194
  legal issues and, 163, 173, 178
  social, 121, 126, 129
  towards others, 8, 11, 129, 173, 178,
    191–197, 204, 209
  universalism and, 191–197, 201
Retirement, 3, 20, 119, 202
Roma children, 47, 48

Same-sex couples
  antiminority politics and, 88–96, 100
  co-appearing and, 152
  diversity and, 51
  experiences and, 26, 34
  gay marriage and, 96
  legal issues and, 26, 34, 51, 88,
    162–163, 168, 178
Sciences Po
  affirmative action and, 15, 110,
    113–114, 119, 122–127
  elite recruitment and, 124–126
  entrance exam of, 114, 123–125
  outreach program of, 124
  Priority Education Agreements and,
    15, 110, 113–114, 119, 122–125, 129
Segregation
  affirmative action and, 108, 110, 113,
    115–116, 119
  demographics and, 66, 79–80
  diversity and, 45, 49–50, 56, 60
  France and, 3, 66, 80, 113

legal issues and, 45, 108, 167, 178
minority concepts and, 1–4
schools and, 45, 108, 113, 116
slavery and, 4, 16, 85, 89, 97, 103,
  149–150, 160, 189
universalism and, 189
urban, 3
September 11 attacks, 141
Seriality, 80–84
Sexual issues
  affirmative action and, 112, 120–122
  antiminority politics and, 7–8, 85–102
  campus safety and, 60–62
  co-appearing and, 135–136, 139, 144,
    148, 152–153
  conversion therapy, 88, 91–92
  demographics and, 66, 78
  diversity and, 44–46, 49–51, 56–62
  ecological policy, 202
  ethics and, 203–205
  experiences and, 26–27, 33–34
  gay people, 7, 49, 51, 52, 91–94,
    96–97, 132–133, 138, 146, 157–158,
    172, 177, 178, 201, 203
  heterosexuals, 26, 96, 135, 158,
    168–169, 202, 204
  homophobia, 4, 51, 95, 100, 127,
    131–132, 139–141, 144, 202
  legal issues and, 158–178
  lesbians, 49, 78, 93, 133, 138, 146,
    152, 159, 169
  minority concepts and, 1, 4, 6, 12,
    15–16
  orientation, 6, 44–46, 49–50, 60, 92,
    94, 158–171, 175, 177–178, 205
  same-sex couples, 51
  sexism, 4, 95, 98, 121, 144, 166–167,
    202
  transgender people, 89, 92, 161–164,
    174, 177
  universalism and, 202
  violence, 4, 51, 59–62, 66, 135, 144,
    158, 166, 177, 205

SUBJECT INDEX

Sikhs, 30, 115
Single investigator system, 58–59
Skin color
  danger and, 4
  discrimination and, 4, 15, 45–46, 50,
    177–178, 203
  diversity and, 45–46, 50
  ethics and, 203
  legal issues and, 177–178
Slavery
  antiminority politics and, 89, 97, 103
  co-appearing and, 149–150
  colonialism and, 189
  as crime against humanity, 16
  Holocaust and, 89
  ideologies of hatred and, 89
  labor and, 4, 16, 85, 89, 97, 103,
    149–150, 160, 189
  legal issues and, 160
  statues of enslavers, 85
  universalism and, 189
Social goods
  cultural issues and, 9, 13, 20–21, 23,
    33, 84, 184–185, 189
  demographics and, 76, 84
  distribution and, 10, 13, 20–24, 28,
    33, 39–40, 76, 84, 184, 188, 190, 202
  domination and, 21, 39, 73, 188–189
  experiences and, 20–24, 33, 39–40
  meaning of, 9
  minority concepts and, 9–13
  moral issues and, 9, 20, 39, 95, 184,
    195
  universalism and, 179, 184, 188–190,
    195
  value and, 9, 21, 23, 39, 126, 190
Socialism, 24–25, 40, 85, 120, 139, 141
Social justice, 20, 22, 37, 205
Social media
  academic institutions and, 43, 61, 63
  antiminority politics and, 105
  Black Lives Matter and, 1–2
  co-appearing and, 131

  diversity and, 43, 61, 63
  Facebook, 78, 132
  solidarity networks and, 1–2
Solidarity
  Civil Solidarity Pact and, 26
  co-appearing and, 132, 139, 142, 155
  commonalities and, 5
  cultural references and, 65
  experiences and, 20, 26, 37
  legal issues and, 173
  minority concepts and, 139
  networks of, 1, 81
  Obama and, 132
  universalism and, 186, 191, 197
Sovereignty
  affirmative action and, 129
  antiminority politics and, 86, 102,
    104
  challenging, 27
  co-appearing and, 153, 155–156
  colonization and, 7, 98, 152
  European Christians and, 86
  globalization and, 104, 193
  nonsovereignty and, 186–191, 198
  responsibility and, 153
  tyranny and, 13, 27–28, 33, 68–69, 85
  universalism and, 183, 186–191, 193,
    198
Sperm, 162–163
Spiral of silence, 54–55
Stereotypes
  affirmative action and, 109, 111
  antiminority politics and, 98
  demographics and, 80
  education and, 15, 209
  ethics and, 209
  gender, 164–165, 168–169
  legal issues and, 161, 164, 169
  prejudice and, 15, 80, 98, 109, 111,
    161, 164, 169, 209
Substantivism, 23
Super-majority system, 75–76
Sustainability, 39, 200

Tax policies, 99–100, 117, 119, 143, 176, 202
Totalitarianism, 25, 28
Transformative justice, 8, 174, 206, 209–210
Transgender people
  antiminority politics and, 89, 92
  legal issues, 89, 92, 161–164, 174, 177
Translation
  co-appearing and, 16, 207
  cultural, 79–80, 181, 184–185
  Enlightenment and, 181
  French, 16, 25, 32, 159, 252n117
  imperfect, 36
Transparenting, 22, 76, 148, 162
Transphobia, 4, 95, 131–132, 141
Trump, Donald
  affirmative action and, 111–112
  antiminority politics and, 2, 89, 92–93, 98–99, 105
  education and, 59–60
  money laundering and, 105
  partisan resources and, 69
  popular vote and, 73
  protest and, 2
  violence and, 2, 99
Truth, 3, 50, 270n129
  anthropological, 183–184
  experiences and, 36–40
  goodness and, 36
  judicial narratives and, 204
  scientific, 87
  search for, 74
Tyranny, 13, 27–28, 33, 68–69, 85

United States
  affirmative action and, 56, 107–113, 115, 122, 128–129
  antiminority politics and, 86–87, 93–95, 98–101, 105–106
  co-appearing and, 131, 134, 137, 141, 145, 151
  demographics and, 66, 68–69, 83

differential treatment and, 110
diversity and, 41–46, 50–52, 55, 58, 60, 62
ethics and, 204
experiences and, 25, 28, 32, 40
Hastert rule and, 69–70
legal issues and, 161, 167, 170, 174, 176–177
minority concepts and, 1–6, 11–14
segregation in, 1, 3, 45, 50, 60, 66, 108, 113, 115, 167
voting and, 3
Universal, as a word, 181
Universalism
  abortion and, 202
  activists and, 184
  algorithms and, 192
  anthropocenic knowledge and, 197–202
  Black people and, 184, 188, 198, 201
  chains of interdependence and, 191–192
  Christians and, 179, 190
  civil rights and, 184
  class and, 180, 199, 202
  communitarianism and, 186, 188
  community and, 9, 11, 14, 29–31, 41–42, 84, 87, 118, 137, 144, 189–190, 194, 197
  conformity and, 183
  contexts of, 191
  convergence of struggles and, 183
  cultural issues and, 180–185, 189, 191
  democracy and, 183, 189, 198, 201
  disabilities and, 202
  distribution and, 184, 188, 190, 192, 199–201
  domination and, 182, 187–189, 202
  ecological issues and, 199–202
  economic issues and, 192, 197, 199
  education and, 202
  egalitarianism and, 39
  empathy and, 194–197

SUBJECT INDEX 369

equality, 182, 191
equivalence and, 183–184
ethics and, 180–197, 201–202
feminism and, 184, 199
French, 182, 184, 193, 199
gay people and, 201
gender and, 199, 202
globalization and, 182, 187, 191–194, 201
health and, 193–194, 198, 202
hegemony and, 181–182, 189
homophobia and, 202
humanism and, 179, 199–200
human rights and, 180, 182, 194
identity and, 184–191, 194–195
inequality and, 186, 195–196
injustice and, 17
interdependence and, 181, 184, 191–197
Jews and, 180
labor and, 191, 195–196, 201
language and, 181, 185, 189
Latinx people and, 200
legal issues and, 182, 186, 189, 191
liberalism and, 187
Logos and, 181
moral issues and, 182, 184, 187, 193–196, 201
multiculturalism and, 191
philosophy of nonsovereignty and, 186–191
pluralism and, 179–182, 189
pluriversalism and, 180
police and, 201
power and, 180, 184, 186–187, 191–196, 202
presence and, 180, 184, 186, 189, 191–197, 200–202
racism and, 199–202
reciprocity and, 188, 201
relational association and, 186, 191
relativism and, 182, 201
religion and, 179

resonances and, 188
responsibility and, 191–197, 201
segregation and, 189
slavery and, 189
social goods and, 179, 184, 188–190, 195
solidarity and, 186, 191, 197
sovereignty and, 183, 186–191, 193, 198
value and, 180–183, 186, 190–191, 195
violence and, 191, 194, 196
vulnerability and, 192–197, 206
women and, 188, 194–196, 202
Urban free zones, 118
US Constitution
antiminority politics and, 87–88, 94
electoral system and, 69
equality and, 108
chain of protection and, 178
school integration and, 242n81

Value
affirmative action and, 126–127, 129
antiminority politics and, 87, 94, 96, 100, 102, 104–105
co-appearing and, 134, 136, 140, 154
of democracy, 11–17
demographics and, 68, 72, 80
distribution and, 21, 23, 203
diversity and, 43, 61–62
ethics and, 203, 206–207, 210
experiences and, 20–23, 31–32, 39
human life, 2
legal issues and, 172–173
minority concepts, 2, 9, 11–17
social goods, 9, 21, 23, 39, 126, 190
universalism and, 180–183, 186, 190–191, 195
Violence
affirmative action and, 122, 127
antiminority politics and, 88, 96, 99
brutality, 1, 5, 143

Violence (cont.)
co-appearing and, 132–137, 142–147, 151
Colorado nightclub shooting, 132, 151
demographics and, 66, 81
diversity and, 46–47, 51–52, 59–62
El Paso shooter, 105
ethics and, 205 210
experiences and, 26, 37–38
gender, 135, 158, 171, 205
hypertrophy of assimilation and, 136
legal issues and, 158, 166, 171, 177
minority concepts and, 2–7, 16
Orlando nightclub massacre and, 16, 131–132, 151
police, 1–2, 16, 47, 60–61, 132–137, 142–147
possibility of, 136
protest and, 2
racial, 2, 4, 47, 60, 81, 99, 135, 137, 143–144, 171, 205
sexual, 4, 51, 59–62, 66, 135, 144, 158, 166, 177, 205
Trump and, 2, 99
universalism and, 191, 194, 196
Voting
co-appearing and, 142, 145, 148
de Condorcet on, 7
equal rights and, 45
ethics and, 209
low-income families and, 142
majority, 73, 75
proportional, 69
relativism and, 73
rights of, 1, 45
United States and, 3
Vulnerability
antiminority politics and, 100
co-appearing and, 146
demographics and, 72
diversity and, 41, 44, 59
ethics and, 206

experiences and, 24, 27, 35
legal issues and, 169, 177–178
minority concepts and, 17
universalism and, 192–197

Weaponization, 5, 44, 62
Whiteness, 2, 6, 50–52, 57, 66, 83, 97, 99, 103, 108, 111, 113–114, 128, 134–138, 140, 148, 170–172, 189, 199, 202, 204
Wokeness, 56, 60–62
"World-totality," 192, 277n106
Women
affirmative action and, 112, 115, 117, 120–121
antiminority politics and, 86, 89–90, 94, 96–99, 105
co-appearing and, 134, 138, 145
demographics and, 66
diversity and, 44–48, 54, 56, 59–60
equal access and, 120–121
ethics and, 209
experiences and, 21–24, 31–34
gynecology and, 169
health and, 89–90, 99, 112, 145, 194, 202
infantilization of, 15, 59
legal issues and, 158–161, 167, 170–177
majority and, 7
minority concepts and, 5–7, 13
quotas and, 66
universalism and, 188, 194–196, 202
as war trophies, 134